Mother Figured

gured

Marian Apparitions and
the Making of a Filipino Universal

DEIRDRE DE LA CRUZ

The University of Chicago Press

CHICAGO AND LONDON

DEIRDRE DE LA CRUZ is assistant professor of Southeast Asian studies and history at the University of Michigan.

The University of Chicago Press, Chicago 60637
The University of Chicago Press, Ltd., London
© 2015 by The University of Chicago
All rights reserved. Published 2015.
Printed in the United States of America

24 23 22 21 20 19 18 17 16 15   1 2 3 4 5

ISBN-13: 978-0-226-31488-4 (cloth)
ISBN-13: 978-0-226-31491-4 (paper)
ISBN-13: 978-0-226-31507-2 (e-book)

DOI: 10.7208/chicago/9780226315072.001.0001

Library of Congress Cataloging-in-Publication Data
Cruz, Deirdre de la, author.
Mother figured : Marian apparitions and the making of a Filipino universal / Deirdre de la Cruz.
pages cm
Includes bibliographical references and index.
ISBN 978-0-226-31488-4 (cloth : alk. paper)—ISBN 978-0-226-31491-4 (pbk. : alk. paper)—ISBN 978-0-226-31507-2 (e-book) 1. Mary, Blessed Virgin, Saint—Apparitions and miracles—Philippines. 2. Mary, Blessed Virgin, Saint—Devotion to—Philippines. I. Title.
BT652.P48C78 2015
232.91'709599—dc23
2015011497

Contents

Acknowledgments

When you've lived with a book as long as I have lived with this one, the people and places that appear or have left their impressions on its pages constitute a world unto its own. At the center of this world are those in the Philippines about whom I write, people who have seen or heard of an appearance of Mary and who have shared with me that experience or knowledge. To each of them, named or not in these pages, I owe a tremendous debt of gratitude. A few individuals refused to be thanked even anonymously. You know who you are.

In the Philippines, I am thankful for the hospitality of numerous individuals and institutions, starting with my *tita*, Techie Dela-Cruz, who never fails to take me in, no matter how long of a lapse it's been. Del Fernandez, Helen Mendoza, and Mayet Ramos have also fed and sheltered me at various times in the years I've been returning to Manila. In Lipa, the sisters of Lipa Carmel graciously allowed me to stay in their guesthouse on several occasions, providing solace and sanctuary in what were often intense periods of research. Archival and library research for this book was conducted in the Philippines, Spain, and the United States, and I am deeply grateful to all those who assisted me in tasks great and small. For allowing special access to archives and private collections or showing especial alacrity, I wish to specifically mention Michael C. Francisco, chief of the Archives Collection and Access Division, National Archives of the Philippines; Lulu del Mar (formerly with the Archivo of the University of Santo Tomas, Manila); Bernie Sobremonte (Archdiocesan Archives of Manila); Angelli Tugado at *Philippine Studies: Historical and Ethnographic Viewpoints*; Fr. Carlo Ilagan, former director of Our Lady of Caysasay Academy; Fr. Gaspar Sigaya, O.P., previously at the Museum of Our Lady of Manaoag Shrine; Ms. Teresita Castillo; the late Mr. Francisco Dychangco of San Pablo, Laguna; Sr. Mary Grace, O.C.D., former mother superior of Lipa Carmel; the late Sr. Bernadette, O.C.D.; Sr. Mary Fides, O.C.D.; Fr. Jordi Roca, S.J., director of the Arxiu Històric de la Companyia de Jesús a Catalunya (Barcelona); Fr. Policarpo Hernández, O.S.A., and the late Rev. Fr. Isacio Rodriguez, O.S.A., prolific scholars in their own right, of the Archivo de la Provincia Agustiniana de Filipinas (Valladolid, Spain); and David Goodrich at the Archives of the Holy Cross Family Ministries in North Easton, Massachusetts. In the Philippines, invaluable research assistance was provided at various stages by Joy Macarandang, Rose Mendoza, and Raissa Rivera, and Maria Cleofe Marpa reviewed my translations of older Tagalog-language works.

Books may be written in solitude, but they are conceived and rethought in hallways and classrooms, in Q&As and car rides, over coffee and cocktails. At Columbia University and Cornell University this book first took shape when I studied under an extraordinary group of faculty. I owe a lot to Rosalind Morris's generous guidance and scholarship on religion and media; she asked me questions I still haven't answered to my best satisfaction. Michael Taussig's heterodox approach to ethnography instilled in me new ways of thinking about the miraculous, the sacred, and the profane. Marilyn Ivy's readings of the uncanny in Japanese modernity inspired some of my own interpretations of phenomena in this very different context. As an anthropological work, this book was deeply influenced by seminars I took at Cornell with James T. Siegel in 1998 and 2005. Despite its transnational scope and examination of universals, as a book that is still, at heart, about the Philippine nation, it is greatly indebted to Benedict Anderson. More than anyone else before or since, John Pemberton showed me how to think and write at the intersections of anthropology and history, and for more than twenty years I have counted on him as a mentor and friend.

The global community of Philippines specialists has provided me with much inspiration, insight, and opportunity for the development of this book. In addition to those scholars I acknowledge by way of citation, I wish to thank here Filomeno (Jun) Aguilar, Oscar Campomanes, Michael Cullinane, the late Doreen Fernandez, Fr. Mario Francisco, S.J., Francis Gealogo, Susan Go, Reynaldo Ileto, Regalado T. Jose, Ricardo T. Jose, Resil Mojares, Ambeth Ocampo, and Luciano Santiago. For engaging in sustained conversations about the Philippines and the vicissitudes of its study, I am grateful to Megan C. Thomas and Smita Lahiri. Vicente Rafael continues to set the highest of standards for engaged and critical studies of the Philippines, and I always appreciate the chance to talk with him about my work and get his feedback. I thank the two experts in Philippine Christianity who reviewed this book's manuscript and provided constructive criticisms, helpful advice, and overall support; Fenella Cannell disclosed to me that she was one of these reviewers, and I thank her personally for her generous engagement. In the end, of course, I alone am responsible for any errors herein.

The University of Michigan has been my institutional home for almost a decade, and participation in its many intellectual communities has transformed my work in numerous ways. A postdoctoral fellowship in the Society of Fellows provided me with a vibrant community of peers and the luxury of actually setting this project aside for a time, which allowed for new dimensions of the study to germinate and develop. I am deeply grateful to Donald S. Lopez Jr., first in his capacity as chair of the Society of Fellows and now as chair of the Department of Asian Languages and Cultures, for protecting my time, for his unstinting confidence in me, and for his guidance in professional matters great and small. In the small city that is the Department of History, former and current chairs Geoff Eley and Kathleen Canning have provided valuable opportunities for me to contribute to the department and thus feel like I truly belong. I have gained so much from my interactions with colleagues in both departments, in the dynamic Doctoral Program in Anthropology and History, and elsewhere on campus, but allow me to single out and thank here Micah Auerback, Varuni Bhatia, Ben Brose, Miranda Brown, Christi-Anne Castro, Katherine French, Zeny Fulgencio, Paul Johnson, Webb Keane, S. E. Kile, Matt Lassiter, Alaina Lemon, Tomoko Masuzawa, Victor Mendoza, Rudolf Mrázek, Rachel Neis, Markus Nornes, Esperanza Ramirez-Christiansen, Youngju Ryu, Andrew Shryock, Carla Sinopoli, Xiaobing Tang, Deling Weller, and Jonathan Zwicker. The administrative staff of both ALC and History have been instrumental in helping me achieve that mythical work-life balance everyone talks about, plus they make working in the office in the summer a little less lonely. It is quite possible, finally, that I would not be at Michigan now were it not for fellow Southeast Asianist Nancy Florida. Beyond having read and commented extensively on the entire manuscript, for which I am so thankful, Nancy has become a most valued interlocutor, cherished mentor, and friend.

I am grateful for the invitations to present portions of this work at the Eisenberg Institute for Historical Studies, the Doctoral Program in Anthropology and History and the Center for Southeast Asian Studies at the University of Michigan, the Department of Communication and Culture at Indiana

University Bloomington, the Center for Southeast Asian Studies at the University of Wisconsin–Madison, the Center for Religion and Civic Culture at the University of Southern California, the Max Planck Institute for Human Development (Berlin), the Department of History at the Ateneo de Manila University, the "Kritika Kultura" lecture series at the Ateneo de Manila University, the Department of Anthropology and Center for Philippine Studies at the University of Hawai'i, the International Graduate Program at the University of Stockholm, and the Department of Anthropology and Southeast Asia Program at Cornell University. Audiences at these and other conference presentations provided invaluable feedback. In 2007 and 2008 I had the great fortune of participating in a workshop sponsored by the National Humanities Center that brought together scholars across disciplines and from around the world who studied visionary phenomena. Convened by historians of Christianity William A. Christian Jr. and Gábor Klaniczay, "The Vision Thing: Studying Divine Intervention" had a profound influence on the direction this book ended up taking and brought me into an ambit of camaraderie that is lamentably now more virtual than actual, but meaningful all the same. I owe Bill in particular a profound debt of gratitude for the relevant material and artifacts he has sent me over the years, for connecting me with other scholars, for reading and commenting on the manuscript in its entirety, and most of all, for his friendship.

In addition to those fellowship programs already mentioned, a number of institutions and grantors made the research and writing of this book possible. These include Columbia University, the Tokyo Foundation, the Wenner-Gren Foundation for Anthropological Research, a Fulbright-Hays Doctoral Dissertation Research Abroad Fellowship, a Charlotte Newcombe Doctoral Dissertation Fellowship from the Woodrow Wilson Foundation, the International Institute of Asian Studies (Leiden), the Asian Studies Center at the University of the Philippines, the Philippine-American Educational Foundation, the Institute for the Humanities at the University of Michigan, and the University of Michigan. Financial support for this publication was generously provided by the Faculty Grants and Awards Program of the University of Michigan's Office of Research. Previous versions of some sections of this book can be found in the following publications: "Coincidence and Consequence: Marianism and the Mass Media in the Global Philippines," *Cultural Anthropology* 24, no. 3 (2009): 455–88; "From the Power of Prayer to *Prayer Power*: On Religion and Revolt in the Modern Philippines," in *Southeast Asian Perspectives on Power*, ed. Lee Wilson, Liana Chua, Joanne Cook, and Nick Long (London: Routledge, 2012), 165–80; and "The Mass

Miracle: Public Religion in the Postwar Philippines," *Philippine Studies: Historical and Ethnographic Viewpoints* 62, nos. 3–4 (2014): 425–44, published by the Ateneo de Manila University. Permission to print from each of these is gratefully acknowledged.

My heartfelt thanks go to the editors, editorial assistants, and others who whipped the final version of this book into shape. Freelance editor Kim Greenwell did a beautiful job uncluttering the manuscript and drawing out my strengths as a writer. Kim also prepared the index, for which I am ever so grateful. I thank Ian Ting, who designed the rosary graphic in chapter 5 at a moment's notice. At the University of Chicago Press, Priya Nelson completely demystified the process of publishing a book, keeping me informed every step of the way, and there was no query too neurotic to be fielded ably and patiently by Ellen Kladky. Working with them and Katherine Faydash has been a true pleasure and a wholly positive experience.

It brings me great relief and joy to finally be able to thank the friends and loved ones who have nourished and sustained me from near and far throughout the years that I have been working on this book. Thomas Abowd, Cy Calugay, Maki Fukuoka, Nina Hien, Smita Lahiri, Zack Linmark, Lisa Mitchell, Amira Mittermaier, Mira Tabasinske, and Megan Thomas have always been there for me, no matter how much time has passed since we last spoke. It gives me strength just knowing I can always reach out to them for support. As dinner parties have turned to play dates, Javier Castro, Mayte Green-Mercado, Hussein Fancy, Jane Lynch, Christi Merrill, and Dan Cutler continue to make Ann Arbor feel like home. Kelly Kempter and Lena Ehrlich create the space for me to attend to body and mind. Miquel Ruiz reminds me that being vulnerable is not a weakness but a need, and I'm so glad he found me again. Four strong, beautiful ladies have been my emotional anchors in recent months, and my unending thanks go to Evelyn Alsultany, Kate Gordy, Mayte Green-Mercado, and Shobita Parthasarathy for their life-affirming support. I honestly don't know what I would do without them.

For providing our son with stable homes-away-from-home, I thank Hongmei Delosh, June Depa, Inez Kaufman, Sherrie Hunninghake, Steve and Wendie Ryter, Dave and Marcie de la Cruz, and Roy and Rochelle de la Cruz. My mom and dad have shown me their love and unequivocal support through the best and worst of times, and I hope they fully share in this accomplishment as a way of accepting my gratitude. So different from each other but still so much my brothers, Dave and Marc de la Cruz have come to my defense as only siblings can, and I love them for it. It's a little scary to think that I've been working on this project for longer than Micah and

Malia, my tween nephew and niece, have been around, but I have enjoyed watching them grow up and am touched by how sweet they are with their little cousin. Loren Ryter lived with me living with this book since its inception, and he has borne the burden of its completion in more ways than I can name. I am grateful for the many ways he has supported me over the years. And Kai, my little ocean, my builder of worlds real and imaginary, assures me in ways both tender and hilarious that imperfect is the best kind of mama to be. This book is for him.

Note on Spelling

Following convention I have spelled all Spanish-derived Filipino proper names, place-names, and words without diacritical marks, except when directly citing texts or authors who preserve their use. For texts wholly written in Spanish I have preserved the use of diacritical marks, in accordance with standard orthography. A few of the original texts and title pages in Spanish see the variable use of accents; in these cases I opted for consistency and either included or omitted them across the board, depending on frequency of use, author, and context. Tagalog orthography varied widely before the mid-twentieth century. In reproducing or quoting from nineteenth- and early twentieth-century Tagalog sources, I have preserved the authors' spelling. Unless otherwise noted, all translations from the Tagalog and Spanish are my own.

Introduction

Of all the alleged apparitions of the Virgin Mary in the Philippines in recent years, none achieved greater notoriety than those that involved Judiel Nieva, in Agoo, La Union. In early 1993, Judiel, then a sixteen-year-old boy with a sickly nature, a middle school education, and the singing voice of an angel, made public the message he claimed to have received from Mary: that she would send a sign of her presence in Agoo on March 6 of that year. Mary had been appearing to the boy every first Saturday of the month and on feast days since 1989, he said, but no one beyond the local community paid any attention until the first Saturday of February 1993, when the statue carved in her image started weeping tears of blood, and the communion host that magically appeared in Judiel's mouth turned to bloody flesh. Pictures of these holy effusions spread rapidly, foreshadowing the miracles to come. By the first week of March, Manila-based news outlets were counting down the days to the scheduled appearance, buses coming from all points of Luzon added trips to their schedules, and the government's Land Transportation Office mobilized "Oplan Apparition," dispatching traffic controllers and emergency vehicles to assist the pilgrims. Residents of the small tobacco-manufacturing town with a population of forty-two thousand prepared as best they could for the human deluge.[1]

The day before the scheduled apparition, traffic was backed up as far as a hundred kilometers in some directions, with the heaviest traffic coming from Metro Manila. Reports confirmed that among those descending on the small town were Filipinos of the highest status and celebrity: senators, congressional representatives, and other government officials, media personalities, business tycoons, and some of the most influential clergy of the Catholic Church. By the end of the weekend, it was estimated that more than one million people had converged on "Apparition Hill" to witness the sign that Mary had promised.

Despite the massive crowd, only a few people reported actually having seen the divine sign. Those who did described red, yellow, and blue lights flashing, then shooting toward a dancing sun that spun and spiraled down toward the horizon before bouncing back into the sky. Even fewer reported seeing the apparition that preceded the lights and took the form of a silhouette atop a guava tree. Many people confessed that they saw nothing but felt Mary's presence nonetheless. Yet all could have heard the messages from Mary read aloud by Judiel, in an event that was broadcast live on the radio and at least one national television network. Received and written down by Judiel in a trance, the messages were a miscellany of statements in English, including "Always pray the rosary," "Satan has made his presence felt in Somalia," and "Without reconciliation there is no peace."

Given the extraordinary scale of the spectacle, it came as no surprise that the bishop of San Fernando, La Union, formed the Diocesan Commission of Inquiry to formally investigate the phenomenon. Philippine bishops walked a fine line between caution and enthusiasm, urging vigilance at the same time that they welcomed the upsurge in attendance at Mass and devotional practice. Months passed and pilgrims continued to come on the days that Mary had designated for her visits. Judiel continued to deliver messages during these appearances, although the fervor that suffused the first apparition event seemed to wane as the media coverage died down. September 8, 1993, marked the last of these apparitions, after which Judiel went into seclusion.

Throughout 1994, as Judiel endured what his spiritual director referred to with gravitas as "the dark night of his soul," pilgrimage to Agoo slowed to a trickle, and the questionable nature of the "miraculous" phenomena became more apparent. Rumors cropped up that members of the visionary's inner circle were squabbling over the distribution of donations and ownership of the land of the apparition site. Experts in the field of atmospheric science explained that changes in cloud composition could easily produce a "dancing sun." And even the most die-hard believers retreated behind such phrases as "it's up to you if you want to believe" (*nasasa-iyo na iyon kung maniniwala ka*).[2]

The Diocesan Commission of Inquiry, meanwhile, continued its investigation and, with the help of a sculptor, found that the bleeding statue was rigged on the inside with canals that spilled out at the inner corner of the image's eyes. Just as damning were the visionary's messages over the years, which the commission found inconsistent, nonsensical, or excessively similar to messages delivered by Mary elsewhere (notably in Europe and North America). In the end, it was the messages that provided the most compelling evidence for the commission to declare in September 1995 that the whole thing had been a spectacular hoax.

But before the "Agoo Apparition" was deemed a hoax, it was an extraordinary public phenomenon, one whose elements pose a formidable challenge to the ways in which "popular religion," and especially Catholicism, has been understood in the Philippines. First, the structure of visibility that made the promised miracles recognizable was not grounded in "local" beliefs or "autochthonous" forms of spiritual power but embedded in an inventory of Marian apparitions, messages, and phenomena whose historical circumstances and locations exist at a great distance from the Philippines. Lourdes, Fátima, Medjugorje—these, not any titles or references in the local vernacular, were the place-names and cases for comparison that circulated at the time of the first apparition and lent it provisional credence.

Second, the Agoo Apparition was largely, if paradoxically, an urban, middle-class phenomenon. The decisions about access, the dizzying relay of publicity in the English-language press, the very important persons in attendance, and that the handlers of the young visionary and flow of spectator pilgrims came from Manila—all suggest that this was not an event staged for the provincial "folk." To this day it is not difficult to find Manileños of a certain age who will sheepishly relate the time they jumped in their car to see what they could see in Agoo.

The Agoo Apparition, finally, provided an opportunity for conversion in the climate of revivified Marian devotion in the years following the People Power revolt in 1986—an event that many of its middle-class participants believed was a Marian miracle of sorts. It was hardly surprising that many of the main players of the revolt were the first to make their way to the apparition site. Thus, from the perspective of one with neither interest nor prerogative to ask whether *verum est*, the more impressive conjuring trick performed at Agoo was that of bringing into relief the religiosity of figures and social types long neglected in the scholarship on Filipino Christianity as exemplary of religious syncretism.

If the case of Agoo suggests the need to revisit some of the dominant paradigms of Filipino Christianity (such as that of the provincial and atavistic "folk Catholic"), the church's denunciation of the phenomenon is just as instructive. For the primary evidence cited against the apparitions' authenticity—that the messages purported to be from Mary drew from a smattering of foreign sources that were sloppily adopted to the local context—betrays a concern that is at once theologically governed and haunted by the desire for an identity that is nonderivative. What makes this convergence of anxieties possible is a logic of the copy, best revealed by the investigative commission's use of the term "plagiarize" to denounce the alleged messages.[3] Whereas once such a term would be used to denote the work of the devil, there was no such suggestion here.[4] Rather, the implication was that there were too many referents readily available for imitation and replication.

The role of the mass media is paramount in this regard, as it was owing to the global dissemination of other apparition events via television and the newspaper—notably that of the then-recent serial apparitions of Mary in Medjugorje, the former Yugoslavia—that the apparitions of Agoo took shape. This was not just an instance of (failed) "localization"; it indexed a fundamental problem of conformity and originality in an era marked by the reproduction of objects and transmissions. On the one hand, it is only within a schema of universally recognized figures and scenarios of divine intervention that such phenomena are apprehended—for example, how did spectators know to look at the sun? On the other hand, there must be some measure of uniqueness for any truth of the divine to be conceded. The slightest tip of this balance, and plausibility is thrown into question. This was made sensationally clear when, some time after the church's official declaration, the press caught up with the visionary Judiel to find that he had transformed into a woman and was pursuing an acting career under the name Angel de la Vega.[5]

This postscript to the case of Agoo attests to what is often perceived as the campy dimension of Marian apparitions. In spite of the seeming triumph of rationality in debunking the phenomena, however, Agoo—within easy reach of popular recollection—still beguiles and mystifies in the Philippines. (Indeed, one of the first questions I was often asked in response to my stated research topic was whether I had heard of the events in Agoo.) This is partly due to the dramatic and carnivalesque metamorphosis of its visionary. But whether as an example of the parodic staging of divine encounter or as a foil to those encounters with Mary that are deeply experienced or believed to be real, Agoo is remembered because it stoked an extraordinary display of religious imagination. This is an imagination at once deeply attuned to widely circulating tropes of the Catholic supernatural and saturated by the desire to have one's community and nation be unique in all the world. Central to what made the Agoo Apparition an episode of such failed seriousness is the knotty condition of universalized religion in a postcolonial locale.

This book is a historical and ethnographic critique of this condition as evidenced in apparitions and miracles of the Virgin Mary in the Philippines. Its setting is primarily the Tagalog-speaking regions, especially Manila and its environs. Its period is roughly the mid-nineteenth century to the present. Its immediate past is that of Spanish colonialism and the conversion of lowland communities to Christianity, dating back to the mid-sixteenth century. And the history to which it contributes is the history of Philippine modernity, whose particular articulations were formed via a concatenation of mestizo enlightenment, anticolonial nationalism, technologies of imperial rule, and capitalist expansion, but whose enchantments have tended to be overlooked or obscured by the explanatory imperative of modernist historiography. Among these enchantments is the steadfast frequency with which Filipino Catholics claim to see the Virgin Mary or attribute miracles to her intercession. This book thus seeks not to explain Christianity's return or reentry into public life, but rather to offer a historical account of its nondisappearance.

As broad as such a history might appear, it is but a miniscule sampling of a universe of phenomena. For many Catholics, it is an incontrovertible truth that the Virgin Mary appears. The question is, When, to a community, an institutional authority, or a nation, do these appearances seem to matter? When and how do they enter the public sphere? Befitting the geographical context of this study, the historian William Christian Jr. has written that "the actual historical topography of apparitions . . . can be compared to that of the sea-bed. The apparitions we know about are the islands above the surface . . . but there are many mountains below the surface we do not see."[6] In this book, to draw out that metaphor, I travel along a chain of apparition islands that emerged in the first instance because someone, at some point, said aloud that they exist—and others paid attention. I examine the forms of appearance that Mary takes, the stories and tensions that proliferate around such appearances, and the practices of devotion to her that reveal particularistic beliefs and local histories, transposed narratives and imagery, and globally circulating discourses of orthodoxy and redemption. I attend to these differences in iconography, influence, and scale as they chart a broader shift from the local to the national and the transnational, and from the material to the representational to the virtual—in short, as they formulate one tale of becoming modern.

MARY VERSUS MARIAN

We might begin this tale by observing that the generic terms "Marian" and "Marianism" are relatively recent designations in the history of Christianity. The *Oxford English Dictionary* reveals the first instance of "Marian" to date back to the Counter-Reformation (i.e., 1635, A. Stafford: "Till they are good Marians, they shall never be good Christians").[7] "Marianism," meanwhile, dates back only to the mid-nineteenth century and was often used disparagingly (i.e., 1845, G. B. Cheever: "Our Mother who art in heaven [says this great system of Marianism, instead of Christianity]").[8] The tone that accompanies each of these citations is not surprising, the former taking the stance of apologia, the latter appearing as an indictment made by one enlightened in the "true" Christianity. But together they signify the novel abstraction of categories from the figure of Mary, Mother of God. The term "Marianism," in particular, betrays the same classificatory imperative and hierarchy of value that gave rise to the concept of world religions.[9]

In the Philippine context like terms would have made their first appearance as the Spanish *mariano* most prevalently in the names of sodalities (*cofradías*) that began to flourish in the eighteenth century under the religious orders.[10] While it is not clear exactly when the English term "Marian" entered Filipino Catholic discourse for the first time, we can be certain that it widely circulated via Pope Pius XII's proclamation of the "Marian Year" in 1953 (for the year 1954), which was celebrated in the Philippines with various feast days and prayer campaigns. In ways similar to the appearance of "Marian" and "Marianism" in the English language, this book argues, the deployment of these terms in the Philippines signaled transformations in ideas about divine presence, community, representation, and potency. For from the introduction of Mary in the Philippines in the late sixteenth century to the last decades of Spanish colonial rule, Mary presided over communities in various incarnations and iconographies, terrestrially rooted, each possessing its own discrete title, powers, and legends. Many of these titles were in the local languages, taking on place-names (Our Lady of Namacpacan), connoting common forms of livelihood (Our Lady of Salambao, where *salambao* is a fisherman's net), or flora and fauna (Our Lady of Caysasay, named after a species of bird known as *casay-casay*). The diversity of devotional practices that flourished around each of these icons and the miracles attributed to them demonstrated that sacredness was plural and deeply tethered to, if not immanent in, the material representation (the image, or *santo*, in vernacularized Spanish), which in turn was attached to the land and geographically bound.

By contrast, the neologism "Marian" suggests an inverse definition, that is, a transcendent figure with a singular identity. "Marian" prioritizes the universal and general over the local and particular. It presupposes a different understanding of divinity, its locus, and its figuration. Furthermore, as an adjective that links a believer to this holy personage qua universal figure, as opposed to a highly place-specific Mary to whom one performs devotion, "Marian" has significant implications for religious subjectivity. Yet, although these are contrastive notions, they are not mutually exclusive. One can have a regular devotion to a particular Mary and still be described, as I often heard my interlocutors speak of themselves or of one another, as "very Marian." But to be "very Marian" means to recognize that the vast plethora of Marys that exist in the Philippines and elsewhere are but a series for which there exists a theological general equivalent.

One claim of this book is that the generalization that makes something like "Marian" subjects or "Marianism" thinkable betrays a deep complicity of religion—and above all, Christianity—with other projects of totalization and ideologies of universalism that constitute the modern world system.[11] This is hardly a novel observation. Historians, anthropologists, and other scholars avowing the postsecular epoch in which we live have drawn our attention in recent years to the co-constitutiveness of Christianity and modernity.[12] But many of these studies have been concerned with the strains of Christianity that most readily share the genealogy of Western liberal thought that has its origins in Protestant reform. As Fenella Cannell has persuasively argued, the scholarly assessment of Christianity and modernity should not privilege Protestantism, lest we develop a myopic view of what "counts" as Christianity and what might be modern about other Christian denominations.[13] What, then, to make of Protestantism's original other, Catholicism? What more can be said of its modernity?[14] And of modern Marianism especially?

THE AGE OF MARY

In 1830, the Virgin Mary appeared to Catherine Labouré in the chapel of the motherhouse of the Sisters of Charity in Paris. This vision, better known by the title conferred to Mary, Our Lady of the Miraculous Medal, marks the beginning of what Catholic circles refer to as the "Age of Mary":[15] a period of efflorescence of Marian apparitions and the revitalization of devotion to Mary worldwide that continues to this day. Since the Miraculous Medal, hundreds of apparitions of Mary have been reported. Few have been officially approved by the Catholic Church. Scholars have readily acknowledged this burgeoning of Marian phenomena, seeing in it a rich reserve for understanding popular and ecclesiastical responses to the social, political, and economic transformations wrought by modernity.[16] The studies of these apparitions of Mary have, rightly, emphasized the contexts in which they took place. Where many of these scholars have erred and studies have fallen short, however, is in understanding visions solely as reactionary phenomena, and their believers as, at best, resistant to change and, at worst, shackled by false consciousness.[17] If one reads many accounts of Marian phenomena closely, putting aside the presumption that such phenomena are simply transparent pretexts for human thought and action, one will find that the interconnectedness of Marian apparitions and modernity—or better, the modernity of Marian apparitions—is far more complex than many scholarly approaches have conceded.[18] Indeed, only an approach that considers multiple agencies and desires—including the seemingly nonmodern pursuit of taking Mary's agency seriously—can render a full picture of the rapprochement between modernity and the supernatural. For this it will be worth examining the vision of the Miraculous Medal, and why it marks the beginning of an epochal shift in apparition phenomena.

Labouré's visions of Mary in 1830 were the culmination of intense religious experiences that began before she entered the order of the Sisters of Charity and included having visions of St. Vincent de Paul, the order's founder, and of Christ in the Blessed Sacrament.[19] On the night of July 18, an angel led Catherine into the chapel, ablaze with light. Materializing before her was a female figure that Catherine first mistook as St. Anne, but upon realizing the apparition to be the Blessed Mother, she knelt at the lady's feet. In this first of several visions, Mary imparted several messages regarding the state of France, including the following: that "the throne will be overturned"; that "among the clergy of Paris there will be victims"; and that "the cross will be despised, it will be trampled under foot . . . the streets will flow with blood."[20]

In November of the same year Mary appeared again to Labouré. M. Aladel, Catherine's confessor, related the vision to one of the leaders of the diocese as follows:

> The Blessed Virgin appeared to a young Sister as if in an oval picture; she was standing on a globe, only one-half of which was visible; she was clothed in a white robe and a mantle of shining blue, having her hands covered, as it were, with diamonds, whence emanated luminous rays falling upon the earth, but more abundantly upon one portion of it.
>
> A voice seemed to say: "These rays are symbolic of the graces Mary obtains for men, and the point upon which they fall most abundantly in France. Around the picture, written in golden letters, were these words: "O Mary! conceived

without sin, pray for us who have recourse to thee!" ... The reverse of the picture bore the letter M surmounted by a cross, having a bar at its base, and beneath the monogram of Mary, were the hearts of Jesus and Mary, the first surrounded with a crown of thorns, the other transpierced with a sword. Then she seemed to hear these words: "A medal must be struck upon this model; those who wear it indulgenced, and repeat this prayer with devotion, will be, in an especial manner, under the protection of the Mother of God."[21]

This is a basic summary of the apparitions, about which several observations regarding their modernity can be made. The first is that the detailed messages that Mary relays to Labouré differ significantly from the communications Mary had with humans in the past. In the renowned appearance of Mary to Juan Diego in sixteenth-century Mexico, for example, the conversations were self-referential; that is to say, the dialogues were primarily concerned with how Juan might convince the ecclesiastical hierarchy and others that she had really appeared.[22] Documentary evidence and investigations of other Marian apparitions in late medieval and early modern Europe also reveal that such visitations were largely about the holy manifestation itself; although messages may have included generic prescriptions for prayer or behavior, they usually referred to matters of bare subsistence or survival and most often resulted in the erection of a shrine or monastery at the site of the appearance.[23] Any further implications or import derived from the apparitions would thus be left to the historian to draw from context.[24] The apparition of Our Lady to Catherine Labouré, therefore, marks a shift in the nature of the content of the communication, in that Mary makes explicit reference to events that shall take place in what we would consider modern historical time. She not only appears *in* the world but also appears in order to speak *about* the world. Although the messages were prophetic in nature and chiliastic in tone, they were completely imbricated in a temporal realm of existence. Thus, before we leap to examine the political significance of Mary's appearance and messages in the tumultuous context of 1830s France—the July Revolution broke out just days after Labouré's first vision—it is worth considering what the behavior of the apparition, as it were, suggests about its perceived agential and communicative (that is to say, mediatic) capacity.

The second feature of the apparition of the Miraculous Medal is its extraordinary representational modality. This is neither a material image "discovered" (as with most apparitions of Mary in the late medieval and Renaissance period, and likewise in the early colonial period in the Philippines) nor simply Mary "in the flesh." It is, rather, the appearance of the Blessed Virgin *as if in an oval picture*. Here, a phenomenology of enframement—note the literal delineation produced by the gold letters spelling out the popular doctrine of the Immaculate Conception—betokens secondness and a constitutive limit to the form of the appearance itself. Although Mary upon the globe is likely a reiteration of the motif deployed as early as the seventeenth-century in the iconography of the Immaculata, the apparition of a two-dimensional representation of Mary that calls for mass reproduction, as the Miraculous Medal does, is yet another first among Marian apparitions.[25]

Finally, there is the impressive propagation of the medal itself and its many remarkable effects. The Miraculous Medal was struck and replicated according to Labouré's visions. The front of each medal featured the image of Mary standing atop the globe, rays of light streaming from her hands. Around the oval, words proclaimed the Immaculate Conception. On the back, as seen by Labouré, was a large "M," surmounted by a cross, below which appeared the sacred hearts of Jesus and Mary. The medals were produced and sold for prices that varied according to the metal from which they were made. And as word of the medals and their favors spread, demand increased. The invocation on the medal was translated into the languages of the various lands to which the medals were destined, and the number of manufacturers of the medals multiplied. Seven years after Monsignor de Quélen, archbishop of Paris, granted approval for the production of the medals, ten million copies were in circulation throughout the world.[26] Accompanying this proliferation of medals was a slew of textual materials: prayer cards, pamphlets, novenas, as well as—of course—the story of the apparitions.

It will come as little surprise that such wide exposure led to other visionary phenomena. In one such case, the medals would reach their own apotheosis in a series of visions experienced by a Swiss religious. In these visions Mary appeared holding one of the medals. She described to the visionary its characteristics and what it symbolized. In other visions the Swiss woman saw the medals suspended in midair, at different levels depending on the material from which they were made, from gold to silver to brass. At one point during one of these visions, the woman heard a sweet voice explaining how each material indicated the level of piety and devotion possessed by the wearer—gold, unsurprisingly, being the superlative.[27]

The story told about the Miraculous Medal by historians and scholars of religion is usually one about religious fervor against secularization.[28] But there are other analyses to be drawn from the visions and their aftermath that may trouble such a pat narrative, notwithstanding the reality of the political struggles that make such a narrative convincing. In this brief consideration, my intent has been to introduce not only some of the themes that shall recur throughout this book but also an outline of method. When we attend to form and phenomenology over functionalism, Marian apparitions and devotion reveal many of the novelties putatively ushered in by secular modernity—new regimes of representation and political agency, changes in perception and modalities of presence, capacities of the mass media and technological reproduction, and ideologies of value, just to note the most obvious hallmarks. Lest there be any misunderstanding, however, my point is not to assimilate Catholicism into a triumphalist, progressivist narrative (i.e., look how modern Catholicism can be!) but rather to throw into shadowy relief the constitutive remainders of the theological and numinous in some of modernity's most cherished and crowning achievements.

SOMETHING ABOUT MARY

Having introduced the broader discursive field and historical context within which this book is situated, I can now speak with greater specificity about Mary in the Philippines. For while devotion to Mary in the Philippines takes as many forms as there are versions of the Blessed Mother herself, there are similarities where the appeal of Mary to Filipinos is concerned that deserve to be outlined.

To demonstrate the uniqueness of Filipino Catholicism, observers and followers often cite the centrality of Mary in devotional practice and popular belief. For the origins of this favoritism we can turn to the history of the late sixteenth- and seventeenth-century introduction of Christianity to the lowland communities inhabiting the archipelago. By many accounts, women (or feminine men) in precolonized societies maintained high social status owing to their many roles, which are best characterized as intermediary in function. From midwives to shamans (*babaylan* or *catalonan*), women negotiated and/or fulfilled both the temporal life cycle and the spiritual needs of the community.[29] When the Spaniards unpacked their pantheon of saints and Jesus Christ, performed their panoply of strange rites, and attempted the inculcation of monotheist dogma utterly alien to the local populace, it was the Virgin Mary who bore the closest structural resemblance to any figure that had previously existed. Here, of course, I am talking about translation broadly conceived, and it is to this legacy of conversion-as-translation that what is often perceived as the undue supremacy of Mary among Filipinos can be, in part, attributed.[30]

Yet while this might provide a convincing explanation for how robust devotion to Mary was engendered in the Philippines, it is largely among scholars that one will find these connections explicitly articulated.[31] The importance of Mary for the communities and individuals with whom I spent time is best gathered from one, frequently referenced New Testament scene, the wedding at Cana:

> On the third day there was a wedding in Cana in Galilee, and the mother of
>   Jesus was there.
> Jesus and his disciples were also invited to the wedding.
> When the wine ran short, the mother of Jesus said to him, "They have no
>   wine."
> [And] Jesus said to her, "Woman, how does your concern affect me? My hour
>   has not yet come."
> His mother said to the servers, "Do whatever he tells you."
>
> (JOHN 2: 1–5)[32]

For many theologians and biblical scholars, the importance of these few brief lines is that it is the first demonstration of Christ's power to perform miracles.[33] In all the times I heard this story in a Philippine context, however, emphasis was placed on Mary's role as Christ's collaborator.

In one public talk, the visionary Teresita Castillo (whom we shall meet in chapter 3 of this book) makes this plainly clear:

> *Paano ipinakita ni Jesus ang pagmamahal sa kanyang ina? Noong unang miracle.*
> *When was the first miracle? Cana. Sinabi ni Jesus noon na hindi pa time niya. Pero*
> *through the words of the loving mother nangyari ang miracle of the wine. So if there*
> *is no Mary, there will not be any miracle at all of Jesus. Just remember that!*[34]

> How did Jesus show his love for his mother? The first miracle. When was the
> first miracle? Cana. Jesus said then that it was not yet his time. But through the
> words of the loving mother the miracle of the wine happened. So if there is no
> Mary, there will not be any miracle at all of Jesus. Just remember that!

Bracketing for now the interesting hybridity of Teresita's language, the lesson she draws from the wedding at Cana is that Christ's first miracle was, above all, a sign of love for his mother, and only secondly a pronouncement of his messianic mission. Several people remarked to me over the course of my fieldwork that this scene resonates powerfully with the experience of dutifully upholding the appearance of abundance in social rites or festivity. As one friend put it: *Naku! Wala silang alak!* (Yikes! They ran out of wine!) *Napahiya si Mama Mary!* (Mama Mary was so embarrassed!) Mary intervenes because of the empathy she feels for the shame that will befall the hosts should they not provide enough wine. Embarrassed (*napahiya*) on their behalf, Mary asks Jesus to ensure that this not happen. Ignoring his rebuke ("my hour has not yet come," or *hindi pa time niya*, according to Teresita), because she knows not only her son's power but also *her influence over him*, she directs the servants to await Jesus's instructions.

Here the connection among Mary, her motherhood, and the miraculous is explicit, at least in Teresita's estimation, and it is this connection that lies at the heart of this book. At the beginning of her lesson Teresita refers to the first miracle as a sign given by Christ to Mary, but the emphasis quickly shifts to Mary as the origin of that sign: no Mary, no miracle ("just remember that!"). This is not to say that Mary herself performs the miracle, but it is "through the words of Mary"—that is, through her mediation—that the miracle takes place. Beneath the exuberant appreciation of the affective bond between mother and child lies a peculiar and subtly subversive thaumaturgy: that Mary, and not Christ, is the source of the miraculous; and this is so precisely because of her power of mediation.

MEDIA TRICKS AND THE MEDIATRIX

The paradox of Mary as both origin and mediator animates this historical ethnography. It connects the colonial period to the present through the convergence of divine and profane, localized and mass, as well as spiritual and mechanical, figures and modes of mediation. Importantly, the nature of this convergence is not deterministic: although the book focuses empirically on appearances of the Virgin Mary (whose name "the Mediatrix" has gained popularity in recent decades throughout the world, including the Philippines), and analyzes them in conjunction with the rise of mass-mediated practices and cultures in modernity, the correlation between the two cannot be reduced to one of cause and effect. It is not, furthermore, just in relation to the mass media that I attend to Marian devotion and phenomena in these pages, but also in relation to a whole array of mediating practices that include speech, various genres of writing, and the production of historical knowledge, as well as those practices long germane to considering the anthropological object of religion: ritual, prayer, possession, and sacrifice.

The conjunction of religion and the mass media is, nevertheless, of central concern in this book, for it focalizes a critique of those studies just discussed that seek to explain modern apparitions of Mary via functionalist paradigms. Where these studies mention the mass media, it is usually in passing, as that which facilitated and accelerated the movement of news and pilgrims across distances. Yet even a cursory glance over the past fifty years reveals the variety of ways in which technologies of the mass media have played a role beyond that of simply providing form for religious content. Such technologies need to be examined for their ability to mirror, restructure, and even produce religious phenomena and experience.

In the apparitions of the Virgin Mary in Bayside, New York, in the 1970s, for example, photography was seized on not only for its documentary capability but also for what was believed to be its deeply revelatory power. Referred to by the devotional community as "Polaroids from heaven," photos taken during the apparitions served as instruments of divination, offering prophetic messages and insights.[35] To give another example, the trope of "serial" visions of the Virgin Mary occurring at a regularly scheduled time over months or years—as is the case with the apparitions in Medjugorje, in the former Yugoslavia—arguably references the rhythms of television viewing.[36] And even these examples seem quaint once one turns to the overwhelming impact of new media in radically reforming devotional practice with innovations like virtual pilgrimage and the ability to e-mail prayer petitions to "Our Lady" at any number of Marian shrines across the globe.

Yet it is not only as a resource facilitating the propagation of devotion, a metaphorics for articulating perception and experience, or a conduit enabling the instantaneous connection to sacred sites that the mass media has helped usher us into the postsecular age. For insofar as religious practices, institutions, and doctrine are always already mediatic, one can invert the question of how the mass media has contributed to the so-called return of religion to ask how certain religious traditions and imaginations may have given rise to, or even anticipated, the possibilities fantasized by the makers and users of media technologies.[37]

To take the two examples cited earlier, it could be argued that photography's power to arrest time in an image or render the invisible visible was prefigured by the iconographical tradition seen in such relics as Veronica's Veil or the Shroud of Turin,[38] and repetition and seriality have long been considered crucial elements bringing about the desired effects of rosary prayer.[39] My point is that there is nothing that one can posit a priori about the relationship between religion and the mass media in modernity. And in our case, even the most homogenizing of modern effects—such as the generalization, part and parcel of all modern economies of representation, which makes something like the category of "Marian" possible—must be examined from several angles in relation to long-standing features of Catholicism, such as its emphasis on the body, its exclusion of women from the institutional hierarchy, and the dialectic that often obtains between church and place.

BEYOND THE LOCAL

The past few decades have seen a profusion of historical and ethnographic studies that focus on modern communities of Christian faithful throughout the world. Under the rubrics of "popular religion," "folk Christianity," and more recently "lived religion," this scholarship has freed Christian devotions from the institutions, doctrines, and theologies of transcendence that once circumscribed them in relation to orthodox norms.[40] These rubrics are not interchangeable, however, and as historian of religion Robert Orsi has pointed out, some of these categories continue to do the work of "policing religion" more than others.[41] But together they have precipitated a sea change in scholarly attitudes toward Christianity that, first, legitimized the diverse nature of Christian practice and belief (beyond simple denominational differences) and, second, identified that plurality as resulting from the particularities of local historical, cultural, and vernacular contexts. A generation or so later, this might sound obvious, yet I spell it out here in order to draw attention to something that has been taken for granted in this scholarly transformation, that is, a tacit consensus about what the "local" means.

The historiography of Southeast Asia underwent broad transformations that paralleled the "local turn" taken by the historiography and anthropology of Christianity, but a decade or two earlier. In the 1960s, U.S.-based historians like John Smail were advocating for "autonomous histories" of Southeast Asia—an alternative to colonial histories on the one hand, and to anticolonial or nationalist histories on the other—that sought to place indigenous narratives at the center of historical writing, even (or especially) if they did not conform to the broader periodizations and epochal shifts identified with large-scale processes like colonialism or conflicts such as the Cold War.[42] In Philippine historiography, this emphasis on local (if not necessarily "indigenous") history finds its most emphatic articulation in the 1982 volume edited by American historian Alfred McCoy and Filipino historian Edilberto C. de Jesus, *Philippine Social History*, which comprises individually authored essays grouped by major region (Luzon, the Visayas, and Mindanao), bypassing for the most part any major national concern.[43] Ethnographies of Philippine Catholicism, meanwhile, have continued to emphasize locality, focusing especially on place-specific devotions through which community identity and history may be articulated and discerned.[44]

Nowhere, however, in Southeast Asian studies was the notion of the local more explicitly elaborated than in the famous 1982 essay by Cornell University historian Oliver Wolters, "Towards Defining Southeast Asian History." When Wolters introduced the term "localization," he gave concise form to a concept that had long been in the making but had lacked a cogent name. Denoting action and connoting an ongoing process, Wolters's "localization" describes how foreign materials are made to fit into local religious, political, and social systems, transforming them and being, themselves, transformed. But this gloss hardly does justice to Wolters's eloquence in justifying the term's purchase and elaborating on exactly what it means:

> The term "localization" has the merit of calling our attention to something else outside the foreign materials. One way of conceptualizing this "something else" is as a local statement, of cultural interest but not necessarily in written form, into which foreign elements have retreated.[45]

In many ways this passage sums up the puzzling contradictions of Southeast Asian history. Here the "local statement" is not given a priori but defined vis-à-vis the foreign as "something else." The foreign—which for Wolters was the Indian ("Hindu"), but for our purposes would be the European colonial—does not enter the local, as one might expect, but rather *retreats into* it. These may be little more than rhetorical idiosyncrasies on Wolters's part, but the ideas behind them have had extraordinary staying power for many Southeast Asianists, as conceding the impact of foreign influences at the same time that they presume that the influences were domesticated or attenuated to some degree. The subtlety of Wolters's formulation is in recognizing that the "local" is brought into relief only through its relationship to an outside, and it is thus inherently instable. The limitation of "localization" is that it assumes that Southeast Asians are only ever on the receiving end of "foreign materials," and thus that their agency, no matter how transformative, is largely reactive.

This is especially true when it has come to what many call "world religions." Hinduism, Buddhism, Islam, Christianity: most of us who work with these traditions in Southeast Asia have pursued their local articulations rather than their universal pretenses, whether we acknowledge a debt to Wolters or not. Yet "localization" cannot account for everything, I discovered, when confronted with Filipino devotional movements that seemed to turn this formulation entirely on its head, with Filipino missionaries becoming the "foreign" to someone else's "local." With the rise of a Filipino diaspora, as well as the increasing deterritorialization of devotional phenomena, figures, and communities through the dissemination of religious materials via the mass media, one cannot count so readily on even provisionally bounded cultural contexts.

But it is not just in relation to place that I suggest in this book that we look at more than just locality. For wherever there is Christian mission, there is an essential commitment to the universality of Christianity: that anyone can be Christian. Now, one need take only a cursory look at the history of Christian mission to see that this principle has not always been evenly maintained in practice (the letters of Francis Xavier sent from a number of places in Asia provide a fine example of this discrepancy).[46] But to ignore this cornerstone of the faith is to overlook the motive power that accounts not only for conversion's "successes" but also for its violence when it comes to dealing with the particularities of human experience.

Just as there are a number of excellent studies of Christian communities that emphasize those communities' local qualities, there are many books, both scholarly and general, that focus on one local Catholic devotion in the Philippines. This book is not one of them. Readers will learn of individual devotions to Mary that emerge out of different times and places, but each of these contributes to an examination whose objective is to historicize how some Catholics have come to suppose, articulate, and propagate the universality of their own faith. In its broadest sense, it is a book about how new universals are imagined and made.

HOW TO FOOTNOTE A MIRACLE; OR, A NOTE ON METHOD

This study is *at once* historical and ethnographic. I emphasize that phrase "at once," for although the reader will note that the book, insofar as it moves chronologically, engages more primary source and textual documents at its beginning and more material collected from fieldwork toward its end, the methodological underpinnings of the study are simultaneously informed by the disciplines of history and anthropology throughout. This is, in the first place, a result of my training, both in an area studies field that has much emphasized interdisciplinarity and as a student of a generation of scholars whose work and teaching often stood at the crossroads of both anthropology and history. But in a book devoted to thinking about mediation and universals, it is not enough to claim that my conjoined methods amount to simply borrowing from both disciplines' well-furnished tool kits. These themes demand that method itself receive some scrutiny, as that which mediates the observable in the production of knowledge.

To be sure, the apparition provides a marvelous opportunity for unsettling ways of knowing. I find William Christian's metaphor about the "sea bed" of apparitions compelling, and most likely true.[47] It may be possible to study the apparitions we know about from a variety of angles, but those that lie in the abyss of unspoken experience will never be known, and therefore cannot be measured, in a manner of speaking. But does this mean that they do not matter? That they are not felt? I think of the actual ocean floor, and how some of the earth's geotectonic shifts take place there, imperceptibly, but eventually to great consequence. Is there not something similar that takes place in the deepest reaches of the historical and ethnographic topography of apparitions? And if so, is it enough to simply acknowledge it, or can we engage it, analytically or otherwise?

I cannot give definitive answers to these questions, since to do so would defeat the purpose in asking them. I am talking about empirically ethereal—indeed, empirically unavailable—events, after all. But merely posing these questions has had demonstrable effects on my research and writing. In the archives, such questions made me acutely aware of the partiality of sources and the ultimate absurdity of the phrase "exhaustively researched." They prompted further musings about the sorts of archives that exist in the appearances and words of holy figures. They compelled me to consider the quality of belatedness that exists in every historical document as itself a subject for inquiry. And they led me to look not only for verifiable connections among figures and phenomena but also for historical resonances: similarities and intensifications of an experiential or affective nature that could not be reduced to clear-cut vectors of cause or influence.[48]

Ethnographically, the thought of this vast repository of inaccessible apparition experience led to certain practices of observation and listening to what did bubble up to the surface. If we take the disproportionality of shared experiences versus unshared experiences to be accurate, we might come to regard such experiences as controversial. This certainly seemed to be the case for many of my interlocutors, and thus attention to rhetorical registers could yield much insight into the social life of their experiences. Was this person presenting a finely crafted narrative, shaped through many tellings? What language(s) did my interlocutor use, and did it mark authority or deference? Was the confession made sotto voce meant to signal that I was being told of a vision in the strictest confidence, or that I should ask more questions about who refused to believe the seer? Were the pauses and looks meant to probe the limits of my own credulity or that of the person with whom I was speaking?

In short, this "sea bed" of apparitions acted as a constitutive outside that shaped how I went about doing research, because it reminded me of the highly mediated nature of what I *could* study. My methods, in turn, could never exist completely outside or prior to this context, because they, too, were materially and intersubjectively mediated. Serendipities, dead ends, reciprocities, and refusals, to say nothing of unforeseen interventions by the physical world, are all part of the messy process of doing both historical and ethnographic research, although very few people will confess this (at least not in print). But if I am to "walk the walk" of this book's theoretical claims and critiques of secular modernity, then these remarks about method are warranted. For if method essentially belongs to the modern process that Max Weber identified as "rationalization," then bringing into relief some of the incalculable dimensions of research may be one starting point for articulating those claims and performing that critique.[49] Then, before leaping to assume a disenchanted stance toward enchanted phenomena, maybe, just maybe, we will stop to reflect on how miraculous it is that anything like a book materializes at all.

AN OVERVIEW

The following chapters chart the transformation of Catholic devotions, practices, and beliefs through changes in what Friedrich Kittler termed "discourse networks": material systems of notation, storage, retrieval, and transmission that not only expand the reach of communication but also provide the means through which communication can take place.[50] There is no reason divine communication should be understood differently, since it is, as I just emphasized, through the mediation of others that divine communication comes to be known. There are three parts to the book, each of which comprises two chapters. These parts loosely correspond to chronological periods and focus on particular forms of the mass media. Within these parameters, through readings of different apparitions of Mary, each section explores certain conceptual arenas or cultural logics that emerge in modernity.

The first part of the book ("Images") generally covers the period of late Spanish colonial rule as it transitions to American tutelary imperialism, and this part is based on print sources. Chapter 1 examines several texts produced or published by Spanish friars that narrate the origins of some of the most significant apparitions of the Virgin Mary in the colonial Philippines. Often serving as the preface to novenas (a nine-day cycle of prayers), these apparition tales reached a zenith of mass production in chapbook form in the middle decades of the nineteenth century. They make history out of popular lore and render complete accounts with only incomplete archival records. These apparition tales are also, at times, violent narratives of exclusion of those communities that posed the greatest threat to Spanish authority. But insofar as these tales are usually written in the local vernacular and attuned to the specificities of place, they invite one to read against the grain of their colonial authors' agendas. These texts represent the worldview whereby the sacred was highly localized and particular, and believed immanent to material forms.

Marian apparitions were unmoored from these conventions in the nationalist period of the late nineteenth and early twentieth centuries. Chapter 2 opens with an apparition tale that betokens a new *representational* capacity of Mary, especially as she is linked to the much revered and beloved figure of Inang Bayan (Mother Country). At a time when other ideologies of value associated with capitalist production emerged as a challenge to the economies of imperial Christendom, mestizo reformists and revolutionaries wrote poetry, essays, and plays that cast their discontent with Spanish rule in an ambivalent allegory of maternal relations. Such reimaginings of the relationship between mother and child paved the way for a double translation that rendered "Filipino" (in the new national-cultural sense of the term) both the figure of the Virgin Mary and the global circulating concept of motherland.

The apparition events at Lipa, Batangas, constitute the focus of the second part of this book ("Visions"). There, in 1948, Mary allegedly appeared and announced herself as "Mary, Mediatrix of All Grace," to a Filipina novice of the Order of Discalced Carmelites. The timing of this apparition is significant, for Lipa was the provincial headquarters of the Japanese Military Administration during World War II, and its inhabitants witnessed both mass killings at the hands of the Japanese and the total razing of their city by American forces. Chapter 3 takes this lens into consideration but also examines the equally significant response of the local church, which after conducting a brief investigation condemned the events in a decree issued in 1951. Unpublished testimonies of the visionary and her mother superior, primary sources from personal collections, and interviews reveal the apparitions at Lipa Carmel as enacting a complex mediation of authority and legitimacy in the postwar period. The story presents, on the one hand, a global monastic order of spiritual renown trying to take root in this war-torn locale and, on the other hand, a global institution whose ranks were undergoing growing pains to "Filipinize" in the newly independent nation.

Chapter 4 views the Lipa miracles from outside of the cloister through an examination of what made them a public phenomenon—specifically, showers of rose petals that appeared on several occasions inside the convent and later began falling on the convent grounds. Over the course of several months, stories about the petals circulated at a national and international level, giving rise to new devotional publics near and afar. The chapter traces the literal and virtual circulation of the petals, examining how they forged networks that mediated social and political imaginaries not limited in space or specific to an institution.

Bookended by the U.S.-led Cold War and the U.S.-led global War on Terror, part 3 ("Mass Movements") enacts an important shift in the book on three registers: from the media of mechanical reproduction to electronic media; from apparitions of Mary as phenomena witnessed by a privileged few to the mass replication of Marian imagery seen by multitudes; and from foreign to Filipino leadership in Catholic mission. Chapter 5 focuses on the rosary, as both a devotional practice and a locus for lay activism. It examines the Family Rosary Crusade (FRC), a Catholic apostolate that was founded in the United States in the late 1940s and proliferated worldwide via a complex of national chapters. The first Catholic organization of its kind to self-consciously embrace the mass media as an effective tool of mission, the FRC transformed the devotional landscape in the Philippines beginning in 1951, and by the mid-1970s it had its own Filipino administrative offices and staff that operated independently of U.S. headquarters. Through enormous prayer rallies, nationwide film screenings depicting the life of Christ, and television spots, the FRC brought new meaning to what it meant to "see Mary," by forging a novel mediascape wherein Mary's image and voice was projected on a variety of visual fields.

Apparition narratives in the Philippines are replete with scenes of misfortune, crisis, fear of the foreign, catastrophe, atrocity, and war. The last chapter engages these themes most directly, at the same time that it further widens the question of Filipinos' intensifying role in Christian mission, by examining two events that were heavily mass mediated and decidedly global in scope. The first of these events took place in September 1999 and was staged by a Filipino Marian devotional group in New York City. Known as the World Marian Peace Regatta, the festival was a daylong birthday celebration honoring the Virgin Mary, performed as a ritual to invoke her protection over the world. Framing this event is a seemingly unrelated diplomatic incident: the 2004 kidnapping of an overseas Filipino worker by a group demanding that the Philippine government withdraw its coalition forces from Iraq. One extraordinary coincidence and the appeal for divine intervention immediately link the two. But what further draws these two events into relatedness is that they both entail imaginaries of the global Philippines that are rooted in a shared history of transnational movement but diverge owing to significant differences in socioeconomic status, physical vulnerability, and the present place of the Philippines and Filipinos in the world.

The history of Mary's apparitions and Mary's followers in the modern Philippines offers a more nuanced understanding of Christianity in and from the so-called Global South. It raises compelling questions about Christianity's claim to universality and the futures of global mission. The conclusion poses some of these questions and invites readers to further pursue some of the central themes of this book, in the Philippines or in other times and places, so that we may better understand the purchase and perils of universals in a global present marked by many forms of sacred violence.

PART I

Images

CHAPTER ONE

The Authority of Appearances

A suitable comparison is that of sculpture, that from stone or wood creates a fully bodied image . . . To see that solid marble or that rough trunk being smoothed down, the sculptor with his hammer and pick in the stone, with his hatchet and adze in the timber, upon the basic form that he made with all his effort he undertakes all over again to perfect it bit by bit . . . until giving shape to its eyes, nose, mouth, all other features, limbs, and parts, to its garb and dress even up to the hems and folds. To arrive at this point: who wouldn't grow exhausted just seeing such assiduousness and meticulousness? And still there remains to polish the marble, give it contours if needed, to lighten the wood, to flesh it out, to give it color and light! It takes no less than this, and far more, to make Christians out of Infidels.

—PEDRO CHIRINO, S.J., *Història de la província de Filipines* (1581–1606)[1]

Pedro Chirino, a seventeenth-century Jesuit chronicler, presents us with an image of conversion in which native infidels are like statues molded from a formless mass into Christians. The meaning of "image" here is doubled, tripled even, as we draw from this passage various connotations of the term. In one sense, "image" (in the original Castilian, *imagen*) refers to the sculpture or bust, physical objects of perception. In another sense, "image" connotes resemblance, which makes possible "a suitable comparison" (*comparazión muy propria*) between infidels and material images, and by extension in this context, the creation of subjects in the likeness of God.[2] And finally, there is the image that emerges from the text in the reader's encounter with it, a biased representation of conversion and the colonial past.

In this chapter, I bring all three of these meanings of "image" to bear on a reading of several texts relating miraculous appearances of the Virgin Mary. Often serving as the preface to novenas (a nine-day cycle of prayer), these narratives reached a zenith of mass production in the mid- to late nineteenth century. As Chirino's evocative description suggests, however, the link among image, appearance, and Christian identity was in circulation long before the age of print capitalism. Thus, the chapter first depicts the important place of religious images in the broader history of conversion to Christianity in the Philippines. It then examines the production of late colonial texts about Mary, the conditions of their production, and the role that apparitions played in mediating the perceived incursions and actual entanglements of colonial modernity.

One of the best points of departure for this overview is the reorganization of native communities into administrative units during the early years of Christian conversion. By all accounts, one imperative of the missionaries was to attract native communities, dispersed and generally isolated, into a physical sphere of Christian influence. This resulted in the construction of centralized settlements modeled after those established in Mexico, the *cabecera-visita*, which demarcated a *pueblo* (later known as a *municipio*, or township). Tethered to a center (the *cabecera*), whose main features were a church and a plaza, were smaller villages (the *visitas*) scattered throughout the vicinity. Each *visita* possessed its own chapel. Historians have cited this arrangement as evidence of the difficulty missionaries encountered in bringing communities within close range of the church. The arrangement was a compromise that required priests to administer at both levels, as reflected in the oft-referenced notion that settlements pertaining to a single *pueblo* be established *bajo la campana*—literally, "beneath the bells," or within hearing distance of their toll.[3] In the Philippines, the *barangay*—a vernacular term that to early European explorers designated the smallest denomination of social organization in existence—was rendered equivalent to a *visita*.[4]

Key here is the importance and centrality of the physical structure of the church as the center of newly founded communities. This emplacement of the church fixed natives as colonial subjects, that is to say, tributary wards, and profoundly affected the physical landscape of the archipelago itself. Churches and chapels stood like so many pinheads on a map that unfolded to reveal an accumulated count of saved souls. Each building was presided over by a human administrator and a holy one. Images of titular patron saints were often installed as an edifying feature of the churches and chapels, lending a particular identity to each proselytizing endeavor. However, in a few cases, per local lore, it was neither the church nor the religious order that chose the spot of veneration, but the titular patron him or herself.

Our Lady of Guadalupe, Lourdes, Fátima, and Montserrat. Our Lady of Knock, Garabandal, Akita, and Clearwater. Wherever the Virgin Mary performs miracles or appears (and frequently the latter constitutes the former), thus is she named. Unlike renditions that derive from doctrinal belief (such as the Immaculate Conception), or artistic renditions of scriptural passages (such as *La Pietà*), the use of place-names as identifiers grounds the Mother of God in the terrestrial. Such renditions anticipate some connection to the human, be it to the inhabitants of the place that bears the name or to the community that attends to Mary's appearance, comprising witnesses, skeptics, sanctioning or disapproving figures of authority, elite patrons, believers, future pilgrims, and so on. As to whether some form of community existed in these places prior to such appearances or emerged as a consequence of them, what William Christian Jr. once noted could not be more apt: "A shrine can put a town on the map, and miracles make a shrine."[5]

Throughout the Spanish colonial period, images of the Virgin Mary proliferated throughout the Philippines, with shrines that bear their names to this day: Our Lady of Manaoag, Caysasay, Salambao, Turumba, and Namacpacan, to name but a few. By conjoining a singular title (Nuestra Señora, or Our Lady) to sites whose names remain in the vernacular, these shrines monumentalize the colonial encounter. At the same time, they stand as repositories of local history, each possessing its own origin story, legends, and miracles. There is not the space here for me to detail the histories of all the patron images of the Virgin Mary throughout the Philippines. Such would be a feat of encyclopedic proportions, given that more than eight hundred of the country's parishes and chapels have Mary as their titular patron, and some art historians and devotees of the Virgin Mary have already attempted this.[6] Because this book is concerned with issues of mediation—with media—I offer instead an examination of several apparition tales and foundational narratives that were published during the period of burgeoning print culture in the Philippines in the nineteenth century.

These apparition and miracle tales were part of the broader publishing phenomenon of chapbooks, which included hagiographies, sermons, prayer books (*devocionarios*), exempla, popular romances, and spiritual manuals. Chapbooks appeared not only in Castilian but also in all of the major languages of the Philippines. In the historiography of Filipino literary forms, these widely circulating texts are considered precursors of such modern genres as the novel. And though they clearly index monastic control over textual production, chapbooks were often written with the participation of native or mestizo acolytes (*ladinos*) who worked as translators or coauthors for the Spanish friars and, in many cases, went on to compose their own texts. The genres of the *awit* (a composition of dodecasyllabic lines) and the *corrido* (a composition of octosyllabic lines) in particular have drawn sustained attention from literary scholars, as these popular romances, often fantastic tales of chivalry and love, allow one to diachronically trace their appropriation by the friars and, later, the innovations made to them by native authors.[7] There has been little interest, however, in the many chapbooks whose themes are not of the epic romance but of the religious manual. It is

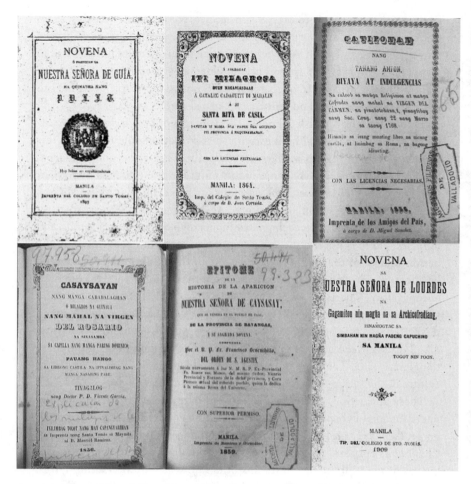

FIGURE 1.1 Nineteenth-century chapbooks. Courtesy of Hathi Trust and Archivo de la Provincia Agustiniana de Filipinas, Biblioteca del Estudio Agustiniano, Paseo de Filipinos, 7, Valladolid, Spain.

a remarkable oversight, considering that novenas or *devocionarios*, hagiographies, and the like were the most proliferative genre of text published in the archipelago in the mid- to late nineteenth century (figure 1.1).[8]

Some of the reasons for this proliferation are straightforward. In 1856, the Spanish colonial government established the Comisión Permanente de Censura (Permanent Commission of Censors), which comprised the *fiscal de la Audiencia* (akin to a district attorney), four laypersons from the colonial government, and four ecclesiastical representatives.[9] At its most frequent, the commission met almost monthly to deliberate, and often condemn, texts that were being imported into the Philippines. It blocked or edited novels, dramas, history books, and philosophical or scientific texts for "ideological" or "heterodox" content.[10] For these censors, chapbooks with patently religious content were inoffensive. In this context, late colonial critics like the bibliophile W. E. Retana would dismiss devotional texts as "[the] thousands of little books of stultifying religiosity in indigenous languages, the only thing that friars wished to propagate, so that the natives of the land and the Spaniards would never be able to comprehend one another."[11]

This last sentence refers to movements that began in the late eighteenth century but accelerated with the opening up of Manila to international trade in 1835.[12] The unprecedented capitalist modernity that resulted combined with the political turmoil of nineteenth-century Spain to produce farreaching consequences. These effects included not only the penetration of liberal ideas coming from the Peninsula but also the formation of a formidable mestizo middle class that sent their *ilustrado* ("enlightened") sons to study in the metropole. There, they absorbed and contributed to emergent fields of knowledge, political debate, and artistic production. The idea that chapbooks of religious content were part of a rearguard attempt by Spanish friars to counteract these developments and keep the native *indio* in a somnambulant state of small-time devotion was wholly plausible.[13]

And yet, given the sheer volume of these religious chapbooks, many of which were published in multiple languages and editions, it is worthwhile to examine a few of them closely. As Smita Lahiri has suggested, friar-authored or friar-published texts can be useful "as diagnostic tools for probing a shifting field of colonial power relations."[14] Hybrid in their composition, *devocionarios* and similar texts draw awkwardly and elegantly from both traditional modes of oral versification, such as the *dalit*, and the standard repertoire of Christian prayer, such as the act of contrition (*ang pagsisisi*, in Tagalog).[15] They are often rife with meta- or paratexts, short dedications or messages that both impose a certain approach to reading and make reference to a space, time, or exchange outside of the text itself.[16] As the Filipino literary critic Resil Mojares has pointed out, novenas and prayer manuals "intended to codify for the faithful the origin and meanings of the divine patron and its representation" often reveal the opposite, that is, "semantic instability" and ambivalence.[17] Put another way, these texts can be read at once as allegories of the intractability of meaning in colonial interactions and as anxious efforts to contain semantic drift. In many apparition cases, this intractability is marvelously and materially rendered in the literal movement (appearance, disappearance, and later discovery) of an image of Mary and the consequent tug-of-war over its localization. The first of several apparitions stories we examine here, that of Our Lady of Caysasay, is one of these.

EVASIONS: OUR LADY OF CAYSASAY

A villager is out doing whatever it is that he does in the everyday course of village life, when he stumbles upon a statue of the Virgin Mary. He prostrates himself before it, tucks it under his arm, and brings it home. The local priest learns of the discovery and goes to where the image is kept. He, too, kneels in adoration before the image and brings it to the parish church, displaying it there for all to venerate. Then, the strangest thing happens. One day the image disappears from its revered post. Time passes, and on another occasion, another villager is going about daily life, when she stumbles across the same image, resting near the spot where it was originally found. The priest brings it back to the parish, but the little image is willful, and again when no one is looking, it returns to where it was found. The image appears to be saying something, speaking by appearing, speaking without properly saying. What—if anything—she is communicating may be contested terrain. Fearing this ambiguity, the priest intervenes, declares the image miraculous, and erects a shrine at that spot.

This is the basic narrative of the story of Our Lady of Caysasay, near the town of Taal, in the province of Batangas, in the archipelago known then as Las Islas Filipinas.[18] But this is also the story of many miraculous images of the Virgin Mary, not only in Filipinas but also throughout the Catholic world.[19] Already this raises the question of circulation: skeptics might ask what the cultures or regimes of circulation were during this period, whether galleons or the mouths of friars or both were what moved these images and stories across oceans. Historians on a quest for resistance, meanwhile, might wonder whether the natives themselves were responsible for the image's movement. Devotees to Our Lady of Caysasay, however, would simply celebrate instead her divine intervention, as they did in 2003, on the four hundredth anniversary of her appearance. For all of the apparition's devoted interpreters, this incident of what André Breton called *la trouvaille*—the discovery at once "surprising and necessary"[20]—of the Virgin in the form of a tiny statuette, little bigger than a hand, was an event and, moreover, a *sign* (figure 1.2).

The particularities of this legend are context specific: the villager is a local fisherman, the friar is an Augustinian, and the title bestowed on the

FIGURE 1.2 Our Lady of Caysasay, four hundred years after, according to legend, she was
fished out of the Pansipit River by Juan Maningcad.

Virgin comes from the vernacular name for a local bird (*casay-casay*). Yet the
persistence of this tale across locales, albeit with some narrative variation,
furnishes a paradigm through which we can understand the extension of
ecclesiastical authority as necessarily partaking of some mystical, if not miraculous, occurrence. The native discoverer, the site of discovery in nature,

the mysteriousness of the appearing and disappearing image, as well as the exceptional figure of the Virgin herself signal the outer limits of colonial (and not incidentally male) authority. The performative enactment of authority takes place by literally *taking place*, that is, by conjoining the finding of the image with the founding of a shrine. The shrine is then made into a *visita*, and thus incorporated into the field of colonial administration as a satellite to the *cabecera* center.

As Resil Mojares reminds us, however, these were far from stable circumstances. Indeed, these stories of found, disappearing, and reappearing images carry a subtext that troubles the tabula rasa fantasy that we saw at the beginning of this chapter. In the ongoing negotiation over signification, how are we to interpret, let alone arrest, the meaning of an image that appears to speak for itself or, in this case, does not speak at all?[21] The hermeneutic authority of the church usually prevails, but the autonomy exercised by the image itself is important to keep in mind. For before it is tied to an institution or adopted into a community, the image is a floating sign (literally, in this case), open though not yet attached to meaning. In appearing, the image speaks nothing other than communicability itself. Though this primary condition may seem obvious, it is easily obscured in readings that hasten to attribute symbolic value to images of the Virgin Mary without considering the historical and phenomenological dimensions of these images' very availability for appropriation. In the next chapter we shall explore appropriation and refashioning for the purpose of redressing the grievances of colonial rule. In a different milieu, at a different moment, the figure of Mary will be one among several that will lift off and away from its orthodox moorings, inhabited by forces and persons other than purveyors of colonial authority. But to understand this process, which I take to be tied to the evolving power of appearances in modernity, we must first examine the precursors that rehearse this figural autonomy. Let us linger, then, with the picture of coloniality offered by Our Lady of Caysasay.

The tale of the Virgin of Caysasay, like so many texts written in the colonial period, bears the perspectives and agendas of its religious author. Although the extant text of the legend of Caysasay is written in Tagalog, it is not the Tagalog of a native speaker but the second language of a friar with explicit goals of proselytization. Rather than an impediment to ascertaining the "truth" of the story, however, this translation is part of the ongoing dialogic encounter that constitutes the text and its meaning—an encounter that spans multiple temporalities, including the future of the devotion.[22] In this case, the temporal discrepancies of the text's production are as illuminating as its narrative content. Let me explain: *Epítome de la historia de la aparición de Nuestra Señora de Caysasay* (Synopsis of the History of the Appearance or Apparition of Our Lady of Caysasay) is believed to have been written circa 1754, by the Augustinian friar Francisco Bencuchillo (1710–76). Yet the events narrated are said to have taken place in 1603, and the edition I have been able to locate was not published until 1859 (bibliographical sources cite an earlier printing in 1856 and a later edition in 1885).[23] Already, then, this tale is fraught with a series of deferred appearances before we even consider the *aparición* itself.

Of course, as explanation, one might point simply to the entirely practical circumstances mentioned earlier, namely, the proliferation of print in the islands by the mid-nineteenth century, which would account for the text's reissue well after it was penned. Were that indeed to be the case, however, we would still puzzle over the stark contrast between the title page (in Spanish) and the versified Tagalog text therein. Even if what is depicted represents a trope of the miracle tale commonly seen across the early modern Spanish world, the text's different temporal framings reference other historical contexts that in turn demand various readings.

Bencuchillo's life as a religious administrator followed an unexceptional trajectory that began with his entrance into the Augustinian order in Spain when he was sixteen years old. He arrived in the Philippines in 1732, at the age of twenty-two, and for the following forty-four years was assigned to serve as parish priest in various towns throughout the provinces of southern Luzon, until his death in 1776.[24] He is known for his written work, which includes hagiographies and novenas in Tagalog, and the study for which he is most famous, *Arte poético tagalo* (first published in 1895).[25]

Bencuchillo's study of Tagalog poetry soberly opens: "There are some that say writing Tagalog poetry is extremely easy, while others know well, or have learned by trying, how difficult it is. I am not as venturesome as the first, nor am I, however, as cowardly as the second, opting as I do instead to take the middle road."[26] This "middle road" leads through a classificatory system that combines what Bencuchillo perceives as easier (read: familiar) modes of assonantal rhyme with ones more difficult (for him) to understand. His study also lists various forms of versification and provides examples thereof. As literary scholar Bienvenido Lumbera has suggested, the samples Bencuchillo includes in his *arte* are, "judging from the awkwardness of the riming and diction[,] . . . his own compositions."[27] *Epítome de la historia de la aparición de Nuestra Señora de Caysasay* is likewise his own composition, written in the *corrido* form, of ninety-one stanzas in octosyllabic quatrains.

From what we are told by scholars of Tagalog poetry, eighteenth-century compositions were more likely to have been listened to in public than read privately.[28] Bencuchillo's composition may have been recited as a sermon or chanted by native congregants, or both. What is clear from the outset, given the text's production in the Tagalog language, is its intended audience. Unlike some versions of *awit*, *corrido*, and the *pasyon* that open with a prayerful address to God and the Virgin Mary, the story of Caysasay opens with an alarmlike call to its listeners:

> *Binyagan gumising cana,*
> *macà naiidlip capa;*
> *maquinig ca nang di iba*
> *iyong icaguiguinhaua.*

> Wake up, convert!
> perhaps you're still sleepy;
> listen to this
> it will bring you comfort.

(BENCUCHILLO, *Epítome*, stanza 1)

The next stanzas shift suddenly away from the intended audience of the poem to the more common invocation of the aid of God and the Virgin in the telling of the tale:

> *Dios cong nacacacampan*
> *lahat na iyong quinapal,*
> *tolonğan acong magsaysay*
> *gagadolong lisa lamang.*

> Dear God, who wrought
> all creation,
> help me to tell this tale
> insignificant by comparison.[29]

> . . . .

> *O Virgeng Inang mariquit*
> *Haring daquila sa Lanğit,*
> *hulogui ang aquing isip*
> *nang dunong mong di mumuntic.*

> Oh radiant Virgin Mother
> Oh great King in Heaven,
> grant upon me
> your vast wisdom.

Na cun mangyaring isulat
pagca maalam mong hayag
toloy namang masiualat
bagsic mong ualang catulad.

So that when I write
your wisdom will be revealed
and all will be led to know
your strength without equal.

(BENCUCHILLO, *Epítome*, stanzas 2, 4–5)

These passages explicitly announce the presence of the friar as author. In turn, the author announces the act of composition, which, at this moment and with divine assistance, is presented as a work-in-progress. He is thus both inside and outside of the text, part of both the legend and its telling. He inhabits a second language (requisite for his mission) in a native genre, but a genre that he himself codified.[30] In this way, Bencuchillo anticipates and mitigates the discomfiting effects of difference. He relies upon a transcendent source, but he defines the rules of articulation, thus crafting an apparent "middle road" compromise that in fact veils the expansion of authority. We shall see this logic play out again in the course of this tale, through the convention of quotation and in the way that the vanishing Virgin is ultimately made to stay put.

The narration of the legend begins with location:

Dito sa sangcapoloang
Filipinas ang pañgalan
sa cabayanang Caysasay
sacop nang Taal na bayan.

Here in this archipelago
known by the name Filipinas
in the heart of Caysasay
within the territory of Taal.

(BENCUCHILLO, *Epítome*, stanza 6)

The poem proceeds in the same formal manner, introducing our hero, Juan D. Maningcad, who one morning heads toward the sea in the pursuit of fish to feed his child:

Doon niya inihaguis
sa cailogang calapit
nang hilahin ay nabatid
huli ay caibig ibig.

There he cast [his net]
into a nearby river,[31]
pulling it in he discovered
a catch most lovely.

Naquita,t, doon nasoot
sa Dála,t, tantong nabalot
larauang calogodlogod
Virgeng Inang pinag bocod.

There he saw entangled
in the net was wrapped
an image most delightful
Virgin Mother apart from the rest.

Lic-hang liniloc na cahoy
na camuc-hang Concepcion
siyang caanyo,t, caocol
nitong larauan nang Poon.

Figurine of sculpted wood[32]
that resembled Conception[33]
as if it were she herself
this Saintly image.

(BENCUCHILLO, *Epítome*, stanzas 11–13)

Not knowing whence this treasure originated, Juan M. kneels before the image, his heart filling with tenderness (*ang loob niya,i, nanlomo*).[34] He picks up the small image, slightly bigger than a hand, and carries it to his home.

From there ensues a pattern of interaction between locals and parish priest that is repeated several times throughout the story. The priest learns either directly or indirectly about the mysterious image. Skeptical, he goes to where the image is provisionally kept to see for himself. The first time this takes place, the priest (or *padre*), accompanied by a judicial representative of the Spanish crown (*hocom na mabini / na cahalili nang hari*), heads to the house of Juan M., as rumors have already spread of the fisherman's catch.[35] The two authorities behold for themselves the splendid find and kneel before it. They decide at once to bring it back to the *cabecera*, declaring a day of fiesta to celebrate.[36]

The image of the Virgin is first cared for by a judge's widow, Doña María Espíritu. She keeps it in a small tabernacle in her home. Imagine Doña María's surprise, the poem relates, when in the evenings she finds that the image has vanished from its secret hiding spot, only to reappear there when she awakens the next day. The woman seeks out the *padre*, and here we hear her words:

> *Panginoon co (aniya)*
> *loob co,i, nababalisa*
> *dito sa catacatacang*
> *inasal nang Virgeng Ina.*

> Oh my Master (she said)
> I am truly disquieted
> by this surprising behavior
> of the Virgin Mother.

(BENCUCHILLO, *Epítome*, stanza 28)

This is the first time in the poem that any direct speech appears, marked here in Tagalog by the term *aniya*. Upon hearing this, the *padre* hurries to Doña María's house. He takes back his words of disbelief when he sees for himself that the image has vanished. The next morning when they open the container, however, the image has miraculously reappeared.[37] Where the Virgin disappears to on these forays remains a mystery, until the *padre* is told that some villagers see her, at night, accompanied by an entourage:

> *Ang candilang caramihan*
> *iniiilao sa daan*
> *ay ang tungo nilang tanan*
> *sa Nayon din nang Caysasay.*

> The many candles
> illuminate the way
> they all head in the direction of
> the Village of Caysasay.[38]

(BENCUCHILLO, *Epítome*, stanza 38)

Upon hearing this, the friar takes no chances and locks the tiny image in the church. But it escapes once again. Time passes, and there is no trace of the mysterious and wandering Virgin.[39]

One day, the poem continues, two women are out gathering wood in the forest and rediscover the image, this time in a tree near the spot where she was originally found. Again the sequence is repeated: they pause to adore her, and they hasten back to the *padre* to tell him what they have found.[40] Here again their words appear in citation, marked by the appearance of first-person pronouns:

Padreng Panginoon namin
mag-albricias ca sa aquin
ngayo,i, nasondoan co rin
pinaghahanap mong Virgen.

Our Reverend Father,
congratulate me
just now I came across
your sought-after Virgin.

(BENCUCHILLO, *Epítome*, stanza 50)

This time, however, the friar is not so kind, nor does he rush to confirm their claims. Instead, he calls them liars and beats them. The women beseech him to punish them no further until he witnesses the image for himself. Following them to the spot, he sees that they were telling the truth and determines at last to leave the image where it is and build a shrine on the spot.[41] It does not follow, however, that the Virgin is named after the location where she was found. The poem elaborates:

Nguni,t, caya pinanganlan
Caysasay ang dahila,i,
ang Virgen ay may casabay
na ibon na Casaycasay.

And yet the name was given
the reason for Caysasay,
for alongside the Virgin there was
a bird known as *casay-casay*.

Sa una ang quinatay-án
nitong benditong Simbahan
cagubata,t, caparangan
ngayo,i, naguing cabayanan.

At first the site
of this blessed Church
was forest and field
but now has become a town.

(BENCUCHILLO, *Epítome*, stanzas 59–60)

Once the chapel is erected, what was formerly unchartered terrain is given a place, a name, and the status of a town (*cabayanan*). The shrine and the miracles, furthermore, have designated the site as sacred, yet within colonial administrative territory. Similarly, at this moment, the Virgin gains a title,

Nuestra Señora de Caysasay, and though she maintains her status of paragon exceptionality, she also is incorporated as a divine agent of the church by means of sanctioned ritual and other protocols of Catholic worship.

At this point the poem shifts abruptly away from the origin legend of the Virgin of Caysasay to relate two stories of miraculous occurrences that fuel the ongoing production of sacred locality. The first instantiates a familiar trope of magical transformation explicitly linked to the earth: so near to so much water, but not a drop to drink. The townspeople of Caysasay are dying of thirst, the story tells us, for the water so abundant in this area is saline.[42] So they pray to the Lord for help. Then one day, suddenly, issuing forth from the Virgin's shrine, comes fresh water that bubbles then gushes and flows:

> Ohao nilang di matiis
> na natutuyo ang bibig
> saquit na ito,i, pinatid
> tubig na matam-is tam-is.

> Their thirst so intolerable
> their mouths so very parched
> this suffering was ended
> by the sweetest of waters.

(BENCUCHILLO, Epítome, stanza 68)

The second miracle and final section of the Epítome is a morality tale about a Sangley (sometimes spelled Sanglay) named Haybing. Sangley is most frequently glossed as "Chinese," though more historically sensitive readings have been keen to point out that this is by no means a perfect rendering of terms. Believed to derive from the Hokkien term shanglu, which is not an ethnic designation but means "merchant trader," Sangley appears in early Spanish chronicles as a third category in what is generally a racial binary of Spaniards and indios.[43] Despite being present for the arrival of missionaries in the late sixteenth century, owing to long-established routes of maritime trade throughout Southeast Asia, Sangleys (Chinese) were perceived by the Iberian invaders as not native to the islands. They became an indispensable player in Spain's economic development of the colony.[44] Yet until the mid-eighteenth century, to the missionary the Chinese were figures of unassimilable difference. Many actually converted to Christianity, in no small measure because of economic incentives provided by the Spanish.[45] But these conversions often proved to be such profound acts of misrecognizing the missionaries' intentions that the Chinese were perceived as a special kind of menace, far more disturbing than if they had resisted conversion altogether. The deep-seated ambivalence on the part of the Spanish occasionally exploded into extraordinary acts of violence, including wholesale massacres of Chinese communities, with victims in the tens of thousands.[46]

Much of this changed in the mid-1700s, when Bencuchillo was writing. There are two main reasons for this. First, in the first half of that century, the violence that characterized seventeenth-century relations was "resolved" more permanently by decrees for the expulsion of Chinese from the Philippines. Though the decrees were exercised largely against non-Christians, some converted Chinese were also expelled for having sided with the British when they occupied Manila from 1762 to 1764. Second, although the Catholicism of the converted Chinese may have been considered opportunistic, some had offspring with local women. Among this mestizo group, by contrast with earlier members of their paternal line, a more ostensibly sincere Christianity appeared to take root. Throughout the middle decades of the eighteenth century, furthermore, the Chinese mestizos greatly benefited from the expulsion of Chinese, taking over their commercial operations.[47] We might thus understand Bencuchillo's poem, and especially the cautionary tale of Haybing, as a reflection of these uneasy transformations of Chinese relations in colonial society.

The story of Haybing first appears almost as an afterthought. There is no specific date given for the time when a decree is delivered to kill all *Sangleys* within the jurisdiction (*hocoman*) of Caysasay.[48] Sadly, despite being a devotee of the Virgin, Haybing is not exempt from the order, thus is he rounded up with all the rest and beheaded. What happens next is no less than the miracle of all miracles—his resurrection. For, the very next morning, in the doorway of the church, who appears but Haybing, intact and alive again.[49] When asked how such a thing happened:

> *Ang sa sanglay na isinagot*
> *ang Ina (aniya) nang Dios*
> *siyang tantong nagcaloob,*
> *at binuhay acong lubos.*

> The *Sangley* replied
> the Mother (he said) of God
> she truly gave
> my life back to me.

(BENCUCHILLO, *Epítome*, stanza 76)

Indebted to her for his renewed and borrowed life (*buhay na caniyang hiram*), Haybing sets out to serve the Virgin Mother, caring for her in the *visita* church. Time passes, and Haybing lapses in his remembrance, forgets his promise and quits his service. Alas, he has turned his back on his debt (*caniyang pinagtalicdan / sa Virgen na caotañgan*), although his duty to the Virgin and the Lord remains.[50] One weekend he is seen plowing his land instead of attending Mass. When asked why, he responded:

> *Togon niya,i, anhin yaon*
> *nalalaon nang panahon*
> *paglilingcod co sa Poon*
> *ñgayo,i, asaua co ang lingon.*

> He did it, he replied
> because for so long
> have I served the Lord
> now it is my wife I esteem.

(BENCUCHILLO, Epítome, stanza 83)

And with this imprudent admission of favoring his wife over the Virgin, Haybing is violently and instantly killed (*si Haybing ay napahamac*), gored to death by his previously docile carabao (water buffalo).[51] Such, it is said with smug resignation, is the Virgin's retribution (*ganito pala,i, ang ganti / nang Virgeng cauiliuili*).[52] This is a Virgin Mary rarely, if ever, seen in the Philippine context: unforgiving, passing judgment, meting out punishment for failed promises, giving and then taking life. The *Epítome* is no longer merely homage to the Blessed Mother and the founding narrative of one town, as the cautionary tale of Haybing is revealed as an allegory of the church's authority.[53] The story of Haybing is thus absolutely essential, for it stages what is necessary for the sovereign's claim to power—death.

This reading might seem a bit heavy handed, yet the motif of the Chinese man who either converts or has his faith renewed by a life-saving miracle, eventually reneges on his Christian duty, then is struck dead by divine intervention (often executed by an animal) is a recurring one. In a chronicle by the Augustinian Casimiro Díaz (1693–1746) there appears yet another miracle story of a Christian *Sangley*, Juan Imbín, who is fatally wounded in an ordered massacre of Chinese in 1639.[54] Taken for dead, he is thrown into the sea. He regains consciousness to find himself floating on a branch of a tree, and he sees before him a beautiful little girl, about the size of the image of Our Lady of Caysasay. As she leads him through the water, crocodiles (or *buwaya*, believed in pre-Hispanic times to be a sacred creature) and killer fish flee, and she guides him safely back to her hermitage on land. Juan Imbín slowly heals, all the while exercising renewed devotion to Our Lady by caring for her shrine. Time passes, his devotion cools, and he goes back to being like all the rest of the Christian *Sangleys,* so the story tells us, neglectful of the beneficence bestowed upon him. One day, plowing a small plot of land, Juan Imbín meets a tragic fate when his trusted carabao suddenly turns and gores him to death.

It is not clear that the Juan Imbín of this tale and Haybing of Bencuchillo's refer to the same person, nor does it really matter. For in spite of the differences in detail, the pivotal events are the same, and they recur in many other tales of Chinese converts and miraculous images. Such tales give us insight into just how threatening and liminal—or threatening because liminal—the figure of the *Sangley* was perceived to be during the colonial period. The stories also show how even the most spiritually edifying anecdotes are haunted by violence and the demand for submission in the context of conversion. Situating the Imbín or Haybing character at the juncture of judicial decree and divine law, these tales portray the *Sangley* as a life brought starkly into relief through association with death. By killing the *Sangley* not once, but *twice,* these tales suggest that more intolerable than the subject who revolts against or simply appears *outside* of colonial rule is the subject who fails to tender the debt incurred by being made an exception to it.[55]

In Bencuchillo's *Epítome* we are presented with topical and narrative variations on the theme of how ecclesiastical authority is established and extended in the colonial period. Strangely, in this regard, the *Sangley* Haybing and the Virgin bear a structural resemblance as figures of internal exclusion. With the Virgin this status is partly given in such theological tenets that highlight her exceptionality among women (e.g., the Immaculate Conception, which, we recall, is taken as the corresponding image of Caysasay). In the Philippine colonial context the status is also conferred by her quality of perpetual foreignness. With a few notable exceptions (to be discussed in the next chapter), iconographically speaking, Mary was always from elsewhere.[56] The impossibility of total domestication was thus a constitutive dimension of her power. How is this impossibility rendered in accounts like Bencuchillo's *Epítome,* whose goals are precisely to set the record straight by turning legend into the official narrative?

As noted earlier, Bencuchillo's "middle road" attitude and prescribed method for composing poetry in a language not his own lay bare a certain logic: the assimilation of something alien within a totalizing field, in this case, that of language. The founding of the shrine at Caysasay and Bencuchillo's poem are both efforts to instantiate this expansion of authority, bringing the previously undomesticated appearance of Mary *bajo la campana.*

Counter to this, however, is the apparent autonomy of this moving image of Mary—appearing, vanishing, and appearing again. What if, just as the moving image of Mary can be seen as an evasion of attempts to bring her into the institutional center of the church, so, too, are apparitions of Mary characterized by an evasion of language? Bencuchillo's poem responds to this by staging her capture in rich narrative detail. And yet, as we shall see, such a capture fails—indeed, it *must* fail—if this material object is to maintain its mute sacredness. A closer reading of the account shall bring this sacredness into relief.

First of all, there is a profusion of words and phrases used to describe the Virgin: "wise Virgin Mother" (*Virgeng Inang maalam*); "radiant Virgin Mother" (*Virgeng Inang mariquit*); "Virgin Mother apart from the rest" (*Virgeng Inang pinag bocod*); "Virgin without compare" (*Virgeng ualang caholilip*); "delightful Virgin" (*Virgeng caayaaya*); "mysterious Virgin" (*Virgeng cababalaghan*); "gentle Virgin Mother" (*Virgeng Inang maamò*); "captivating Mother" (*Inang cauiliuili*); "Virgin who takes in the needy" (*Virgeng mapag ampon*); "Virgin who intercedes" (*Virgeng mapagcalara*); "dear Virgin" (*Virgeng mahal*); "compassionate Virgin Mother" (*Virgeng Inang naaua*); and of course, there is also the description of the found image itself. Naming and describing the Virgin in these myriad ways is not particular to Bencuchillo's text, as there is a prayer known as the Litany of the Blessed Virgin that consists entirely of a list of her titles.[57] Although the manifestation of the Virgin in this case takes material form, there remains something irreducible to that form, something that language tries to name. At the same time the sheer abundance of descriptions in this poem belies the impossibility of fully domesticating the meaning of Mary's appearance. Bencuchillo's poem, like the litany, remains haunted by something in excess of signification that no amount of effusive recitation can fully apprehend.

Second, although there is little direct speech in the legend as Bencuchillo tells it (marked either by *aniya*, or "he/she said," or first-person pronouns), the speech that does pepper the verses is that of either women or the tragic *Sangley*, Haybing. Quotation brings these characters of difference into the textual fold, their presences felt and registered at the same time that they are domesticated and harnessed in relation to the friar at the receiving end of speech. When these voices are heard, furthermore, they are heard reporting the movements or actions of the Virgin: Doña María telling the priest that the image had disappeared from the tabernacle; the wood-gathering women reporting their discovery near the well; Haybing attributing the miracle of his resurrection to the Virgin. No one explicitly interprets those movements;

not even the priest says, "This means that . . ." or "The Virgin must want that . . ." Significantly, the extent to which one can speak for the Virgin is equivalent to the degree to which one can speak *of* the Virgin. We have only utterances that report what witnesses have seen. As testimonies go, furthermore, these utterances are necessarily structured by belatedness: they point to Mary's presence only after the fact. The Virgin has always come before: before the utterance, before the poem. A gap opens up between the moment of witnessing and the moment of telling. This gap is the auratic distance that produces, and in turn is demanded by, the sacred.

The story of Haybing serves to punctuate this. It is, of course, a story of apostasy. We hear his voice in the poem declare that it was the Virgin that saved him. But we hear his voice again when he renounces his service to the Virgin Mary. Hardly another line in the poem passes when—*whack!*—he is struck dead. It is almost as if the poor *Sangley*, in addition to misrecognizing the extent of his debt to the Virgin, also failed to heed the acceptable limits of speech. When we hear Haybing speak the second time, he admits his own dissimulation, that his appearance of piety was false. Just as the convention of quotation serves to bring the sacred Virgin into relief through reports of her presence, the rendering of Haybing's blasphemy as an utterance succeeds in making the force of violating the sacred felt.

In Bencuchillo's poem, the Virgin goes from being an undomesticated appearance to a retributive agent that governs appearances, such as that of the disingenuous convert. Such was the didactic intent of the *Epítome*, to stage for the Tagalog listener or reader a lesson in proper Christian behavior. Indeed, the prose section immediately following the poetic narrative of the apparition, *Ang manğa susundin sa pag nonovenas* ("How to pray a novena"), offers a detailed prescription of why and how to pray the accompanying novena (or in Tagalog, *pagsisiyam*): when one should start it, which practices should be performed around it, what one should be contemplating, and how one should physically comport him- or herself while praying.[58] Reading the text, one moves directly from these instructions to the prayers (*panalanğin*) that constitute the nine-day cycle. At the end of it all, however, appears one last section of the text, a *dalit*, or hymn, of eighteen stanzas that returns the reader to the octosyllabic form of the narrative. The *Dalit sa Catouaan sa Mahal na Virgen sa Caysasay* (Hymn of Joy to the Virgin of Caysasay) opens thus:

> *Aba bitoin sa dagat*
> *sa cadagatan sumicat*
> *hologui cami nang sinag*
> *ningning mong ualang catulad.*

Hail, star of the sea
across the sea you rose
a beam cast upon us
your unparalleled radiance.

(BENCUCHILLO, *Dalit*, stanza 1)

Over the course of the stanzas, the *dalit* recaps the narrative synopsis of
the apparition and her miracles. But even this recap is interrupted in every
second stanza by a refrain (marked by the Spanish abbreviation, *Estriv.*, for
estribillo):

> *Cami iyong paquiquingan*
> *Virgeng Ina sa Caysasay.*
>
> Oh hear us
> Virgin Mother of Caysasay.

With this single element, and despite the intentions of its Spanish author,
the *dalit* opens the text to a different mode of engagement. In the refrains
of address to Mary lies the possibility of outright interpellation of her as a
listening subject. No longer is the text centered on characters speaking *of*
the Virgin in a distant past but on the audience (be they listeners or readers)
speaking *to* the Virgin in a punctual present.

RECUPERATIONS: OUR LADY OF MANAOAG

If the *Sangley*—with his fickle devotion and favoring of fleshly wife over
heavenly Virgin—stood as one threat to conversion and colonial rule until
the mid-eighteenth century, what threats would the Blessed Mother be put
to fending off in later years? In his book *Breve noticia acerca de la aparición de
Manaoag (Brief Account of the Apparition of Manaoag)*, written in Spanish in
1891, Salvador Millán, a Spanish Dominican, gives us some idea:

> Until very recently, the life of the natives of the Philippines resembled the lovely
> palm trees that graced their pleasant countryside, swaying in a gentle breeze,
> sheltered by a benevolent sky, and beneath the providence of God, who sent rain
> and dew for their growth and vitality. Such it was for the people of the Philip-
> pines . . . Very recently, the situation has been changing: the sky, once serene,
> grows overcast; the breeze becomes a hurricane; the tranquil rain, a torrential
> downpour; all signs lead one to believe that what was once a garden will soon
> become a sad and parched field . . .
> Until very recently, the natives of the Philippines believed without question
> the truths of the faith that they had learned from the missionaries: if they com-

mitted sins, they were merely sins of weakness, attendant to human nature; but their souls remained ever docile before the holy teachings and religious truths. But these days, what a disgrace! Already among the locals one hears certain doctrines, malevolently planted by those born overseas, who in their foolishness believe themselves superior in the eyes of the *indios*; they claim to be intellectuals [*plaza de ilustrados*], when they are nothing but poor spellers of some insolent newspaper . . .

Fortunately, these doctrines find little response among the inhabitants of the Philippines. But there are some hapless Filipinos—thankfully few—who without understanding or knowing what's being said, parrot these doctrines, believing that they might gain favor with those who teach them, and that this will earn them a privileged place in their communities, and through this, recognition among their countrymen.[59]

Whipped into a frenzy by what can be only the storm of progress itself, Millán unleashed his vitriol against none other than the *ilustrados*, the elite class of educated mestizos and creoles in the Philippines at the end of the nineteenth century.[60] Many of these young men sojourned in Europe, where they studied, wrote and published (some in the "insolent newspapers" to which Millán refers), caroused, joined Masonic lodges (perhaps the subject of Millán's references to "doctrines"), fraternized with Spanish progressives, and from a distance were able to see and articulate the injustices wrought by clerical colonialism in the Philippines. The *ilustrados* and everything they stood for were not the only targets of Millán's ire: he also targeted "railroads that bring commercial culture to the islands" as well as "Protestants."[61] These "perils" and others are documented in the chapter "Only the Virgin of the Rosary Can Save the Philippines from the Dangers That Threaten It" (*Sólo la Virgen del Rosario puede librar á Filipinas de los peligros que le amenazan*).

Like Bencuchillo's poem, Millán's account is a retroactive one, whose significance is amplified only by its narrative delay. The dedication of this *noticia* opens as follows:

It causes the soul great grief to think that in the three hundred years or so that the Sanctuary of Manaoag has been in existence, notwithstanding its enjoyed renown, comparable even to the most famous of shrines in Europe, its story has never been published, which, in addition to its edification, would serve as well to satisfy the legitimate curiosity of its devotees.[62]

Such is one goal of Millán's publication. His account seeks, in the face of threatening forces, to recall the founding of a sacred place by depicting the appearance of Mary, a superlative figure of origination.

After four introductory chapters, the origin story of the founding of the shrine at Manaoag begins. Like Caysasay, its grounding in geographical place is featured:

> Thirty kilometers from the town of Lingayen, capital of the province of Pangasinan, toward the east one finds a picturesque valley, like an amphitheater composed of small hills that close in on it from all sides and serve as a defense against hurricanes and tropical storms.[63]

It is here that the miraculous visitation of the Virgin takes place. The story is well worth presenting in its entirety:

> One day a devoted *indio* was passing by the foot of the hill where the sanctuary now stands, when all of a sudden he heard a gentle, ineffable voice that called him by his name. He looked toward the hill summit, from whence the voice came, and was shocked at the sight of the whitest and most resplendent of clouds. Ruffling the top of a leafy tree, [the cloud] levitated toward the sky, creating transparent, vaporous ripples like an intricate mosaic. [The *indio*], not without fear, headed in the direction that had so captivated his attention. Just as he got there, before his eyes appeared a celestial vision [*una visión celestial*], that, filling his soul with sweetness, drew to it all of his potencies and senses. In the middle of the cloud appeared a lady dressed in white and radiant with beauty, and in her arms she held a child of celestial beauty. The lady held in her right hand a rosary, and both she and the child gazed ever-so-sweetly at the fortunate *indio*. The lady explained that she was the Virgin of the Rosary and [this was] her Holy Son, and that they desired a sanctuary be built in their honor and in that very spot, so that those devoted to them could take to it from time to time, to implore her maternal protection.
>
> The celestial apparition [*aparición*] lasted but a few moments, after which the cloud slowly rose toward the sky, until it disappeared from the view of the ecstatic seer, who, barely recovered from his profound stupor, approached to kiss the tree made holy through its contact with Mary. Suddenly he stopped, because among the tree's branches he saw an image [*imagen*] the same size of the Virgin of the Rosary with the Child, also of the same size, in her arms. [The *indio*] told all of this to the missionary, who, accompanied by the other Christians of the mission, went to the designated place. [The missionary] carefully took the image and brought her to the church of Santa Monica, where she was venerated until a wooden church could be erected in the spot of the apparition.[64]

There are both striking differences and obvious similarities between this and the appearance of the Virgin at Caysasay. The site in nature and the native visionary are features shared by both. There is also the fact that both Bencuchillo's *Epítome* (written in the mid-1700s and published in the mid-1800s) and Millán's *Breve noticia* (written and published in 1891) purport to bring out of obscurity events that took place at the beginning of Spain's early settling of the Philippines. Indeed, it is perhaps the timeliness of their respective publications, or more precisely, their writings' displacement in time, that reveals the full force of what they attempt to convey. As deferred inscriptions, the tales effectively mirror the thematic content therein, that is, recovery. The narratives tell of images of the Virgin that are "recovered" from places where she unexpectedly appeared. But these narratives are further subsumed within tales of the founding of places and the erection of shrines. Their histories, in other words, are acts of recovering origins, origins that, like all origins, can emerge only at the moment of their displacement in time.[65] Trapped in this space of haunting, one doubled by manifest forms of perceived menace (the *Sangley* or the *ilustrado*), the importance of the Virgin Mary to these authors is clear: as a figure of superlative origination, of origin, furthermore, immaculate—*without difference*—Mary buttresses against the losses (impending and actual) that precipitated the telling of the stories themselves.

One last similarity between these two tales of Mary's apparitions is that Manaoag is also a tale of an image found. Yet the relationship of that image to speaking is significantly different. With the story of Caysasay we saw that the image of the Virgin spoke without properly speaking, that she spoke by appearing. In the tale of Manaoag, by contrast, she not only speaks but also *calls*. This is particular in its implying an expectation of response. This call, furthermore, is but the first in a series of manifestations, one divorced from appearance. Her second manifestation as a "celestial vision" in turn is bereft of the kind of materiality of the subsequently appearing "image." Why, we might ask, must an apparition of the Virgin now comprise a series of various forms of making herself present? What does this difference suggest about the shifts in appearance in general?

In the story of Caysasay, what would be considered the "vision" is, if not one and the same, directly associated with the material object of the image: tactility and visuality occupy the same object of perception. In the tale of the apparition at Manaoag, in contrast, what manifests itself is not a singular being or thing but multiple aspects of presence that correspond to differentiated senses of perception: hearing, sight, touch. The image that is left behind is but a trace of what had appeared and then vanished. By indexing absence, the image, in its voluptuous materiality, laments the impossibility of sheer presence.[66] The image is an afterimage, a *prosthetic* image, a placeholder marking the visible threshold of the real. Allow me to interject here a revealing statement about the compulsion to touch religious images made by one of my interlocutors, a self-described "Marian devotee," in 2001: "It's like a photograph . . . You know that the photograph is not [the actual person], and yet it helps you feel close to them, so much so that you might reach out and caress the photograph, or even kiss it." This is, of course, by no means a perfect analogy. Yet the comparison prompts us to reflect upon how the image of Manaoag and the photograph might be similar beyond their shared power of indexicality, by which I mean the material and visual residue of something that came before (figure 1.3).

In the nineteenth century, religious images were greatly affected by the very industrialization of image production that had given birth to the photographic form. In the Philippines, art historians tell us, one sees these effects on religious images (or sculptures, called *santos*) in two distinct, though somewhat related, developments. The first development announces itself in Sinibaldo de Mas's *Informe sobre el estado de las islas Filipinas en 1842* (Report on the Conditions of the Philippine Islands in 1842), where he notes under the heading "Industria" the great number of images being "scrupulously finished" by various sculptors whose names were, for the first time, becoming known.[67] Indeed, many historians of Philippine *santos* lament the paucity of sculptor names associated with images carved before the nineteenth century, commonly citing a "lack of data" as the reason.[68] What these historians overlook, however, is that only when the product of one's labor enters into circulation, becomes the property of another, and potentially moves farther and farther away from its provenance does the importance of noting that provenance emerge.[69] Furthermore, by the second half of the nineteenth century, sculpting *santos* achieved the full-fledged status of a profession. During the years 1876–78, one provincial governor hired several sculptors from Paete, a town already renowned as a seat of the *santo* industry, at wages that they themselves dictated. In 1879 sculpture was included among the various arts accredited by the Academia de Dibujo y Pintura (Academy of Drawing and Painting), which opened in 1855.[70] And by 1880, finally, a professional guild or association of sculptors had been founded.[71]

The second development that links religious images to photography as circulating objects of value has garnered considerably less attention than the professionalization of the art form, though it is no less important for understanding the *santos'* rapidly expanding capacity to signify. The nineteenth century in the Philippines was a time of prosperity for the mestizo elite. Fully participating in newly opened international trade, this stratum of Philippine society accrued significant wealth from control and/or ownership of export-producing land. In this context, scholars have argued, private

FIGURE 1.3 Souvenir photograph of the author and Rose Mendoza, independent researcher and friend, with Our Lady of Manaoag, 2001.

sponsorship and upkeep of *santos* became increasingly common, as parish priests recognized the considerable advantages of parceling out the often-extravagant cost of staging processions and religious celebrations. It seems reasonable, then, that the treatment of *santos* as private, familial property would arise around the same time that images became endowed with other kinds of value (through the growth of an industry dedicated to their production, for example).[72] Although the *santo* could be treated as an inalienable member of the family, the private possession or sponsorship of *santos* would become one of the most recognizable—and highly public, since they might be annually paraded about—signs of status and wealth.[73] It was not unheard of, furthermore, for the *santos* and their requisite accoutrements (outfits, jewelry, as well as the *carrozas*, or carriages, they rode on) to be coveted bequests in hacienda owners' last wills and testaments.[74]

These digressions into photography, the industrialization of images, and the *santo* as a visible marker of private wealth can be distilled into one basic point. By the late nineteenth century, when Millán was writing Our Lady of Manaoag's history, religious images were being produced and circulated in new ways. One result was the proliferation of different kinds of value attached to the religious image itself. Now bearing the signature of its maker, the religious image was alternately a means for perfecting an aesthetic form, an indicator of wealth, and/or a sentimental heirloom. In other words, religious images could now *represent* far more than their divine referents. Representational value becomes mutable only when the forms to which it adheres are generalized. Generality is that quality produced by a movement of abstraction, a "point of view according to which one term may be exchanged or substituted for another."[75] The reigning example of the principle of generality is the commodity form once abstracted that is money. It is not only in the domain of economy, strictly defined, however, that the principle of generality operates. In the context I am examining here, the principle of generality is that which enabled the emergence of a Virgin Mary who could represent more than the mother of God, who could represent, as we shall see, the nation.

Though Millán's history stands as an invocation of Mary for the purpose of maintaining colonial order, as a deferred tale it arrived too late: generality had already happened. Written in the twilight of the nineteenth century, and in contrast to Bencuchillo's endeavor, Millán's depiction of the apparition at Manaoag appears to reflect the changing modes of perception as they were radically reconfigured under modernity: presence as evanescent, the image as trace, the voice disembodied. And what about that voice? After all is said and done—the agendas laid bare, the historical conditions enumerated, the logics of origins' deferred appearance disclosed—this voice is the most mysterious remainder. For in the early Dominican chronicles, even though there is no mention of Mary's apparition, Manaoag, the name and the place, nevertheless appears.[76] *Manaoag*, it should be noted, derives from the Pangasinense *man-taoag*, which means "to call."[77] Perhaps we should read this as lending veracity to Millán's story after all: proof that his was not just a retroactively narrated tale contrived to recuperate origins in the name of the church. But perhaps this call—not in the colonial language but in the local tongue—points to something beyond recuperation: sheer communicability itself. "To call": a call as full, or as empty, as an echo.

FROM THE SINGULAR TO THE SERIAL: A TALE OF TWO (OR MORE) GUADALUPES

From the beginning of Spanish colonial rule, the task of evangelization and the administration of the sacraments were organized according to discrete territorial units, each of which pertained to a specific religious order.[78] In the preceding apparition stories, we readily see the purchase afforded by miraculous appearances of Mary for religious authorities in these local domains. For the authors of those stories, the appropriation and production of "foundational narratives" was one way to deal with the incursion of modernity. This incursion was experienced as a penetration of forces that came largely from without, be it in the figure of the perpetually foreign *Sangley*, the Protestant, or the alienated native son. In these two examples it is easy to read the extension of authority from authorship and to see the agenda to which Mary's signifying capacity was put. Yet not all such texts of this genre were so transparently reactionary, or indeed, so parochial. Even more numerous than foundational narratives of local Philippine shrines were novenas that translated into a Philippine language an already-circulating history of an apparition or a pious biography from Castilian, French, or Latin.

In many ways, this genre of translated devotional literature is very much like the popular romances of the *awit* and the *corrido* discussed earlier. With their references to faraway places, moralistic or religious messages, and florid verse or prose, these novenas presented, to a degree, a spatiotemporal universe unmoored from any actual context in which *indio* or mestizo readers might find themselves or understand as actually existing elsewhere. Yet miraculous image and apparition stories stand as instructive exceptions. As the historian David Brading has shown in his study on Our Lady of Guadalupe in Mexico, devotional texts in the nineteenth century were often highly concerned with the historicity of miraculous events, given more positivist, if not avowedly secularist, challenges to their veracity.[79] Thus, betwixt the epic romance and the local foundational narratives such as those just examined, the many devotional texts (also known as *devocionarios*) dedicated to chronicling the history of a miraculous image or apparition constitute a genre unto their own, introducing into Philippine vernacular worlds a sacred geography at once deterritorialized and temporally situated. As we shall see in the following example of one 1870 novena to the Mexican Lady of Guadalupe, the effect of this was often strangely telescopic, collapsing place-names and references by translating a devotion that was already multiply local.

The title page alone of the 1870 history and novena to Our Lady of Guadalupe indicates several frames of reference. It reads in its entirety:

> *Historia at novena*
> *nang*
> *Mahal na Virgen*
> *Ntra. Sra. de Guadalupe*
> *Pinag ayos at pinag husay sa uicang Castila nang isang religiosong Agustino.*
> *Tinagalog nang isang sacerdoteng devoto nitong marilag na Señora.*
> *At ipinalimbag nang naturang Religioso.*
>
> History and novena
> of
> the Blessed Virgin Our Lady of Guadalupe
> Edited and arranged in Castilian by a friar of the Augustinian order.
> Translated into Tagalog by a priest devoted to the magnificent Lady.
> Printed by the aforementioned religious.[80]

From the start, and in contrast to the texts we have already examined, the "authors" of the *Historia at novena nang Mahal na Virgen Ntra. Sra. de Guadalupe* are ambiguous. Most of the historical narrative in this novena appears to derive from Mateo de la Cruz's *Relación de la milagrosa aparición de la santa imagen de la Virgen de Guadalupe de México* (1660), a significantly abridged version of the Augustinian P. Miguel Sánchez's *Imagen de la Virgen María Madre de Dios de Guadalupe* (1648).[81] Both of these texts were printed in Mexico, and it is via *Relación* that the 1531 apparitions of the Virgin Mary in Mexico came to be known across the Atlantic.[82] Thus, the Augustinian referenced on the title page of *Historia at novena* could be either Mateo de la Cruz or an unnamed friar in the Philippines contemporaneous with the novena's 1870 publication. We are not provided the identity of the translator, but it is possible that, in the *ladino* tradition, he was a native or a mestizo equally fluent in Castilian and Tagalog. Written entirely in Tagalog prose, *Historia at novena* takes the chapbook form and totals seventy-five pages.

Following a brief preface that extols the Virgin Mary in her role as protectress in the conquest of the New World, the text unfolds to tell the story of Our Lady of Guadalupe in a series of chapters that culminate, as do many texts in the *devocionario* genre, in a novena prayer. It begins with the famous story of the apparition: A native by the name of Juan Diego hears a voice calling his name from a hill one Saturday in the year 1531. Looking in that direction he sees a woman who demands that he approach. Announcing herself as "Mary, Virgin Mother of God," she tells Juan to ask the bishop to build a sanctuary at that spot. Juan complies, yet without success, returning to the bishop twice before asking that the Virgin send with him a sign of her appearance to give the bishop. The Virgin instructs Juan to climb the hill where she had appeared, cut the roses he found there—remarkable in and of themselves for appearing on such cracked and arid land—and bring them to the bishop. Juan does so, and upon unfurling his cape (or *tilma*) of flowers, a colorful image of the Virgin miraculously appears.[83]

In the Tagalog *Historia at novena* the setting of the narrative is that of the centuries-old tale: Mexico (Méjico), New Spain (Nueva España), even the name of the arid hill (*bundoc na tuyo*) historically known as Tepeyacac where Mary first appears is unchanged. There are no significant innovations on the version of the apparition story originally penned by Sánchez (and abridged by Cruz). Yet the text of the *Historia at novena* unfolds in interesting ways, among which is a shift in orientation to include developments of the devotion in the Philippines. In a chapter that follows the apparition story titled "Fundacion ó pag babangon nang Convento at Santuario nang mahal na Virgeng Nuestra Señora de Guadalupe dito sa Filipinas" (Establishment of the Convent and Shrine to Our Lady of Guadalupe in the Philippines), the text describes the curious erection of the shrine to Our Lady of Guadalupe on the banks of the Pasig River, near Manila. Originally founded in 1601 as a church whose patron was Nuestra Señora de Gracia, the presiding advocation of Mary was changed in 1604, when a few Spaniards residing in Manila petitioned to have a church in the Philippines dedicated to the Virgin so beloved in "New Spain." Their request was granted and the switch was made, one that included installing in the Filipino shrine the image of the Mexican Virgin, identical to her counterpart on the other side of the world.[84]

As if to extend this correspondence between the two shrines of Guadalupe and their images, the text of *Historia at novena* goes on to relate, in two sequential sections, the miracles that Our Lady has performed in Mexico

(*Manĝa milagrong guinaua sa Méjico nang mahal na Virgen Nuestra Señora de Guadalupe*) and in the Philippines (*Manĝa milagrong guinaua nang mahal na Virgin Nuestra Señora de Guadalupe dito sa capuluang Filipinas*). These lists are translated from Cruz's *Relación de la milagrosa aparición de la santa imagen de la Virgen de Guadalupe de México* and Gaspar de San Agustín's *Conquistas de las Islas Filipinas*, respectively. The differences between the kinds of miracles brought about through the intercession of Our Lady of Guadalupe in both places are not particularly significant, as the majority of all the miracles described relate to individual healings. Among the Mexican cases a few stand out, such as the story of the great four-year flood (*gunao*) whose waters subsided thanks to Our Lady's intervention and the plague that abated after a group of children beseeched her to save their community. Meanwhile, the thirteen Philippine miracles are taken directly from the convent registry, and each case bears the name of the priest who verified the wondrous phenomena.[85]

The parity that the *Historia at novena* attempts to articulate between the Mexican and the Philippine images opens up what Resil Mojares, speaking of yet another Guadalupe image in the outskirts of Cebu City, describes as "broader, less bounded spaces (region, nation, world), in which shrine, community, and catchment are enmeshed."[86] Indeed, this is the more common characteristic seen among the multitude of novenas published in Philippine languages in the late nineteenth century, where the context is not the Philippines but a foreign land where apparitions also occur and saints dwell.[87] This opening of worlds precisely beyond the local takes place through the translation of these "elsewheres" into the vernaculars, which not always results in the syncretism of "folk Catholicism" but rather in the coexistence of elements both foreign and local, as we see here. At the same time, as we are also about to see, translation also sometimes resulted in the strange projection of the local into the abroad.

The first of such projections appears immediately following the preface to the *Historia at novena*. It is the title of the first chapter of the book, which reads:

> *Tongcol sa pag paquita nang mahal na Virgen Ntra. Sra. de Guadalupe sa isang tagalog na si Juan Diego ang panĝalan.*
>
> On the apparition of the Blessed Virgin Mary of Guadalupe to a Tagalog named Juan Diego.

As previously noted, there are no narrative differences between this Tagalog version of the apparition story and the text from which it is translated,

Cruz's *Relación de la milagrosa aparición de la santa imagen de la Virgen de Guadalupe de México*. But the visionary Juan Diego appears as a *tagalog* throughout the text, and "Méjico" is described as populated by *manga tagalog at castila* (Tagalogs and Castilians).[88] More curious still, some Nahuatl terms, such as *cocolixtli* (a kind of hemorrhagic fever), remain untranslated but are marked as terms specific to the native language of the Tagalog region yonder (*sa catagalugan yao*[*n*]). Comparison across texts in this *devocionario* genre shows this to be an idiosyncratic application of the category "Tagalog," but judging from lines that render an inclusive "those from Mexico" and "those from the Philippines" (*sa manga taga Méjico at gayon din naman sa tagarito sa Filipinas*), along with references to "Tagalogs here" (*manga tagalog dito*) and "Tagalogs there" (*manga tagalog doon*), it is far from an application made in error.[89] So what do we make of this odd projection of the category "Tagalog" into a Mexican setting?

Here readers are reminded that in the pre-Hispanic era "Tagalog" was likely not an emic designation; it was accorded the status of an ethnolinguistic category only upon the arrival of Spanish missionaries in the sixteenth century. Still, by the nineteenth century, the category became real enough to inspire spectacular inventions of tradition in compositions by mestizo writers such as Pedro Paterno about "ancient Tagalog civilization."[90] As a racial category, "Tagalog" would figure concretely only in the early American colonial period. It was then that the technology of the census ramified what had largely been, under the Spanish, a primitive system of tabulation for the purpose of either tribute collection or profiling demographic distribution.[91] In summary, while the reification of "Tagalog" has its own long history, only in the nineteenth century does one see the term used by colonizers, natives, and mestizos alike.[92] Reference to the census, in particular, points us to the more general logic of seriality upon which all of these developments rely.

In *The Spectre of Comparisons*, Benedict Anderson's gloomy follow-up to his classic work on nationalism, *Imagined Communities*, he discusses the "logic of seriality" and its relation to modern politics and subjectivities. Anderson examines two "profoundly contrasting types" of seriality, which he designates as *unbound* and *bound*. Unbound seriality produces universal categories and a standardized vocabulary of "types" whose emancipatory potential lies in their modularity. Individual subjects need only imagine their possible, if ideal, enrollment as citizens, activists, artists, and so forth, in an infinite possibility of series. Undergirding this notion of seriality unbound are commensurability and translation, or more precisely, translatability: "that languages are transparent to each other, interpenetrate each other, map each other's domains."[93] Bound seriality, by contrast, is ruled by the principle of the integer, "the impermissibility of fractions."[94] It is thus the instrument of governmentality and is best seen in the technology of the census, in voting, and in the reification of ethnic identities. The purpose of Anderson's essay is part corrective, part response to the critiques of *Imagined Communities* in the decades following its publication, a period that bore witness to the dissolution of nationalisms born of decolonization and post-totalitarianism into identitarian politics and ethnic violence.

Far beyond its elaboration on the conditions of possibility for the nation, what the logic of seriality introduces is nothing short of a "new grammar of representation," and more profoundly, a new experience and apprehension of *representability*. Turning back to our history of the apparition of Our Lady of Guadalupe, we might understand the curious appearance of "Tagalog" as indexing the emergent consciousness of series unbound and bound. Notably unlike the two previous apparition stories, which were deeply rooted in a singular geographic locale, the story of this apparition maps, via the confounding interchangeability of "Tagalog" and the implicit *indio*, a seamless and total world. That this is an imperial world, and that Mary stands as a figurehead in it, is beyond doubt. But even Mary is subsumed by this serial logic, as "Guadalupe" itself emerges as a series, mapping parallel histories that occupy "homogenous empty time."

In 1904, a year after the United States published its first census of the Philippines, Mary manifested in yet another form. That year, a religious sodality, the Marian Congregation of the Society of Jesus (the Jesuits), published a lengthy volume titled *La Virgen María, venerada en sus imágenes filipinas* (The Virgin Mary, as venerated in Philippine images). Described as a "collection of accounts, published and unpublished, of the images of the holy Virgin venerated in this country, illustrated with multiple plates, including in addition, two appendices that list all the Marian advocations in the archipelago, and other historical information," the book contains brief descriptions of no fewer than sixty images of Mary, as well as their individual histories, legends, and feast days.[95] Drawing from missionary chronicles and *devocionarios*, each section reads like a catalog entry of one to five pages, an exposition of facts and figures that the authors further compile in tabular form in an appendix. Our Lady of Guadalupe—version Manila—appears in the collection, as does Our Lady of Manaoag and Our Lady of Caysasay, although not all the images originate from an apparition of Mary, and not all are considered "miraculous." In the rationale provided in the introduction, the images featured were chosen for being the "most visited and venerated in the archipelago," examples of the "multiple advocations" beneath which "our Immaculate Queen is venerated."[96] In this serialization, we see the assertion of a theological general equivalent, the subsuming of Mary as an individual and singular local patron by the universal figure to which the descriptor "Marian" would refer.

But this aspiration to the universal does not simply issue from the grid that flattens out the histories and details of each individual image into the columns of provenance, location, date of origin, and feast day. It is not just a transcendental signified to which all images of Mary shall refer; it also must be mediated by a third term, which, in the case of *La Virgen María*, announces itself in the title page and introduction as "el pueblo Filipino."

CHAPTER TWO

First Filipino Apparition

DREAMING OF INANG BAYAN

There is a legend that tells of an ominous dream had by one of the leaders of the Katipunan, the secret society of late nineteenth-century revolutionaries.[1] Several of these men had fled from their headquarters, the offices of *El Diario de Manila* (where they were known to have printed their pamphlets and propaganda), and into the barrio of Balintawak, Caloocan. There, Melchora Aquino, a shopkeeper better known in the pantheon of national heroes as "Tandang Sora," gave them shelter.[2] One night,

> one of [the men] dreamt of a beautiful woman dressed in local garb who held in her arms a very beautiful child dressed in farmer's garb with cropped red pants. His hand wielding a bolo he cried, "FREEDOM! FREEDOM!" The beautiful woman approached the dreamer and said: "BE CAREFUL!"
>
> The dreamer awoke and told his companions of his vision, saying that the Virgin and Child had the faces of Spaniards but were dressed like Tagalogs.
>
> Because of this [the men] did not proceed back to their work in Manila but waited a bit longer in Balintawak. It was not long before news arrived that the Veteran Civil Guard had requisitioned the *Diario de Manila* offices and captured a few of the Katipunan.[3]

This version of the tale appears on the back of a prayer book printed in Spanish in 1926 titled *Novenario de la Patria* (Novena of the Motherland), written by Monsignor Gregorio Aglipay, a former Catholic priest who in 1903 became the first bishop of the Independent Philippine Church (Iglesia Filipina Independiente).[4] The brief synopsis is presented as an excerpt from an article that supposedly appeared in the local newspaper, *La Vanguardia*.[5]

The article, furthermore, is based on hearsay: "It is reported that while he was still living, Aurelio Tolentino would tell of how one night, while he and his companions Andres Bonifacio, Emilio Jacinto, and others were sleeping at the house of Tandang Sora in Balintawak, one of them dreamt . . ."[6] These multiple mentions echo a logic we saw in two of the apparition tales discussed in the previous chapter: it is a retroactive narration of the miraculous event, a deferred appearance of Mary in print, written in the mode of recollection.

But where the tales of Our Lady of Caysasay and Our Lady of Manaoag were stories that recalled the origins of sacred local shrines, the legend of Our Lady of Balintawak, as the advocation would be called, is appended to a prayer text that pays homage to the origins of the Philippine nation. There is no ambiguity as to what this figure represents; the subtitle of the *Novenario* makes clear, "The Mother Country Is Symbolized by the Dreamt Lady of Balintawak" (*La Patria se simboliza en la soñada Madre de Balintawak*). The Tagalog translation of the novena, *Pagsisiyam sa Virgen sa Balintawak* (Novena to Our Lady of Balintawak), makes the correspondence between the mother country and the Virgin Mary even more explicit; its subtitle reads, "The Virgin of Balintawak Is the Mother Country" (*Ang Virgin sa Balintawak ay ang Inang Bayan*). Yet this was neither a performative nor a radical moment of symbolization; it had been long prepared by the words, actions—and, of course, dreams—of Filipino nationalists for decades.

Likened to the sublime by one Filipino cultural critic, and the subject of countless pieces of drama, art, and literature, Inang Bayan (Mother Country or Motherland), endures as one of the most prevalent figurations of the Philippine nation.[7] Yet like so many figurations born of the modern logic of seriality (in this case, the seriality of *patria*), and as the subtitle of the novena clearly suggests both in its original and in its Tagalog version, Inang Bayan is the result of translation. It is, moreover, a *double* translation, of the quasi-divine figure of the Virgin Mary and of the globally circulating concept of the nation, into Filipino.[8] This chapter traces the moments and sites at which one can see these very processes of translation take place. Aglipay's novena represents the culmination of this process. But prior to this, the maternal allegory proliferated in ways not always or immediately tied to Mary—circulating as a form that could be taken up and molded into a character, an idea, and ultimately, a symbol for the nation.

In Philippine historiography, the deployment of the idiom of mother and child in popular perceptions of nationalism is well-covered terrain, and readers familiar with the vernacular texts herein may find their inclusion reiterative of what others have said.[9] My purpose in revisiting them in their context of late colonial modernity is to lay out the conditions of possibility for understanding the kinds of transformations in religious perception and Marian devotion that we will see later in the book. The birth of Inang Bayan or "Motherland" cannot be fully understood unless its deeply local antecedents and emergent forms of historical consciousness, epistemologies of comparison, and newer influences are accounted for. Let us begin, then, with one foundational moment in the forging of this particular representation, when a clamorous echo of mother and country resounded in a series of nationalists' cries.

THE MOTHERLAND TRILOGY

There exists a trio of Tagalog-language poems, composed between the years 1886 and 1896 by men of *indio* ("native") or mestizo ancestry, in which one sees the early foreshadowing of the nation personified as mother. Notably, as the titles—*Hibik ng Pilipinas sa Ynang España* (Filipinas' Lament to Mother Spain), *Sagot nang España sa Hibik nang Pilipinas* (Spain's Reply to Filipinas' Lament), and *Katapusang Hibik ng Pilipinas* (Final Lament of Filipinas)— reveal, it is not the Philippines that is figured as motherland, but rather her (indeed, it is always assumed that the voice of Filipinas is female) colonial guardian.[10] Composed in the years immediately preceding the revolution of 1896, the poems are a form of dialogue carried out in Tagalog that ventriloquizes Spain. The maternal voice was projected by men of *indio* or mestizo ancestry far flung throughout the globe. In these poems, this voice was a singular vehicle for lamentation, and lamentation's acknowledgment.[11]

Penned by Hermenegildo Flores and Marcelo del Pilar, respectively, the first two of these poems, *Hibik ng Pilipinas sa Ynang España* and *Sagot nang España sa Hibik nang Pilipinas*, set this exchange in motion. Flores was del Pilar's teacher in Manila, and both were active participants in the Propagandist Movement, the reformist campaign that flourished in the 1880s. The best-known vehicle for the *propagandistas* was *La Solidaridad*, a newspaper published first in Barcelona, and later in Madrid, of which del Pilar was the most acclaimed editor. But the movement itself began earlier, while del Pilar and others were still in Manila, with the bilingual publication of *Diariong Tagalog* (Tagalog Journal). Both poems are written from a first-person perspective, beginning with an address from daughter to mother, then the mother's reply. Written in Tagalog, in the *awit* form, that is, in dodecasyllabic quatrains (sixty-six in *Hibik* and eighty-two in *Sagot*), both stand as vociferous critiques of the "frairocracy" that early nationalists saw as a hindrance to progress in the Philippines.[12] By some critics' estimation, these poems are not literary exemplars.[13] The poems are noteworthy, however, for the ease with which they articulate the voices of mother and child to imagine a dialogue between the Philippines and Spain. The exchange reads as a hybrid of epistolary correspondence, prayerful supplication, and the convention of Spanish Siglo de Oro drama known as the *loa,* in which one of the players delivers a florid address to acknowledge and praise someone in the audience. Thus framed, the colonial relation is subtended not by opposition but by filial continuity.[14] Flores's *Hibik* opens:

> *Ynang mapag-ampon Españang marilag,*
> *nasaan ang iyong pagtingin sa anak[?]*
> *akong iyong bunsong abang Pilipinas*
> *tingni't sa dalita'y di na maka-iwas!*

> Oh beautiful and protective Mother Spain,
> where is your concern for your child?
> I am your youngest born, miserable Filipinas
> Look! You cannot ignore my suffering.

> *Ang mga anak kong sayo'y gumigiliw,*
> *sa pagmamasakit ng dahil sa atin*
> *ngayo'y inu-usig at di pagitawin*
> *ng mga fraileng ka-away mong lihim.*

> My children strive to please you,
> by sacrificing for us both
> now they are persecuted and kept in the dark
> by the friars, your traitorous enemies.

(FLORES, stanzas 1 and 2)

The poem immediately establishes the relationship between Filipinas and España as one of intergenerational obligation and maternal care. Interlopers in this familial relation, the friars are figures of treachery and deceit, come to ruin the inheritance that Filipinas and her children stand to gain. Instead of receiving education and enlightenment, the latter are deceived by the friars, who only sow evil (*magdaya sa mga anak ko't sabugan ng sama*) and scrape up every last possession of the Tagalog people (*may di pagkasimot ng ari-arian ng bayang tagalog?*).[15] With their thirst for riches (*uhaw sa yaman*) and a love of luxurious residences,[16] the friars accumulate wealth via their perverse barter of indulgences for donations and extort the population with their false promises:

Ang pangako nila sa mga anak ko
ay magbigay lamang sa mga convento
ng kualta'y sa langit naman patutungo
at ligtas sa madlang panganib sa mundo.

Their promise to my children
is if they only donate to the convents
they will indeed go to heaven
and be freed from all the dangers of this world.

(FLORES, stanza 23)

If nationalism imagines generational continuity, Flores's *Hibik* presents a vivid juxtaposition whereby the illicit consort of the religious orders and their illegitimate accumulation of wealth is measured against the birthrights of each generation of Filipinas, from mother to daughter to children.[17]

Del Pilar's sequel to Flores's lament, *Sagot nang España sa Hibik nang Pilipinas* is, first and foremost, a testimony to Filipinas' having been heard: a fantasy of primal recognition played out in the allegorical figure of the mother. It opens:

Puso ko'y nahambal nang aking marinig
bunso, ang taghoy mo't mapighating hibik;
wala ka, anak kong, sariling hinagpis
na hindi karamay ang ina mong ibig.

My heart was appalled when I heard
your cry and dolorous plaint, my child;
you have no sorrow, child, that's yours alone,
for your mother always shares it with you.

Wala kang dalita, walang kahirapan,
na tinitiis kang di ko dinaramdam:
ang buhay mo'y bunga niring pagmamahal,
ang kadustaan mo'y aking kadustaan.

You have no suffering, no affliction
that I don't undergo with you:
since you're the fruit of my love,
your humiliation is also mine.

(DEL PILAR, stanzas 1 and 2)

In this mirror of recognition we can begin to read del Pilar's reply as advancing the subjecthood of Filipinas qua Filipinas, at the same time that it reinforces the filial continuity that underwrites the notion of inheritance. Del Pilar continues the *Sagot* with a series of stanzas that itemize all of the extraordinary resources Filipinas has to offer: tobacco, coffee, rice (*palay*), indigo, cotton, hemp (*abaca*), sugarcane, timber, sulfur, lead, copper, iron, gold, silver, and more—all are yielded by Filipinas' fecund soil (*lupa*).[18] But no sooner is this litany of resources recited than the true nature of their value is revealed:

> *Tantong naliligid ang mga lupa mo*
> *ng dagat ng China't dagat Pacifico,*
> *balang mangangalakal sa buong sangmundo*
> *pawang naaakit dumalaw sa iyo.*

> Your land is surrounded
> by the China Sea and the Pacific Ocean,
> so that merchants all over the world
> are drawn to visit you.

> *Talaga nga manding ikaw ang hantungan*
> *ng sa ibang nasyong sinimpang puhunan;*
> *ikaw nga't di iba dapat makinabang*
> *nang yamang sa iyo'y gawad ng Maykapal.*

> Indeed you are the repository
> of the capital of various countries;
> you and only you deserve to profit
> from the riches bequeathed by the Creator.

> (DEL PILAR, stanzas 9 and 10)

As much as we see the popular motif of mother and child, thus, we also see here the entry of the commodity and the economy of agricultural export.[19] Heritability converges with calculability, as we see in the following:

> *Ang lupang nilawag at pinaghirapan*
> *ng magulang nila't mga kanunuan*
> *ngayo'y asyenda na't nahulog sa kamay*
> *ng hindi nagpagod at di namuhunan.*

> Land that was cleared and tilled
> by parents and ancestors
> has now become estates [haciendas] owned
> by those who invested neither labor nor money in it.

> (DEL PILAR, stanza 28)

Again, in their false promises of the afterlife that coerce the dying to hand over their possessions, the illegitimacy of the friars' bequests versus that of one's family's rears its ugly head:

Pag may mamamatay na tila mayaman
prayle ang aagap magpapakumpisal
at inuukilkil na ang pamanahan
ng aring inimpok ay kumbento lamang.

When a man is dying and he seems rich,
the friars are quick to give him confession,
and they din into him that the convent alone
be made heir to his possessions.

Hinlog, kamag-anak ay dapat limutin
sa oras na iyon, siyang sasabihin,
kaluluwa't yama'y dapat na ihain
sa prayle't ng huwag impierno'y sapitin.

Relatives, close and distant, should be forgotten
in his last hour, he is told,
for soul and property should be offered
to the friars to save him from hellfire.

(DEL PILAR, stanzas 42 and 43)

In referencing these poems, several scholars have rightly drawn attention
to their use of vernacular idioms, especially the emotional bond between
mother and child, to effectively communicate their critiques to a wider
Tagalog-speaking public likely not of the *ilustrado* class.[20] But scholars have
overlooked the equally articulated theme that is the scandal of misbegotten
wealth. The poets make more than a general accusation of hypocrisy, for
stanza upon stanza of both the *Hibik* and the *Sagot* describe in abundant detail exactly how the friars lie, cheat, and steal from their congregations; the
types of luxuries in which they indulge; and the long history of their deceit.[21]
This does not contradict the familiar schema of filial obligation and maternal
care that taps into "popular consciousness" but rather complements it. The
poets render a slippage between the friars' artificiality of relation—described
at one point by del Pilar (Mother Spain) as poorly chosen "guardians"—and
their perfidious diversions of inheritance, wealth, and land. There is more,
thus, to these first two poems of the motherland trilogy than the sentimental
trope of mother love, much less devotion to the Virgin Mary. Instead, there
is a tension between the Christian economy of salvation and the restricted
economy of capital, a tension that is ultimately resolved as the latter sup-
plants the former in the eyes of the Propagandists. A reciprocal relation of
maternal or filial love provides a natural foundation that acts as a measure of
intrinsic value against the flux of capital within and through the Philippines.

Exploring these economistic dimensions to the poetic exchange between Flores and del Pilar, that is, between Filipinas and Mother Spain, a different picture of colonial modernity from that which Reynaldo Ileto and others have examined through these poems emerges. True enough, both *ilustrado* authors hope to garner receptivity among their larger audience by framing their compositions with the popular idiom of mother-child bonds and its emotional vocabulary of debts of gratitude (*utang-na-loob*), pity (*awa*), and sympathy (*damay*). But the message they convey equally solicits their readers' (or hearers') comprehension of the material reasons behind their own oppressed state, which have much to do with the untenability of imperial Christendom and its means of wealth extraction, such as tribute and forced labor, in a landscape increasingly defined by capitalist production. To ignore this is to miss the opportunity to consider the myriad ways in which average colonial subjects may have understood their own condition beyond mere appeals to the affective or emotional, entangled as they most certainly were in the cash-crop economy that dominated the colony during the late nineteenth century.

By the time the third poem of the motherland trilogy is composed, what were fantasies of recognition, filial continuity, and heritability in the first two poems have become fantasies of abandonment, violence, and revenge. *Katapusang Hibik ng Pilipinas* ("Final Lament of Filipinas") appeared in the year of the start of the revolution of 1896, and it is attributed to none other than the first leader of the Katipunan, Andres Bonifacio. At its most basic level, Bonifacio's poem is suggestive of how the broader Tagalog audience may have comprehended the earlier poems. And like Hermenegildo Flores's first *Hibik*, *Katapusang Hibik* also takes the voice of Filipinas, addressing Mother Spain. But unlike the two Propagandists' companion poems, the voice of the revolutionary leader is devoid of any affection or sentimentality:

> *Sumikat na Ina sa sinisilangan*
> *ang araw ng poot ng katagalugan,*
> *tatlong daang taong aming iningatan*
> *sa dagat ng dusa ng karalitaan.*

> At the horizon, Mother, has risen
> the sun of Tagalog fury;
> for three centuries we kept it concealed
> in the sea of woes wrought by poverty.

> *Walang isinuway kaming iyong anak*
> *sa bagyong masasal ng dalita't hirap,*
> *iisa ang puso nitong Pilipinas*
> *at ikaw ay di na Ina naming lahat.*

> We your children stood without support
> during the terrible storm of pains and troubles;
> all in Filipinas are now of one heart—
> you're no longer a mother to us.[22]
>
> (BONIFACIO, stanzas 1 and 2)

Bonifacio's poem is not merely anticlerical, it aims to incite a violent separation from Mother Spain.

The language of justification for this bitter renunciation extends the themes of heritability and economy from the previous two poems, but only in order to dispel the fantasy of guarantee that filial relations possess against corruption and abuse:

> *Wala nang namana itong Pilipinas*
> *na layaw sa Ina kundi nga ang hirap*
> *tiis ay pasulong, patente'y nagkalat*
> *recargo't impuesto'y nagsala-salabat.*
>
> Filipinas has inherited nothing[23]
> by way of comfort from her mother, only pain—
> our sufferings grew: revenues for this and that,
> charges imposed and taxes levied left and right.

> ....

> *Ang lupa at bahay na tinatahanan*
> *bukid at tubigang kalawak-lawakan*
> *at gayon din naman mga halamanan*
> *sa paring kastila ay binubuisan.*
>
> For the lot and the house in which we lived,
> stretches of fields and rice paddies,
> and even the very plants we raise,
> we had to pay tax to the Spanish priests.
>
> (BONIFACIO, stanzas 7 and 9)

In the eyes of Bonifacio's Filipinas, Mother Spain has conspired with the friars to bequeath only hardship.

It has been argued, most famously by Philippine historian Reynaldo Ileto, that the sentiments such as those expressed by the Katipunero Andres Bonifacio were easily accessible—were even made possible—thanks to the popular familiarity and practice of the *pasyon*, the Passion play of Jesus Christ. "Just as the start of Christ's passion is marked by his emotional and painful separation from Mary," writes Ileto, "so does the struggle of the

Filipinos, following the contours of tradition, begin with separation from Mother Spain." [24] Indeed, various versions of the *pasyon* attest in their length to the important influence of this scene of separation.[25] And yet recourse to the *pasyon* as the most important influence of this poem proves somewhat unsatisfactory if one considers that such an influence would render implausible the violence that permeates lines like the following:

> *Gapu[s]ing mahigpit ang mga tagalog*
> *makinahi't ibiting parang isang hayop;*
> *hinain sa sikad, kulata at suntok,*
> *ito baga, Ina, ang iyong pag-irog?*

> Binding the Tagalogs with ropes,
> garroting and hanging them like beasts,
> weakening them with kicks, beatings, and blows—
> Mother, is this the way you love?

> . . . .

> *Aming tinitiis hanggang sa mamatay*
> *bangkay ng mistula ayaw pang tigilan*
> *kaya kung ihulog sa mga libingan*
> *linsad na ang buto't lamuray ang laman.*

> We have endured unto death:
> like a corpse that is still being tortured,
> so when finally thrown into the grave,
> our bones are broken and our flesh a mess.

> . . . .

> *Ikaw nga oh Inang pabaya't sukaban*
> *kami di na iyo saan man humanggan*
> *ihanda mo, Ina, ang paglilibingan*
> *sa mawawakawak na maraming bangkay.*

> O negligent and malevolent Mother,
> we're no longer yours come what may;
> prepare the graves, Mother,
> for the many who are to die.[26]

(BONIFACIO, stanzas 4, 6, and 11)

Even in the most drawn-out scenes of the Tagalog versions of the *pasyon* that involve Mary and Jesus, unorthodoxy takes the form of a disproportionate emphasis on Mary's suffering, first upon Christ's bidding farewell, and then at the hour of her son's crucifixion.[27] Thus, while there is undoubtedly some interpretative accuracy in citing here the influence of the *pasyon*, just as it was reasonable for Flores and del Pilar to couch their message in the popular idiom of the mother-child bond, doing so fails to account for this description of a Calvary committed with the consent, if not at the very hands of, the Mother.[28] The idiom of maternal separation has surely taken on a life of its own at this point; the availability of Catholic narrative and forms to appropriation signals, too, the possibility of their unmooring from conventional signification. It would be no coincidence that around the time *Katapusang Hibik* was composed, Bonifacio and his fellow Katipuneros allegedly received that mysterious visit by a woman who *as of yet had no name*. And it is not insignificant that this apparition would appear, not out in nature, fished out of a lake or perched on a tree branch, with the ultimate sanction of church authorities, but in the realm of dreams—where it is the nature of signs to mean more than what they first appear to.

STAGING SEDITION

Dreams also figure prominently in the unfinished cycle of dramas, gathered under the rubric of "seditious plays," written by Aurelio Tolentino in the first few years of the twentieth century. Although he is recognized as a literary giant of his time, historians and critics have examined Tolentino and his works with equivocal regard.[29] A member of the revolutionary Katipunan, and later, an organizer for the armed resistance movement against the Americans, Tolentino is often portrayed as deeply nationalistic, and he was imprisoned multiple times for his actions. A strong advocate of the use of Tagalog as the national language, he was equally fluent in Spanish, although his native tongue was that of his home province, Pampanga. He often reworked already published or written materials from the three languages. His best-known writings (including those to be discussed shortly) were courageous critiques of American colonial rule, even if not exactly lauded for their artistry. In contrast, his two major novels, *Buhay* (1909) and *Ang Buhok ni Ester* (1914–15), written well into the American period, have been read as more politically and socially conservative, reflecting, for some, a more acquiescent disposition to the foreign regime, veiled by aesthetic indulgence. He championed the rights of laborers, at the same time that he accepted commissions to write operettas (*zarzuelas*) for major tobacco-manufacturing companies. In short, Tolentino's life and works epitomized the vicissitudes of the bourgeois patriot in colonial times.

Tolentino had originally intended to write a trilogy of plays, a plan that was permanently thwarted when the second of the cycle, *Kahapon, Ngayon at Bukas* (Yesterday, Today, and Tomorrow), was condemned by the U.S. government after a riot broke out on its opening night performance, on May 14, 1903 (the riot was said to have been started by Americans in the audience who rushed the stage and attempted to smash the sets).[30] Tolentino was charged with sedition, found guilty, and sentenced by an American judge to two years in prison. *Kahapon, Ngayon at Bukas* is the best known and best regarded by historians of all the seditious plays because of the sensation its performance and trial created; this in turn has bestowed upon it iconic status vis-à-vis the genre more broadly.[31] My discussion of the seditious plays is mostly limited to this unfinished trilogy, *Luhang Tagalog* (Tagalog Tears) and its loose sequel *Kahapon, Ngayon at Bukas*, and focuses especially on the dream sequences as they work through the maternal allegory in both. But first a few words about these seditious plays more generally.

Staged plays such as these nationalist dramas developed out of several performance traditions: the staging of the *pasyon* (also known as *sinakulo*), and secular dramas called *comedias* (known in some areas as *moro-moro* for their leitmotif of Christian-Muslim conflict), often referred to in their Tagalog form, *komedya*. The *comedias* originated as a three-act form developed by Lope de Vega in late sixteenth-century Spain, and historical records reveal that versions of the *comedia* had been produced in the Philippines concurrently with its emergence in the Peninsula.[32] It was only in the eighteenth century, however, that the *comedia* became commonplace (composed more frequently by native or *ladino* writers), burgeoning as an art form in the nineteenth. Similar to the *corrido* genre discussed in the previous chapter, *comedias* were typically filled with battles and royalty, as well as the melodrama of forbidden courtship and sequestered princesses. They structured the imagining of conflict, love, and betrayal that one sees in the nationalist dramas of the early twentieth century.[33]

Tolentino's unfinished trilogy was no exception. Indeed, we might read the difference in characters and plot between *Luhang Tagalog* and *Kahapon, Ngayon at Bukas* as enacting this very shift: from the *comedia* of popular entertainment to its nationalist progeny. In this Tolentino proved himself to be, if not the most talented playwright, then at least a brilliant assessor of the technics of nationalism. For the success—and scandal—of the second play was thanks to its difference in continuity from the first, its translation in performance of the mother figure into Inang Bayan (sometimes spelled *Inangbayan* or *Ynangbayan*, "Motherland").

The first play in the cycle, *Luhang Tagalog* (Tagalog Tears), takes place in the year 1499, before Spain set foot in the islands, and depicts the betrayal of the *datu* (chief) of Balintawak, Gat-Salian, by his father, Lakan-Salian, who has allied with Chinese soldiers under the leadership of the great warrior Hinghis-Khan.[34] By the end of the play all are dead, Balintawak has been burned to the ground, and only the traitor-father Lakan-Salian survives. The second play in the cycle, *Kahapon, Ngayon at Bukas* (Yesterday, Today, and Tomorrow), displays greater narrative sophistication than its predecessor from the start. Rather than simply opening where the last play left off, the drama begins a generation or so later, when the massacre at Balintawak is being commemorated. Immediately the audience is introduced to the character Inangbayan (Motherland), who chides those participating in the commemoration for being far too joyous and boisterous for the tragic occasion. Thus, while the setting of *Kahapon, Ngayon at Bukas* is still the distant (one might even say mythic) past, the temporality introduced is that of modern memorialization, and the agent who imparts this new consciousness in the people is none other than this feminized figure of the nation.

In the dream sequences of both of Tolentino's plays one sees the work performed by the mother figure, and more explicitly, the transformation of maternal figuration from a quasi-divine character reminiscent of the Virgin Mary into Inangbayan. In *Luhang Tagalog* there is no character Inangbayan, and while the female characters such as Bituin (or Star, the wife of the *datu* Gat-Salian) are far from portrayed as submissive, the drama mostly revolves around the *datu* and his traitorous father. The dream in *Luhang Tagalog* is Gat-Salian's unconscious perception of his father's dastardly plan to take his life, for when he wakes from it, his father has just attempted to kill him. This attempt the audience (or reader) sees. What the audience is not shown is Gat-Salian's dream, which he merely describes to his wife and his noble assistant, Bundok (Mountain):

> I dreamed that my father had become a great ghost, his eyes ablaze. He flayed me with his gaze, scourging me mercilessly with a serpent that he held in his hand. I cried out, begging for help. I called you, Bituin, and I called upon Bundok and other captains, including my soldiers, but nobody heard me, and none of them even turned his face toward me from afar. In despair I called to my mother, who has long been in Heaven, and she came from Heaven to me, wrapped in waves of the purest cloud; she saw me weeping, sighed heavily and cried out: "My son! My poor son!"
>
> ... She called me insistently and with arms extended to receive me: "Come, my son," she said. "I will take you with me and lead you into the presence of

God." I tried to throw myself into my dear mother's arms but was overcome; an irresistible force held me back. When she saw that all my efforts were useless, she knelt down before the phantom that made me suffer, before my father, and implored him to set me free. Instead of listening to her entreaties, he only snarled the more, grasped me by the hair, and shook me violently. My body trembled like a leaf and thousands of bloodthirsty, devouring spirits appeared before me, ready to eat me up. They opened their mouths and displayed their huge grinning fangs and terrible sharp claws.[35]

Gat-Salian continues to describe the terrifying vision of all his subjects massacred and Balintawak burned to the ground. Thrown to the lions by his father, Gat-Salian is devoured flesh and bone, until, he says:

My soul returned quickly to the arms of my compassionate mother, who embraced me warmly, and . . . Oh! I heard the gnashing of the teeth of my executioners, who were chewing up the bones, which were all that were left of the body they had seized upon to devour. All was over. Already I was . . . ascending with my mother to the throne of God.[36]

Coming from heaven, "wrapped in waves of the purest cloud," is a weeping and compassionate mother who intercedes, and into whose arms the dying take flight. We've seen these images before: they are in the origin story of Our Lady of Manaoag, and in the famous iconography of Mary as Mater Dolorosa and in the Pietà. Gat-Salian dreams of his own wretched death and the destruction of his dominion, and he calls for his mother's succor, a call to which she promptly responds. That the dream and the attempt on his life occur simultaneously betoken the meaning of the Tagalog term *bangungot*, a word most frequently translated as "nightmare," though it bears an explicit association with death.[37] Bituin, the wife of Gat-Salian, attempts to placate him, saying, "You are not a child, why should that bother you? Did you not say it was only a dream? . . . It is over now and faded away." "True," replies her husband, "but there remains in my mind a fearful impression prophetic of gloom and in my heart frightful presentiments."[38]

We find this foreboding sense of doom to be practically identical to that felt by the character Malaynatin ("Our Consciousness," indicating the American government), the dreamer of Tolentino's second play, *Kahapon, Ngayon at Bukas*. When asked by his wife, Bagongsibol (literally "New Spring," the newcomer, or America herself), "Why do you pay attention to lying dreams?" Malaynatin replies: "This heavy dream of mine has lodged in my heart a most painful dread."[39] Yet this is the only extent to which the dreams in both of Tolentino's plays are similar. In *Kahapon, Ngayon at Bukas* the dream sequence takes place in act 3 (or *Bukas*, "Tomorrow"), that which corresponds to the American period. Unlike the dream-as-narrated by the character Gat-Salian in *Luhang Tagalog*, here the audience is privy to Malaynatin's vision. Picture Bagongsibol, made up to reference America herself. She enters happily with an eagle on her arms:

BAGONGSIBOL: Beautiful eagle, queen of all that is mighty, fly and cover the world with your wings!

> *Suddenly she looks at her eagle.*

BAGONGSIBOL: Who has injured my precious eagle?

> *A flash of light and Inangbayan appears.*

YNANGBAYAN: Just a small bullet, cast lightly.

BAGONGSIBOL: So it was you! And how could you hurt it so, with so light a throw, without force?

YNANGBAYAN: It was an electric bullet [*ang bala'y may electricidad*].

BAGONGSIBOL: Ynangbayan! Traitorous one! You'll pay for this!

> *Bagongsibol charges Ynangbayan. Suddenly there appear*
> *numerous tombs before Bagongsibol. Ghosts rise up from them.*

YNANGBAYAN: Before our tombs did you solemnly swear that one day you would grant freedom to Ynangbayan. She loves you with all her heart. Do not deceive her, for God shall punish a liar.[40]

Just as Marcelo del Pilar found it possible in poetry to speak as Mother Spain, so, too, can an audience of Filipinos enter into the dreams of America in this dramatic form. A convention of substitution is mobilized. Inhabiting the perspective of the colonizer, one encounters an image of the other's— that is, one's own—motherland. Memory is Inangbayan's ally, here personified as the ghost witnesses of America's pact. Her weaponry is not that of kris and dagger but that of modern warfare (electric bullets!).[41] In this play, the mother figure does not intercede on behalf of those nearing death (as we saw in *Luhang Tagalog*) but actually summons the dead and, moreover, speaks on their behalf (nameless, necessarily, as the dead are).[42] Inangbayan's power over death is most explicitly dramatized in act 2 (or *Ngayon*, "Today"), when she literally rises from the grave where the characters loosely representing the Spanish friars and the Spanish government had buried her alive. In summary, while both of Tolentino's plays are replete with scenes of death, only *Kahapon, Ngayon at Bukas* is *haunted* by death, that is, filled with signs of death: ghosts, tombstones, mourning, commemoration, a litany of killing devices, and so forth. The extent to which Inangbayan positively engenders (and genders) the presence of the nation is thus determined by the extent to which she deals in these signs, that is, the extent to which she and death commingle. Kalayaan (here translatable as "freedom") may be Inangbayan's husband,[43] but death is her inamorato—an illicit twist on the nativity scene that has so emblematized the beginnings of the Philippine nation.

NOVENA OF THE MOTHERLAND

Aurelio Tolentino understood well the communicative power of dreams, and of dreaming as a field in which translation takes place and new significations are both heralded and authorized. Whether dreams were exclusively Tolentino's favored means of expression, or a commonly circulating motif among nationalists, the frequent and enduring reference to his seditious plays and fable of the apparition at Balintawak make plain that dreaming was simply one variant of the imaginings that gave form to the Philippine nation. Tolentino may have been responsible for spreading the legend of the dream in which Our Lady of Balintawak appears to the young Katipuneros, but in the hands of many of those fighting for Philippine independence, the legend itself became a foundational narrative for establishing a new devotion to the nation.

The text with which we began this chapter, *Novenario de la Patria* (Novena of the Motherland), was one of the doctrinal organs written in the middle years of the Iglesia Filipina Independiente (Philippine Independent Church). One of the most fascinating outcomes of late nineteenth-century Philippine nationalism, the Iglesia Filipina Independiente (henceforth IFI) was established as the national church after conditions long in the making led to a permanent separation from the Catholic Church in Rome. Fueled by anti-friar sentiment, its founding was galvanized by the 1902 accord reached between American governor-general William Taft and the Vatican. Taft had been sent by President Roosevelt to negotiate the withdrawal of the religious orders from the Philippines, and he returned with a compromise whereby the vast holdings of the friars would be sold, but the friars themselves would remain. The release of estates and the complete expulsion of the friars was the condition upheld by many of the secular Filipino clergy ("secular" meaning "not belonging to a religious order"), as well as some of the most outspoken nationalists of that time.[44] On August 3, 1902, in response to the failure to meet these conditions, the IFI was formally launched by one of Philippine national history's most splendid characters, Don Isabelo de los Reyes.[45]

The foundation of an "indigenous" or national church in the Philippines was not, in and of itself, an extraordinary development in the regional, if not global, turn of the century. In Japan in 1901, Uchimura Kanzo established the Nonchurch Movement, a very loosely organized Christian sect that eschewed any liturgy, sacraments, or ordained clergy. A few years later in 1907, the Pyongyang Revival marked the beginning of the monumental spread of Christianity in Korea.[46] Although the IFI differs significantly from these examples for being an institution that splintered off from the Catholic Church, rather than having sprouted forth from the matrix forged by histories of Protestant mission, it instantiates the broader convergence of nationalism, anti-imperialism, and Christianity in an earlier era of decolonization.[47] Its main founders, de los Reyes and Gregorio Aglipay—the latter of whom was named *obispo máximo* and remains the namesake of the church today— were both active participants in the revolution against Spain from 1896 to 1898. De los Reyes, in particular, saw the new church as simply one spoke in a wheel of nationalist formation that included vernacular presses, labor unions, and political parties.[48]

Given that the conditions inciting the schism were sociopolitical rather than doctrinal or ideological in nature, it comes as no surprise that in the early years of the IFI, the church appeared to adhere to all aspects of Catholicism except allegiance to Rome.[49] Within the first few years of the church's development, however, it became increasingly clear that Isabelo de los Reyes's agenda was to introduce—"like the sharp intrusion of a foreign body into a living organism," as one Jesuit critic put it[50]—secular, rational ideas that would rub acutely against orthodox Catholicism's grain. By the time of the *Novenario*'s publication in 1926, thus, the IFI was far from being just the Catholic Church in Philippine dress, and Our Lady of Balintawak was not just the Virgin Mary in native drag. She was, rather, the nation itself. The deployment in this text of the novena form (the nine-day cycle of prayer and meditation) underscores the extent to which this new mother would demand every bit of devotion from her children as Nuestra Señora had in the past.

The first thing to be noted about the *Novenario* is that it was originally written in Spanish.[51] It is structured like all Catholic novenas, divided with the intent of being recited over nine days. Each day's recitations include an opening and closing prayer (*oración*) that frames the readings (*lecturas*). Yet this is no ordinary prayer booklet, for already in the opening address, nestled among the platitudes of praise to God, one reads the following:

OPENING PRAYER

Oh God, our true Father! From the depths of our hearts we raise the purest sentiments of love and gratitude for the endless proofs of your most gentle fatherhood. Like a most affectionate father, you steadfastly provide for all our needs, however little we labor, and protect us from danger. Make us upstanding and worthy of your affection. Make us comply with your commandments of charity and labor, because charity shall make us happy and free us from unpleasantness, and labor is the great remedy which you have placed within our reach to satisfy our needs and just desires.

Oh supreme Intelligence, glorious beacon of the Universe! With all the fervor of our souls do we beseech you to lend us one ray of your natural light, so that by means of the sciences we may know the wonders of your supreme power, glimpse your sublime nature, and learn the necessary virtues for our dignity and well-being.[52]

From the start the *Novenario* announces its strange hybrid method: it is a prayer, but one that will be communicated first and foremost through the faculty of scientific reason. Reason becomes the means through which God is extricated from the mediating practice and doctrines of "religion." This is remarkably worked out in the three readings assigned for the first day alone: (1) "God, According to the Ancient Religions," (2) "Our Idea of God," (3) "What the Idea of God Teaches Us."[53]

Each of the three readings for each day of the novena offers a sober reflection on the development of "God" throughout human history, couched within which are correctives provided by science to man's errors in thought and belief. *Paleontología, hidrografía, química,* and *geología,* for instance, have thoroughly disproven Genesis, "according to which the world began as a dawn created the first day—but this is an enormous error since dawn originates from the light of the sun that only the fourth day emerged . . . And we shall not even speak of the infantile tale that presents God as a potter who makes man from mud and the first woman from man's ribs!"[54] Indubitably God exists, the authors of the novena assert, but not in the likeness of men, as the "ancient religions"—that is, Catholicism—would have you believe. God is, rather, an "intelligent, supreme, and mysterious Power [*Potencia*] that produces, gives life, directs, animates, and preserves all beings; the great soul of the Universe; the beginning of all life and universal movement."[55] Resurrection exists, but only insofar as "all the energies that appear lost upon the extinction of life will in fact pass in the forms of electricity, heat, hydrogen, etc. . . . the laws of physics and chemistry prove that nothing disappears, neither energy nor matter."[56] Schopenhauer makes an appearance in the novena, in the company of biologist Ernst Haeckel and the physicist William Thomson. Among these illustrious thinkers is cited another well-known physician, Dr. José Rizal, who is reported to have said, "If Jesus had been God, his works would not have had such value."[57]

Should there be any question as to the IFI's beliefs, a reading on the seventh day of the novena explicates:

19TH READING: THE NEED FOR A NATIONAL AND SCIENTIFIC CHURCH

Via the preceding readings listeners shall understand that however venerable the biblical legends and teachings of Jesus may be, they are not free from scientific and moral errors, and cannot be the foundation of a Church worthy of the enormous progress of modern science. Furthermore, a National Church is absolutely necessary to defend the sacrosanct ideal of our independence against the machinations of foreign religious orders that conspire against it, and it is essential that the modern, scientific, and patriotic teachings of Rizal, Mabini, and other Filipino masters oppose those Judaic and neo-Christian pagan tales that are utterly absurd and contrary to all the sciences.[58] Herein lies the motive for the foundation of the Iglesia Filipino Independiente.

We forsake neither Jesus nor Moses; we only correct the errors that have been attributed to them. On our altar [in the parish of María Clara, San Lázaro, Manila] you see three memorialized figures. We do not adore them as idols—we are not savages worshiping wood—but only as they preside here as monuments, or beacons, of our ideals.[59]

The three figures are Moses, "who symbolizes the Old Testament, so that you will know that we deeply revere his ten commandments"; Jesus, "so that we may adopt with all our hearts his mellifluous teachings of charity and universal brotherhood without distinction of race or religion"; and finally, Our Lady of Balintawak, who

symbolizes our Motherland [*Patria*]. The child Katipunero represents the Filipino people—the *rising generation*—that longs for independence. Both figures shall constantly remind you of the immense sacrifices of our country's redeemers.[60]

What is striking about these descriptions is the assertion of representation, by means of which the teleological modernity of the IFI's project makes itself so compellingly felt. These figures are symbols, not idols; they represent the *patria* (motherland) and the *pueblo* (people). It is now the European Catholics whose practices, such as that of venerating *santos* (which in the vernacular refers as much to the physical icons as it does to the pantheon of personages), are seen as idolatrous. But this is not all. For while these figures are representational and not to be mistaken for their venerated referents, they also "preside here as monuments of our ideals." And as monuments *of* (not *to*) these ideals of independence, the figures of Moses, Jesus, and Our

Lady of Balintawak perform a service different from representation: they are both from and outside the collective consciousness that demands constant remembrance and dedication. They are, in other words, prosthetic forms by means of which the nation is given presence.

Having drawn attention to the figures upon the altar of the church as metonyms for the nation, the remaining days of the novena and the readings therein appropriately turn to the Philippines' most illustrious national heroes. The readings are not, however, about these men's lives and deeds but rather about their convictions and beliefs, as spoken through their numerous writings and letters. With titles such as "The Creed of Rizal" (reading 20), "Advice of Rizal to women" (reading 22),[61] and "The Testimony of Rizal" (reading 24), these readings seek not to portray a distant pantheon of heroes but to establish a mode of communicating fidelity to the nation by listening to and citing those who most famously reflected upon it. In addition to José Rizal, the saintly Apolinario Mabini—easily the most brilliant intellect of the revolution—is honored and given voice through the inclusion of his famous "Decálogo," or Ten Commandments, modeled after that which is learned as part of the catechism of the Catholic Church.[62]

That many of these writings take the form of familiar Catholic doctrine and recitation is not insignificant. But while such mimicry served, in part, to critique the church, the texts do not seem to have been written with wholly iconoclastic intent.[63] For all the scathing satires spun from this technique, many sincere texts were also written. Indeed, the very effectiveness of these appropriations stemmed from the fact that they drew upon and redeployed devotional forms and recitations that were familiar and meaningful to all, be it for ceremony or quotidian practice. Such appropriations were thus a powerful way to infuse daily life with national and moral consciousness. Like the images on the altar of the parish of María Clara, the texts evinced an awareness of the emblematization of sacred, or quasi-sacred, notions and modes of address.

And yet these tokens of disenchantment—the near Protestant ethos we see in the *Novenario*, the fully agential subject interiorly possessed of reason[64]—are not without their mystical foundation. Recall one last time the apparition story that opened this chapter and that appears on the back of the novena. It appears as a paratext, or *parergon*, in the strict sense of the term, "a piece of work that is supplementary to or a by-product of a larger work."[65] It is also *parergon* in the sense of the Derridean supplement, "inscrib[ing] something which comes as an extra, *exterior* to the proper field . . . but whose transcendent exteriority comes into play, abut[s] onto, brush[es] against, rub[s], press[es] against the limit itself and intervene[s] in the inside only to the extent that the inside is lacking."[66] All the more relevant here is that Derrida is talking about the *parerga* that lie neither wholly inside nor outside Immanuel Kant's *Religion within the Limits of Reason Alone*, the "General Observations" that examine those "*morally*-transcendent ideas," that is, the supernatural, where "all use of reason ceases."[67] An origin at the margins, transcendent yet not necessarily divine, describable yet nameless, it is the apparition of the Lady at Balintawak that gives rise to the work (of prayer) itself.[68]

This chapter and the previous one have attempted to chart shifts in the phenomenology and symbolic power of apparitions of the Virgin Mary throughout the late colonial Philippines. In this broadening capacity to signify—from a mute material object grounded in physical location, to an apparition whose constituent dimensions reflect the fragmentation of the human sensorium, to a metaphorical stand-in for the nation—we witness one trajectory in the dominant narrative of modernity: the birth of a certain mode of representation, language as referential, religion as a metadiscursive construct, and so forth. This was by no means a smooth and single path. I have tried to emphasize elements that disrupt a straightforward narrative of epistemic shifts, such as the emergence of origins at the moment of their displacement in time.

Despite this, something remains. What began as an examination of apparitions—in considering appearances—has drawn us time and again to the matter of *voice*. Be it in prayer, in the call, or even in muteness, voice relates to these appearances of Mary in different, and often confounding, ways. Our Lady of Caysasay showed us how authority is generated by speaking for she who does not speak. A call lingers long after (or is it long before?) Our Lady of Manaoag appears in the annals of history. A poet finds in the maternal allegory, long anticipated by Mary, a figure through which to speak of and to speak for the nation. Our Lady of Balintawak appears and speaks of danger; in return she is honored with the perfect transmission of speech in prayer. Among these instances, voice variably authenticates and evades presence, says two things at once, becomes the register of self-representation, and performs allegiance and devotion. Such variation proves that there is nothing primordial about the voice, nothing consistent. Voice can stand next to, precede, lie within, and remain an echo long after appearance. Voice refuses location, be it the body or shrine or nation. Yet there voice is, haunting each appearance with its indeterminate relationship to it—including the very textual depictions we have examined, which even at best can only present images of speaking.

PART II

Visions

CHAPTER THREE

Mary, Mediatrix

In my first interview with Teresita Castillo (or Teresing, as most know her), how we got on the topic of writing dictionaries had everything to do with what she would and would not talk about. She would not talk about the late 1940s, when she was a seventeen-year-old postulant in a Carmelite convent in the town of Lipa, and the Virgin Mary appeared to her announcing, "I am Mary, Mediatrix of All Grace." She would not talk about the public miracles that accompanied the apparitions: the showers of rose petals that fell from the sky on the convent grounds. She definitely would not talk about the hasty church investigation of the apparitions: how the priest interrogating her pitched an ashtray at her head, how she was accused of lurid encounters with her mother prioress, or how she was forced to leave her beloved cloistered community when the church declared in 1951 that the "extraordinary happenings . . . at the Carmel of Lipa . . . *excluded* any supernatural intervention."[1] And she would not talk about how, for the past fifty years, she has been ready to die. For once one sees the face of the Virgin and sees what heaven awaits, why would anyone want to stay on this earth?

After refusing to discuss everything for which she is known—and everything about which I wanted to speak to her—Teresita settled on a seemingly benign topic: her role in producing some of the best-known volumes of English-Tagalog and Tagalog-English dictionaries, a project that occupied nearly thirty years of her life.[2]

Teresita began by describing her first grief-stricken years after leaving the convent in Lipa. She moved back into her parents' house in the nearby town of Tanauan but remained inconsolable. She tried to participate in various projects and pilgrimages, but those, too, failed to quell her incessant weeping. Sometime in the mid-1950s she was brought by the archbishop Rufino J. Santos to an Australian Redemptorist priest, a man with a most befitting name—Fr. Leo English—who was asked to provide Teresita with "mental work . . . to get Carmel out of her mind."[3] Fr. English was starting on the letter "A" of his English-Tagalog dictionary. He pursued the project in between the days of his mission work and needed the help of an assistant to bring it to completion. At first Teresita was both terrified and reluctant, insisting to Fr. English that she knew nothing about typing or research and was fully fluent in neither Tagalog nor English. "But you must obey the archbishop," Fr. English admonished. "You're under my care now, and you will have to learn."[4]

So, first, Teresita learned to type. Her tentative one-finger technique brought more scolding from the priest, who barked instructions until she was able to type using all of her fingers. Once she could do this, the formidable project began. The tools of the work, according to Teresita, were as follows: two copies of the thousand-plus-page *Scott Foresman English Dictionary*; a pair of scissors; twenty-six envelopes; a stack of blank sheets of paper; some glue; and the typewriter. The instructions were equally clear cut: Cut each and every entry and its definition. File them in the envelopes marked with the letters "A" through "Z." Be sure not to confuse the two dictionary copies, since the printing is double sided; one dictionary is for all of the entries from the front of a page, the other for the entries on the back of that same page. When finished, start again with the entries in the "A" envelope (hopefully they remain in some alphabetical order!), glue an entry onto the blank sheet of paper, stick it in the typewriter, and write the Tagalog translation after it.

Eyes that had once seen so much now saw only words—hundreds of thousands, even millions, of words. When Teresita finally completed a first draft of the dictionary, Fr. English instructed her to type eight more copies, as he wished to circulate them for comment (one copy, according to her, was 1,200 pages). Next, she began work on the Tagalog-English dictionary by using a similar cut-and-graft technique with the English-Tagalog version that she herself had produced. The projects had, without a doubt, distracted Teresita from her grief. She no longer wept, for as she put it, she could not properly read through tears.

The task of Teresita the translator was not the romanticist vision proffered by Walter Benjamin: calling forth that essence of language that transcends the plurality of languages, speaking in and as an echo of the original.[5]

More labor than love, Teresita's contribution, only briefly mentioned in the acknowledgments, became as emotionless as the typewriter on which she worked.[6] At the height of the dictionaries' production she would toil seven days a week, from eight in the morning until noon, and from two to six or seven in the evening. She worked on it everywhere, even during a long boat trip to Australia with Fr. English in the early days of the project. Finally, in 1986, decades after it began and nine years after the publication of its counterpart, the Tagalog-English dictionary was published. Teresita's life as a lexicographer ended, along with the self-evacuating tedium that had filled it. Now she laughs aloud with pleasure each time she needs to look up a word.

In my first conversation with Teresita, this was all I learned. After ambling beside her down the stairs in the house of the acquaintance who set up the meeting, we thanked each other. She patted my forearm and for a moment stood smiling at me. With another pat she turned and walked toward the kitchen, where friends and family turned their heads to receive her. The good friend of hers who introduced us marched up to me and, punctuating with a single jerk of the eyebrows, asked, "Did you get what you wanted?"

Did I? What I wanted was testimony, the story of the apparitions as told by none other than the visionary herself. Not that this would have been the first or only time she had told the story, and I was surely not the first to interview her. Indeed, I had spent a good deal of time preparing for the meeting by reading all the material I could gather about the miracles of Lipa and the young Carmelite postulant who had first witnessed them. I planned to note any discrepancies between what she might tell me and what I had read, but what I wanted was not consistency in content but insistence in telling, in other words, how present was the voice that told. I wanted to hear her testimony, and in so hearing be assured of the unity and integrity of the story and its source. I wanted the force of her narration to compel my own belief.[7]

Instead of compelling narrative, however, I got only words. Literally, words—cut, pasted, and tapped out to the *pak-pa-pak-pak* of the typewriter; words unmoored from the "I" that supplies the performative power of testimony—"*I* saw this. *I* was there." Behind these words there was no one, not even Teresita.

I open this chapter with this vignette because it vividly illustrates the profound implications (as well as expectations) of the relationship between a sign and its source. This relationship, which we can extend to encompass not only language and testimony but also phenomena and their causes, is at the center of all consideration of miracles and apparitions. In this regard, the case of Lipa is no exception. Consider the following excerpt from the negative verdict delivered by the local bishops' investigative committee, signed April 11, 1951:

> We, the undersigned Archbishops and Bishops, constituting for the purpose a special Commission, having attentively examined and reviewed the evidence and testimonies collected in the course of repeated, long and careful investigations, have reached the unanimous conclusion and hereby officially declare that the above-mentioned evidence and testimonies *exclude any supernatural intervention in the reported extraordinary happenings* . . . of the Carmel of Lipa.[8]

Put another way, the church's ad hoc committee found no supernatural *source* to which the "reported extraordinary happenings" could be attributed. Upon issuing this decree, Rufino Santos (then the apostolic administrator of the diocese of Lipa), issued a set of orders to the nuns that included suspending all visits and letters to the convent.[9] Although meant to be temporary, these orders were enacted with the severity of an injunction to keep silent under pain of excommunication. For thirty years, the visionary and the community of nuns obeyed.[10]

When I first met Teresita in the early 2000s, it had been twenty years since the injunction to remain silent had been lifted. A few books and news features had appeared about the apparitions, and Teresita was giving more interviews. Thus, it was not obedience to this order that made Teresita reticent in our first conversation. Whatever the reason, throughout my time researching and writing about Lipa, even as I got to know Teresita better, I found myself turning time and again to this initial interview, for it attuned me to the significance of *not* talking, to the bearing of reticence and evasion, to what takes the place of the subject sought. It made me aware of the negative modes of expression that both complied with the church's authority and worked around its refusal of recognition—modes of expression that served, because they had to, as the modus operandi of belief.

Just as this experience in the field helped structure a particular practice of ethnographic listening, the reality of the archives demanded a particular practice of historical reading that excavated experience and event out of absence. As those who research the Lipa apparitions know, the church's 1951 decree was paired with orders that the nuns burn the diaries of those directly involved. Proceedings from the investigation have never surfaced, despite the most intrepid attempts to find them, even by those within the ranks of the church hierarchy.[11] Thus, the problematic relationship of signs and sources asserts itself again, but this time in the doing of history. One cannot write about Lipa the way that historians have written about Lourdes, or about any other apparition in the modern or early modern period for which the investigation was documented and those documents were extant and accessible.[12] Moreover, the condemnation of the apparitions and miracles of Lipa is utterly constitutive of the events as they are recalled in the present. From the beginning of the history of this devotion—at its origin—lies the denunciation of fraud.

The structure of this chapter reflects this refractory history as it examines the apparitions and miracles that took place inside of the Carmelite convent in Lipa in the late 1940s. It (re)constructs the events using a range of approaches that reflect the motley sources left and produced by Lipa Carmel's history of silence and censure. Together, this chapter and chapter 4 constitute a broad examination of the miracles of Lipa, from the late 1940s, when they occurred, to the early 2000s, when I carried out most of my research. This chapter focuses on the contemplatives' cloister—a germane metaphor for the history of concealment and the boundaried space within which events initially unfolded and were, for a time, confined. The primary actors within this space are religious: the visionary and her fellow sisters, the local bishops, and the Order of Discalced Carmelites. The following chapter examines what happened when the extraordinary phenomena and miracles erupted beyond the confines of the cloister walls, leading to the formation of a devotional public that would eventually lure the story of Mary's appearance at Lipa out from the shadows. Although both of these events draw from and contribute to what had become, by the mid-twentieth century, a recognizable repertoire of Marian apparitions and miracles worldwide, neither of these stories can be told without the firm footing of location—the stage upon which the extraordinary happenings took place (figure 3.1).

THE FOUNDING OF LIPA CARMEL

Ephemeral, thin as air, the locus born of a magic spell must be inscribed on solid ground. It has taken form in a setting.

—MICHEL DE CERTEAU, *The Possession at Loudun*

Nowadays, from Manila, one can get to Lipa City (henceforth simply called "Lipa") in about an hour and a half, assuming there is no traffic. Leaving the metropolis behind, the South Luzon Expressway (SLEX) slices through vast tracts of paddy, the green gently sloping in the distance, and along the highway the land is studded much less gently with self-contained rest stops boasting Starbucks and premium Caltex gasoline. All along the way there are

FIGURE 3.1 The chapel of Lipa Carmel, Batangas Province, 2004.

billboards heralding the latest and nearest development property; billboards advertising foodstuffs; billboards for this, that, and their own sake. Amid these commercial displays are the signs that bring real relief—Batangas, Lucena, Legaspi, Canlubang, Mayapa, Calamba—place indicators that ground history as much as territory, signs promising that you will arrive. Following these signs brings one off of the SLEX and onto the Southern Tagalog Arterial Road (STAR), a two-lane highway dotted only with notices sitting on the median that kindly suggest Give Way, Have a Nice Vacation, Relax and Enjoy the Trip. Here the surrounding landscape is startlingly different. The forest and coconut trees on both sides lend the highway a tunnel-like feeling as it climbs in altitude. Past the provincial border town of Santo Tomas and Tanauan (the birthplace of the famous architect of the Philippine Revolution, Apolinario Mabini, as well as the visionary of Lipa), then passing the few massive and oddly vacant industrial and technology parks, one finally comes to a fork in the road that with a right turn leads immediately to the city limits of Lipa.

Heavenly visions notwithstanding, Lipa is no stranger to apocrypha. Founded by Augustinian missionaries in 1605, Lipa was twice relocated in the eighteenth century to escape the destructive eruption of the Taal Volcano, famous for its location in the middle of Taal Lake, a freshwater lake that itself fills a large caldera. In the late nineteenth century, Lipa became one of the wealthiest cities in one of the wealthiest provinces in the Philippines when a convergence of factors led to a boom in coffee production, resulting in burgeoning wealth for many of its elite families.[13] Teodoro M. Kalaw, one of Lipa's native sons and among the most celebrated writers in the Philippines, once wrote of the town's golden era:

> These were the days of prosperity for Lipa . . . The *señoritos*, dressed in the style of the day, in shirts spangled with sequins that glittered in the sun, went about their business, mounted on spirited Arabian horses . . . [The] ladies came to use golden slippers with diamond incrustations . . . Money was splurged on clothes, interior decoration and pictures; on rare crystals and china ordered from Europe; on curtains of the finest silk, on stuffed chairs from Vienna, on exquisite table wines and foods.[14]

Wealthy nineteenth-century Lipeños were steeped in a culture of *hispanidad*, attendant to which was a reverence for the Catholic establishment that included the thirty-year tenure (1865–94) of Lipa's parish priest, a Spaniard from the province of Burgos named Fr. Benito Baras. Baras was nothing if not industrious; the years under his leadership saw a new parish church and rectory, cemetery, and bridge that connected Lipa to the nearby town of Tanauan and the road that would come to serve as the main highway to Manila.[15] No physical signs of growth could compare, however, to the symbolic luster cast when the queen regent María Cristina granted to Lipa the status of "villa" in 1887.[16]

Lipa's nineteenth-century excess was matched only by its twentieth-century destruction. For Lipa was the provincial headquarters of the Japanese Military Administration during the occupation from 1942 to 1945. Buttressed by hills and forests, with an air base built by the Americans in the 1930s, its location was strategically ideal for Japanese forces. The entire province of Batangas was at the time under the military command of Colonel Fujishige, a man who, according to one prominent historian, liked to call himself "General" and whose paranoia only grew as food and staple shortages were felt, economic pressure increased, and word spread that American forces were on the verge of returning.[17] Fujishige's response amounted to some of the greatest atrocities committed in the entire wartime period: convinced that the population of male civilians had all become guerillas, Fujishige ordered that they be round up and executed.[18] It is for this reason that Batangas suffered the most civilian casualties of any Philippine province: between October 1944 and May 1945, an estimated twenty-five thousand people were killed.[19]

"Lipa"—the name that originally referred to the nettled brush abundant in the region—became linked with these atrocities, which are now referred to in popular parlance as simply the "Lipa massacre."[20] There were, however, several episodes of mass killing committed by Japanese forces in the month of February 1945.[21] One of these episodes took place on February 27, 1945, when at least five hundred male civilians from Anilao and Antipolo were rounded up, lured by the promise of receiving passes that would permit their movement throughout Japanese-controlled areas.[22] After arriving at one of several designated locations in and around Lipa, they were marched to a minor seminary that had been established just a few years earlier by the erstwhile bishop of Lipa, Alfredo Verzosa.[23] On those premises, on an embankment facing the Pamintahan brook, the men were bayoneted, and their bodies dumped below (figure 3.2).[24] The seminary was later burned to the ground, and upon that scorched plot of land Lipa's first Carmelite monastery was founded in 1946.

Hardly a year had passed after the massacre at Pamintahan when Bishop Verzosa initiated correspondence with the prospective founder of Lipa Carmel, Mo. Theresa of Jesus (affectionately known as "Ma Mère," and then the prioress of Manila Carmel). Verzosa had long wanted the Discalced Carmelites to have a home in Lipa;[25] indeed, one of his pastoral goals during his long tenure as bishop (1916–51) was to establish seminaries and branches of religious congregations throughout his diocese.[26] But the Carmelites had other incentives to build a fourth convent in the Philippines, as Mo. Theresa had written to the vicar-general of Manila: "we have completed our number and are obliged to refuse the numerous applications of good vocations for contemplative life."[27] By the end of March 1946, Mo. Theresa surveyed the future monastery of Lipa Carmel, church authorities in Manila bestowed their blessing on both the bishop and the congregation, and several nuns received the indult for exclaustration (permission to leave the cloister) to begin building their new home.

In the letters and chronicles regarding the monastery's foundation, the nuns' descriptions eerily evoke the war—which included of course not just the mass killings but also the brutal razing of the city to the ground by American air strikes and land offenses. On May 31, 1946—the feast day of Our Lady, Mary Mediatrix of All Grace[28]—Bishop Verzosa orchestrated a religious ceremony to officially welcome the sisters to Lipa.[29] In the ruins of the Lipa Cathedral, with no roof and only crumbling remnants of the thick walls that dated back to the Spanish colonial period, matrons of the local

FIGURE 3.2 Santos Bautista stands at the edge of the ravine at the Pamintahan brook and points to the spot where hundreds of men from Lipa were bayoneted by Japanese soldiers and left for dead. Photograph taken on September 25, 1945. Courtesy of the National Archives of the Philippines, Japanese War Crimes Closed Reports.

elite sat decked out in their sparkling jewels, adjacent to the nuns draped in their thick black veils. The sisters' temporary housing, similarly destroyed, is described thus: "On the border of the house can be seen the ruins of a formerly nice residence of the Asilo de Sagrado Corazon [Refuge of the Sacred Heart] . . . The house is painted white and the roof is covered with an army canvas tent to prevent leakage . . . Each window is screened by a double piece of army mosquito net . . . One enters by the door which is made of a bullet-riddled sink."[30] The formidable and extended presence of the U.S. military, meanwhile, is utterly evident. The nuns' official relocation from Manila to Lipa in May 1946 was made in a military plane named *Bar Fly*, and American officers accompanied the nuns on the flight.[31]

Yet such details are assimilated into the nuns' copious descriptions of the work it took them to make their provisional home inhabitable until the monastery and adjacent chapel could be constructed. Signs of normalcy, such as the rigid schedule of disciplined prayer, strain to assert themselves in these letters. One of the sisters writes, "We recite the Little Hours here at about seven o'clock after Mass; Vespers and Compline at about 2:30 p.m., and Matins at eight. We hear Mass at Madre Laura's small chapel, which shakes with our movements."[32] The sister's chronicle continues in this vein: how much strength is required to pull the water from the well, what they cooked that day, how they spent their recreation time, how she switched to a smaller pillow because the big pillow made it hard to breathe. The aftermath of catastrophe haunts these chronicles, yet direct references to the war are conspicuously absent. This absence may not be so remarkable, given the women's dedication to a life isolated from the rest of the world, even if it is their own backyard. Revealed in the words of the sisters is an apprehension of their experience as it resonates first and foremost with that of their spiritual forebears, and even Teresa of Ávila herself. Sr. Mary Cecilia, who would become the congregation's—and Carmel's first Filipina—prioress upon completion of the convent, and who played a key role in the apparitions, wrote of the welcoming ceremony: "The warm and enthusiastic welcome made by both clergy and people recalled to mind similar touching scenes related with such vivid descriptions by the immortal pen of Carmel's Great Mother and Foundress, St. Teresa of Avila, in her 'Book of Foundations.'"[33]

Even at the ceremony held on August 15, 1946, to bless the cornerstone of the convent—an event attended by Lipa's luminaries and members of the Philippines' political elite, such as former first lady Aurora Quezon—little note was made of the war-torn context. Auxiliary bishop of Lipa and chaplain of Carmel, Alfredo Maria Obviar, made no occasion of the event to mourn the thousands dead or to reflect on rebirth and redemption, speaking instead in sterile terms about the future center of spiritual activity: "We are gathered here today to witness [saksihan] the blessing of the cornerstone that shall become the residence of the holy nuns of Carmel . . . One day we shall look upon the Monastery of Carmelites standing at this spot, and we will be able to proclaim that they are inundated with God's blessings [pagpapala]. How great is our hope that they will share these with us."[34] A well-known tertiary (a lay member of the Carmelite order), meanwhile, recited verses in Spanish he had penned extolling the virtues of the Blessed Mother.[35] Only the address given by U.S. Army chaplain Rev. Edwin Casey situated the monastery's founding squarely in the recent history of its surroundings:

> In this hour when your nation is rising from the ashes and ruins of war, He has inspired the good Mothers of Our Lady of Mt. Carmel to raise up a spiri-

tual arsenal of prayer and good works, by establishing a Carmelite Monastery here . . . The good Mothers of Our Lady of Mt. Carmel are optimists, like the Little Flower. They are rising out of the ashes, ruins, desolation, and pessimism that are the results of war. They are amongst the first and rightly so. St. Therese [of Lisieux] could not bear with anything like pessimism or discouragement or gloominess.[36]

How much can one make of an absence, in this case that of the dead and of those who killed them? How does the unspeakable violence of just one year before leave its traces in what is and isn't said?

BACK TO THE (HAUNTED) FUTURE

Today, a private hospital abuts the site of the massacre at Pamintahan. There is no marker, no monument, or any indication that atrocities occurred so near. Compare this to Lumbang, a barrio outside of Lipa where another massacre was committed within a week of that in Pamintahan. In Lumbang a monument in Tagalog reads:

LET IT BE KNOWN TO ALL THAT HERE LAY THE REMAINS OF MORE THAN ONE THOUSAND (1000) PEOPLE, CHILDREN AND ELDERS, FROM BARRIOS LUMBANG AND SOLOK, AMONG OTHERS, WHO WERE KILLED BY THE JAPANESE DURING THE WAR, ON MARCH 4, 1945.[37]

My research assistant, Joy, born and raised in Lipa, knew more or less where the massacre site in Pamintahan was when I made a return trip to Lipa in 2004. She knew at least that there was a hospital immediately adjacent to it when she led me there one searing afternoon. The hospital, named after a prominent local family, is a single building erected at the corner of two dead-end streets.[38] One of the streets leads back toward a main city thoroughfare. The street perpendicular to it runs along the edge of the city center, and at the time, protruding as if from the hospital itself, was a rusted wall of corrugated tin, too high to afford a view to what lay on the other side. A door cut in the wall allowed for a peek into what looked like a construction pit of precarious soil ledges and concrete foundation, but it was padlocked, preventing entry. When we asked the security guard if we could enter the walled-off area, another hospital employee in professional *barong* (man's shirt) immediately appeared at his side, wanting to know what we wanted. He, in turn, fetched the security manager, a man named William whose mirrored sunglasses appeared to be a permanent facial fixture. After demanding my identification and scowling in protest, William finally obliged, leading us along the other side of the hospital and then behind it, onto a small footpath that led through an anthurium garden to the edge of the construction site, opposite the corrugated wall.

The construction pit, it turned out, was the result of the hospital board's decision to extend the building with another wing. The project had been grounded, however, because they kept hitting tunnels that had been built by the Japanese, some of which led all the way to the San Fernando air base on the far side of the city. The board knew they might find human remains from the massacre, but the tunnels were unexpected. Even more shocking, however, was the variety of remains discovered. "Long bones," said William, looking past us toward the pit. "They found long bones in addition to the Filipino ones." Indeed, research at the archdiocese revealed that the site was also an old Spanish cemetery. William could not say exactly how these remains upon remains had influenced the current suspension of the building project, but he was certain that the place was haunted (*pinagmumultuhan*).[39] A young priest I spoke with in a parish near Lipa suggested something similar in relation to the apparitions of Mary in the late 1940s. When I casually asked why he thought some people didn't believe the visionary, he replied: "All those that were killed by the Japanese there behind Lipa Carmel [in Pamintahan], their spirits [*mga kaluluwa ng mga pinatay ng Hapon*], maybe that's what appeared to Teresing."

HOW TO READ A TESTIMONY

The few descriptions of what happened and appeared to Teresita in 1948 can be found in two main sources: an account written by Mo. Mary Cecilia (henceforth Mo. Cecilia), Lipa Carmel's prioress at the time of the apparitions, and a testimony typewritten by Teresita herself circa 1990.[40] Teresita's testimony underwent minor revisions for a version she produced in 1997 for archbishop of Lipa Gaudencio Rosales as part of a new church investigation into the miraculous events (to be discussed in chapter 4). This later version is accompanied by a signed affidavit notarized by an associate justice of the Sandiganbayan (a federal antigraft court). Both versions possess the flat cadence of a legal document, as if telling the facts demanded that Teresita speak matter-of-factly. Yet, while Teresita's testimonies describe her multiple encounters with the devil and the Virgin Mary in the late 1940s, the belated production of the documents bears witness to the order accompanying the church's 1951 decree to destroy all the diaries and materials in the congregation's possession. All the more puzzling, then, is the existence of the account by Mo. Cecilia, which bears no date and did not surface until 1983, but which both laypersons close to Lipa Carmel and the nun who first circulated it assume to be contemporaneous with the apparitions.[41] History is never sure, as Michel de Certeau reminds us, but it is perhaps even less so when the "interspace" of historiography is not that which is opened up by the relationship between present interpretation and past archives, but that for which the most reliable point of departure is forty years after the fact.[42]

So how do we read such testimonies? Of what do they provide evidence? In the pages that follow I weave together various nonchronological ways of understanding Teresita's and Mo. Cecilia's accounts.[43] Readers will recognize strains of phenomenological, sociological, literary, and theological approaches to reading these texts, none of which is satisfactory on its own. Though a more elegant argument could surely be made using a single mode of interpretation, my reading seeks an analysis faithful to the multiply nested protagonists and events in this story: the postulant inside the cloister, the cloister at the massacre site, the massacre site in a localized theater of total war, the congregation as one foundation in one missionary vector in an international order, the congregation within a diocese within a national church, and so forth. Indeed, it is not too far fetched to see Teresita's testimony as making a world in miniature of the history this book aims to tell.

ENCOUNTERS DIABOLICAL AND DIVINE

Teresita's desire to be a nun was fraught even before she entered Lipa Carmel. She was the youngest of six children, and by her account the favorite; as such, Teresita's adolescence featured all the comforts and pampering that come with belonging to the upper class (figure 3.3). Her father, Modesto Castillo, was a reputed Freemason and the governor of the province of Batangas from 1922 to 1930, and again from June 1946 to December 1947, when appointed by the president Manuel Roxas. The Castillo children all studied at the best schools in Manila. Recognizing Teresita's musical gift, her parents paved her educational path accordingly and planned to present her with a grand piano for her graduation. Poignantly, it was the arrival of this gift, to no recipient, that occupied Teresita's thoughts when she crept out of her house at 4:00 a.m. on her twenty-first birthday, July 4, 1948. Teresita met the jeep of the auxiliary bishop and chaplain of Lipa Carmel, Alfredo Obviar, at the back of the ruined municipal building in her hometown of Tanauan, sixteen kilometers away from Lipa. Arriving before dawn, she heard her birthday Mass in Carmel.[44]

FIGURE 3.3 Teresita Castillo as a teenager. From Keithley, "The Petals of Lipa," in *Batangas: Forged in Fire.*

Long aware of their youngest child's aspirations to join the contemplative order, the Castillo family sent Teresita's brothers to the convent to recover her. The description Teresita provides is shocking and sensational:

> Towards the evening, my eldest brother [Florencio] came, calling my name. He was my favorite brother. He fired a shot upwards and realizing that his shouts were of no avail, he turned his fury on the massive doors and started pounding on them with violence. Thinking that he might be pacified if I [saw] him in the parlor, Mother Prioress led me to the parlor. He was there and as I sat down, he pointed his gun at me to shoot me. He told me that he preferred to see me dead rather than be a Carmelite. The Out-Sisters [professed nuns who work outside of the convent] were terrified so they called the police station for help. The Out-Sisters called for some policemen, but God intervened and my furious brother left before the police arrived.[45]

Three weeks passed, during which, according to Mo. Cecilia's account, Teresita persevered in her "firm determination to put forth great effort in becoming the perfect Carmelite."[46] Her brothers and sisters persisted in their harassment in the meantime, begging her to return to her family. As such, when it arrived, Teresita's first supernatural encounter was a continuation of this dramatic assault, only in a different form:

JULY 31, 1948

My first encounter occurred during the Great Silence which means that nobody may talk with anybody except for emergency reasons. I was in our cell praying hard for my family when I heard three knocks. I did not see anyone come in. After a while, I heard a man's voice, very rough and guttural in nature[,] as though coming from a deep, hollow container. He gave me a vivid picture of how my family was. He said that my father, who was at that time the presiding judge of the Court of Industrial Relations, could not study his legal cases. I was told (and this was confirmed by others) that after each meal he would leave two spoonfuls of rice for me. He used to stand by the window waiting for my return. This was indeed a very touching attitude of my poor father. I suddenly felt homesick, so much so that I was on the verge of crying. Then I heard the voice again telling me that he will leave signs of his presence in our cell. With shaking knees and trembling hands, I somehow managed to grope for our little lamp, and sure enough there were two black footprints and their shape was so different from that of a human being.[47]

The first diabolical transgression was the breaking of the rule of silence. The supernatural entity makes no appearance but speaks as if from a bottomless well. As we shall see, this perceptual distinction marks the difference between the nameless entity and the "devil"; for intentional or not, Teresita uses the term "devil" only once the specter visually manifests himself to her. Yet this first encounter is not without visual suggestion, namely, the "vivid picture" the voice describes of Teresita's morose father. The term "picture" does not describe the literal materialization of an image before her eyes but rather the coherence that is precipitated by storytelling.[48] Before he is the "devil," this supernatural entity is simply a narrator. And while the sudden eruption of his voice terrifies Teresita, the torment stems from this uncanny coherence, without identity or fixed location, which tells of something taking place somewhere else.[49] It is this displacement that makes Teresita suddenly long for her family, an icon of origin, and feel "homesick." The footprints left behind, "black" and "so different from that of a human being," serve as an odd signature, attesting to a presence but providing no name.

The torment continues the following evening:

AUGUST 1, 1948

The same voice came back to me at around 3:00 a.m. He kept repeating the same thing to me.[50]

Even in this second encounter, there is no subjectivity attached to the voice, no connection to the experience of the subjects it reveals.[51] Indeed, in this same entry, Teresita momentarily wonders whether the disembodied voice is "a trick of my family to get me out."[52] Now, "really afraid," she is none-theless distracted by wondering whether her brother might have sought the help of the mayor, whom he knew well, to bring her home.[53] The alternate possibility—that of *no* connection between the voice and her brother in par-ticular or the conflict with her family in general—renders all experience immaterial. Forced to consider this other possibility, Teresita can only ask aloud, "Why pick on me?"[54] The situation seems determined by nothing other than chance—an impression forcefully dramatized in the next brief entry that appears in her testimony:

FIRST FRIDAY OF AUGUST

Devotional cards were drawn by the Community in honor of the Sacred Heart. I got "Victim." I told myself, "What's next, *Mr. Whoever-you-are?*[55]

On the following day, August 7, 1948, an altogether-different voice greets Teresita. Something entirely new, however, precedes this encounter:

It was a Saturday when I smelt a very sweet fragrance like that of white lilies while I was on my way to our cell. I thought perhaps a close relative of mine (an old belief) died, or something like that.[56]

Chance has no place in the otherworldly locus circumscribed by a permeat-ing scent. As Michel de Certeau notes, "Odor constitutes the territory of time out of time,"[57] in this case an "old belief" about death—or "something like that." What exactly odor signifies might be mistaken, but the haunting pres-ence of odor is clear. In this entry a new convention is ordained: the scent of flowers no longer signals death; instead, it heralds the presence of Mary.[58] The testimony continues:

When I reached our cell, I immediately heard a very sweet voice, a voice beyond description which said: "My daughter, sufferings will always be with you until the end of your life." I did not see anyone, and the words came as a shock to me. I was stunned, speechless, and motionless, but not so afraid. I asked myself whose voice was that. It was very different from the previous one.[59]

Still shocking for its coming without visual referent, this voice is not nearly as frightening. This voice silences Teresita not with terror but because there seem to exist no words to describe it. It does not need to be feared because it does not betray the gap between narrative and experience. On the contrary, this voice only speaks of, and addresses itself to, Teresita's recent torment, thus closing the gap by providing a caption to her experience. Still uncanny, this voice nevertheless reestablishes identity. Teresita can now be a victim who suffers rather than a victim of unbearable chance. This authorization of

suffering gives Teresita the strength she needs to stand up to the devil when
he finally makes his appearance:

AUGUST 11, 1948

At about 3:00 a.m., I was awakened by the shaking of my bed which lasted one
minute. Then I heard the hoarse voice. He told me that I had an obligation to my
parents, to take pity on them. If they died of loneliness, I would have to answer
for that . . . Suddenly he appeared before my eyes. I was terrified with unbearable fear. He was terribly ugly. He was short, about five feet tall. He was surrounded by fire. His glaring eyes were bloodshot which could not look straight
at me but looked to the left side of our cell. His foul odor convinced me that
he was something totally evil. Without warning, he hit me. By Divine Provi-
dence, I managed to get hold of the holy water. *The devil* disappeared after being
sprinkled by me with the holy water as I had been told to do by Mother Prioress.

 I ran to Mother Prioress. When she saw the marks on my wrist, she embraced
me for the first time. I was crying. She put my head on her shoulder and patted
my back. Mother Cecilia comforted me, and I saw tears in her eyes. That was
the time I really missed my parents. I was almost ready to give up my vocation,
when suddenly I realized that if I did so, the devil would be the winner and I,
the loser. I was scared but my fear did not last long. *With God's grace, I was determined to win the battle.*[60]

What before manifested itself as phantasmic—the disembodied voice and
the black footprint—now coalesces with all other modalities of presence:
Teresita *hears* the voice, she *sees* the devil, she *smells* his "foul odor," she *feels*
his striking her. What was before a terrifying specter—terrifying because
spectral—is now an outright monster. And thus madness loosens its grip on
Teresita. She becomes responsive in ways she could not when she endured
the first torments. She cries, notices the reaction of the mother prioress, really
misses her parents; in other words, she is connected again with the world and
the people in it. And contrary to what we might think, this encounter with the
devil works not against, but in conjunction with, the previous "sweet voice"
that Teresita would later realize is the Blessed Mother. The two instances
combine to restore order, to reconnect signs to sources. Teresita is now the
authorized locus of suffering, and the afflicting voice belongs to none other
than the devil. Further, she now understands that she is embarking upon a
battle to be fought, with a clearly delineated enemy, a spiritual war.

RESTORING RELATIONS

We need not interpret these apparitions as the restless souls of those massacred by the Japanese or the melancholy delusions of familial separation in

order to read Teresita's encounters with the divine and diabolical as none-theless resonating with these historical events and real affectivities. Above all else, this beginning to Teresita's story evokes the theme of senseless suffer-ing. Her experiences are an imperfect stand-in for the experiences of those who suffered and died during the war, which is to not say, however, that her experiences are reducible to mere epiphenomena. As much as the war-torn context of Lipa may have informed the events that took place within the Carmelite cloister, it is important not to lose sight of the equally significant dynamics and pressures at work both within and traversing the convent's walls. A fledgling congregation, the nuns had to prove their mettle at the express invitation of Bishop Verzosa by building their community in dire material circumstances and physical conditions. The seven Carmelites whom the bishop authorized to establish the foundation in 1946 came from Manila Carmel, a far more comfortable residence in a prosperous neighborhood of the big city. The move, which they couched in terms of "deep sacrifice," was an arduous undertaking.[61] By the time of the apparitions the congregation had almost doubled in number, but its beloved matriarch and spiritual an-chor, Mo. Theresa of Jesus, the French founder of Carmel in the Philippines affectionately known as "Ma Mère," had returned to Manila. At the same time, interpersonal tensions arising from rivalries, jealousies, personal and collective doubts about Teresita's experiences, and simple differences of tem-perament surfaced in these quarters of intense and intimate living, as they undoubtedly have in cloistered communities for as long as there have been monastic orders.

Toward the end of August 1948 other members of the community of Lipa Carmel begin to populate Teresita's story. There is the powerful presence of Mo. Cecilia, the prioress of Lipa, who became Teresita's closest confidante throughout the time of the suffering and the apparitions. Enter also Alfredo Obviar, the male heroic figure of the story and then auxiliary bishop of Lipa and the chaplain of Carmel. When the devil drags Teresita down the stairs, it is Mo. Cecilia who struggles against him to pull Teresita up, dispelling Tere-sita's sense that she was naked during the fight.[62] And it is Bishop Obviar who kindly explains to Teresita that such is the power of devilry: "He can make you feel you had nothing on but in truth you were wearing your pos-tulant dress." [63] Little by little, the distress of chance that marks the opening pages of Teresita's testimony is abated by the involvement and implication of others. And the all-too-earthly ordeals of credibility, envy, and spite arrive in its place. "Trouble started in the Community from this day on," writes Teresita.[64]

"Suffering" soon becomes an experience with multiple sources, dimensions, and subjects. When "hurting words were said," and when "jealousy and envy cropped up, followed by malicious accusations of familiarity and favoritism," Teresita accounts for it as the "sufferings both Mother Prioress and I had to go through."[65] One of these sufferings takes the form of Teresita feeling that her whole body is pricked by pins and needles; she experiences this pain for days. Teresita offers this pain as penance on behalf of priests and nuns, some of whom, Mary tells her, are in danger of losing their vocations. If the devil gives form to the nameless forces that seem beyond Teresita's control, forces that make her a victim of chance, the pinpricks she suffers can be understood as a somatization of the hostilities and ambivalences expressed by her brothers and sisters in the faith. In a broader sense, this particular affliction attends Teresita's realization that priests and nuns, "representatives of Christ on earth," are only human.[66] As arresting as this physical pain appears in her testimony, the ordinary circumstances surrounding it are simply those of getting used to convent life, which in point of fact include practices of self-mortification, such as the use of a cilice.[67]

Only Teresita and the prioress, Mo. Cecilia, know about the painful pinpricks, as well as the periods of blindness that Teresita suffers in the days leading up to and immediately following the apparitions. Through this shared knowledge, a close relationship between Teresita and her prioress develops. At this point Mo. Cecilia receives interior locutions from the Blessed Virgin Mary, warning her of her postulant's impending afflictions and instructing her on how to act and support Teresita through them.[68]

Teresita's three periods of blindness end as abruptly and arbitrarily as they begin. The first episode comes in the wake of the demons that Teresita felt ripping off her dress. Tellingly, Teresita's first reaction is "agony to think that perhaps my blindness would be the cause of rejection" by her new community.[69] The second time she awakes unable to see, but upon leaving her cell to attend Mass, her sight is restored. On the third occasion Teresita's blindness serves specifically as a sign. Before celebrating a Mass, Monsignor Obviar tells Teresita to ask Mary to provide a sign of her presence. Mary appears to Teresita and motions her to approach saying, "This, my child, is the answer to your Chaplain's request."[70] The last thing Teresita claims to have seen is Mary's right hand moving toward her eyes. This time, she is not just struck blind; her left arm is also paralyzed, as confirmed by the convent's infirmarian, who pricks Teresita's arm with a needle. Teresita claims to feel nothing and physically does not respond. Here blindness signifies for the community, as Teresita becomes the field upon which this mark of blindness is writ. Her suffering is the instrument through which her capacity to mediate between Mary and the community is realized. This capacity is first engendered when the Virgin Mary appears to Teresita over a series of fifteen days starting on September 12, 1948.

THE APPARITIONS

In Teresita's testimony, the appearance of a separate chapter heading, "The Apparitions for Fifteen Consecutive Days," is revealing, for September 12 is not the date of Teresita's first encounter with Mary. As we previously saw, Mary spoke to Teresita a week earlier. A few days after that first encounter Teresita followed the fragrance of white lilies to her cell, where the Blessed Virgin Mother was sitting on her bed; they interacted on no fewer than five occasions after that. So when we are told that the apparitions commence only in mid-September, we are seeing an attempt to frame Lipa in relation to the most famous of modern apparitions of Mary, namely at Lourdes and Fátima, where the important phase of the story is Mary's serial appearance over consecutive days or months.[71] As if to anticipate its future citation or inclusion in the annals of Marian apparitions worldwide, this section of Teresita's testimony exhibits narrative containment and a quality of being ready to excerpt that we do not see elsewhere. That is to say, the very structure of this section acts as a kind of self-legitimation, bringing its contents into stark relief to fit a pattern of past apparitions.

If this seems a bit too contrived on the visionary's part, one could argue that the section's shift in tone makes sense for indicating a separate phase of activity, one that places Teresita squarely in the role of messenger and liaison between the Virgin Mary and the cloistered community. Nevertheless, there are more than a few striking similarities between the apparitions in Lipa and those the church deemed "worthy of belief" elsewhere. For example, the entry of Mary's first appearance on September 12 reads:

> At around 5:00 in the afternoon, I was walking in the garden (not much of a garden because it was a new foundation) and started to pray the rosary. When I reached the third mystery, I noticed that a vine I was passing by shook to the extent that I could not help but look at it. Since there was no wind, I thought perhaps a big lizard or snake was passing through the vine because of the way the vine was shaking. Suddenly I heard a woman's voice that said: "Fear not my child." Recognizing the voice, I immediately knelt down, turning my head from left to right, expecting to see someone. Then the voice continued: "Kiss the ground and whatever I shall tell you to do, you must do. Eat some grass, my

child." (Perhaps this command was to test my obedience and simplicity.) "I want you to come to visit me here in this spot for fifteen consecutive days."[72]

Anyone familiar with the story of the apparitions of the Virgin Mary in the Pyrenean town of Lourdes in 1858 may be struck with déjà vu while reading this. The references to wind and praying the rosary are two features of the first apparition at Lourdes. The instruction to kiss the ground and eat grass was given to the young visionary Bernadette Soubirous at Mary's ninth appearance to her. Mary also told Bernadette to return to the grotto for fifteen consecutive days. Likewise, Mary's physical appearance to Teresita may not be an exact replica of Mary at Lourdes, but it is strikingly similar:

> I saw a very beautiful lady with her hands clasped and a golden rosary hanging in her right hand. Her dress was pure white, so very simple and held at the waist with a narrow belt. Her feet were bare, resting on a cloud which was two feet above the ground. Her face of indescribable beauty was radiant. Her sweet smile did not have a trace of sadness.[73]

Theologically speaking, the most important element both apparitions share is Mary's revelation of her name. Toward the end of her appearances at Lourdes Mary declares "Que soy era Immaculada Councepciou" ("I am the Immaculate Conception"). On the last of her apparitions at Lipa she states with equal command "I AM MARY, MEDIATRIX OF ALL GRACE."[74] At Lourdes, this pronouncement to the young, unsophisticated girl of fourteen was, in the words of historian Ruth Harris, "the culmination of a theological tradition that stretched back to the Middle Ages ... [and] the latest in a series of miraculous events within living memory that had pointed the way to the promulgation of the dogma of the Immaculate Conception in 1854."[75] Similarly, as we will see in greater detail in chapters 4 and 6, Mary's self-identification at Lipa would come to serve as divine evidence of another of her theological capacities, one yet to be formally defined as dogma but enjoying increasing support in many Catholic quarters in the past few decades.

Some aspects of Mary's appearances at Lipa conform to patterns that we have seen in apparition events reaching all the way back to the late medieval and early modern period, including those we examined in chapter 1, such as the request to make the site of her appearance sacred by performing a blessing at that spot.[76] In a related message, Mary expresses the desire for "a statue of myself to be made so my little ones can see me. Describe me to your Chaplain," she continues, "I wish my statue to look as you see me and [be] as big as that of Our Lady of Lourdes which stands inside the cloister" (figure 3.4).[77]

FIGURE 3.4 The nuns of Lipa Carmel with the original statue of Mary, Mediatrix of All Grace. Standing to the left and right of the statue are Mo. Mary Cecilia and Teresita Castillo. Reproduced with the kind permission of Lipa Carmel.

Other features of the Lipa apparitions, namely the messages, betray specific concerns of the community, such as the novice's credibility. Unbelievers among the congregation are singled out; the envious are made to feel petty. At one point Mary beseeches the nuns to fight for the soul of one unbelieving sister with prayer, so that her "hatred turn to love and trust."[78] At the same time a few messages reveal culturally specific hallmarks of Filipino Catholicism, such as the fixation on Mary's dolorous witnessing of Christ's crucifixion:

> Great was my suffering when our eyes met on His way to Calvary. Our hands were just an inch away from each other. I wanted to reach Him, to make Him feel that I was around and that I will be with Him and stand by Him up to His last breath. But God did not will it so. His arm was too weak to extend another inch to reach mine. Then meditate on this, and see how much the Mother and Son worked and suffered together to save the world.[79]

In these formally framed apparitions of Mary—part pastiche, part lens into local worlds—one of the most notable aspects is the language in which

Mary speaks: English. At the time of the apparitions, English was still a relatively foreign language. Despite the intense efforts under U.S. colonialism to spread the use of English throughout the public school system, Spanish was still very much in use among the upper-class and church hierarchy (all correspondence to Bishop Verzosa, for example, had to be in Spanish, since that was the only language he knew apart from Ilocano, his native tongue, and Latin), and local vernaculars even more so among the population at large.[80] What might an English-speaking Mary have signified? Should we take English to be coterminous with American and see Mary Mediatrix as a deferred arrival of the so-called liberator? Or is English here merely the historically determined incarnation of the foreign? In other words, was it the foreignness of English or its association with the recent history of American presence in the Philippines that mattered?

There is a single oblique reference to the broader context of the apparitions that speaks to this matter of English. According to Teresita's testimony, Mary's message on November 12, 1948, is as follows:

> Pray, my child. The people do not heed my words. Tell my daughters that there will be persecutions, unrest, and bloodshed in your country. The enemy of the Church will try to destroy the faith which Jesus established and died for. The Church will suffer much. Pray for the conversion of sinners throughout the world. Pray for those who rejected me, and those who do not believe my messages in different parts of the world. I am really sad, but consoled by those who believe and trust me. Spread the meaning of the rosary because this will be the instrument for peace throughout the world . . . But be not afraid for the love of my Son will soften the hardest of hearts and my motherly love will be their strength to crush the enemies of God. What I ask here is the same as in Fatima.[81]

As observant Catholics and observers of Catholicism worldwide know well, the apparitions at Fátima amounted to the most powerful symbols of popular, anticommunist Catholicism in the twentieth century: Mary as she appeared to three sheepherding children in rural Portugal, in 1917, and the rosary as the most effective tool to defeat communism. Devotions to both defined Catholicism in the global Cold War period, and they are significant in this message for arriving on the eve of one of the Philippines' most brutal civil wars, the Hukbalahap rebellion.[82]

Although this later became a major point of focus in the press once news of the apparitions had spread, it is the only such direct reference to the Cold War milieu in both versions of Teresita's testimony. Perhaps, then, when it comes to language, it is enough to say that it demanded remark, as when

Teresita explicitly states, "She spoke to me in English."[83] Here, the medium of the message of the Mediatrix is highlighted, and perhaps it is this noting of the medium that makes it meaningful. In its foreignness as much as in its historical relevance, English simply serves to bring the fact of mediation into relief.

There are more messages in addition to the ones I've mentioned in this section, many of which Mary spoke outside of her fifteen consecutive appearances, over nearly two dozen communications. Overwhelmingly, these messages centered on the religious. Even the message referencing Fátima concluded with Mary asking all the sisters to "do a lot of penance for priests and nuns."[84] Over and again Mary asks Teresita for prayer and penance on behalf of fallen members of the church. Under the entry for August 19, 1948, Teresita writes, "The Blessed Mother requested of me a kind of suffering I had to undergo for a priest."[85] The account of the next visit on September 1 reads, "She told me that our Mother Church would lose many vocations and that was why she was appealing for prayers, penance[,] and sacrifices."[86] And again a few days later, "She told me that this day's pains [the pinpricks] should be offered for several priests who were in danger of losing their vocation."[87] Then a week or so later Mary said, "Please pray for priests and nuns and help me by doing some penance for them. Pray for them as you have not prayed before. The Sacred Heart of my Son bleeds anew for every fallen priest or nun. To some, pride was the obstacle to go back to the true fold, and shame hardened their hearts."[88] What are we to make of these messages and their emphasis on the religious? At least two interpretations come into view when we consider the crisis facing the Philippine church in the postwar period on the one hand, and the genealogy of Teresian Carmelites on the other.

AT STAKE: THE INVESTIGATION OF THE APPARITIONS AND MIRACLES OF LIPA; OR, THE CATHOLIC CHURCH IN THE POSTWAR ERA

Ultimately, we can only speculate as to the reasons for the church's hasty decision on the apparitions at Lipa Carmel, since no official records of the investigation exist. As noted earlier, proceedings of the investigation disappeared in the 1960s and have never surfaced. Furthermore, the primary persons aside from Teresita implicated in the phenomenal happenings—namely, Mo. Cecilia (the mother prioress of Lipa Carmel at that time), Bishop Obviar (auxiliary bishop of Lipa and chaplain of Lipa Carmel), and Bishop

Verzosa (bishop of Lipa)—all passed away before the ban of silence was lifted from the community in the late 1980s. So, too, had the Italian papal nuncio and six Filipino bishops who signed their names on the 1951 decree. Nothing from that period exists in the archives of the University of Santo Tomas, where the interrogation of Teresita and Mo. Cecilia took place, or in the Archdiocesan Archives of Manila. And June Keithley, the Filipina broadcast journalist whose relentless zeal for the case brought her all the way to the Carmelite Generalate in Rome, found little of consequence in their files. Thus, our tools of speculation are limited to Teresita's belated testimony, bequeathed lore and popular memory, and textual sources referencing the broader political context of the local and global church. Let us work backward and begin with the last of these, situating what we know to be an investigation executed at the local level in the culture of Marianism that prevailed at the highest levels of the hierarchy at that time.[89]

In certain respects, considering the devotional life of the man who ruled the Holy See at the time, there is every reason to believe that a Marian intervention in the wake of total war would have been welcomed. Pope Pius XII (r. 1939–58) was deeply Marian, particularly favoring the devotion to Our Lady of Fátima, the Virgin who appeared in Portugal in 1917. On November 1, 1950, while the investigation of Lipa was well under way, Pius XII stood in front of an audience of millions outside St. Peter's Basilica in Rome and proclaimed the dogma of the Assumption of Mary. This proclamation— the first to have exercised papal infallibility as declared in 1870, during Pius IX's reign—holds that when Mary was taken up to heaven, her body and her soul were intact.[90] Such corporeal integrity is rooted in the belief in the Immaculate Conception, that Mary herself was born without original sin and thus her body was incorruptible in death, the dogma of which was declared in 1854. The proclamation of the dogma of the Assumption in 1950 had two mutually reinforcing consequences: the revivification of Marian spirituality and mass devotion to her cult, and the glorification of the pope via this spectacular and inaugural exercise of performative power. This may illuminate the case of Lipa, for it betokens the place of Mary vis-à-vis institutional authority. Cast in the familiar role of handmaid to the church, Mary served the pontificate's aspirations to power.

Furthermore, in southwestern Europe, the years between 1947 and 1954 saw an extraordinary efflorescence of religious apparitions, thanks in part to the spread of the story and devotion to Our Lady of Fátima.[91] Ironically, however, and despite the Marian devotion of Pius XII, this efflorescence produced unfavorable responses among other members of the church hierarchy. Nervous about the perceptions about Catholics that the burgeoning of reported visions would produce on the world stage, many clergy reacted with skepticism and, in some cases, censure. Among those expressing extreme skepticism was Alfredo Ottaviani, adviser to the Santo Oficio (the office of the church's governing body that oversaw and safeguarded all matters of Catholic doctrine), whose article "A Warning against False Miracles" was widely circulated among Catholic dioceses. Warning against a "religiosity that is blind and out of control," Ottaviani's decree urged the faithful to take a more discerning stance toward the supernatural.[92] This is all to say that even if the investigations into the Lipa phenomena never progressed beyond the local hierarchy, at the church's global center there was deep ambivalence over apparitions of Mary. Ottaviani's warning certainly reached the Philippines, albeit to limited reception in Spanish-language church publications like *Boletín eclesiástico de Filipinas*.

In the postwar period, where the Philippine church was concerned, the most important decisions regarding its leadership came, too, from Rome. While there was growing consensus that the highest seat of the church (archbishop of Manila) in the new nation should be occupied by a Filipino, it is debatable whether this should be read as a sign of recognition of sovereignty or a concession to quell the long-standing clamor to Filipinize the church that was revived under the "Asia for Asians" ideology propagated throughout the period of the Japanese occupation.[93] In either case, the delineation of what sovereignty, or "independence," would mean was made quite explicit, as evidenced in this communiqué delivered by the Filipino auxiliary bishop Rufino J. Santos:[94] "An independent Philippines shall be bestowed the exceptional favor of having a Filipino Archbishop of Manila. But an independent Philippines is not, because it never was nor shall ever be, independent in their devotion to Christ, nor of said devotion's visible leader, the Pope in Rome."[95] Santos was speaking specifically here of the appointment of Gabriel Reyes, former archbishop of the diocese of Cebu (one of two archbishoprics in the Philippines at that time), to the post of coadjutor archbishop of Manila. This transfer gave Reyes immediate rights of succession to the Manila throne, occupied for thirty-three years by an Irishman named Michael O'Doherty.[96] O'Doherty passed away in October 1949, marking the end of foreign leadership of the Philippine church—at least in official terms, since all of these accessions were administered, and to a certain extent determined, by one Monsignor Egidio Vagnozzi, the apostolic delegate from Rome.

Vagnozzi was an archconservative with papal aspirations and high professional ambitions.[97] Several diplomatic posts (Washington, Lisbon, Paris, Manila) did nothing to temper his traditionalist orientation, and he garnered a reputation, especially among the American Catholic hierarchy, as a reactionary meddler. (He was predictably critical of the drafts on liturgical reform championed by the Second Vatican Council, decried as heretical Pope Paul VI's unprecedented efforts toward interdenominational dialogue, in 1965, and attempted to quash any sites of interest in the unorthodox ideas of the Jesuit thinker Pierre Teilhard de Chardin, to cite just a few of the infamous interventions that defined his career.) Vagnozzi's tenure as apostolic delegate to the Philippines began in March 1949. When the Vatican established diplomatic relations with the new republic, Vagnozzi's post was elevated to that of apostolic (or papal) nuncio. The announcement of diplomatic relations and the first public message delivered by Vagnozzi in his new promoted capacity appeared in the April 1951 issues of both the Philippines' popular Catholic weekly *The Sentinel* and the internal publication of the church, *Boletín eclesiástico*. In these, Vagnozzi's formal statement is immediately followed by the verdict titled "Official Statement on Reported Extraordinary Happenings at Carmel of Lipa."[98]

We may never know what the truth of this timing was, what decisions were made in the politically volatile playing field that was the postindependence (though never independent of Rome, as the future Cardinal Santos had reminded) hierarchy of the Philippine Catholic Church: exactly what submissions, coercions, and sacrifices were measured and made by the six Filipino bishops who appended their signature to the statement, perhaps, in the name of Filipinization. Yet if we take a closer look at the six bishops who signed the 1951 verdict on Lipa, we see that five of them were promoted in the years immediately following independence, around the time that the miracles and apparitions were taking place:

1 Gabriel Reyes, as we already mentioned, was appointed coadjutor archbishop of Manila in August 1949, giving him rights of succession after O'Doherty, who died in October of that year.[99]

2 Cesar Maria Guerrero, who actively cooperated with the Japanese Military Administration, was tried for treason against the United States and then pardoned by President Roxas in 1948.[100] He was awarded a brand new diocese (San Fernando) in May 1949.[101]

3 Mariano Madriaga, bishop of Lingayen, is the only one of the signatories who had held his post since before the occupation, in 1938.

4 Rufino Santos was appointed auxiliary bishop of Manila in 1947, and

he served as apostolic administrator of Lipa (since Bishop Verzosa was so heavily implicated in the case). When Gabriel Reyes met his untimely death in 1953, Santos took his place as archbishop of Manila, and later, in 1960, he was named the first cardinal of the Philippines.[102]

5 Juan Sison went from being an ordained priest to auxiliary bishop of Nueva Segovia in 1947.[103]

6 Vicente Reyes went from being a priest to being named auxiliary bishop of Manila in June 1950.[104]

Perhaps the case of Lipa was simply an occasion for these promoted bishops to apply their new authority. Perhaps the apparitions, in a cloister in the provinces, were simply too much of a nuisance to a church whose leadership was desperate to reign in its ranks. Perhaps, as was suggested to me by one of Lipa's parish priests and champion of the devotion to Mary Mediatrix, *takot sila* (they were afraid) that a positive verdict on the apparitions and miracles would provoke a global phenomenon in their backyard, the limelight and pressure of which they could not bear.

Among the devotional community of Lipa Carmel, there is no lack of speculation or hypothesis regarding the original church investigation. But there is little doubt that one nasty nuncio named "Bagnosi" played a central role.[105] My many interlocutors' thoughts about Vagnozzi can be summed up thus: *mababa ang tingin sa mga Pilipino*. He looked down on Filipinos. Vagnozzi could not believe that the Blessed Mother would choose to appear to a Filipina. Vagnozzi was incredulous at the thought that Mary might choose to appear in the Philippines at all. "That was the mentality then," explained one of the nuns, laughing uneasily. "I could expect that from him, because, you know, the Americans at that time." Vagnozzi, it is believed, pressured the Filipino bishops to sign the verdict under pain of excommunication: "They [the bishops] were afraid . . . [R]emember that's when the Philippine hierarchy was just beginning," one sister explained. "Vagnozzi was the culprit," said one elderly gentleman, leaving it at that. While I would not necessarily interpret these comments as clear expressions of nationalist sentiment, it is clear that Vagnozzi was identified as a kind of other, but with a foreignness that had many names and organized itself around various tokens of identity. The nun who sheepishly referred to the "mentality" that had prevailed at that time thought that Vagnozzi was an American. Others made explicit their knowledge of his title, nuncio, as one that arrived from and was tied to someplace other than the congregation of bishops (*mga Obispo*) who so many believe were forced to sign. By and large, the reiterations of Vagnozzi's racism presupposed his *not* being a Filipino. In the face of so much unknowing that only speculation can fill, "Bagnosi" represents a point of origin, fixed yet variably fashioned, back to which one can trace the continual sign of disapproval that so defines the history of the miracles of Lipa. I realized this upon the rare occasion that a more sober explanation for the negative outcome of the investigation was offered, such as the suggestion by another Carmelite that the information provided by those interviewed simply could not be corroborated. When it comes to determining the exact motives of the church commission, we have on the one hand conjecture necessitated by silence and deduced from context, and on the other hand popular consensus largely fixed upon a single character.

Teresita's own contribution to this speculative mix, meanwhile, scarcely elucidates. The section of Teresita's testimony that describes the church's investigation is quite brief compared to the rest of the text, and understandably so, given the emotional scarring it caused. In it she describes the terrifying occasions when she was brought to the hospital of the University of Santo Tomas in Manila, where she was intensely interviewed by one psychiatrist whose name she cannot recall and a psychologist of the Dominican order, Rev. Fr. Blas. The relentless questioning in the role of "devil's advocate" (Fr. Blas himself had announced upon meeting Teresita that it would be his charge to play this role), and the intimidation and anger she felt coming from the two men were imaginably torturous for her. At one point, she claims that Fr. Blas ordered her to sign a statement effectively admitting that the apparitions were the result of her imagination.[106] Teresita refused, and the priest left his office in a huff.

When he summoned her back the following day, Teresita stood firm in her refusal. It is here that Teresita recalls the appalling incident, infamous and oft repeated among the community of Lipa Carmel: "Fr. Blas was so angry that he took hold of a crystal ashtray on the table and hurled it at me. With God's grace I was able to bend so the ashtray hit the wall. He took the document of his, crumpled it[,] and threw it into the garbage can and then he hurriedly left the room."[107]

When the investigation was over and the verdict released, Teresita voluntarily left Carmel. She did this upon the recommendation of Ma Mère, who said that she would be asked to leave in any case, but resignation would at least preserve the chance to return. (She never did.) Soon after arriving at her parents' home in Tanauan, Teresita paid a visit to "the nuncio" to tell him that she had left the convent. "Little did I know," she writes in her vivid depiction of the scene, that His Excellency Msgr. Vagnozzi was so angry with me . . . As soon as he saw me, he shouted at me and drove me out saying, "Get out of my house you little devil!" I immediately stood up and knelt for his blessing before I leave [*sic*], but he refused. He headed for the big door and shouted again, "Get out! Get out!" He stood by the door, waiting for me to get out. My knees started to shake and [I] felt so weak, that when I was about to pass before him, I stopped and looked at him with fear. He got what I wanted to tell him, because he gave me a little more space where I could pass not within his reach. Out I went and then I heard a loud slamming of the big door . . . On my way home to Quezon City, I started to think of the possible reason why the Nuncio was so mad at me. Was it wrong if Mama Mary appeared to me? Was it my fault? I did not invent the story. I did not even wished [*sic*] it, nor did I dream to see Mama Mary. Nothing of this sort entered my mind when I joined the Carmelite Order.[108]

"Little did I know," Teresita writes, that the investigation would put her in the center of a maelstrom equal to that of the convergence of forces, sublimely good and evil, that previously had left her at a loss for explanation, that had made her a victim of chance. Again in her testimony, up until the very end, we hear reflections motivated by one question: why me? And while we can sense Teresita's resignation to fate, her submission to being the locus of suffering, the sources of her affliction keep shifting. The faces that first terrorized her metamorphose into other faces. Recalling the interrogation by the psychologist, she writes, "I was afraid of him, even more afraid than the day I saw the devil's face for the first time."[109] And again upon concluding the painful episode with the nuncio, Teresita admits, "Heaven only knows how afraid I became to see a priest."[110]

This is not to say that the priests had become demons in Teresita's eyes. What I think emerges both in Teresita's chronicle and the story of Lipa as it has developed over the past few decades are forces unleashed by events that in the immediate wake of their coming to pass were yet unspoken, yet unspeakable. Such were the atrocities of war. These forces first course through channels already worn down by old mythologies and previous orders—the hierarchical structure that subordinates a community of nuns to a congregation of bishops, say—but discrete identities cannot contain the flood, and in the end these identities themselves prove instable.[111] This is, of course, one definition of possession. And where Lipa was concerned, there could have been the performance of exorcism. But then there would have to be speaking. Instead there was denial, and with that, silencing. Secrets are buried so that power can prevail. Yet while secrets might lie at the very core of power, it is not only the powerful who keep them.[112]

HARBORING BELIEF

The idea of harboring belief came to me as I sat on the other side of a window grille in the convent of Lipa Carmel. Although I was no longer taken with the habits of enclosure, or rather, with what I fantasized to be the habits of enclosure, it was impossible to ignore the architecture of separation that dictated the parameters of contact. The visiting room was always dark and drab, since no sunlight from the public side of the convent could enter, and only when the heavy wood shutters embedded in the wall were opened from the inside was any natural light let in. This itself was dim compared to the daylight that fell unimpeded on the inside of the cloister, light that a visitor could perceive through the doorways that opened to the sisters' own side of the visiting lounge, sunshine so evocative you could practically smell it.

On this day I was chatting with Sr. Bernadette, then in her seventies.[113] Although she was not a member of Lipa Carmel at the time of the apparitions, she joined the community just two years after the church's decree. The "Dark Night," as the nuns called it, had already fallen. Sr. Bernadette elaborated: "In 1953 we were not even allowed to talk about it; we were told that it would be a mortal sin! Everyone was so afraid."[114]

Indeed in the early days after the church's declaration, the ban of silence on both the religious and the laity was enforced with this threat. Sr. Bernadette confirmed the church commission's order to destroy all materials directly pertaining to the events. Nothing was to be spared, not even the image of Our Lady, Mary Mediatrix, that had been sculpted according to Teresita's description.[115] The nuns felt that they had no choice but to obey the order, but destroying the statue—the most iconic emblem of proof that Mary had appeared—was something they could not bring themselves to do: "so she was hidden in the bodega." Sr. Bernadette leaned into the window grille: "She came so close to being ruined! She was almost chopped up! So what someone did? They painted her blue. And then someone put a heart, to make her, you know, so she was like the image of the Immaculate Heart. At first she was kept in a box, and then taken out of the box but still veiled. But I saw her! I mean, I knew it was her!"[116]

Throughout the years of the Dark Night, the image, still disguised as the Immaculate Heart, inched its way out of the cloister's common areas, from the bodega to the private altar, and from the altar to the recreation room. By the late 1970s the nuns all agreed that the image was in dire need of retouching. Sr. Bernadette lamented, "She was so dirty! So the first thing we did was to paint. We painted her white." After that, it was only a matter of time before the heart disappeared, and Our Lady, Mary Mediatrix, was restored to her former self. "The real thing," affirmed Sr. Bernadette.[117]

All of this took place without anyone in the community speaking a word. The sisters' belief was tacit, mediated obliquely through mundane decisions about their shared home, advancing ever so slightly, retreating when need be, as the image itself had. Yet the nuns remained obedient to the rule of silence; in fact they used that silence to protect the object of their devotion as they might harbor a fugitive. Hence "harboring belief" as a mode of profession: an affirmation without declaration, neither wholly interior to the individual self nor fully constituted in overt social action. There was no ritual framework that drew attention to the fact of belief qua belief, and no credo that announced belief in its plenitude. Instead, belief played a game of hide-and-seek with its source, revealing itself in the intervals between veiling and unveiling, in disguise, in the movement between the knowledge and disavowal of the dual identity of the image of Mary. One is tempted to say that belief took a form of expression that was itself apparitional: there but not there, present but hidden.

The sisters found themselves in a unique situation of divided loyalties that produced this act of holy disguise. Yet to the sisters, I noted, versions of the apparition events settled along the all-encompassing trajectory of individual and communal Carmelite vocation. Take, for instance, the story of Sr. Bernadette's (née Lydia Bautista) first visit to Lipa Carmel, as described in a homily quoted in her death circular:[118]

> "On a certain November 12 . . . her mother brought her to the Lipa Carmelite convent. She was a teen-ager then and not a religious person at all. That November 12 happened to be the day of the last apparition of Our Lady in Lipa. It was on that day of Our Lady's last apparition in Lipa that Lydia Bautista, a carefree teenager, felt a clear and categorical call to be a Carmelite contemplative." Referring to this particular grace, Sr. Bernadette mentioned that after hearing Teresita's message that day regarding the Mediatrix, she felt that her personal work had been defined for her: "*Spread my devotion and pray for priests.*"[119]

How one was "called," the trials of postulancy, the regimens of work and prayer, the cycles of changing leadership, the feast days and other occasions for celebration within the community—the more one lives by the Rule, the more these become steps in performing the path leading to divine illumination and unity with God. Ideally, all experiences are assimilated into what Teresa of Ávila, the founder of the Order of Discalced Carmelites, called the "Way of Perfection." For the cloistered community of Lipa Carmel, the miracles, apparitions, and more lastingly, the engendered devotion to Mary Mediatrix, find potential abode in the "Interior Castle" first envisioned by the saint, the blueprint of which lies at the core of Carmelite life.[120] Hence the community refers to the period of enforced silence following the church's decree as the "Dark Night."[121]

Thus, Mary's appearances, and especially the repeated injunctions to pray for priests and nuns, must also be understood in reference to the genealogy that reaches back to the great mystic. But there is another important descendent of St. Teresa to invoke here, a saint whose writings and deeds may, in the end, best illuminate the visionary's perceptions of the phenomena that took place within the cloister walls.

THÉRÈSE AND TERESITA

Under the entry dated October 3, 1948, about a week after the last of Mary's consecutive visits, Teresita describes the following occurrence:

> After Mass, we generally go up to our cell and on my way, a very strong fragrance of roses was all over the corridor. And as I reached the staircase, all of a sudden I saw petals falling before me. My first impulse was to look up to find where those petals were coming from. I saw nobody, but petals kept falling on every step of the staircase . . . I saw a Sister climbing up the stairs a few steps behind me. When I reached the second floor of the convent, I looked back and to my amazement, all the steps were thickly covered with petals. I went down carefully to call Mother Cecilia. When she saw the numerous petals on every step and also on the way to our cell she was for some time speechless and motionless. I myself could hardly believe what I saw.[122]

The carpet of rose petals was not the only extraordinary thing that happened that Sunday. Later that same day, Teresita fell into a trance. While in this state she saw St. Thérèse of the Child Jesus (d. 1897); it was her feast day. Merry angels surrounded St. Thérèse, then departed one by one. Standing alone, St. Thérèse told Teresita "that simplicity teaches us to be humble and obedient, to remain as little as possible because Jesus and Mama Mary cannot refuse any grace needed."[123] Although she said nothing further, she engaged the young postulant in a playful exchange of "flying kisses."[124] When she left, Teresita begged her to give Jesus and Mary a kiss on her behalf.

In her bliss, Teresita recalls a story her mother once shared with her. It was soon after Thérèse was canonized in 1925 that Teresita's mother asked for the new saint's intercession. Mrs. Castillo already had one daughter but very much desired another. The saint apparently granted her wish, and a second daughter was born on July 4, 1927. This blessed favor, we are told, is the reason for Teresita's given name. Yet a shared name is only the most literal connection between the Filipina visionary and the French saint. The more one knows about St. Thérèse—"the Little Flower"—of the Carmel of Lisieux, the more apparent it is that Teresita emulates her namesake and that the supernatural occurrences at Lipa parallel the phenomena associated with her. Indeed, from another standpoint, the story of Lipa is as much an additional chapter in the French saint's hagiography as it tells of another miraculous appearance of the Virgin Mary. But the legacy of St. Thérèse is vast, and the literature about her is legion. To understand her impact on the events at Lipa Carmel, we need to get a hold of St. Thérèse primarily as she figured in the pious imaginations of female Carmelites living half a world away from the convent in Normandy where the young woman blazed her path to glory. That is to say, we need to understand Teresita's Thérèse.

The first place to start is with the resonances between Teresita's testimony and St. Thérèse's masterwork *Histoire d'une âme* (Story of a Soul). Written between 1895 and 1897 at the behest of three of her closest companions (two of her sisters and her mother prioress), St. Thérèse's autobiography is the cornerstone of her legacy and was almost certain to have been read by the women entering Lipa Carmel, if not as adolescents, then surely as postulants. *Story of a Soul* found worldwide fame soon after it was published in 1898, a year to the day after Thérèse died of tuberculosis at the age of twenty-four. Overflowing with sentimentality, the autobiography comprises a romantic recollection of her childhood, the chronicle of her conversion, her trials of faith, and an effusive exhortation of what she called her "science of love"—a theology of love as the *only* Christian virtue necessary, the alpha and the omega of Christian devotion.[125]

For Teresita, who confessed in the first version of her testimony that St. Thérèse's autobiography "is a book I never get tired of reading over and over again,"[126] what seemed to hold the greatest appeal was Thérèse's faithful disposition as couched in the rhetoric of diminution, or more explicitly, the quality of "littleness." Grounded in several scriptural passages, such as "Whoever is a little one, let him come to me" (Proverbs 9:4),[127] and possessing a range of meanings from insignificant to physically small and certainly childlike, the language of "littleness" that pervades Thérèse's apologetics laces Teresita's own writing. Teresita refers to herself often as a "little one" or "my little self," emphasizing her infantine wonder at the miraculous occurrences that befall her on the one hand, and her powerlessness in the face of various torments on the other. This self-description also allows Teresita to characterize her relationship to Mary (who also calls her "my little one") as that of a child to her mother. Interspersed throughout her testimony are fanciful descriptions such as the following, which echoes St. Thérèse's writings on "little deeds":[128]

> I kept myself busy by studying the rules of Carmel, memorizing some Latin prayers, and adjusting myself to a very different kind of life. Laundry work was the hardest for me, and not knowing how to wash clothes, both my hands soon had small holes in them. [These] reminded me of the little violets, small they may be, but when bunched together they become a very beautiful offering to Jesus. Painful, yes, but very pleasing to the Mother of God.[129]

In addition to the principle of littleness, Teresita deploys a variety of motifs that find their parallel in Thérèse's writings. On one occasion, for example, Teresita describes going into a trance, during which Mary accompanied her through a beautiful garden that "looked to me like it had all the kinds of flowers in the whole world."[130] In this reverie she muses, "The thought of the greatness of God was inevitable. How God really loved us to create all those lovely flowers with different shapes, colors, and perfumes for us to admire."[131] Compare this to a passage in the opening pages of Thérèse's autobiography: "And so it is in the world of souls, Jesus' garden. He willed to create great souls comparable to Lilies and roses, but He has created smaller ones and these must be content to be daisies or violets destined to give joy to God's glances when He looks down at his feet."[132] Flowers, birds, and gardens all figure centrally and as the backdrop to the apparition events in Lipa Carmel as Teresita describes them. Her invocation of the French picturesque that saturates *Story of a Soul* and exposition of devotional lessons gained throughout her own spiritual journey reveal her undeniable emulation of Thérèse—an emulation that is, paradoxically, for all its professions of humility, downright aspirational in its expressed desire for sainthood.

From a literary point of view these aspects of Teresita's testimony are clearly derivative, but this should not be read as postcolonial mimicry, even as the testimony cannot be extricated from postcolonial conditions. Rather, the clear resonance with and occasional paraphrasing of the French saint's autobiography are Teresita's attempts to transform her experiences of singular suffering into assertions of spiritual privilege and inheritance—to claim a place in the mystical genealogy that includes the *other* Teresas.[133]

Historically speaking, moreover, this link in a longer monastic chain consists of more than Teresita's personal supernatural encounters and self-representations. Lisieux Carmel and Lipa Carmel are not connected just because of their visionary inhabitants: the Carmel of Lisieux is central to the foundation of the Carmelites in the Philippines. The illustration on the cover of the second volume of *The Roots of Teresa's Nuns in the Philippines,* written by the Filipina sister Mary Teresa Sideco and published in 1999, says it all (figure 3.5): there is a big, leafy tree, and at the base of the trunk appears the inscription "Avila, Spain, August 24, 1562."[134] This is the date that the Spanish mystic Teresa of Ávila revolutionized the Order of Carmelites with the founding of the convent of St. Joseph. Above that on the trunk appears, without date, the inscriptions "Paris," then above that "Poitiers," then moving up the trunk "Lisieux 1838," "Saigon 1861," "Hanoi 1895," "Hue 1909," "Jaro 1923," "Manila 1926"; and then finally branching off from there appears "Lipa 1946." The tree's canopy is dotted with Carmelite foundations elsewhere in the Philippines, and overseeing all in an inset portrait is the medieval saint. One cannot find a more literal picture of relatedness and spiritual kinship than this. Although it might seem fairly incidental that Lisieux Carmel was the sending foundation for missions to the region of the world that would be called Southeast Asia, Thérèse's fervent desire to join her coreligionists in Saigon was hardly so.[135]

Thus we see the inextricable connections among religious communities and historical trajectories that pull together colonialism, Christian mission, and the construal of mystical descent. A fledgling community like Lipa Carmel consciously drew out these connections to both edify and justify its foundation. Not only do Filipina Carmelites trace their existence back to Lisieux Carmel, however. Conversely, Thérèse of Lisieux's expressed enthusiasm for Asian mission (indeed the church declared her a patron saint of missions in 1927, a remarkable conferral considering she never went anywhere) makes the founding of Lipa Carmel in her name appear almost foreordained, as if the mission field she so fantasized entering surely included the Philippines on its horizon. At points both individual and collective, both in retrospect and prefiguratively, St. Thérèse of Lisieux serves as the linchpin of Lipa Carmel's spiritual heritage.

St. Thérèse is thus as central as the devil and the Virgin Mary in the supernatural battle waged in the corridors of Lipa Carmel. She serves as an inspiration and a model of behavior for Teresita as she experiences both ordinary travails and sublime encounters. Drawing St. Thérèse into this triumvirate, as Teresita's testimony and the monastic historiography do, suggests yet another important way of accounting for the miraculous events of the late 1940s: in their own ways, all three figures perform the work of legitimizing

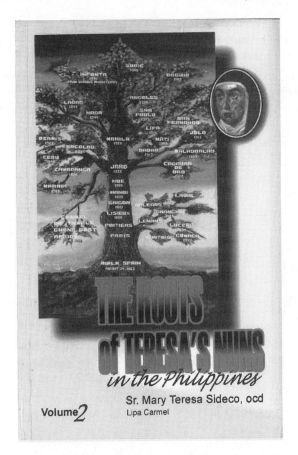

FIGURE 3.5 From trunk to treetop, the branches of St. Teresa's Order of Discalced Carmelites in the Philippines. Cover illustration, Sideco, *The Roots of Teresa's Nuns in the Philippines*, vol. 2.

the new community. For one, as the history of possession and female monasticism has shown, the devil loves attacking nuns—and has an especial appetite for Carmelites in particular! St. Teresa of Ávila, whom Teresita refers to in her testimony as "grandmother," said herself that "the devil cannot bear to see how much Discalced friars and nuns are serving the Lord."[136] True to perverse form, in the logic of legitimation, suffering a diabolical attack is a sign of great sanctity. Where Mary is concerned, it almost need not be said that she arrives with great sacralizing power. There would be no pilgrimage were it not for the belief that heaven and earth intersect at the places where

Mary has appeared.[137] The persons and communities that she literally graces with her presence become themselves intercessors of sorts, and no more so than when that community's raison d'être is to sacrifice and pray for and on behalf of the world. And we have just described how St. Thérèse lends further legitimacy to Lipa Carmel, both in the many ways that Teresita relates to her and as a metonym for her community of Lisieux, from which Lipa, as the illustration of the Carmelite tree depicted, sprang.

But St. Thérèse's influence does not end there. As we saw in the opening of this section, there is a most material dimension to her association with the apparition events that took place in Lipa Carmel in the 1940s. The showers of rose petals that fell within the cloister walls recalled St. Thérèse's famous (if apocryphal) last words: "After my death, I will let fall a shower of roses."[138] Rose petals are the saint's signature, and Catholics through the decades have reported showers of petals as signs of her intercession. But when the petals began to fall in the vicinity of Lipa Carmel in November 1948, they also represented a bridge to the outside world, tangible proof of the supernatural that could be witnessed by all.

CHAPTER FOUR

Petals for the Public

On November 11, 1948, rose petals fell outside of the Carmelite monastery in Lipa. Petals had fallen inside the convent in the weeks surrounding the fifteen consecutive days of Mary's appearances to the Carmelite postulant, Teresita Castillo, but once they appeared outside the cloister walls the apparitions of Mary were transformed into a truly public event, and news of them began to spread. Inside the cloister the petals acted as either blessings or proof. They fell in Teresita's cell on several occasions; before the nuns on the feast day of St. Teresa of Ávila and for the celebration of Philippine Carmel's silver jubilee; and in private for Auxiliary Bishop Obviar, chaplain of Carmel, who thereafter began to believe Teresita's claims. Outside the cloister, the falling petals were a phenomenon in their own right, precipitating a horizon of material and symbolic possibilities for each person who witnessed, heard about, and in some lucky cases, obtained them (figure 4.1).[1] Over the course of several months, the petals and stories about them circulated and proliferated at a national and international level, giving rise to new devotional publics that closely attended to the events at Lipa Carmel from nearby and afar.

This chapter examines the creation of this public by tracing, via a variety of sources, the circulation of the petals and stories about them. It is of a piece with the previous chapter, providing an altogether-different yet complementary perspective on the events. Whereas chapter 3 focused on the apparitions inside the cloister as they legitimated the new monastic foundation and allowed for a circumscribed imaginary of mystical descent, this chapter shows how the rose petals came to mediate social imaginaries and identities beyond the cloister. The immediate context of the postwar period

FIGURE 4.1 Crowd witnessing a shower of rose petals outside of the Carmelite convent in Lipa, circa 1948. From Keithley, "The Petals of Lipa," in *Batangas: Forged in Fire.*

and the situatedness of Lipa in that history remain an important backdrop to this chapter. Just as one can interpret the divine and diabolical encounters within the convent in terms of recent traumatic events recast through the more familiar Christian narrative of suffering and redemption, one can also ask what it means for petals to fall from a sky that only a few years earlier saw major air strikes demolish an entire city. Nevertheless, as I argued before, the phenomenon of the rose petals should not be reduced to a mere epiphenomenon of "real world" events and conditions; as elsewhere in the book, I understand the rose petals both as a phenomenon to be mediated (e.g., through press reports, photographs, testimonials) and as media in their own right.

This chapter covers a lot of terrain, geographically and temporally speaking. It moves chronologically, starting with the spectacle of the petal showers in the late 1940s. Owing to the 1951 church prohibition against speaking about the apparitions and miracles, there is a long pause in any activity related to the apparitions until the mid-1970s, when one devotee of Mary Mediatrix takes the first steps to reopen the case. The chapter picks up there, charting the development of Lipa's revival throughout the 1980s and 1990s. It brings us, finally, to the recent past and resurgent hopes that the church might deliver a positive verdict on the apparitions and miracles, laying to rest the decades-long controversy.

WITNESSES, PILGRIMS, AND THE PRESS

The first news of the showers of rose petals on the grounds of the Carmelite monastery at Lipa appeared on November 17, 1948, in the newly resurrected *Manila Times*.[2] Jim Austria, the society editor, wrote a first-person account of his visit to the nunnery that strikes a dramatic tone for the reportage in this national paper. Austria painted a picture of stark juxtapositions: the gloomy and dark severity of claustration to the exquisite and delicate petals falling from the sky, out in the open. Baffled by the shower of petals that "fell in graceful swirls straight down, almost like a drizzle, to a single spot" in front of him, Austria described the scene and his interactions with the mother superior as if reporting from exotic and alien territory, "miles away from the roar of the printing presses."[3]

Yet it was precisely owing to the printing presses that the miraculous showers came to be known, as little word of the apparitions had traversed the confines of Carmel prior to Austria's article. As the showers of petals increased in frequency over the following several days, Austria reported on the corresponding swell of pilgrims coming first from Manila and then from farther reaches of the archipelago. Among the first of the pilgrims to arrive was a coterie of elite Catholics from the nation's capital, led by none other than Aurora Quezon, former first lady of the Philippines (who also attended the ceremony laying the cornerstone of the convent in 1946). A few days after that, "notables" in the administration, including the chief justice of the Philippine Supreme Court, the secretary of agriculture, and the director of the Philippine Relief and Trade Rehabilitation Administration, "braved the rain to eyewitness the 'miracle of the roses.'"[4] The events unfolding in Lipa captured not only the political elite's attention, however. Less socially and politically prominent people likewise arrived in droves, coming by the car-

and busload. Students, aid workers, and families, as well as parish, civic, and artist groups traveled from as far as the Visayas (the islands of the central Philippines), gathering in crowds as large as thirty thousand on the convent grounds.[5] By the time the showers ceased at the end of March 1949, petals had fallen on no fewer than fifteen separate occasions.

According to accounts, what happened on these occasions varied. At times the showers consisted of just a few petals drifting to the ground. At other times petals would fall in a deluge, or continuously over the course of a half an hour. The petals were often pink but sometimes white. Fragrance was often present at the time of the showers, but not always, and some witnesses noted the scent of *azucenas* (lilies) and ilang-ilang, in addition to the scent of roses. As if to expand the supernatural force field beyond Lipa Carmel, the locations of miraculous showers multiplied. Petals started to fall outside of the convent grounds: in a nearby garden; at a local marketplace; in a classroom; even in Sampaloc, Manila, on a street adjacent to a street named Lipa.[6] Reports came in of people claiming that single petals miraculously appeared on their persons or among their belongings after they left the monastery.[7] Miracles begot miracles: in the wake of one shower on the convent grounds, the image of Mary made in the likeness of Teresita's vision "swayed rhythmically from side to side, each movement occurring in between one minute intervals."[8]

As the phenomenon of the showers of petals grew, the *Times* became not only a constant source of reportage but also a forum for witnesses and skeptics to testify to what they had seen, failed to see, or had seen and not believed. In this forum we see the kind of reflexive discourse that some theorists have claimed is the hallmark of a public as engendered by the circulation of texts.[9] In an article headlined "Shower of Roses in Lipa Convent Interests Scientists, Educators," for example, *Times* reporter Austria dedicated half the text to a word-for-word statement by Mr. Salvador Araneta submitted to the paper; the statement itself was a response to a previous article in which Araneta had appeared.[10] In another article, Dr. Francisco Villanueva wrote of his investigative visit to Lipa, his interview with the mother superior and a few Lipa officials, "gathering materials for my books."[11] Just a few months later, Villanueva's *The Wonders of Lipa*, the only book contemporaneous with the miraculous events, was published. The book drew much of its evidence from the articles that had appeared in the *Times* in the first several weeks of the petal phenomenon. Would that that might complete the discursive circle, a brief notice appeared in the *Times* announcing the publication of the book in May 1949.[12]

Many of the people mentioned and contributing to the newspaper coverage bear surnames associated with some of the country's wealthiest families and political elite. The observations articulated by this particular public were thus specific to their concerns and interests. Those interests were highly topical to a national scene, which at that moment was dominated by the ascendancy of the Hukbalahap, the peasant uprising taking place in Central Luzon. Not surprisingly, then, participants in this reflexive discourse emphasized what they interpreted to be the anticommunist message of the apparitions and miracles. The article "Chief Justice and Noted Scientist Convinced Petal Shower a Miracle" claims that Dr. Manuel L. Roxas (not to be confused with the president of the same name who died almost one year prior), described as a "well-known Filipino scientist," believed that "the apparition is a warning or a message to the people to beware of communism," that the "enemy of God and the people' is rapidly approaching our shores," and that this was comparable to the "similar ideology" that threatened Europe in the times of Mary's appearances at Lourdes and Fátima.[13] In a subtler, Durkheimian tone, yet one no less framed by Cold War rhetorics, in this case of race, U.S.-trained Filipino professor of political science Maximo Kalaw said that "when so many worthy people believe in such a thing[,] . . . there must be something to it." He went on to call the miracle the first of its kind in a "brown world."[14]

Insofar as one can outline the contours of this particular public, therefore, we might say that it was delineated by an enthusiasm that was less religious than ideological, and that drew its anticommunist line from the Catholic Cold War propagated on a global scale but devised primarily by followers hailing from the United States. That is to say, the ambit of this public was not limited to the Philippines. The American press coverage in particular deployed a Cold War framework unremittingly, yoking the apparitions and miracles of Lipa, like those at Fátima, to divine sanctions to take up the fight against communism.[15] Indeed, in 1949 and 1950 the Lipa miracles became a pet topic for anticommunist crusaders on the American Catholic talk circuit from Biloxi to Santa Fe; their speeches were announced and covered by local dailies nationwide in addition to the Catholic press.[16]

Yet in spite of the ideological thrust assigned to the Lipa miracles by the mainstream Filipino and American press and the prevalent anticommunist sentiment of its attendant public, it is the nature of a public that although it may be captivated for a time, it cannot be contained. The circulation of the *Manila Times* articles led to the imbrication of other perspectives, and vice versa, perspectives that bespoke a range of sensibilities. Take the perspective of Lorraine Carr, an American journalist who lived in the Philippines with her doctor husband in the postwar years and who described the rose petals as "the most fascinating story" she had covered.[17] In her memoir, thinly veiled as fiction, *To the Philippines with Love,* Carr dedicates an entire chapter to the miracles. Slightly more astute than some writers before her, she acknowledges the performative capacity of the press, that is, its power to order the world:

> And these things [the apparitions of Mary] were revealed. The daily papers in Manila headlined this story: "The Miracle of the Rose Petals at Lipa." There were other big stories in the news: the Huks had raided a barrio in Tarlac and had beheaded twelve farmers; Chiang Kai-shek had flown from Formosa and had dined with President Quirino to discuss world events; evacuees were pouring in from fallen Shanghai. All were big stories, but they went below the fold; the story of the rose petals was headlined.[18]

Although Carr relies heavily on the *Manila Times* reportage for the Lipa chapter, especially for the experiences described by witnesses, the chapter's narrative elements betray much more than self-conscious awareness of Carr's own textual production. Having read the articles with great interest, the main character "Lorraine" decides she wants to make the pilgrimage to Lipa. Just as many Americans did in reality, Lorraine employs a slew of domestic servants, who, in the book, serve as exemplars of the Filipino everyman-everywoman. In Carr's chapter on the Lipa miracles, the two showcased servants—José, the houseboy, and Josie, the cook—represent two points on a spectrum of Filipino religious belief.

José is completely gullible, captivated from the start by the story of falling petals, listening intently to the witnesses when in Lipa and then "trembling with excitement" when he comes across a petal of his own.[19] Lorraine feels she needs to protect him in his naïveté, relating: "José, we won't tell anyone about your good luck. Let's keep it a secret!' He agreed. I simply could not have the family chide him. For *he* believed."[20] Josie, meanwhile, is a fair-weather believer. When the stories of the showering petals appear, she expresses skepticism, recalling to Lorraine a hoax she uncovered as a child when she came across her parish priest pumping water through a tube into a statue of a saint believed to be weeping tears. But when Josie's father becomes blind and crippled with rheumatism, she accompanies him to an indigenous healer who does, indeed, cure him.

In the chapter on Lipa, Carr tacks back and forth between the convent's miracles and her domestic workers' encounters with supernatural phenomena. Her conclusion exemplifies the kind of patronizing functionalism often seen in ethnographies of the day:

> The miracle of the rose petals of Lipa had brought good to the islands . . . This beauty of the rose petals filled a need in the minds of the Filipinos. They had just endured a long and brutal war. In times of stress, such as these, they felt a strong urge for something greater than their puny selves. It is small wonder that people will turn to religion, to "miracles," even to superstitions and soothsaying[.] They need something to cling to that will give them a feeling of security in an insecure and troubled world.[21]

To the Philippines with Love is a dreadful piece of writing. But it is instructive in how it engages the dominant public conjured by the circulation of stories about the miracles of Lipa in the mainstream press represented by the *Manila Times*. Although the book ends by tossing off a note about communism, it is not a text of anticommunist propaganda. Its perspective on the miracles is informed not by Cold War ideology but by postcolonial nostalgia, by white love for the Philippines in Carr's "memories that will forever bind me to the islands."[22] The miraculous rose petals were the stuff of those memories, mediating her expression of love for the childlike ways of Filipinos and her real, albeit condescending, affection for her native staff. The miracles, in other words, enable an altogether-different kind of devotional subject to emerge. Notwithstanding the title of the book, Carr's actual audience was a devotional public of Americans, those who had served or lived in the Philippines, or those who perhaps had fantasized about a life of white privilege in the imperial tropics.[23]

In contrast to Carr's colonial sentimentality is one Filipino's sensibleness toward the Lipa phenomenon in the *Manila Times*. The botanist Dr. Eduardo Quisumbing's investigation of the petals was the subject of frequent cross-referencing in the newspaper: first in an article noting that petals had been sent to him for classification, then again in an article reporting on his visit to Lipa Carmel, and a third time in his verdict on the petals' provenance (authored by himself).[24] Director of the National Museum, which was established in 1901 by the Philippine Commission (the appointed body of American officials charged with administration of the colony), Dr. Quisumbing betrays no trace of ideological motivation in his rigorous testing.[25] He insisted on withholding any comment on the showers until he investigated the matter himself. He examined the petals given to him but qualified up front that none among them except for one was actually retrieved by the parties who had provided them. Of his visit to Lipa Carmel he wrote: "I had

an opportunity to make an ocular inspection of the premises . . . I interviewed people in the streets, those outside the premises of the Carmelites,
and prominent people in their homes. None could tell me definitely that they
saw the fall of the petals from a considerable height . . . [T]he petals were
either seen already on the ground or about to fall."[26]

Having identified the varieties of rose flora in the town of Lipa, whose
names distilled the Philippines' long and complex histories of colonialism—
there was the *escarlatang-pula* (combining Spanish and Tagalog terms for
"red"); the *escarlatang-puti* (*puti* is Tagalog for "white"); and the Helen Gould
(an American varietal), among others—Dr. Quisumbing concludes that those
petals "'showered' . . . show close resemblance to the petals of Escarlatang-
pula and to Jaquiminot."[27] As for where the petals literally fell from, Dr.
Quisumbing concludes in a deadpan tone:

> The "shower of petals" could have but two origins: namely heavenly or earthly.
> Of the heavenly, the petals could not have come from any of the heavenly bod-
> ies around the earth. The nearest to earth is the moon. Scientifically and more
> specifically botanically, origin from the moon is impossible and out of the ques-
> tion . . . Of the earthly origin, the petals could have a foreign origin or a local
> origin. That the petals might have come from France or Greece is fantastic, as
> scientifically, this is impossible. One has to consider the various atmospheric
> factors like distance, direction and velocity of the wind at that the time of the
> showers and other weather factors. That the petals might have come from the vi-
> cinity of Manila, giving an example, and dropped in such limited space, despite
> the wind and other weather factors, is impossible, scientifically speaking. The
> shower, fall, or discovery of the petals within the convent is beyond me to ex-
> plain. That some of the showering or appearance of the petals are coincident
> with the apparition of the Blessed Virgin is not for me to explain. I was terribly
> disappointed that I had not witnessed the showering of the petals during my
> visit to Lipa on November 29, 1948.[28]

It is easy to read this conclusion as farcical, but in fact its message is ambiguous. On the one hand, Dr. Quisumbing seems to be suggesting that the
very notion of "showering petals" (he often put this in quotation marks) is
absurd, as absurd as rosebushes on the moon or petals floating through the
atmosphere from Greece. On the other hand, he is doing what investigators
of supernatural claims have done for centuries: subjecting the phenomenon to rigorous testing to eliminate all possible scientific explanations. Only
after this process can the phenomenon, if still unexplained, be considered a
genuine exception—the first step to making a miracle.

In his productive, even congenial, skepticism, Dr. Quisumbing provided a counterpoint to the kind of publicity generated by the elite actors and agendas dominating the coverage of the showers of petals in the most widely circulated newspaper at that time.[29] He reminded readers that the materiality of the petals themselves and the exact nature of their relationship as a sign to a source were of paramount significance, and that investigating them soberly and soundly was the only way to determine their validity as supernatural phenomena. In this he was not alone. Indeed, for many of those who witnessed the showering petals and their profound effect on the local community, skepticism was not just a way to protect oneself from the possibility of a hoax or the influence of a foreign ideology; it was a pathway to belief.

THE TRUTH OF UNREASON

When I saw the old man scowling in the hallway, I thought for sure that my minutes were numbered. Joy, my research assistant, and I had clearly intruded on the elderly couple's afternoon, and while Mrs. Milan graciously turned off the television to sit with us, Mr. Milan only grunted from the hallway in response to my greeting. Mrs. Milan was a former Carmelite sister in Lipa, one of the few who had worked outside the convent, taking care of visitors and procuring provisions for the cloistered community. She was present at the time of the miracles in 1948, and she accompanied Teresita to the University of Santo Tomas hospital in Manila when she was interviewed about the apparitions. Mrs. Milan left the sisterhood sometime in the 1950s, in part because of health problems, and in part because she fell in love with the man now standing in the hallway. Mr. Milan's stance told me much about *kabarakuhan*: a Batangueño term derived from *barako* that describes both a famous local coffee varietal and a kind of masculinity touted in the province, alternately brazen and brave, disparaged and admired, fearless and feared. When Mr. Milan approached from the hallway I was sure our brief conversation was over. I was mistaken. For just when I thought we would have to pack up, he interjected, and like a narrator delivering his audience to an opening scene, he began:

> Back in those days, I was neither churchgoing nor kind. I was always drinking. Every Saturday my mother would go to the Carmelites and ask them to pray that I'd change. When the shower of petals began[,] she knew about it because she was always at church. She said, "Guillermo, go to Carmel." "Why?" "Don't you know? It's been showering petals for days." "Mother," I said, "you're so easily deceived by these nuns. They're the ones dumping the petals so that they can make money. They're staging the miracle." I wouldn't believe it. Maybe if I saw

it falling from the sky and picked it up myself. But I don't care who you are—even the Holy Father in Rome, if he gave me a petal, said it was showering, I still wouldn't believe it. So you know what I did, I borrowed a camera, a *candid camera*, to catch those nuns throwing those petals . . .

The first thing I did was go around the convent, check out all the windows. They were all closed. Except for one in the front, one everyone was looking up towards, where they said the petals were coming from. I went to an avocado tree. There was a branch you could sit on. I didn't move, and I hardly blinked. So there I was. Then people started screaming: "Shower! It's showering!" I still didn't believe it. But the Blessed Virgin was going to change my mind.

I saw one, a petal, coming from directly above. How could it come from the window when it was coming from above? And it was windy, but even then the petal drifted straight down; it wasn't caught by the wind. So when that happened . . . [laughs] it was really the Blessed Virgin.[30]

At first disbelieving, Mr. Milan sets out to prove that the source of the miraculous showers was the nuns. Using his own eyes and the verifying power of the camera, he plans to catch and photographically capture them in the act of deception. In doing so, it seems that he is motivated by the ostensibly infallible capacity of this technology to render all things visible, and to do so lastingly. Yet if we listen closely to his story, it is not just another instance of "seeing is believing." In fact, both sight and the camera drop out of the picture, so to speak, at exactly the moment he comes around to believe. Again I quote: "How could it come from the window when it was coming from above? And it was windy, but even then the petal drifted straight down; it wasn't caught by the wind." What makes itself visible to the eyes of Mr. Milan and the eye of the camera only mediates another truth. It's not that he sees and thus believes; rather, he believes because the shower of petals, the direction they came from, the way they fell, is precisely unreasonable. It isn't the truth of appearances, therefore, but the truth of unreason, showed up by appearances, that convinces him.

In this sense Mr. Milan's method of discernment was quite similar to that deployed by the church commissions charged with investigating miracles. Such commissions always render synthetic judgments, a posteriori, rigorously tested against the world. Only after exhausting all reasonable explanations can they consider the truth of unreason. For the church the name of this truth is "supernatural." For Mr. Milan it was "Blessed Virgin." Still, the commission that investigated the miraculous showers of petals did not rule in favor of unreason—at least not at first glance. The explanation the commission was rumored to have believed has become as legendary as the miracles themselves—indeed, one cannot talk about the petals without mentioning the allegation that the nuns staged the showers of petals using an industrial-sized blower, which they set up in an undisclosed location, possibly the roof.

Comments about the blowers abound. Mely Kison, a Lipa native who was instrumental in reopening the case in the 1980s told me: "When the nuns were first accused of having a blower they thought they [the investigators] meant a *hihip*, a little tube of bamboo that you use to keep the fire going when you're cooking. They had no idea what they were talking about! Can you imagine? All the nuns on the roof making the showers by blowing through a *hihip*?"[31] Some people I spoke to reasoned as Mr. Milan had, testifying that the nuns simply could not have generated the petals' pattern of flight against the wind. Others focused on the absurd prospect of a blower, as one young woman I spoke to opined: "There's no way. A blower would make too much noise, and it's huge; you would see it!" Or as another mentioned, "My father was an engineer, and he always said that a blower was impossible. Not on that roof. Impossible." But perhaps the most convincing, and certainly most frequent comment of all was this: *wala pang kuryente.* There was not yet electricity. Here the truth of unreason, equivalent in these testimonies to the truth of the miraculous, is arrived at through another ingenious appropriation, whereby the church commission's own assertions are tested against the world and found to be completely without "logical basis."[32]

The rose petals are considered miraculous by many not just because they fell in defiance of natural laws. Following the news of the showers, claims emerged that several petals yielded holy images: the face of Christ, the scene of the Crucifixion, the Madonna and Child, the Last Supper, and various saints.[33] For those who believe the petals to be of divine origin, when it comes to these effigies, reasoning again shows up the truth of unreason by means of professed (if not always accurate) knowledge of technology. Just as "there was not yet electricity" in Lipa of the late 1940s, the techniques and apparatuses that might, at present, imaginably produce such incredible artifacts—such as computers, or my favorite comment, laser beams!—were not yet in existence. Like the legendary Shroud of Turin or Veronica's Veil, the effigies that appeared on the petals are believed to have been produced by the truest indexical means possible—they are traces or residues left behind by the invisible presences they depict.

In Christian iconology the word used to describe such images is *acheiropoietos*.[34] Broken down, this simply means "not made by hand." And although the substitution of a divine agent for "hand" is implicit in this particular term's usage, we can note other media that produce similar manifestations. Indeed, although Walter Benjamin did not make recourse to such a cumbersome term, he described photography as structured by a similar absence when he stated that it "freed the hand of the most important artistic functions."[35] Although for Benjamin it was an eye through a lens that supplanted the hand, it is not difficult to see an affinity here between this ancient concept and the modern instrument of reproduction. I have seen a few of these petals, and the effigies are truly baffling, rendered visible by contrasts of light and shadow, without any damage to the parts of the petal's anatomy such as its veins or its thickness, and without disruption to its two-dimensional surface (figure 4.2). The images on the petal appear much like a photographic negative. Furthermore, except on the rare occasion that one has an opportunity to examine one of these extant petals with his or her own eyes (which was only once in my case), photography is necessary to their propagation, because it is only by means of photographs that viewing these petals is possible.[36] There is thus complicity between the effigy-bearing petals and photography, just as the popular certification of the petals as genuinely from heaven entails their occupying a place, albeit as exception, among the possible fields of technological reproduction. A shared structure of phenomenality makes it impossible to consider the petals without imagining other artifacts produced by mechanical means, even if it is to ultimately disavow any causal connection between them.

HEALINGS LOCAL AND ABROAD

For those who believed the source of the effigies to be divine, unmediated by any apparatus, their locus of production was precisely invisible. The petals, whether bearing images or not, were traces that marked a presence since departed—a presence that left behind a tangible residue, a kind of heavenly molt. The idea that the petals were not only from but also *of* the divine accounts for yet another miraculous feature: their healing power.

Published accounts from the period are rife with reports of ailments cured after drinking water either infused with a petal or directly from the Carmelites' cisterns, or of wounds healed by the physical application of a petal.[37] The ailments and afflictions in such stories are eclectic, but common motifs appear that suggest the accounts' local significance. One of these motifs is that of being doubly saved, not only from illness but also from having to seek treatment far from local doctors. In one case we learn that "a very wealthy businessman" visited the Carmelite monastery mere days before a

PETAL   1948

FIGURE 4.2 Photo of a 1948 Lipa petal bearing the image of Mary and the infant Jesus. Photograph courtesy of Chito Segismundo.

scheduled trip to the United States, where he was to have an operation for a stomach ulcer. He was cured after applying a petal directly to the diseased part of his body and drinking the water there. His trip to America no longer necessary, he then donated the money he would have spent on his travel and treatment to the erection of a new church. In a similar case, a deaf boy, told that his disease was incurable without a surgical procedure performed only in the United States, was healed when his mother applied a rose petal to his ears. In gratitude, and with a poetic flourish, the boy's mother donated a loudspeaker and microphone to the convent to be used during the recitation of the rosary.[38]

Another motif of the miraculous cures is that of "believe or suffer." One Lipeño experienced this firsthand when he refused to accompany his wife to Carmel and found himself swollen and almost unable to walk upon entering the town's cathedral, where he had forced his wife to go instead. He immediately reverted back to his normal self once petal-infused water was applied to his body.[39] Another male skeptic visiting the monastery experienced sharp stomach pains that abated only after asking forgiveness from the Blessed Virgin.[40] Here we see a revival of the retributive Mary depicted in earlier apparitions of the colonial period, but now she is not the sole object of devotion but associated with these proliferating fragments of otherworldliness. When word started to spread—most influentially through the mass media—of the petals' curative powers, demands for petals came in from around the world. Some of those demands were met, sending the petals into circulation far beyond the Philippines.[41]

At least two healing cases came from the United States. In Jamaica Estates, New York, one man suffering from heart trouble secured a petal thanks to his daughter's correspondence with a Filipino physician. He claimed that within a few weeks his blood pressure dropped and his "cardiagraph" showed significant improvement of his condition.[42] Another case of healing through a Lipa petal was reported from Baltimore, Maryland, where a Filipino priest studying there lent a petal given to him by his sister, a nun from Lipa Carmel, to the physician attending a young girl with pneumonia and pleurisy. When the petal was applied to the girl's body, we are told, her fever dropped back to normal, and subsequent applications brought about a complete recovery.[43]

One circulated petal created a sensation that for a short time resulted in a sizable healing ministry.[44] In a marvelous reversal of history, that is, of religious influence exerted from a distance, a Lipa petal reportedly worked wonders upon the inhabitants of a tiny village known as Vadillo de la Guareña, in Zamora, Spain. Sent by a Dominican friar from the Philippines to his brother, the village teacher, the petal found its way into the hands of the teacher's wife. Señora María de la Concepción Ginestal Zapata de García Hidalgo—or "Concha," as she signs her letters to her brother-in-law—had been suffering for more than a month from an open sore on her leg that oozed pus and caused shooting pains. According to the brief article excerpted from *ABC* (the conservative national Spanish daily) that serves as the basis for the feature that appeared in the Manila publication *Santo Rosario*, Señora Ginestal placed the petal on her wound and watched "in astonishment" (*con asombro*) as it healed without scabbing.[45] In place of the wound a small white blemish appeared, and over the course of a few hours it transformed into the shape of a crucifix. At the time of the *ABC* report the cross-shaped mark had lasted more than two full days, and the woman's pain had disappeared. "The whole village witnessed with their own eyes the extraordinary occurrence," the article concludes, "which they considered to be a miracle."[46]

The author of the *Santo Rosario* article, making obvious his corroboration of the details in the *ABC* feature, relates how he sought out in Manila the friar who first sent the petal to Spain. The friar gleefully indulged the reporter by presenting several items of correspondence between himself and his brother and sister-in-law in Spain attesting to the miraculous cure. The *Santo Rosario* reporter marvels not just at the miracle but also at what followed in its wake: "a torrent of letters demanding petals . . . that fell upon both the small village of Vadillo and the Sanctuary of Dominican Fathers in San Juan del Monte [Manila]."[47] That the mass media produced this deluge is clear from the sentence preceding the above: "The marvelous occurrence could not be confined to the limits of Vadillo when the press and the radio stations (both provincial and national) divulged the incident to all of Spain."[48]

As ingenious as they were willing to share their providential fortune, the Ginestals of Vadillo devised a number of different ways to make the most of their lone petal. The first was to take the petal itself on tour, just as a saint's relic might travel from place to place. Here again several forms of the mass media were integral to these developments, as newspaper articles and radio interviews announced the petal's upcoming expositions. But it was not solely as an instrument of publicity that the mass media significantly enabled the growing sensation of the healing petal; rather, the mechanical reproduction intrinsic and operative in the mass media itself became a model for the petal's propagation. For the couple's second tactic for spreading the petal's wondrous potency was to (re)produce it in thousands of proxy objects: prayer cards (or *estampas*) brought into contact with the petal and then distributed. When applied to the bodies of the diseased and debilitated, these copies had the same curative effects, according to Ginestal, as the original petal itself. A woman who had suffered for four years from a perforation in her bladder; a two-year-old boy whose head and face had been covered with eczema practically since he was born; three or four paralytics; several developmentally disabled people—all healed by the petal-infused *estampas* that worked their magic at multiple sites, and *simultaneously*.[49] Far from diminishing the holy power found to inhere in a singular petal, the manufacture and circulation of these *estampas* broadly distributed it. Still incredible, access to and experience of the miraculous became less the exception and more the rule.

The magical power of curing *through contact*, carried out *at a remove* from the unique and originally powerful object: this is the lesson in miracles—which is no less a lesson in modernity—provided by the magazine feature "Lipa-Vadillo." The story recounts the proliferation of a miracle, brought about by the radical transformation of distance and sense perception—again, contact at a remove—conceivable only in the age of technological media. Yet no sooner do I make such a claim then I wonder whether it were not, in fact, the other way around: if this enabling and efficacious structure of simultaneous distance and closeness was in fact none other than the auratic power of the cult object, reactivated and reencountered in these mass-mediated forms, then drawn out with each *estampa*.[50] The order of the mimetic relationship seen here is impossible to determine for certain, and it is this that makes these petals so extraordinary—more extraordinary, I dare say, than the apparition of the Virgin herself. Uniquely partaking of artifice, nature, and the divine, the petals and their proxies were something between—a hybrid of—technological reproduction and holy relics: the work of God in the age of mechanical reproduction.[51]

The circulation of these petals fed a socio-geographical imaginary as much as a divinely enthralled one. Indeed, this was one of the petal's pronounced and lasting effects, as seen at the end of the first "Lipa-Vadillo" article (the very title of which suggests the translocal): "Thanks to one extraordinary petal . . . [Vadillo is] a new entry in the Filipino world of folklore! So too has the name of Lipa filled the hearts of all those Spanish faithful."[52] In addition to the miracles of healing and the *acheiropoietos* manifestation of images upon their delicately thin surfaces, the petals possessed the power—again highly reminiscent of the mass media—to telescope distant places, far from one another, into the same field of knowledge ("folklore") and feeling ("filling the hearts"). "Vadillo" and "Lipa," Spain and the Philippines, can suddenly be thought in the same instant. That this recalls a colonial history is by no means lost on the author of the Castilian-language article, who specifically mentions the shared legacy of "faith, culture, and language." Yet this is less a reassertion of the colonial, I think, and more the delineation of a vector of connection—*un puente tendido*, or "an extended bridge"—one among many that constitute a shared world at large: "the incidents that befell the Carmelite Convent of Lipa have had in other corners of the globe a more spectacular reaction ... [but] in Vadillo, for the family at the center of our story, the tale of a letter from a relative and the presence of one petal shall suffice."[53] Through their very circulation the petals capture—in the sense of render, or let us say, picture—as much as they are imagined to captivate, a world.[54]

But pictured worlds and the publics that inhabit them can vanish just as quickly as they appear. So it was with the devotional public that formed around the miracles of Lipa, an imagined community of supranational dimensions whose members admiringly reflected upon their own burgeoning ranks as much as they performed acts of adoration and supplication to Mary as she appeared in this Philippine town. When the church issued its negative decree regarding the apparitions and miracles in 1951, it effectively, almost magically, made the whole thing disappear. Upon disseminating their decision, the bishops in charge commanded that the Carmelite sisters be silent about the events or risk committing a mortal sin. The church could not enforce such an injunction for the devotional community at Lipa and at large, but it nonetheless emphasized the grave error of believing in the apparitions and miracles. Local devotees of Mary Mediatrix recall that members of the hierarchy did this through sermons, telling congregations that there was no truth (*walang katotohanan*) to the miracles, that they must stop going to Carmel, and that the image of Mary would be removed.

Elsewhere, the church sought to debunk and arrest the Lipa story through the very channels that first broadcast it to Catholic communities worldwide. In the United States, many who once spoke fervently about the "Asian Fátima" simply fell silent or outright denounced what was now considered a hoax. Some, like Fr. Alphonse Heckler, director of Tell the People, one of many organs of American Catholic anticommunism, gingerly but unquestionably disassociated his movement from Lipa. Writing in a mass mailing to members of the apostolate, he explained:

> The pronouncement of a commission of Bishops of the Philippine Islands ... obliges us to remove the story of Lipa from our talks and writings ... As far as the Tell-the-People movement is concerned, the declaration of the Bishops does not affect us. The basis of our work has always been the requests of Our Lady of Fatima. The story of Lipa merely lent weight to Mary's urgent pleas at Fatima for prayer and sacrifice ... The Bishop of Green Bay willingly approved the revised edition of our folder Tell This to the People, a copy of which is herewith

enclosed. All reference to Lipa has been removed. Please follow this policy in your work so that we may continue to have the approval of the Church and the blessing of Mary, who Herself always obeyed God's appointed representatives on earth.[55]

With statements like this, with silence, and with forceful suppression, the story of Mary's appearances and the miraculous showers of rose petals were resigned to oblivion, as was the public that had emerged because of them. But not completely lost to the church's condemnation (and even actual conflagration) were some of the thousands of petals themselves.

REOPENING THE CASE OF LIPA: ORIGINS

The story of Lipa's revival, almost thirty years after the church's negative decree, begins with a lone petal and a persistent layman. Francisco Dychangco, better known as "Ka Paco" to his family and friends, was a young architecture student in Manila when the rose petals fell on the grounds of Lipa Carmel in 1948. He made several trips to the monastery but never had the good fortune to witness a shower. He had also heard the rumors that the Blessed Mother was appearing to a Carmelite novice. But at the time he approached both alleged phenomena with sober agnosticism, neither "discount[ing] the possibility of the truth of these happenings" nor propagating belief in them.[56]

All of this changed in 1975, when Mo. Albert (née Alberte Frederique Beranger W. Gennetais), a former prioress of Lipa Carmel, passed away. Mo. Albert had held the office at Lipa for nine years starting in 1958, less than a decade after the church's negative decision on the apparitions. As the community of Lipa Carmel slowly returned to normalcy, Mo. Albert sought to make vast improvements to the monastery and its facilities; these would be considered her "golden years."[57] After leaving Lipa, Mo. Albert went on to play an important role in the founding of the Carmelite monastery in San Pablo, Laguna, Ka Paco's hometown. This is presumably where she and Ka Paco got to know each other, since he was a dedicated patron of several local parishes and religious communities. (Indeed, he eventually became a tertiary, or lay, Carmelite.) When she died, Ka Paco asked another Carmelite sister if there were any religious objects that Mo. Albert had left behind. This sister surreptitiously gave him a rose petal, encased in plastic, with a note that read: "To Ma Mère [the French founder of Carmel in the Philippines], rose petal from Our Lady, showered March 1949."[58]

At that moment, owing perhaps to the legitimacy conferred by the prioress's possession of the petal, or to finally holding a precious petal from Lipa in his hand, Ka Paco began to rethink the events of Lipa. He asked a number of Carmelite sisters for the real story, but they remained, as he put it, "tight-lipped."[59] His persistence paid off when he met a prioress of another religious order, a nun who was formerly a Carmelite at Lipa and present at the time of the apparitions and showers. She was willing to share her experience of the supernatural occurrences. What resulted from their conversation was an epic pursuit to reopen the case, spearheaded by Ka Paco but eventually involving a number of religious and laypeople in the Philippines and abroad.

We learn a lot about this pursuit through Ka Paco's diary, seventy-five pages separated into two volumes of a typewritten log that spans the years from 1982 to 1993. In it, he records every meeting, every letter sent and received, and every datum transmitted or acquired relevant to the apparitions and miracles of Lipa. As texts go, it provides a meaningful counterpoint to the testimony of Teresita examined in the previous chapter. If Teresita's testimony depicts the experience of divine encounters, then Ka Paco's diary details the myriad and mundane encounters that collectively push these experiences out into the open, revising them along the way for public consumption and ecclesiastical recognition. It reminds us that the world of visions and miracles comprises not just reverie but also rumor, the wielding of influence, and in this case, bureaucratic management of details and judicious corroboration of facts.[60]

Such a text also furnishes invaluable, if oblique, commentary on the purchase and perils of religious publicity and supernaturalism at a time when Catholic institutions and lay communities in the Philippines wielded significant political power. During the years covered in the diary, the Philippines saw a rise in protest against the dictatorial regime of Ferdinand and Imelda Marcos, the People Power revolt that ousted them in 1986, and the rocky political and military transition that followed. In all of these developments, but in the second in particular, the church and the Catholic laity played unprecedented and consequential roles.[61] Only a few direct references to these events appear in Ka Paco's log, however. As important as these broader social and political developments were, as in the previous chapter the historical context is best understood as climate rather than direct cause: sometimes subtle, sometimes seismic, shifts in ideology and ethos that enabled a certain receptivity on the part of actors and institutions to reconsider the events that took place decades before. It is clear from Ka Paco's diary that one of the most important dimensions of this receptivity, especially after

1986, is the power of the laity in what one of his influential priest-cum-allies calls "the new Church."[62]

At the same time, at a very different level, Ka Paco's diary relates the tale of his own metamorphosis from busybody to mover and shaker. It is a story of the making of a Filipino evangelist, one who comes to understand how to navigate the labyrinthine channels of the Catholic hierarchy, market his message effectively, and embrace his own personal struggles as a mysterious yet fundamental part of his mission. Ka Paco recounts his growing awareness of the importance of networking among the various personalities of the religious hierarchy. He seeks the counsel of local bishops who are open to reconsidering the case or who outright profess their belief in the apparitions, using them as references to gain access to other members of the hierarchy. To bishops less in favor of revisiting the phenomena he gives the opportunity to escape his doggedness while advancing his cause by inquiring up the chain of command—at one point all the way to the nuncio (the apostolic delegate from the Vatican) himself. He is strategically reticent when interviewing one of the signatories of the original church decree, the bishop Vicente Reyes, who seems particularly resistant to reopening the case. Indeed, he learns to tread carefully in all of his interactions with the religious, making sure that his efforts do not wind up being counterproductive.

Simultaneously, amid the endless meetings with the bishopric, priests in high or relevant places, and Carmelite communities in Lipa and elsewhere, Ka Paco cleverly constructs a public face for his mission and its message, which suggests a larger will and collective. He begins by founding the Marian Research Center (MRC), a clearinghouse for correspondence and evidence. Its inaugural project is a "gallop [sic] poll" Ka Paco devises to gauge interest and belief in the Lipa apparitions.[63] Although the mistaken adaptation here of the foremost institution of polling operations may strike some as amusing, it reveals Ka Paco's recognition that some credible scale of objective assessment is needed to advance the cause. Ka Paco engages and intervenes often in the press, mediating several journalists' desire for sensational content with his own need to craft and control the message of both Mary's apparitions and the burgeoning interest in them. By the end of his recorded activities (1993), when he travels to the United States to visit his extended family, he gives informal talks to Filipino communities about the apparitions. He speaks to a variety of groups not only about the apparitions but also about "how the case of Our Lady Mary Mediatrix was started by the MRC."[64] In short, he learns what every successful modern evangelist knows: that promoting one's message entails promoting the promoter.

There is very little feeling expressed in Ka Paco's diary. But this is not to say that he makes no mention of personal hardships; though scant, they serve an instrumental purpose as spiritual "trials" obstructing his efforts. For example, between the telegrammatic and often bone-dry descriptions of where Ka Paco went, whom he saw, or what someone said on a given day, we find the ordeal of John Paul, his adoptive grandson. The teenage boy undergoes test after test and treatment upon treatment for symptoms that we later learn are manifestations of an aggressive cancer. In one of the few handwritten addendums to his diary at the end of the day of April 23, 1984, Ka Paco notes: "I want to abandon my work [for Mary,] as I can no longer endure the pain, both physical and mental, that I feel due to little John Paul's sufferings."[65] But he persists when told that "working for Our Lady entails great sufferings for my purification," and that John Paul, who finally succumbs to the disease, can "help in the recognition of the happenings in Lipa Carmel" from heaven.[66]

Above all else, Ka Paco's diary opens a window onto just how risky the generation of publicity could be for the Lipa case, even given favorable circumstances, when exposure could mean support for the cause or vulnerability to ridicule and the opening of old wounds—or worse, further condemnation. Its contents instantiate the themes of secrecy and revelation I introduced in chapter 3, outlining the phase in the history of the Lipa miracles whereby a new devotional public was forged out of and then participated in the movement between silence and permissible speech, concealment and measured exposition, disclosure and reticence. As we see in what follows, Lipa's revival in the 1980s and 1990s owes to a series of key interventions through which matters of secrecy and exposure were featured in public discourse or space.

THE RETURN OF THE IMAGE

By 1988, the Marian Research Center had made significant progress in garnering support among both the religious and the laity for a new investigation of the Lipa miracles. Archbishop of Lipa Mariano Gaviola had taken an ambiguous position on this, sometimes appearing to entertain the possibility of reopening the case, other times seeming only to avoid anyone who might mention it. The question of exposing the original image of Mary Mediatrix that was sculpted according to Teresita's description of her vision, and had been disguised and hidden for four decades, emerged as a separate, but obviously related, issue. On this Archbishop Gaviola stood firm, threatening that "to rush the exposition of the image may destroy the whole case."[67] This did not stop Ka Paco and fellow devotees of Mary Mediatrix from carrying a copy of the image in procession on pilgrimage elsewhere in the Philippines, which they did in August of that same year. Here physical circumvention and the idea that a copy of the image was of less value than the original allowed devotees to obey the church line while still promoting the image and its devotion.

It was not until 1990 that Archbishop Gaviola consented to the public exposition of the original image, on the occasion of the death of one of the Carmelite nuns of Lipa.[68] The connection between the passing of Sr. Alphonse and the first public exposition of the original image is widely known among the devotional community of Mary Mediatrix. But it is the nuns' interpretation of that connection that best captures the delicate politics of publicity at this time. Sr. Alphonse was among the nuns who experienced the showers of petals inside the convent in the late 1940s. She was, as a former prioress (who preferred not to be named) told me, not very educated but very sincere, humble, and simple, so much so that her younger sisters found her incapable of telling a lie: when Sr. Alphonse revealed that she had witnessed the falling petals, they believed her. On her deathbed, Sr. Alphonse called for Archbishop Gaviola to make her general confession. They talked for two hours, and because no one believed such a simple mind and pure heart could have filled that much time with the recounting of sins, the sisters surmised that she must have been speaking to the archbishop about Our Lady and the miracles of four decades past. When Archbishop Gaviola made the announcement to bring out the original statue of Mary Mediatrix at her burial, one of the nuns broke down in sobs.[69] "Sr. Alphonse did in her death what she could not do in her lifetime!" this sister told me, adding, "She did it from up there [pointing up] . . . She died, and then they brought out the statue! We had been waiting for that! Everybody silently!" No amount of public support or pressure could accomplish what the silent obedience of the cloistered community and one last revelation of one of their members could. Invisibility gives way to visibility via signs transmitted from beyond any public sphere.

PUBLICITY NEGATIVE AND POSITIVE

Sometimes the theme of exposure took the form of scandal that was then converted into positive publicity. This was the case in 1982, when the weekend magazine of the establishment newspaper of the Marcos regime, the

In the late 1940's, nuns at the Carmelite Convent in Lipa, Batangas saw rose petals falling from the ceiling. This incident led to the pouring in of donations and the building of a chapel.

20 WEEKEND DECEMBER 26, 1982

FIGURE 4.3 In 1982 the "Miracle of Lipa" was cited by *Weekend* magazine as one of the five greatest hoaxes of all time.

Philippine Daily Express, published a feature titled "Oh Those Wild and Crazy Hoaxes!"[70] The article lists the miracles of Lipa, or "A young nun-to-be's shower of rose petals," as one of the five greatest hoaxes of all time, ranked right after *The War of the Worlds* (figure 4.3). Ka Paco was deeply offended by the flippant feature and wrote a letter to the magazine's editor that appeared a month later: "Wanted," read the mailbag headline, "Testimonies for or against the Lipa event."[71] In the letter Ka Paco demanded that the article's author authenticate her sources, and he put out a formal call soliciting information or testimonies from anyone who had witnessed the phenomena of the late 1940s. Within a short time, the post-office box of the Marian Research Center was filled with replies from people who had never forgotten their own experience. Eventually, with the help of others, Ka Paco collected more than five thousand signatures of people who could attest to the miracles both in the past and owing to contemporary interventions of Mary Mediatrix. These were forwarded to Archbishop Gaviola.

Although much was taking place behind the scenes, very little came of this exchange in the newspaper and signature drive until 1989, when June Keithley Castro, a well-known Filipina journalist, decided to include the case of Lipa in a documentary series she was producing on apparitions of the Virgin Mary throughout the world. The timeliness of this video series is significant, for it was conceived by Keithley in the immediate wake of the People Power revolt of 1986. This event, in which Keithley is credited for having galvanized the public to take to the streets by informing them of the military's movements via radio broadcasts from a clandestine location, was believed by many to have been a miracle brought about by the intercession of Mary.[72] Many of the participants (and importantly, political inheritors) of the popular uprising thereafter became impassioned devotees of the Blessed Mother, using their prior professional skills and ample resources to found and propagate various kinds of Marian organizations and devotions. This documentary series, titled *The Woman Clothed with the Sun*, was Keithley's personal contribution to these endeavors, the result of her conversion, brought about by the monumental, mass event that was the EDSA uprising.[73] For the Lipa episode of the series, she obtained permission from the archbishop to interview the Carmelite nuns who were present during the miracles of the late 1940s, as well as the visionary, Teresita.[74] When the documentary aired on national TV in October 1991, the story of the apparitions and miracles of Lipa were fully reintroduced into the public sphere.

In the meantime, the efforts spearheaded by Ka Paco's Marian Research Center became enough to convince Archbishop Gaviola to reopen the case by forming a special commission that comprised a few members of the church.[75] Progress of the investigation depended largely on local church leadership. At the end of 1992, the archdiocese of Lipa was handed over to Gaudencio Rosales, a man deemed less sympathetic to the lay-led efforts than his predecessor, and the investigation stalled during his tenure. Then in the summer of 2004, a new archbishop of Lipa was installed, the former military chaplain Ramon Argüelles, and with that, hope was renewed that the investigation would resume, the original decree be overturned, and the apparitions and miracles of Lipa be declared authentically supernatural once and for all.

PERSPICACITY AND CIRCUMLOCUTION

Throughout this newer period of pending and relative openness, the interactions among the cloistered community of nuns, the devotional community, and the local church hierarchy, continued in the ways I have thematized here, circumscribed by deep ambivalence over publicity and fear of overstepping one's bounds vis-à-vis the church's condemnation in 1951. The reticence that emerged as a consequence gave rise to extraordinary abilities among the devotional community to read between the lines. When I was conducting field research in Lipa in the early to mid-2000s, it was not uncommon to hear people deconstructing the priests' homilies after Mass, as if each were a code that needed to be cracked. For example, that the new archbishop did not even mention the name "Our Lady, Mary Mediatrix" was a very bad sign, while the fact that the bishop known to be heading the new church commission had mentioned her name was a very good one. Circumlocution was imperative. Knowing what and what not to talk about, when and with whom, knowing when not talking was as telling as talking, as well as knowing when someone had simply said too much: these constituted the protocols for professing belief in Our Lady, Mary Mediatrix. We might want to think about the effects performed by such modalities of speaking, how these relays between disclosure and reticence produced a captivating air of uncertainty about the facts at the same time that they displayed a host of creative strategies for articulating belief in the face of various kinds of repudiation. Add to this a church that appeared compromised by its own past secrets, and one can begin to get a sense of the fraught quest for the truth of the miracles of Lipa Carmel.

But just how important is the truth?—we might ask. There are many religious devotions that require scarcely more than legend to legitimate their practices, as well as many that, like Lipa at the turn of the twenty-first century, were neither clandestine devotions nor fully sanctioned by the church. The Philippines is famously populated with syncretic or "folk Catholic" practices for which orthodoxy, much less "truth" in any positive sense, is hardly a belief-determining factor. So would it not be better in fact to do away with the true-false binary, given that its upholding is the very charge of, and thus fortifies, orthodox authority? Undoubtedly, except in the case where falsehood enables the production of belief. The stories that were the pulse of the community around Lipa Carmel parried skepticism at the same time that they revealed the declaration of hoax as constitutive of devotion. This, in conjunction with the possibilities revealed in the previous chapter, namely, that what appeared might not have been Mary, created the unique circumstances that spurred the unabated desire for church recognition. Recognition would set everything right in terms of the relationship between a sign and its source, between identity and appearance.

ROUTINIZATION AND ORTHODOXY

In 2005, it appeared that the devotional community could stop reading between the lines. Archbishop Argüelles issued an official declaration that appeared to confer, after all this time, recognition. Or did it? He wrote:

I will no longer keep it secret, whatever the consequences may be, that personally I never doubted the Lipa apparitions that took place in the early years of my childhood. As I grew up later as a seminarian, young priest and then bishop, even now as archbishop I would always find solace, peace and strength in spending time praying before the image of Our Lady in the Carmel of Lipa. It is to her that I always entrust my mission and seek solutions to my problems. But I will never question any decision made by the official Church regarding the matter. Nor do I intend to create unnecessary controversy by reopening issues that should better remain quiet for no matter how long a time.[76]

With this statement Argüelles defined the terms in the final chapter of the controverted history of the Lipa miracles. Walking the line between orthodoxy and popular devotion by cleaving a division between the personal and the institutional, the archbishop sought to put an end to the clamor for official church recognition. But this was not the last of his statements or actions. Although he remained quiet on the matter for several years, on November 12, 2009—notably the date of the last of Mary's apparitions to Teresita in 1948—Archbishop Argüelles issued another statement that appeared to contradict his previous pronouncement:

I, the undersigned Archbishop of the Archdiocese of Lipa declare and publically announce:

1. That pursuant to the Instructions and conditions issued by my predecessor, the late Archbishop Mariano G. Gaviola, the decree of 1951 is hereby reversed;
2. That the public veneration of the image of Mary, Mediatrix of All Grace in the Carmelite Monastery of Lipa be continued and made available for the prayer of the pilgrims for true peace in our nation and the sanctification of the clergy;
3. That the contemplative and prayerful atmosphere of the Carmelite monastery as willed by the reforms of St. Teresa of Avila be properly maintained for the edification and spiritual growth of the pilgrims who join the prayers of the contemplatives of the said place;
4. That all bans written or unwritten intended to curtail or diminish the devotion to Mary Mediatrix of All Grace be lifted;
5. Finally, that a new commission be formed to review the documents on the alleged apparitions of 1948 and to compile additional documents from the period up to the present.[77]

On the first of these items Argüelles immediately qualified to the press that he was not speaking of reversing the church's judgment on the supernatural nature of the apparitions and miracles but simply upholding the reversal instated by Gaviola in 1991, when he allowed the permanent exposition of the image of Mary Mediatrix. Nonetheless, the establishment of a new investigative commission was big news that precipitated an avalanche of rerun and original features on the events of the late 1940s. Videos, articles, and other publications took advantage of a panoply of media platforms for circulation.

From Argüelles's official statements as well as informal interviews, one might gather that he was swayed by the continued efforts of the laity devoted to Mary Mediatrix. In one interview he stated that the "Mediatrix phenomenon is the greatest thing that ever happened to the Church of Lipa in the last one hundred years and even from time immemorial,"[78] and he has made frequent mention of the "fervor" of the faithful in his diocese, the "increasing number of pilgrims" traveling to Lipa, and the "friendly pressure" he encountered "to declare the apparitions authentic."[79]

Yet there were other factors to note in relation to the 2009 decree that suggested a timelier agenda, one that sought to increase the archbishop's authority and raise the profile of the archdiocese. April 2010 to April 2011 was the diocese's centennial year.[80] Creating an occasion to redouble local and national attention to the "Mediatrix phenomenon"—indeed, that for which the province was arguably, religiously speaking, most famous—would thus have been worthwhile in the lead-up to the jubilee. But there was more simmering behind this surprising development than just additional publicity for the archdiocese in its centenary celebration. For, as long as Argüelles had been in power, and along with the modus operandi that had come to typify communication among the local devotional community, there had been talk of a proposal to transfer the image of Our Lady, Mary Mediatrix, from the Carmelite monastery to a new parish that would be built nearby. By the time the jubilee began, the site for the proposed parish had been chosen (thanks to a generous land donation by a member of one of Lipa's prominent families) and a parish priest assigned. Then, at dawn on September 12, 2010, on the occasion of the annual pilgrimage to Lipa Carmel in the centennial year, this relocation was literally enacted with a procession of the image of Mary Mediatrix to the proposed parish site.[81]

In an interview, Fr. Rodem, then the parish priest of the proposed shrine, spoke in highly rationalized terms about the necessity of establishing a separate location for the benefit of Mary Mediatrix devotees. "Carmel could only do so much," he explained. "People can come (to Carmel) and discover Mary, but who will be the ones aggressively going out and propagating the devotion?"[82] He suggested the need for a center where pilgrims could be welcomed and attended to without burdening the cloistered community. The idea implicitly reinforced Carmel's silent and contemplative rule, and Fr. Rodem evocatively described Carmel as the "lungs of the Church."[83] The new parish could not compete with Carmel, just as no single organ of the body can compete with another. He spoke of the monastery and the new parish as "complementary," the parish "the fruit of what is already going on at Carmel."[84] There were other practical motivations, too, he explained, as the new parish would cater to seven *barangays* (loosely translated as "villages") and more than twenty thousand souls, relieving a nearby parish of a glut of administrative obligations. Baptisms, marriages, registries: these could not be carried out at Carmel.

Although it was clear to me that Fr. Rodem's engagements with both his superiors and his detractors had provided him many opportunities to rehearse these justifications, I sensed no disingenuousness on his part. This is not to say, however, that structural factors and a certain politics of domestication were not at work in the decision to found a new parish under the patronage of Mary Mediatrix. The idea that the monastery is not an appropriate site for public congregation—even if it has a sizable chapel, as Lipa Carmel does—is coextensive with the notion that contemplatives are not suited to administer to the outside world. Fair enough. But the ceremonial progress of the image of Mary Mediatrix to the new parish site forcefully enacted the ongoing process of church routinization of the devotion and its controverted history. The removal of the iconic image from its charismatic center—the site made sacred by the blessings of Mary herself—to another institutional home signaled far more than just a change in the management of administrative tasks; it was the symbolic induction of a very localized apparition into a more orthodox Marian schema.[85]

Take, for example, Fr. Rodem's seemingly spontaneous lesson on the designated feast day of Mary Mediatrix. In our conversation, he mentioned in passing that the new parish, though not yet built, had just celebrated their patron's fiesta on May 31. With characteristic facility, he anticipated my confusion over why the parish had held it then and not on September 12 (the date of the first apparition of Mary to Teresita and long the de facto feast day) by launching into an explanation that cited the 1921 declaration of Pope Benedict XV that theologically linked Mary Mediatrix of All Grace with the Visitation, the feast day of which is May 31.[86] In accordance with this pontifical announcement of eight decades past, a number of dioceses in the Philippines declared that year, by means of a pastoral letter, that May 31 would be the official feast day of Mary Mediatrix of All Grace.

Shifting the religious calendar was not the only way that Marian orthodoxy subsumed the Mary of Teresita's vision. Held in conjunction with the pilgrimage that culminated in the procession of Mary's image to the proposed parish of the Mediatrix was the First National Marian Prayer Congress, a three-day conference that hosted a long series of lectures delivered by Rev. Dr. Manfred Hauke, a German specialist in the field of dogmatic theology, which was open to the public.[87] The congress was cosponsored by the archdiocese and the newly minted Pueblo Amante de Maria Mariological Society of the Philippines (PAMMSPhil), a quasi-scholarly group that aims, among other things, to "know the Theological basis for the devotion to the Blessed Virgin Mary, based on Scriptures (solidly in the teachings of the New Testament) and tradition (Doctrine and Life of the Church) . . . [and] contribute towards the reform and authentic renewal of the veneration of Mary and Marian devotion, which must be fundamentally biblical, soundly Christological and soundly liturgical."[88] PAMMSPhil was a project of Archbishop Argüelles, founded as a tertiary organization to propagate Marian tenets more in line with those of the universal church. The apex of PAMMSPhil's aspirations is the society's overt advocacy of what is known in Catholic circles worldwide as the "fifth Marian dogma," that is, the belief that Mary is the "Co-Redemptrix, Mediatrix, and Advocate." Sparing the reader the esoteric intricacies of Mariology for now, I will simply sum up the relevance of this movement to the history of the miracles of Lipa as this: inasmuch as Lipa is known as the place where Mary identified herself as Mediatrix of All Grace, should the pope declare, ex cathedra, that belief in this capacity of Mary is binding, Lipa would, like Lourdes before it, be the place where this theological truth was foretold. At stake, then, in Argüelles's reopening of the investigation of the apparitions and miracles of Lipa was not just attention to the archdiocese's centennial but also the possibility that Lipa might become the new epicenter of Marian pilgrimage worldwide.

Many people in the devotional community of Lipa Carmel share this wish, even if they do not frame it in terms of the fifth Marian dogma. Indeed, the most frequent response to the question I always posed about the effects on the community should the church recognize the apparitions and miracles of Lipa was couched not in terms of vindication, or historical wrongs being righted, but in terms of inclusion: Lipa would become *parang Lourdes*: "like Lourdes." Or *parang Fátima*: "like Fátima," referring to two of the most famous shrines to Mary's apparitions in Europe. So easily does the logic of seriality inherent in the category of the Marian permeate even the so-called popular perspective. The operation of the universal category in both everyday discourse and liturgical celebrations is powerful indeed— powerful enough to make disappear those enchanting materializations that made much of this revival possible in the first place: the rose petals.

THE POWER OF THE "NOT AUTHENTIC"

In contrast to the lure of becoming "like Lourdes" and the desire for church recognition stands a story told to me by one of Lipa Carmel's nuns. This nun, whom I shall call Sr. G., entered the convent in the early 1960s, at a point when the prohibition against speaking of the apparitions had been absorbed into the ethos of silence that ruled the contemplative community. Despite the time that had passed, however, members of Sr. G.'s family pleaded with her to "enter in any other Carmel except that one," protesting that the nuns there were all swindlers (*manloloko*), that they had used a blower to make the petal showers, and so forth. At once obstinate and mischievous, Sr. G. defied their wishes, promising only partially in jest that by the time they visited her she would have found out the truth! Her curiosity about the miracles notwithstanding, Sr. G. heard not a peep about the apparitions or miracles, most especially from those who lived through them.

One day, she and another nun in charge of cleaning the sacristy (the room where priest and altar server vestments, sacred vessels, and other objects used in Mass are kept) came upon a petal enclosed in glass with a rim that could be removed. The petal and its case were inside a box that was inside a cabinet. The box was labeled "not authentic," but as Sr. G. explained to me, "'not authentic' doesn't mean that the relics are not authentic; it just means that they have no authentication papers."[89] Along with her coconspirator, she reasoned that since they were not present at the time of the apparitions and miracles, they were not directly subject to the prohibition against speaking about or venerating Mary Mediatrix. So they asked permission from their prioress to have the petal, which they then shared between them. Sr. G. took to carrying it around with her, and whenever someone would ask for prayers, especially "if it's a very difficult case," she would write their names on a very tiny piece of paper and carry it next to the relic. She would say to Our Lady, "If this is a real petal from you, please grant this." After telling me this, Sr. G. paused, then marveled: "And you know, every time I would put it [next to the relic], all the [prayers] were granted."

In a history awash in gray with respect to the matters of truth and falsehood, Sr. G.'s story reaches marvelous new heights in playful doublings and circumvention. "Not authentic" does not mean that the petal is fake, Sr. G. instructs; it just means that it has not conformed to a particular church protocol: these are two separate yet compatible truths (although experts in canon law might strongly disagree). Meanwhile, conversely invoking a legalistic line of reasoning, she and the sister who discovered the relic reason that they must be exempt from the prohibition, which surely had temporal parameters. Sr. G.'s story reveals an intimate desire for divine truth that diverges from the wish for official church recognition as voiced in the devotional public sphere. What mediates this desire is the rose petal in its irrepressible materiality and ability to delight as a found object, *la trouvaille*.[90] Perhaps more than any other story presented here, Sr. G.'s recollection suggests much about the nature of the miraculous as it is particular to the phenomenon of the showers of rose petals in the history of Lipa.

Indeed, there is something curious about the verdict ("Official Statement") delivered in 1951 by the church commission. It reads in its entirety:

> We, the undersigned Archbishop and Bishops, constituting for the purpose a special Commission, having attentively examined and reviewed the evidence and testimonies collected in the course of repeated, long and careful investigations, have reached the unanimous conclusion and hereby officially declare that the above-mentioned evidence and testimonies exclude any supernatural intervention in the reported extraordinary happenings—including the shower of petals—of the Carmel of Lipa.
>
> MANILA, APRIL 6, 1951[91]

This statement, which appeared in both the internal and widely circulated bulletins of the Philippine Catholic Church (*Boletín eclesiástico* and *The Sentinel*), makes no effort to identify beyond generic reference the persons and incidents investigated in the case of Lipa Carmel. The exception to this appears in the final line, in the offset clause that explicitly mentions the "shower of petals." Why, we might ask, did the church commission feel compelled to note only this feature among the diverse array of phenomena, figures, and occurrences connected with the alleged miracles of Lipa? What was it about the showers of petals, above everything else, that the church needed to single out and invalidate?

The petals were not ephemeral rumors or stories that would circulate by word of mouth. They were not appearances that would reveal themselves to a single person whose lone testimony would provide the only proof. Nor were they documents of reportage that detailed only what others claimed to see. They were, rather, proof of a most material sort, witnessed and possessed by not just one but by many. They were artifacts that appeared mysteriously, yet within a matrix of conditions—social, historical, technological, many of which have long been considered the hallmarks of modernity—that enabled their circulation and replication. It is this that posed the greatest threat to the church's effort (one might say mandate) to contain what was rapidly becoming a mass phenomenon—a mass miracle—and it is for this reason that the "showers of petals" were made the focal point of the verdict.

Taking place when they did, the peculiarly *public* nature of these showers of petals cannot be emphasized enough. Even with the most famous of modern apparitions of the Virgin Mary, such as that of Lourdes in mid-nineteenth-century France, the public that emerged in response to the events was not privy to the punctual acts of divine intervention but formed around the personages mediating the intercession, such as the child Bernadette. In Lipa, by contrast, it was imaginable that anyone—townsperson, tourist, dignitary, skeptic, passerby, sacristy cleaner—could have experienced these showers or come across a petal if only he or she were at the right place at the right time. If timing and proliferation come to trump grace and singularity in the act of making a "witness," perhaps it is only a small leap to take for one to begin to believe that he or she can, as the saying goes, expect miracles.

PART III

Mass Movements

CHAPTER FIVE

Of Crusaders and Crowds

In the Philippines of recent years, one need not be a visionary, a pilgrim, the prayerful, or the blessed to see the Virgin Mary. Via public service announcements that frequently play on a number of national television networks, she appears, one of the more recognizable renditions of her face filling the screen (figure 5.1). And not only does she appear; she also speaks, in a voice so ethereal that it seems to come from beyond the screen. Her lips do not move, yet she beseeches viewers: "I ask every family: Please pray the rosary!" Should there be any doubt that the "I" who speaks this message is Mary, a name appears, as if signed, across the lower right-hand corner of the screen: Mama Mary.[1]

These traces of the Virgin—the disjointed pairing of image and voice and the signature writ by an invisible hand—exemplify a new kind of Marian presence, distinct from those apparitions we have seen thus far in the origin stories of popular shrines and in the historical record. Although produced by Filipinos for a Filipino audience, the Mary who appears in these commercials is not from Philippine iconography but is rather the image of the Virgin as she is said to have appeared in Medjugorje, in the former Yugoslavia, in the 1980s. The language spoken is neither a Philippine language nor the media language of Taglish, but English. And far from being deeply localized versions of Mary grounded in geographical place, legend, and vernacular, these images are ubiquitous and uniform. Like the rosary itself, the appearances do not stand as singular events but are generated and maintained by logics of repetition and circulation. They appear without relation to place, are copies rather than originals, and are familiar but unre-

FIGURE 5.1 "Please pray the Rosary." This public service announcement produced by the Family Rosary Crusade of the Philippines ran for years on national television networks.

markable as a consequence of being played so often. They are not the least bit momentous. Yet they are Marian apparitions nonetheless; only theirs is the paradoxical form of spectral embodiment, of presence conveyed at a distance. This kind of "presence-ing" is also the promise and effect produced by other forms of technological media. Thus, in this public service announcement we finally arrive at what the previous chapters could only anticipate: the union of Mary and the mass media, filling the same phenomenal domain.

It is perhaps unsurprising—possibly even fitting—that the source of such new forms of appearance of Mary in the Philippines would be elsewhere, from the place where televisual hegemony has historically reigned supreme. The producer of these repeated public service announcements is the Filipino office of what was originally an American apostolate: the Family Rosary Crusade (FRC). Founded by Fr. Patrick Peyton, an Irish immigrant to the United States who believed that the Virgin Mary miraculously cured him of tuberculosis, what began as an occasional reminder to pray the rosary on American Catholic radio programs in the mid-1940s had grown into a full-fledged media ministry by the 1950s. The FRC used mass rallies, television, and films to propagate devotion to the Virgin Mary through rosary prayer.[2] That its heyday coincided with the broad consolidation of U.S. military, political, and economic dominance after World War II is no accident, just as the ministry's spread would greatly benefit from the Marian revival of the pre–Second Vatican Council church of Pius XII. Indeed the Family Rosary Crusade, a movement whose founder, Peyton, overtly analogized its campaigns to a military assault, could be born only of the matrix of 1950s Catholic conservatism, the Cold War, and the cool medium that would make the FRC's battle against communism one that it could fight on the most public, and private, of fronts.[3]

But what would happen when the FRC went abroad and took root, as the organization ultimately did in the Philippines? This chapter examines the Family Rosary Crusade in the Philippines from 1951, when Peyton first visited, to the 1990s, when the public service announcement regularly aired. In the pages that follow, I provide an overview of the FRC's activities, attending to the ways in which the universal aspirations and ideological agendas of the crusades sometimes fell short of, and sometimes exceeded, the organization's intentions and were transformed in the Philippine context. As much as this is an examination of the American-led FRC in its imperial dimensions during the global Cold War, it is equally a study of the religious deterritorialization seen in the television commercial—the making of the general theological equivalent that for Filipinos would go by the name "Mama Mary." Finally, by drawing on the narratives of those in the Philippines who took over the FRC's mission, this chapter demonstrates how lay Filipinos have themselves become deeply interested in, if not devoted to, the production and policing of orthodoxy.

Before delving into an account of the Family Rosary Crusade, it makes sense to spend some time with the instrument that lies at the center of the FRC's mission: the rosary. An artifact of some paradox, the rosary ingeniously fuses both metaphor and literal, repetition and narrative, recursivity and linearity, the power to distract one from spiritual matters and the power to tether one to divine power. As a matter of historical and anthropological fact, the rosary is the most important of all Marian devotional practices, including in the Philippines. So let us pause for a moment and see what exactly it is.

THE MECHANICS OF THE ROSARY

The object used in the practice of rosary prayer is a single strand of beads, which includes a total of fifty-nine beads, fifty-four of which form a circular chain (figure 5.2). This chain is brought to a close with what is usually called a "center," an emblem that often bears an image of the Virgin Mary. From the center hang the remaining five beads, and at the very tip of this short strand is a crucifix.

The sequence of prayers recited in rosary practice strictly adheres to the configuration of beads and consists, for the most part, of multiple sets of ten Hail Marys, preceded by an Our Father, and concluded by the doxology "Glory be to the Father."[4] One of these sets is known as a "decade." An entire rosary is made up of fifteen decades, though most people pray only five at a time, and it is only five decades that one chain of beads most commonly represents.[5] Before reciting the decades, the prayer is initiated, as with many a Catholic practice, by making the sign of the cross. The crucifix leads this gesture and is held with the thumb and index finger. Before moving to the first bead (that adjacent to the crucifix), the fundamental tenets of Christianity are stated in the prayer of the Apostles' Creed.[6] With the first bead is said the Our Father, then three Hail Marys, followed by the doxology.[7] Moving toward the center, with the last bead in the tail strand of the rosary, comes another Our Father, and with that begins the first of the decades.

Each decade corresponds to what is known as a "mystery." Thus, a common recitation of the rosary represents five "mysteries." These "mysteries" refer not to unfathomable secrets but to events: they relay significant pas-

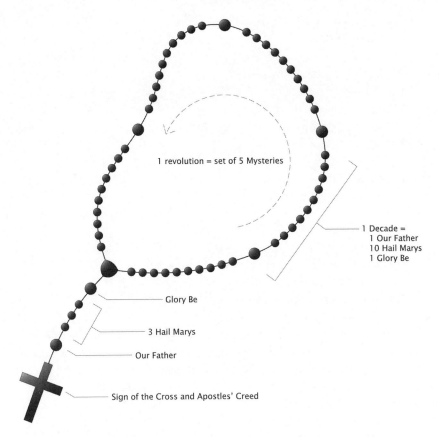

1 revolution = set of 5 Mysteries

1 Decade =
1 Our Father
10 Hail Marys
1 Glory Be

Glory Be

3 Hail Marys

Our Father

Sign of the Cross and Apostles' Creed

FIGURE 5.2 Rosary beads

sages in the life of Christ, including his incarnation, mission, passion, and resurrection, according to the narratives in the Gospels of the New Testament. Each mystery is announced prior to the Our Father that starts a decade. Furthermore, for each day of the week a specific set of mysteries is prescribed for meditation. The first set of mysteries, falling under the rubric of "Joyful," include the following:

The annunciation of the archangel Gabriel to Mary
The visitation of Mary to Elizabeth
The birth of Jesus at Bethlehem
The presentation of Jesus in the temple
The finding of Jesus in the temple

The second set of mysteries, known as "Sorrowful," include the events of the Passion of Jesus Christ:[8]

The agony of Jesus in the garden
The scourging at the pillar
The crowning of Jesus with thorns
The carrying of the cross by Jesus to Calvary
The crucifixion of Jesus

The third and final set of mysteries is referred to as the "Glorious Mysteries," and these chronicle the following:

The resurrection of Jesus from the dead
The ascension of Jesus into heaven
The descent of the Holy Spirit upon the apostles
The assumption of Mary into heaven
The coronation of Mary as Queen of Heaven

What is noteworthy about this sequence of events in the mysteries of the rosary is that it begins and ends with the Virgin Mary. In a manner reflecting the material structure of the strand of prayer beads itself, the narrative finishes where it begins. Although it chronicles the particular journey of Christ, the chain of repeated prayers always delivers the orator back to Christ's mother.

This return reveals both the mechanics and the efficacy of the rosary as an instrument of prayer, which is to say, an instrument of communication. "To Jesus through Mary," is the oft-spoken adage associated with the rosary, and in its ecclesiastically prescribed usage, although Mary is the recipient of prayers—the destination signaled by the final mystery that positions her at Christ's side in heaven—her role is but to act on the supplicant's behalf in petition to God the Son. Substitution does not end here with Mary as proxy, however. As one contemporary theologian instructs, when one prays to Mary, one is praying "*like* her . . . [I]t is *in* and *through* her that we view all the mysteries we meditate on, even those of which she may not have had firsthand knowledge . . . It is with her eyes, so to speak, and her heart that we enter into the mysteries of her Son."[9] Addressing prayers to Mary, one puts oneself in Mary's place, seeing what could not have been seen otherwise, seeing what Mary herself might not have seen. Here imitation and invocation converge, as vocal repetition instigates visual perception, and prayer becomes the performative act of *bearing witness* to the incarnate Word.

It should be emphasized that this magical production of the Word "viewed" from words voiced is the ideal objective of rosary prayer as ordained by modern purveyors of Catholic doctrine. In reality, the repetitive nature of the practice, as well as the multiple and ambiguous places and purposes of Mary in its operation leave much room and possibility for the failure to unite *phonè* and *logos*. Recognizing this, church leaders have warned of the less desirable—and even dangerous—effects of attention led astray. St. Louis-Marie Grignion de Montfort acknowledged in the early 1700s "the distractions which almost inevitably attend to the constant repetition of the same words," and that no less than the devil himself was always "ready to pounce on every Hail Mary that comes his way and write it down in his deadly notebook."[10] Over time, the anxieties around the failure to focus during rosary prayer took on more modern attributes in the fear of "automatic" or "mechanical" recitation, or as Pope Paul VI put it in his 1974 tract *Marialis cultus*: of the rosary becoming "a body without a soul."[11] At the same time, as we will see in this chapter, the mechanicity *in potentia* of the rosary could find its uncanny embodiment in other machineries, in other technological media. Organizations like the Family Rosary Crusade recognized such technical affinities, making the most of religious mass media to ensure the proper transmission of the prayer's form and content.[12]

POSTWAR MEDIASCAPES

Officially declared "independent" in 1946, the Philippines of the post–World War II period was still thoroughly bound to the United States in what was euphemistically referred to as a "special relationship." Among the conditions of this relationship, sometimes called "warm friendship" by Filipinos and Americans alike, was the temporal extension of contracts to maintain military installations on the islands, American access to exploit and develop natural resources, and postwar rehabilitation aid that was contingent on U.S.-determined terms of free-trade agreements.[13] Never was the semantic value of "independence" so fundamentally rent, and this only at the military and economic level, to say nothing of culture.

As we saw in chapter 3, the Catholic Church was at the time experiencing its own birthing pains in becoming Filipino, begging the question as to what exactly, in this post-"independent" moment, being "Filipino" meant. Although foreign hold on the most powerful seat in the institutional hierarchy, the archbishop of Manila, was relinquished in 1949 to Philippine-born Gabriel Reyes, he, and especially his successor, Rufino Santos, were far from the vanguard in the push to Filipinize the church. Santos (who would become cardinal in 1960) was the solidly clerical product of both Spanish-language training and the tutelage of longtime archbishop of Manila, the Irishman Michael O'Doherty (who held the seat from 1916 to 1949). In addition to presiding over the investigation of the Lipa miracles as apostolic administrator of Lipa, Santos is perhaps most infamous for supporting the defeat of the 1956 bill that would have made *Noli me tangere* and *El filibusterismo,* José Rizal's two anticlerical novels, a mandatory unit of all high school curricula. In short, although both Reyes and Santos were Filipinos, the church they led was ambiguously so. As was the case in the political arena, the Filipino face of the national church did not necessarily reflect the sympathies and dynamics of power that lay beneath it.

Meanwhile, what was strange enough about American popular culture—which is to say, mass-mediated culture—of the 1950s was stranger still when transplanted into the Philippine milieu. Television is instructive in this regard. In its nascent phase, during that crucial decade, TV programming in the United States was far more politically schizophrenic than it was homogeneous. Television was both the most powerful generator for communist hysteria and its robust antidote. While McCarthy pumped panic into the tuned-in public, Ozzie and Harriet reflected back to that very same public an imago of domestic security and plenitude. Any drama that would appear to bridge fear and forgetting, such as the purported link between the communist reds and the redhead, took place off camera.[14] Before television producers really came to terms with the medium's own uncanny nature and ironic potential in the 1960s, that is, before one entered the Twilight Zone or could pay a call on a family of ghouls, before housewives became genies or witches and a German prisoner-of-war camp could actually be funny, televisual programming oscillated between purging and sublimation, disclosure and disavowal.[15] What 1950s television presented to American viewers was not one single story but a mosaic composed of paranoia and dreams.

The origin story of television in the former American colony, meanwhile, is quite different. Given the "special" place of the Philippines in the American sphere of influence, it is not surprising that television would make its debut in the fledgling nation as early as the early 1950s. It is even less surprising, perhaps, that an American major in the Signal Corps, James Lindenberg, is considered "father of Philippine Television" in histories of the Filipino mass media.[16] Lindenberg founded the Bolinao Electronic Company (named after the hometown of his wife and hereafter noted as BEC) in 1946, using scavenged equipment and spare parts from the rubble of the war. Although obtaining a license from Congress to set up a television station was easy, Lindenberg's project of bringing television to the islands was thwarted by strict import-control laws (especially on luxury goods) passed in late 1949 by the administration of President Elpidio Quirino.[17] Although his sights were still set on television, Lindenberg and the BEC settled for the time being on radio.

In Filipino kin terms, if Lindenberg was "father of Philippine Television," its *ninong* (godfather) was Judge Antonio Quirino, none other than the brother of the ailing national leader. Antonio Quirino faced numerous obstacles in his efforts to obtain a license from Congress to establish television stations, because his intentions to use them as a propaganda vehicle for his brother's campaign for reelection in 1953 were less than subtle.[18] By 1952, nonetheless, he was able to "acquire" a 70 percent share of the BEC, christening the new corporation the Alto Broadcasting System ("Alto" for the first names of its owners, Aleli and Antonio), or ABS. In September 1953, the first television program was broadcast live from the garden of the Quirino mansion in the walled city of San Juan, Metro Manila, over the only station in existence, which Judge Quirino humbly ordained with the call letters DZAQ.

According to Charlie T. Agatep, who, along with Vero Perfecto, hosted the maiden show, there was not much to the broadcast of three hours and fifteen minutes.[19] There was no script, no plan, and the one black-and-white orthicon camera (the type used until the mid-1960s) spent much of the evening panning over the elite crowd in attendance (which invariably included Judge Quirino, and perhaps the president himself). Agatep recalls, "Without a floor director to give us signals, our cameraman would pan back to Vero and me as we made one-line jokes à la Bob Hope . . . We were hilarious."[20] There were no entertainment acts, no press, and only a handful of advertisers. It is not unreasonable to assume, furthermore, that many of those who had access to view the broadcast on the two hundred or so black-and-white TV sets in the Philippines at the time were, in fact, the same people already attending the taping. The broadcast ended with a children's show and a popular soprano singing a couple of *kundiman* songs, and it signed off with an announcement to "tune in again at 6 p.m. tomorrow for that classic movie, 'The Count of Monte Cristo.'"[21] For the next couple of months the few hours of daily airtime was filled not with live broadcasts but with whatever film Agatep could get his hands on: Donald Duck reels and "employee relations films" and, if he was lucky, "The Three Musketeers."[22]

As such, the founding moments of Philippine television hardly mirrored what was being beamed into American homes in the 1950s. Whereas in American programming, Cold War politics and the anxieties it perpetuated contended with tranquilizing images of postwar prosperity, in the Philippines television was, from its inception, blatantly, and moreover, reflexively (live from the Quirino mansion!), political. While American television made visible the machinations of government (the live hearings of the House Un-American Activities Committee providing the most engrossing drama), in the Philippines it was, in a manner of speaking, government that made television. This political sponsorship was, furthermore, plainly visible; indeed, it was the primary content of the debut telecast.

The actualization of television as a media form was mired in Philippine national politics, at a time when interpretations of sovereignty and nationhood were still being contested. This defining feature of television's beginning in the former U.S. colony—politics not as mere content for form but as the conditions for the emergence of a given form—might have asserted a kind of national difference and identity, were it not so steeped in an even greater sense of anxiety and dread inspired by the iron curtain. And that brings us to one crucial dimension of Philippine-U.S. relations at that time that shaped the struggle for independence, variants of the same massive scare: the Quirino presidency was largely defined by its efforts and ultimate success in annihilating the peasant rebellion, allied on and off with the Partido Komunista ng Pilipinas (Communist Party of the Philippines), of the Hukbalahap.[23] Thus, the aforementioned inversion of media and politics aside, be it the HUAC or the Huks, in both places television was haunted by the specter of communism.

Bathed in the light of the electric bulbs glowing through the *capiz*-shell lanterns that we can imagine dotted the Quirino's garden was a mise-en-scène of postcolonialism in all its ambivalence: broadcast that September evening was the Philippine government both qua Filipino and qua proxy in the geostrategic waging of America's Cold War. The Quirinos would not remain at the helm of this program long, however. For despite Judge Quirino's attempts to turn TV into a vehicle for his brother's reelection campaign, Elpidio Quirino lost—and moreover, he lost to a man who even more convincingly interpreted the doubled role of both Filipino and client of the Americans. In 1953, Ramón Magsaysay, former secretary of defense in Quirino's administration, good friend of U.S. colonel Edward Lansdale, wildly popular and staunchly anticommunist "guy" of the people, took the presidency by a landslide.[24]

It was in this terrain of blurred allegiances that the Family Rosary Crusade, headquartered on Sunset Boulevard in Hollywood, California, took root. The first generation of radio and television programs produced by the FRC in the Philippines were locally dramatized broadcasts of scripts first performed in the United States by the likes of Bob Hope, Loretta Young, and

Bing Crosby, only now performed by Filipinos. Yet for the first ten years or so, television was still accessible only to the very rich in the Philippines and had not yet reached the masses.[25] But the FRC was already experienced in propagating the rosary worldwide by way of public spectacle, through two very different yet very effective media: the rally and the film.

ROSARY RALLIES

One cannot understand the power of the public prayer rallies staged by the FRC unless one is familiar with the complex plan in which they were embedded, the program that gave the organization its name: the crusades. The rosary crusades comprised three phases of activity, which by the late 1950s provided the standardized format deployed worldwide, including in the Philippines. The first phase was the utilization of the mass media for advertising, likened by Peyton, per his penchant for military metaphors, to an aerial bombardment.[26] Radio, TV where applicable, billboards, newspapers, magazines, film trailers, even stamp cancels were used to herald the impending arrival of the crusades to one's city, town, or diocese. During this period, Peyton, or one of his close proxies, met with local clergy, teachers, charity leaders, and other religious and lay constituencies to explain the crusade and enlist participation by circulating information about the upcoming events in their parishes, schools, and community organizations.[27]

The second phase, which Peyton saw as "the movement of troops to capture the objective," was the crusade itself, which lasted approximately six weeks.[28] On the first Sunday or Monday of the program, each participating bishop issued a pastoral letter formally announcing the crusade to all parishes in the diocese. On the following five Sundays, the priests would preach a series of homilies that Peyton had authored, bearing themes such as "basic reasons for devotion to Mary," how to pray the rosary, the importance of the rosary to family life, and others.[29] On these Sundays bulletins produced by the FRC headquarters in the United States were distributed among all families in the parish. Little by little over the weeks, parishioners would receive more and more information about the rally that would mark the crusade's climax, at the center of which was the charismatic founder of the movement, Fr. Patrick Peyton himself. Details such as where the rally was to be held, how to caravan or find transportation, and so forth, were gradually disclosed as local organizers of the event accomplished what often were impressive logistical feats of successfully negotiating with municipal leaders, transportation officials, and prominent businessmen, as well as some corporate sponsors.[30]

If all went as planned, these few weeks generated considerable buzz throughout the diocese or district: teachers told their students, who told their parents; hospital workers told their patients, who told their families; seminarians told their cohort, and so on—thus building anticipation for the rallies. The sheer amount of religious publicity for the rallies was extraordinary, and perhaps unprecedented. All forms of the mass media were used to achieve full saturation of visual space, via posters and bumper stickers, billboards, and newspaper ads, as well as radio announcements and, for those who had access to it, television.[31]

The first major rally was held in 1959, in Manila, where an estimated 1.5 million people filled the Luneta, the enormous park that sits adjacent to Manila Bay and is a site of great historical significance.[32] This rally was deemed such a success that Peyton returned to conduct a nationwide series of crusades in 1962. All told, the two campaigns and their climactic rallies involved more than thirty cities and were attended by at least three million Filipinos—a remarkable number considering the entire population of the country at that time had not yet reached thirty million.[33] This count of three million was, of course, only an estimate, yet it is one underscored by photographs, which provide a form of doubled witnessing that attests both to the enormity of the crowd in attendance and the impossibility of calculation. The subject of their limited capture is precisely the mass.

Photographs of the sheer crowd (figure 5.3) at these rosary rallies, that is, photographs in which the crowd appears horizontally boundless, offer a perspective that is at once transcendent and immanent. They provide a bird's-eye (or God's-eye) view and evoke the feeling of being there, one step away from being swallowed by the crowd. This is their power. At the same time, a litany of numbers accompanied most published pictures of these crowds. An FRC magazine feature on the rallies, for example, reads "nearly two million persons," "no less than 200,000 who attended," "a crowd of 400,000," "some 500,000 people gathered," "about 200,000 stood for three hours on a muddy rally ground," "some 50,000 stood at the rally on a hot afternoon."[34] Although Catholicism has long relied on counting as a constitutive part of salvation, such an "avalanche of printed numbers" seems less an instrument of calculation than an attempt to contain any seepage of the mass beyond the frame erected by the camera lens;[35] indeed, attendance estimates would often serve as captions to the photographs of crowds. For the event that took place at the Luneta, the *Manila Times* published a breathtaking two-page panoramic photo of the crowd, immediately beneath which was a text box that asked, and answered, "How big was the Rosary rally crowd?"[36] Here, numbers within captions would seem to do-

FIGURE 5.3 Family Rosary Crusade Rally. Luneta Park, Manila, 1959. Courtesy of Holy Cross Family Ministries.

mesticate, rather than enhance, the photos' sublime quality. But it wasn't just numbers that served this purpose. In other rally photos (figure 5.4), the composition itself dampens the oceanic feeling, with Peyton alone providing a focal point for transcendence in the foreground, and the appearance of cameramen who stand both embedded and apart from the crowd, disclosing the manufactured quality of the representations.[37] This tension between sublimity-fervor and domestication-discipline that one perceives in the photographs of the crowds does more than just exemplify the aesthetic of a modern genre. It emblematizes the dynamic and workings of the crusade's entire program of evangelization.

Although the religious crowd, in practices such as pilgrimage and feast days, has long been an important feature of Philippine Catholicism, and although rallies were commonplace political events in the early part of the twentieth century,[38] there is one religious event we can look to as a clear precedent of the rosary rallies: the Thirty-third International Eucharistic Congress, held in Manila on February 3–7, 1937.[39] Part celebration of the Eucharistic Mass and part world exposition, the congress of 1937 was at

FIGURE 5.4 Family Rosary Crusade Rally. Luneta Park, Manila, 1959. At the right on the stage is Fr. Patrick Peyton. Courtesy of Holy Cross Family Ministries.

that point the largest gathering in Philippine history. An estimated 250,000 people converged at the Luneta, the same site where the first rosary rally would be held twenty years later. For five days, residents of Manila, foreign delegates from various states, representatives of the papacy, and members of religious communities both domestic and from missions abroad came together in a spectacular display of pageantry designed to intensify catechesis on the Eucharist and fortify devotion. Although the congress and the FRC rallies were not directly linked in terms of sponsorship and mission, they nonetheless must be seen as part of the broader landscape of Catholic mass movements worldwide from the late nineteenth to the mid-twentieth century, movements to which the production of images and reportage was constitutive. Aerial and panoramic photos of the crowds and grounds circulated widely in both the Catholic and the secular press, becoming models for the staging of future events. Some of the photos even acquired an iconic status that imaginably had intense effects, both positive and negative, on those who were part of the crowd.[40]

Notwithstanding the impact of crowds and their articulation with photography, we should still ask, who were these people who gathered—in the thousands, the tens of thousands, the hundreds of thousands—to hear Fr. Peyton speak? [41] Apparently, all kinds, if we are to rely on FRC reports, the press's assignation of "types," and visual evidence provided by the photos: religious sodalities (*cofradías*) with their unfurled flags of affiliation, families, society matrons, vendors, people with disabilities, ordinary folk, farmers, and youth. There were those who planned their journey to the rally site for days, and those whose curiosity was piqued moments before by a radio announcement giving the blow-by-blow of a giant American dressed all in black alighting from a small prop plane at an airstrip near their town. And what took place at these rallies, aside from the crowd?

Imagine a town, large enough to be the provincial capital, small enough to be shut down for the day. The movie house and cockpits are closed and banners bearing the slogan "The Family That Prays Together, Stays Together" canopy the streets.[42] Not even the biggest church could accommodate the people who came. Narrow roads and building walls groan with the weight of congestion as buses, cars, and *calesas* (horse-drawn carriages) get as close as they can to the open field, which belongs to the local high school or university or to the capitol building's grounds. Imagine even more people spilling from the vehicles when Trafcon—short for Traffic Control, an ad hoc formation of members of the Philippine Constabulary and the local chapter of the Knights of Columbus—turns their drivers back. First-aid stations that dot the field are slowly swallowed up by the crowd. And toward one end of the grassy arena, there is a makeshift stage, covered with white and blue (the colors most associated with Mary), appearing now like an island in a black sea, or as one spectator from the stage describes it, "a huge mosaic of cobblestones."[43] On the stage, in a neat row that stands notably in contrast to the throng, dignitaries—the provincial governor or town mayor, select members of the local elite, perhaps even someone from the U.S. military, the bishop—preside over the scene. And there, finally, center stage, is the man everyone has come to see and hear: Fr. Patrick Peyton.

Certain protocols of ceremony are observed. The pre-rally commentary segues into an opening hymn to the Blessed Mother, which is followed by a welcome address, predictable oratory that is less predictably registered in any number of languages: Cebuano, English, Tagalog, Kapampangan, with all the pomp deemed necessary to herald the significance of the event. Then comes the collective recitation of the rosary, but only five of the fifteen mysteries. At times a few of the dignitaries would lead the prayer; at other times the leaders would be a carefully selected assembly of representatives from various social classes. There would be one more round of introductions before the "Rosary Padre" finally took the stage. In his notable brogue, Peyton might tell the story of how he founded the FRC in gratitude to the Blessed Virgin, who saved him from tuberculosis when he was a young seminarian. He would tell of his other crusades that brought him into contact with people throughout the world. He would speak of prayer in general, and the rosary in particular, as the panacea for everything from the smallest of family conflicts to the greatest of global strifes. And he might leave the audience with clever little metaphors, such as "Group prayer serves as a spiritual megaphone," and "[Faith] is something like radio. God is there for everyone but He only comes to those who turn the dial of Faith."[44] Then he would descend from the stage into the crowd and, towering over it with his height, bless the rosaries thrust forward by anonymous hands.

Peyton was a charismatic figure of classically Weberian proportions. One letter to the *Manila Times* described him as capable of "lifting his hearers above the ground; regaling their hearts with soothing mysticism. As he speaks, one feels that he lives in a supernatural sphere."[45] Peyton became, for many, a celebrity whose star power was heralded by the extraordinary amount of advertising for these events and enhanced by the perceived ease with which he moved from one city to the next, in a private plane loaned to him by one of Manila's more prominent families. One vice governor described him in one breath as a "modern apostle whose only home is an aeroplane" and a "world renowned personality."[46] The *Manila Times* commentator noted that even the greatest political rallies, many of which provided incentives such as food, money, and transportation, could not top Peyton's draw.[47]

Further, the audience was filled, it seemed, with people who came precisely to feel moved. One Filipino FRC volunteer I interviewed drove this point home. Speaking of a rally in Surigao, the volunteer confessed:

> So I was joking with this old person. While Fr. Peyton was speaking, I said, "Tita [or "aunty," an informal term of address], do you understand what the priest is saying?" [*tita, naiintindihan mo ba ang sinasabi ng paring 'yan?*] "No." "Er, do you believe what's being said?" [*naniniwala ka ba sa sinasabi niya?*] "Absolutely!" [*Oo, naman!*] He he, that was the best. She can't understand what's being said, but she believes! And the majority were like that.[48]

This was not the only time I heard this story or one like it, as it surfaced in other interviews I did with Filipino FRC volunteers, suggesting that this was a common experience, and perhaps even something of a test. As much as these stories stood as testimony to Peyton's charismatic aura, for the volunteers, they were also a source of amusement. This amusement was neither mocking nor sarcastic but seemed to recognize that there was something ironic about uncomprehending belief; or rather perhaps, that the nature of belief in these settings was more of an outwardly oriented response than an interiorized state of conviction. In these stories, furthermore, the professions of belief emerged precisely at the moment of an avowed disconnect between speaker and listener, brought about by hearing a foreign, even incomprehensible, language.

Of course, the experience of hearing without comprehension would not have been unfamiliar for these crowds, accustomed as they were to Catholic Mass (which prior to the Second Vatican Council, was performed in Latin).[49] For the FRC volunteers to remark on the issue of understanding, therefore, suggests that the experience of attendees at these rallies was something wholly different from their regular routines of worship. Part revivalist meeting, part solemn rite, and part rock show, the FRC rallies forged a new kind of congregational space that drew from many different idioms and precedents. But while this made them powerful culminating events, the rallies were by no means the goal of the FRC. The revivalist-like experience of the crowd and its potential excesses had to be immediately contained by the crusades' third phase of pledge drives, which Peyton depicted as "occupation forces to maintain the victory."[50]

PLEDGE DRIVES

Immediately upon completion of the rally, where and whenever it was held, the "pledge week" phase of the crusades would begin. Parish volunteers known as "crusade leaders" would be dispatched, in pairs, to go house to house in their community, collecting promises from the families therein to practice the Family Rosary. Armed with a *Handbook for Crusade Leaders* and a worker's badge, these volunteers would prepare to "be spiritual salesmen of the Family Rosary . . . know [their] product thoroughly[,] . . . and plan in advance various methods of effective approach."[51] The *Handbook* presented volunteers with a variety of possible objections they might encounter and suggestions for how to deal with them.

The main instrument of the pledge drive was an index card, inscribed on the front as follows (figure 5.5):

> To obtain peace for the nations of the world, and the love and protection of God and Mary for myself and the members of my family, I solemnly pledge the daily Family Rosary.[52]

On the back were lines to list the name of the head of the family, the street address, and a series of spaces to be filled out by the crusade leaders upon visiting homes. These included the following:

1. Total number (Catholics and non-Catholics) who signed pledge in this family.
2. Number of non-Catholics who signed.
3. Number of Catholics who refused.
4. Reason for refusal.
5. Space for Additional signatures.[53]

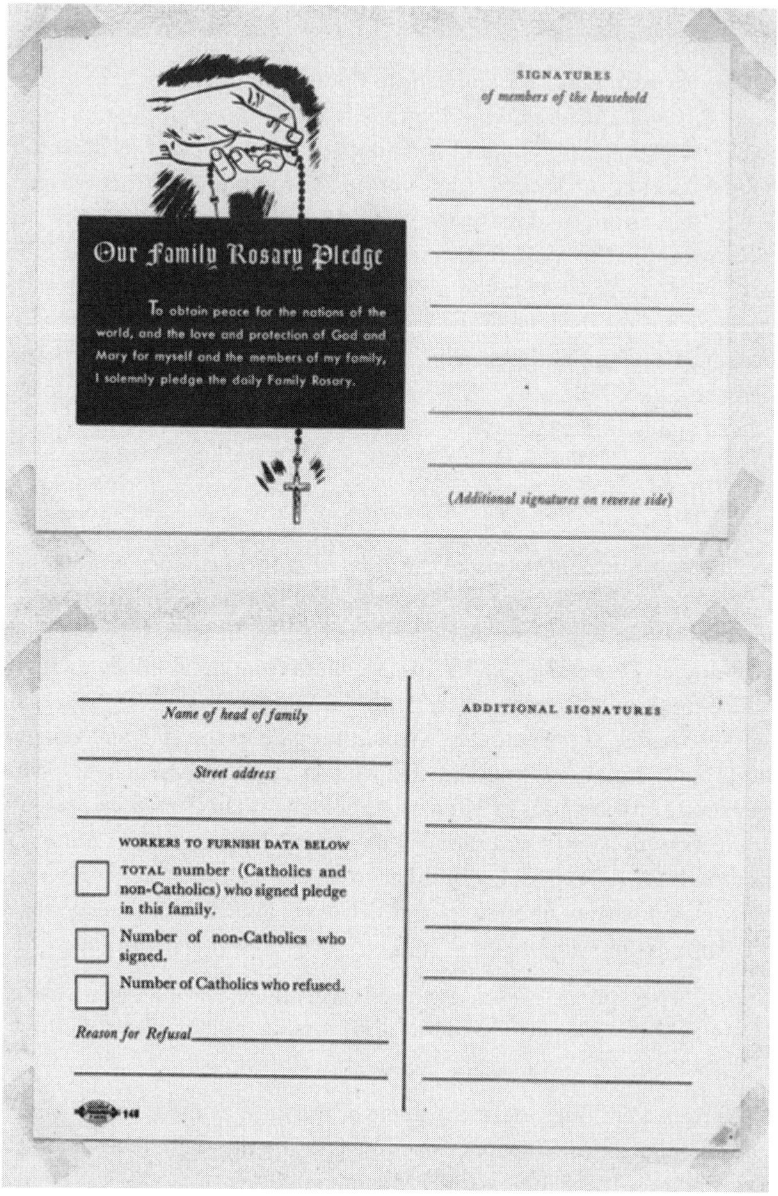

Our Family Rosary Pledge

To obtain peace for the nations of the world, and the love and protection of God and Mary for myself and the members of my family, I solemnly pledge the daily Family Rosary.

SIGNATURES
of members of the household

(Additional signatures on reverse side)

Name of head of family

Street address

WORKERS TO FURNISH DATA BELOW

☐ TOTAL number (Catholics and non-Catholics) who signed pledge in this family.

☐ Number of non-Catholics who signed.

☐ Number of Catholics who refused.

*Reason for Refusal*_____

ADDITIONAL SIGNATURES

FIGURE 5.5 Rosary pledge cards were the means by which families demonstrated their commitment to pray the rosary and the success of the "Crusades" was measured. Courtesy of Holy Cross Family Ministries.

Pledge week was essentially a form of census taking, a point that then archbishop of Manila Rufino Santos himself made.[54] In a memo from his office
to all vicars forane for the Manila crusade of 1959, he urged 100 percent
compliance by recommending that the vicars meet personally with each parish priest under their jurisdiction, that each priest urge his parishioners to
be at home during the pledge gathering days, and that results be promptly
submitted to the archbishop at the end of the pledge drive.[55]

Where families might fall through the cracks, Santos recommended "the
simple, practical, possible, and in fact, easy method" of using the children
of the parish.[56] In another letter, in this case addressing public and private
school teachers as the "second line of defense for the Family Rosary Crusade," Santos suggested that during pledge week, teachers "from day to day
question their students to ensure that their homes have been visited by the
two laymen [crusade workers], and if their family signed the pledge."[57] "The
teachers can help enormously," he continued, "by getting the students to
report on the progress of the house to house visitations . . . with regards to
relatives, neighbors, and friends."[58]

The archbishop's recommendations to teachers did not fall on deaf ears.
The high school students at St. Scholastica's, for example, one of Manila's
most prestigious girls' schools, produced an eighty-page souvenir bulletin,
in which the students' reflections and actions during the six-week crusade
were meticulously recorded.[59] Likely encouraged by their teachers, the students even innovated on some of the procedures of the pledge drive, gen-
erating their own individual reports that went beyond the information requested on the official pledge cards to include the number of brothers and
sisters age seven years and older, the number of maids and houseboys, other
relatives, and any other people residing in the house.[60] Here it is quite clear
that at least one of the issues encountered in the implementation of the
FRC in the Philippine context was the fundamental difference in how kinship—or the "family"—itself was defined, and that the schoolchildren innovated on the drive's methods to better capture what their families actually
looked like. Fine-tuning these innovations further, the reports attempted to
account more clearly for individuals' religiosity, measure their fidelity to the
reception of the sacraments and to the Family Rosary, and assess their will-
ingness to sign the pledge and attend the rally. The students even generated
and monitored summary reports as the crusade and pledge week went on.[61]

That the pledge drive generated an enthusiasm for surveillance seems
beyond doubt. But to what end? There is no evidence that any of the specific
information collected on the cards went beyond the parish level, as San-

tos requested only the *number* of pledges from the parish reports, data that were forwarded in turn to FRC headquarters and were *the* measuring stick for the success of the crusades. In a letter dated January 18, 1960, about a month after the Manila crusade was held, a secretary for the office of FRC Manila wrote to Fr. Quinn, Peyton's right-hand man, to report that thus far, the pledge drive had yielded a total of 1,170,875 individuals signing, including 5,032 non-Catholics and 6,375 sick people. The secretary does go on to note that no Huks had signed—but neither, she writes in the same sentence, had any lepers.[62]

On the one hand, this disclosure seems to indicate awareness of an overarching agenda to be vigilant and identify anyone of communist persuasion. On the other hand, it suggests that by this time Huks existed as just one category of individual, perhaps outcast, among many—including lepers. Furthermore, although Santos wanted to launch a second campaign immediately, he gave directions simply to gather an additional one million signatures. In other words, there are no specific directives to target or even follow up with the families and individuals who may not have signed the pledges the first time around. We might thus think of the censuslike pledge drive as a campaign of surveillance without a clear objective apart from the obvious: to make sure everyone was pledging to pray. Although we cannot neglect the discourse of anticommunism and the military metaphors that percolated through the Filipino crusades via the directives of its American founder and U.S.-based propaganda, we would also be wrong to conclude that this was first and foremost what the volunteers and participants at all levels had in mind as they went about their tasks.

Indeed, a closer look at some of the correspondence and volunteer reports reveals that concerns addressed or resolved by the crusades were often much more local or idiosyncratic in nature. For some, like one nun in Cebu who "worried about conditions in the remote barrios where the Protestant missionaries are making great progress," the rosary crusade was the "saving plank for real true Catholicism."[63] For others, like one sister of the Good Shepherd Convent and Orphanage in Baguio City, the practice of the Family Rosary was quite effective in preventing orphans from running away.[64] For yet others, women especially, the rosary crusade was about keeping their men. One woman, speaking of the effects of the crusade on her community in Jaro, Iloilo, wrote: "We thank the Blessed Virgin for thawing the hearts of the menfolks in our crusade," one of whom had expressed that, now, "he has something to come home for."[65]

It may seem rather obvious to point out, even if only by its name, that the

Family Rosary Crusade also had at its ideological core the reentrenchment of conservative domesticity and gender roles that one saw not only in American Cold War culture but also in the postwar period of the Philippines and well into the 1960s. Still, how this FRC-dictated reentrenchment played out or was articulated in the Philippine context often left room for surprising ambiguities. Only men, for instance, could be the pledge collectors. And while this was justified under the rubric of the paterfamilias and the predominant stereotype that women were "naturally" more pious, it sometimes had to be explicated in peculiar terms. In the final sermon of the crusades, for example, the priests were instructed to prepare the congregation for pledge week by making the following comparison: "In the story of the First Christmas, there was no room for Mary and Joseph because the innkeepers only saw a pale, tired young girl accompanied by a strong, handsome, man. This week, when Mary comes to your doorstep, you will see only two men. They are her ambassadors. She wants to dwell in your home."[66] In context, the image projected by this comparison appears rather unorthodox, and perhaps even a little queer. The idiom of the Holy Family—with its "strong, handsome man"—suddenly morphs into two men, alone, seeking space in your home for the Blessed Mother. In a place where spectacular festivals of public devotion to Mary, as well as the dressing, maintenance, and trade in Marian images have long been a domain occupied by *bakla* men, it may not be so far fetched to see these "ambassadors" as attenuating, if not undermining, the masculinity of the paterfamilias that the FRC desired to project.[67]

Filipina women, meanwhile, though prohibited from collecting pledges, performed a range of roles in the FRC. In the early 1960s a coalition of women's groups spearheaded the formation of the FRC Auxiliaries and took charge of much of the fund-raising for the various missions.[68] Usually belonging to the class of society matrons, these women organized fund-raising events that included everything from can recycling to rummage sales, to mah-jongg tournaments, and often gave money of their own.[69] It was owing to the Auxiliaries that the millions of pledge cards, hundreds of thousands of handbooks and posters, and other materials used for the FRC rallies were made available.[70]

However, just as the male pledge collectors asserted an ambiguous masculinity as both heads of households and submissive sons of Mary in the homosocial formation of volunteer brigades, so, too, did women find ways via FRC channels to assert their individual, albeit prudent, desires. These channels often took the form of correspondence between Auxiliaries women and Fr. Peyton himself:

Dear Father Peyton: Reading your letter was just like talking to you in person . . . [T]hank you very much for that beautiful and blessed bracelet that you are sending . . . I shall always wear that as my rosary beads . . . as a reminder of your good and wonderful self.[71]

Dear Father: There have been so many changes in people since your wonderful crusade—we call it A.P.—"after Peyton."[72]

Dear Father: Please know that I could never forget your kindness . . . and your words of encouragement . . . to which I cling . . . with my most honest desire to live up to your beautiful expectations and hopes for mankind.[73]

Some of the women's writings to and about Peyton were downright blush-worthy, such as the report filed to FRC headquarters about the crusade in Caceres (Naga), Camarines Sur. It reads:

The look in those blue Irish eyes seemed to heal wounds and scars in the soul. The slightest brush with his cassock lightened seemingly unbearable trials and earthly cares! A light touch of his hand blotted out pains and heartaches! How else can one write about him but to say that he is divine?[74]

These are love letters of a certain sort; they trace epistolary relationships that Peyton seemed only too willing to enter into—indeed, he responded to every one—as they were important to keeping his mission alive and fostering support on the ground. But from the perspective of the FRC women they were chances for intimacy at a distance, opportunities legitimated by the long Catholic tradition of the relationship between priest confessors and pious women, yet potentially disruptive of the commitments that women were expected to make as mothers and wives in the Cold War reentrenchment of domesticity.

INSTRUMENTS OF ORTHODOXY

After the crusades of 1962, the FRC in the Philippines slowly took root with the establishment of its own leadership, and by the mid-1970s the FRC Philippines had its own administrative staff and offices that operated independently from Family Rosary headquarters in the United States.[75] These years saw an increase in media programming on the radio and increasingly throughout the 1960s until martial law was declared in 1972, on television. One of the most significant media projects at this time, however, was the mobile film outfit known as the "popular mission." A kind of roving cinema, the popular mission grew out of the first phase of media bombardment for the 1959 and 1962 crusades, during which, in addition to press publicity, radio spots, and the overall saturation of media space, religious films produced by the FRC in the United States were shown in local movie houses as part of the run-up to the crusade events. It was not until the late 1960s, however, that the popular mission took off as an ongoing project that was fully run by Filipino FRC employees, with neither the presence of Fr. Peyton nor the supervision of one of his American proxies.[76]

Also known in its original Spanish as the *misión popular*, this program brought a five-hour-long film, *The Life of Christ*, into the poorest urban areas and remote provinces. The film depicted each of the fifteen mysteries of the rosary. In coordination with numerous dioceses, usually shown outdoors and projected on any available surface, the film played to tens of thousands of people throughout the Philippines, from northern Luzon to Sultan Kudarat. Produced by the Family Rosary Crusade and filmed in Spain in 1956, the film had the look and feel of those classics that epitomized the biblical epic of that time, such as Charlton Heston's *The Ten Commandments* (1956) and *Ben-Hur* (1959). Though *The Life of Christ* did not star a Brynner or have a DeMille behind it, it aspired to be a production of similarly colossal proportions, with a cast of thousands and wildly ostentatious sets.[77] Its Iberian actors could have believably played Jesus and Mary to Filipino audiences, whose primary visual referents for such figures were *mestizo* and *mestiza* (fair-skinned) iconography (figure 5.6). The telling of the story through this relatively unfamiliar medium—particularly in those communities with little prior exposure to film—had a significant impact. Accounts related to me by two Filipino FRC volunteers—Larry, who worked for years as a technician on the project, and Ben, who was one of the main instructors—fulfill the most clichéd expectations of naïve response to the medium, reactions enjoyed and manipulated by the organizers themselves. Larry talked about how he would suddenly increase the volume at dramatic moments, such as "We will crown the King!" (with thorns) or when they nailed Christ to the cross (rendered by him as "*boog!*"), and watch gleefully as viewers screamed, "*Arayyy!*" (ouch) or started weeping.[78] Ben told a story of how at one film showing, during the crucifixion scene when Christ beseeches, "Father, forgive them," a drunk passerby suddenly sobered up, knelt before the screen, and cried, "Forgive me! [*Patawarin mo ako!*] Forgive me! How'd you get here?"[79] He recalled when people back at the FRC headquarters heard about the incident, they laughed and laughed at the man who believed the film to be real. This laughter, in contrast to the amusement expressed at the rally attendants' uncomprehending belief, was indeed condescending. Yet there

FIGURE 5.6 Scenes from the Family Rosary Crusade's *The Life of Christ*, a series of short films that dramatized the fifteen mysteries of the rosary. Spanish actors mouthed the English words that were later voiced over; the films remained undubbed and without subtitles until the late 1990s, long after the popular mission had ended. *Left to right:* The Annunciation (the Joyful Mysteries), the Crucifixion (the Sorrowful Mysteries), the Ascension of Jesus into heaven (the Glorious Mysteries).

was still a wondrous element to it, according to Ben, as the man had no idea what was actually being said in the movie, since it was entirely in English.[80]

The *Life of Christ* films were translated (into Tagalog alone, it need be noted, and in no other languages that would have been the mother tongue of a good majority of viewers in the provinces) only when the VHS versions were made available in the Philippines in 1999, long after the popular mission had ended. During the 1960s and the years from the late 1970s to the mid-1980s when the films were touring the country, only the English version was shown, with neither subtitles nor simultaneous translation. The film was thus similar to the rally as a public and visual spectacle, in the sense that it was capable of compelling not only attendance but also *belief*, and it did so in spite of language. Still, the purpose of showing the film was explicitly didactic—to teach the proper meaning and method of rosary prayer—and it therefore demanded, at least in principle, that language be communicative, that it not be left unmoored from any message. To ensure this, film showings were buttressed at every turn, or rather every reel, by instruction and exegesis delivered by one of the organization's Filipino crusaders.

A FILIPINO CRUSADER

Ben was one of these crusaders, the popular mission's head instructor. His job was to train the numerous members selected by the dioceses to lead the workshops during which the films were shown. These workshops took place in approximately twelve locations simultaneously, as there were twelve projectors. When this task was completed, the small team—consisting of Ben,

Larry the technician (who also worked in Ben's capacity by training people to run the projectors), and two, perhaps three, additional people (often priests)—moved on to another part of the diocese. Ben claimed that, depending on its size, they might stay up to a couple of months in one diocese to ensure that all the parishes had a chance to screen the film. Even though Ben was often present at a particular showing and could himself attest to attendance and the experience of the audiences, his main charge was to instruct the instructors.[81]

At once modest about the important role he performed for the mission and enthusiastic to talk about his experience, Ben confessed up front that he was an unwilling participant at first. A self-described "family man," he went to Catholic school and dutifully attended Mass, but in the Philippines that does not necessarily imply being an especially devout Catholic. Accordingly, Ben felt that he was not qualified, either spiritually or in his doctrinal knowledge, to lead the mission. When one of the local FRC leaders asked him to join, he refused. Even when Fr. Peyton himself called to cajole Ben into joining the mission, he declined, citing his responsibilities to his family, a plan in the works to migrate to the United States, and his lack of knowledge about scripture and the rosary. It was only after a portentous vision came to him in his sleep that he began to change his mind:

> I had a dream. Yeah, a dream of a lady with a child and the rosary. That's the first dream that I have: that the lady gave me the rosary. I woke up, I sat up, then extended my hand. It seems I am receiving the rosary. Then I sleep again.
>
> That same night, maybe early morning, the same lady with a child, she gives me a sack of *kamote*. And I find out there's lots of people lining up, different people, with the rich, the old, young, and poor. And every time that I hand out the *kamote*, it turns to gold. So I don't mind that dream.[82]

Thankfully, I had not immediately expressed what I assumed to be the meaning of his dream, for Ben continued:

> I told [a friend] about that dream, that I don't know how to interpret that dream. She told me, the dream is really the Blessed Mother through Fr. Peyton calling you. Then I have a confessor in Santa Cruz [a neighborhood of Manila], and I said to him, "Father, I had a dream I don't know how to interpret; it's bothering me." Then I told all the stories. He said, "That dream, the Blessed Mother really wants you to accept the rosary. Then when you extend your hands you're accepting." I told him too about the *kamote* . . . and he said, "*Kamote* is very common, but when you give it to people it turns to gold. So whatever you say, they're getting the full meaning."[83]

Ben summed up the interpretation thus:

> *Kamote*, it is very common food, for the poor, for any. But it turned to gold, they [his friend and his confessor] said, meaning even the way I talk, the way I express, the way I deliver, what I say it's gold to them. It becomes gold, like they get the message.[84]

Ben found the dream pleasant ("I don't mind that dream"), but he found not knowing its meaning troublesome ("I don't know how to interpret [it], it's bothering me"). The identity of the woman appearing in the dream was not obvious to him. Neither was the meaning of the dream. But it was enough of a message that Ben sought out the help of his friends and advisers to interpret it. What Ben knew was that the dream presented a set of signs that required translation. In this sense the dream was like the rally, summoning attention without necessarily conveying meaning—at least not without further mediation.

Even after conferring with his adviser and clarifying the message of the dream, Ben was still hesitant to join the popular mission. He couldn't believe that this flattering invitation was especially meant for him, a Visayan who was fluent in neither Tagalog nor English and by his own measure was "very, very poor in communication." Furthermore, and most important, he had a family to support, kids in private schools, and a new baby. It was only when one of the directors of the FRC and his own brother offered to support him financially that he agreed to join the popular mission. Gold may have been his layman's word transformed by divine inspiration, but it was money that saved Ben from his layman's concerns.

The status of "layman" is worth looking at here, for one of the things Ben repeated was Fr. Peyton's insistence that he was an ideal candidate for spreading the devotion of the rosary precisely because he was a "layman" (in our conversation this term remained in English). Ben's dream about the *kamote*, a common food, confirmed this for all who encouraged him to get involved. Through this curious semantic twist, "layman" came to mean one who was exceptionally chosen to do God's work and one who possessed a superlative capacity for communication. This capacity was as much about translation as it was about straight talk: only after translation made the *Life of Christ* films meaningful to the Filipino family, only through metaphor, could "meaningful" and "contemplative" prayer be achieved.

To teach sincerity in prayer, Ben would present the example of the child who spouts "I love you" over and over without reference or context versus the child who says it infrequently but from the heart. To teach the lesson of forgiveness in the last of the sorrowful mysteries, Ben would describe a scenario of the *lasenggo* (drunkard) and *babaero* (womanizer) husband stumbling home to a wife who could choose either to chastise him or to accept his failures. For the women in the audience, Ben would draw a comparison between Mary, all mothers, and the mother hen who gathers her chicks beneath her wings while they sleep to keep them safe from snakes and frogs.[85] All of his comparisons were devised to resonate with what was imagined to be everyday life in the barrio. But translation meant more than just extracting lessons that ordinary people could relate to from the formula of rosary prayer and *The Life of Christ*. From Ben's first foray with the popular mission it meant speaking in languages that were not his native tongue, which was Ilonggo. In addition to Tagalog and English, in both of which he was perfectly conversant but denied as "his own," before he gave his first seminar, he was provided a crash course in Cebuano, the majority language of the Visayas region. "So that you are one of them, so that they can understand," he explained as his motivation.[86]

In the course of our conversation, Ben spoke in numerous registers. He moved between English and Tagalog, settling for the most part somewhere in between, but he also switched back and forth between description and performance, and between recalled or reported speech and direct instruction, as if he were once again before an audience of potential enthusiasts. Corresponding to these registers was an oscillation between analysis and emotive emphasis. He would break down the prayers of the rosary to ensure that the meaning and reference of every single line was understood, but he was just as likely to dispense a heartfelt illustration or saying. This, I concluded, was what made him an effective preacher, at once thorough and appealing to feeling.

At the same time, these sometimes improvisational, sometimes wellscripted attempts to translate, or localize, the message of the *Life of Christ* were circumscribed by the fixed format in which viewers were instructed to watch the films. This structure was standardized across the FRC's popular missions worldwide, as evident in the guide, published in numerous languages, used by instructors.[87] The structure was as follows: Before each mystery, the leader was to provide an introduction that both summarized where viewers were in the narrative and advised them of what was to come in the next mystery. Viewers were asked to watch for certain actions or dispositions among the characters: "Pay attention to how delighted Mary and Joseph appear in the stable," "You're about to see Christ standing before Herod and Pilate," and so forth.[88] Once the film section (i.e., mystery) was shown, the instructor would then offer an explanation (*paliwanag* in Tagalog) of what they had just seen.[89] It was at these junctures that Ben and other instructors would clarify the emotive aspects or moral decisions in the film to their viewers—but not before training them in a kind of visual literacy via the discursive framing of each section of the film's narrative. From the perspective of instructors like Ben, this literacy was crucial in encouraging Filipino Catholics to perform the rosary *properly*. For these missions were not about converting non-Christians to Catholicism but about teaching Catholics to be more orthodox. As Ben put it: "We explain that the rosary is the living Bible—if you meditate. I think it was Paul VI who said that if you pray the rosary without meditation, *katulad ng ating katawan walang espiritu*. Like a body without a soul."[90] Larry, one of the FRC technicians, echoed this: "Everyone knows how to say the rosary, but they lack meditation [*ang kulang, meditation*] . . . When they see the film, everything is made clear to them [*maliliwanagan sila*]. So that when they do the rosary, they can imagine everything that's happening like it does in the film [*Kaya pag nag-rorosaryo sila, maiimagine na nila na ganoon ang nangyayari*]."[91] Not just prayer, but proper prayer, was the overall goal of the popular mission.

One of the great ironies of the popular mission, and the rosary crusades in general, was that it attempted to inculcate sincerity in the praying subject using media whose form and content were sometimes at odds, be it the pledge card, which amounted to sheer statistics, or *The Life of Christ* in a foreign language. Perhaps the most obvious example of this was the famous slogan "the family that prays together, stays together." Although translated in the Tagalog handbooks for instructors as *ang mag-anak na dumadalanging sama-sama, mananatiling magkakasama*, my sense is that, in actual use in the field, the slogan was immune to translation. I lost track of the number of times Ben used the English phrase in our conversation, it so frequently anchored his many anecdotes and explanations. On the one hand, this appeared to be a rhetorical technique, returning again and again to a memorizable principle, to repeat it like a mantra. On the other hand, the phrase was essentially a jingle, and as such, it served as a kind of commercial inserted between the different mysteries of the rosary, like advertisements during a television broadcast. The more Ben repeated this slogan, the more the crassness of its sales pitch sounded out of tune with the sincerity of his conviction.

It was only when, in an unguarded moment, the motto failed to convince even him that the force of prayer—rather than the forceful marketing of prayer—was felt. Toward the end of our conversation, Ben related an inter-

view conducted on a radio program in Cotabato (Mindanao) while he was
on the mission:

> [The radio interviewer] said to me, "So while you are preaching about the
> family—the family that prays together, stays together—er, how can you be here?
> Here you are, preaching about the importance of the father in the family. So
> what are you doing here? How could you [leave your own family?]"[92]

Only then did I begin to understand what Ben was referring to when he said
earlier, without elaboration, how he endured many "trials" (*pagsubok*) while
he was on the mission. I asked him if this separation from his family was
one of the trials he had mentioned earlier:

> Yeah, that was a big one, because while I was in Mindanao my wife got sick.
> They thought it was breast cancer. There I was in Cotabato, and for three days
> was she unable to eat. My daughter, who was grade two, I think, grade three, she
> went on a Wednesday to church to say a novena. It was raining, and my wife
> said, "Don't go already." But they went there and she [the daughter] said to the
> Blessed Mother, "Mama Mary, my mama is our mama *and* our father. You sent
> my daddy to Mindanao to spread the rosary, so I want you, Mama Mary, to tell
> your son to make my mom better when we get home." So innocent, eight years
> old! When she got home, she said, "Mama, you're gonna get better. Papa Jesus
> will heal you through Mama Mary." That's one trial as I was saying to you ear-
> lier. [He pauses.] But it's OK . . . You just go about your mission and don't talk
> about it to other people. [He falls silent.] It's OK, that . . . you know . . . just . . .
> prays together, stays together.[93]

Here the FRC motto rang incomplete. Yet it was precisely in this pause,
what I took to be a momentary eruption of self-doubt, that hope was recol-
lected against the shadow of real loss. For immediately after this, Ben bright-
ened as he relayed how this prayer, almost admonishing, cast out by his
daughter, who knew neither the right formula nor the proper deportment,
had worked. The day after the eight-year-old set about bargaining with Mary,
his wife began to eat, and the lump in her breast disappeared.

The history of the Family Rosary Crusade in the Philippines is a history of
localization in the age of the mass media. Despite the highly organized and
bureaucratic structure of its programs and the uniformity of its materials,
the organization called attention to what Oliver Wolters termed "local statements," through the process of translation and other adaptations to local
contexts on the ground. Local concepts of family, structures of belief, as

well as attitudes or experience with technological media are among these statements. These local features attenuated some of the FRC's overarching goals, such as that of fighting communism, because they averted ideological concerns in favor of more phenomenological experiences: what it was like to participate in a pledge drive, to be in the midst of a mass gathering, to encounter film for the first time.

At the same time, the crusades gave rise to a new subject in the history of Christianity in the Philippines, the Filipino "crusader" who, invested in orthodoxy and backed by the authority of a global organization, would make it his mission to propagate devotion to Mary among his fellow citizens. The crusades also transformed the mediascape of Manila, if not the entire Philippines, as their campaigns increasingly occupied visual space not only through the spectacles of rallies and films (the popular mission ended in the late 1980s) but also through public advertising, radio, and television programming. Although strict government control over the media during the years of martial law (1972–81) meant little airtime for the organization, the end of the Marcos regime brought a new era for broadcasting, and by the end of the 1980s, the FRC had acquired its own broadcasting equipment. To this day, it produces regularly scheduled Catholic-themed radio and television programs, documentaries, and public service announcements, such as the long-running spot of Mama Mary who appears, asks people to pray, and signs her name.

CHAPTER SIX

Coincidence and Consequence

The time is July 2004, nearly three years after September 11, 2001, and the Philippines is a member country of the "coalition of the willing" in the U.S.-led occupation of Iraq. On July 7, Angelo de la Cruz, an overseas Filipino worker (OFW) who drives trucks for a Saudi-based firm, is abducted near Fallujah. On July 8, a videotape is released showing de la Cruz surrounded by masked men calling themselves the Khalid ibn al-Walid Brigade. The men threaten to behead him should the Philippine government refuse to withdraw its fifty-one military personnel within seventy-two hours.

In response to the kidnapping, Philippine presidential spokesman Ignacio Bunye declares that Malacañang (the name of the presidential palace and shorthand for the administration) is resolute in its original plan to keep the Filipino troops in Iraq until August 20, the mandate's original expiration date. The soldiers are instructed to remain on active duty. Under the orders of President Gloria Macapagal Arroyo, Philippine labor secretary Patricia Santo Tomas puts an immediate halt to processing any contract workers destined for Iraq.

On July 10, the last day before the deadline, the television network Al Jazeera broadcasts a video of de la Cruz making his "final plea" to the Philippine government to withdraw troops. Although the administration does not disclose any further details of the kidnapping to the public, late in the night of the same day, in a national television newsflash, Santo Tomas announces that de la Cruz has been released and is en route to Baghdad. Although the source of this information in unnamed, and the release of de la Cruz still not verified by the Department of Foreign Affairs, President Arroyo confirms the news with a text message sent to de la Cruz's family in the province of Pampanga, assuring them that their father will soon be home.

Both leaders have spoken too soon.

Within hours, de la Cruz's captors, balking at the international media frenzy surrounding the premature announcement, state that he is still in their custody. Although they extend their original deadline by an additional forty-eight hours and change their demands from immediate withdrawal of troops to a promise to remove all personnel before July 20, their threat to take de la Cruz's life still stands. The Philippine government refuses these new conditions, insisting that it will maintain its original pullout date of August 20. The next day, the kidnappers report that de la Cruz has been moved to a place of execution.

Caught between Washington and a nation clamoring to have its native son return, Arroyo issues an ambiguous commitment to the Iraqi group: they will order the removal of Philippine troops but will give no specific date as to when the actual departure will take place. Then, desperate to avoid further diplomatic humiliation and citing the extreme delicacy of the situation, Malacañang institutes a news blackout on all its dealings with the hostage crisis.

On July 14, the very day after the blackout is imposed, there are reports that 250 kilometers north of Manila, in the cathedral of Baguio City, a statue of St. Thérèse is shedding tears of blood. The first to witness the weeping image is a young man named Christopher Fergis, who noticed the trickle the day before as he knelt praying the rosary before it. Although the cathedral is not his regular parish, Fergis tells reporters that he was drawn there after dreaming of the Virgin Mary for several days in a row. While it is unclear, according to his statements, if Mary imparts any specific messages in these appearances, he claims: "When I was in front of the St. Therese statue, I heard voices coming from nowhere . . . telling me we should pray for unity and pray for our leaders."[1]

Fergis is not the only one who draws an overt link between the hostage situation and the alleged miracle. Other witnesses to the bleeding image confess that they also spent recent days praying for de la Cruz's release. The mainstream press likewise makes a connection between the two events, with such lead-ins as "While Catholic devotees prayed for divine intervention to help save the life of truck driver Angelo de la Cruz, a 26-year-old man reported seeing blood drip from the statue of St. Therese of the Child Jesus at the Baguio Cathedral."[2] Even the layout of several newspapers' front pages presents the miracle of the bleeding statue as if intervening in the political

FIGURE 6.1 Even in the layout of several newspapers' front pages, the miracle of the bleeding statue appears to intervene in the political drama. *Philippine Daily Inquirer*, July 14, 2004.

drama, taking up column space alongside news reports originally filed by Al Jazeera, features on nationwide protests and vigils, and editorial analysis of the administration's actions (figure 6.1).

As we have seen in other chapters of this book, religion, including extraordinary events of a putatively religious nature, often makes the news.

But there is something remarkable in this instance that deserves our consideration. In the timing of this particular miracle, we see an interaction between religion and the mass media that is structured not by a stable relation between content and form (i.e., the utilization of the mass media for the dissemination of religious or religion-related content) but, rather, by a relation of convergence and, moreover, substitution: where the mass media is silenced—and moreover, political mediation fails—religious mediation appears in its place.

In this chapter, I take up these matters via certain key events involving Filipinos at home and abroad. My analysis draws on more recent manifestations of Mary and devotion to her, especially as they reflect the resurgence of Marianism in the Philippines after the People Power revolt of 1986. At the same time, as evidenced by the opening scene of crisis, the purview of this chapter encompasses both the Philippines and Filipinos in the world. The chapter examines the ways in which religion and the mass media (both respectively and in conjunction) are heavily imbricated in the extensions of labor, transnational movement, global geopolitical conflicts, and the ever-present shadow of U.S. imperialism that helps define those. Indeed, by the end of this chapter I will have brought into relief, through seemingly unrelated events, several connections in the complex web of international alliances, national allegiance, and media spectacles that held Angelo de la Cruz hostage in its threads—even as one group alone claimed responsibility for his kidnapping. Rather than provide a strict account of what led to the hostage crisis, however, I use the lens of contemporary Marianism to historicize the associative paths that generate popular interpretations of crises and danger (such as that involving de la Cruz and that which he faced), as well as of the strategies of power and control to which those paths give rise.

I begin with a 1999 festival celebrated in honor of the Virgin Mary's birthday. Although the ethnographic treatment of the celebration may first appear as yet another example of the sort of convergence of centuries-old figures of Catholic mediation and modern technologies of the mass media that this book has already traced, my analysis seeks to elucidate how and why Filipino Marian devotees have "gone global" in the past thirty years and, by implication, how these devotional groups could serve as another junction in the state of affairs that include the kidnapping of Angelo de la Cruz. Whereas other chapters in this book are more linear, here I use multiple frames of temporal reference to find patterns and reveal connections that participants themselves have made among seemingly random phenomena. The chapter then concludes where it began, in the space opened up by miraculous intervention—the space where the kidnapping of one Filipino "everyman" is just one incident in a hostage crisis of global proportions, suffered by people of countless devotions and sustained by numerous convictions and creeds— which continues to define our present.

WORLD FLUVIAL, NOT GLOBAL FLOWS

It was September 2001, and in another part of the world, something catastrophic was taking place. I, however, was in Manila. And like any cellphone-wielding inhabitant of the metropolitan region, I heeded the text message the moment it arrived. It read: UR N TV! TURN 2 CH9. I turned, and sure enough there I was, on TV. But it was a different me, from what was then a not-so-distant past, standing beneath a tree on a bright fall afternoon in New York City. Other images filled the screen: a close-up of someone listening intently, a priest gesticulating on an outdoor stage, a statue of the Virgin Mary, a wide shot of a crowd on the green. Occasionally the TV would fill with the New York City skyline, and there, above the jagged edge of concrete and glass, the twin towers of the World Trade Center could be seen from the Brooklyn side of the East River.

The images reeling before me were from two years prior, in 1999, when a group of Catholic Marian devotees traveled from Manila to New York to orchestrate a lavish event in honor of the Virgin Mary's birthday: the World Marian Peace Regatta. On the grounds of Battery Park, a few hundred Catholics from all over the world convened for the celebration. There was a stage set up on the west edge of the green that was occupied by musicians, people leading the recitation of rosary prayers, visionaries swearing testimonies to what they had seen, and priests, theologians, and other Marian devotees. Throughout the day the crowd held its own steady rhythm, expanding during times when whoever stood center stage could not quite hold collective attention, contracting toward the stage when there appeared someone or something that could. Off to the side of the stage there were tables where one could purchase all sorts of religious items and browse through books with titles like *In Our Days: Mary's Prophecies on the Last Years of the 20th Century*, *Satan's Answers to the Exorcist*, and *A Scientist Researches Mary Mother of All Nations*. Displays were set up before which one could ponder images of angels and saints, the unborn, and Pope John Paul II leaning on his staff, digitally superimposed on a misty forest background, among a candy-colored field of tulips, or at the edge of the Grand Canyon.

The main feature of the celebration, that which gave the event its name,

FIGURE 6.2 A pageant of Marys. Photograph by Loren Ryter.

was a fluvial parade of images of the Virgin Mary. The images came from all over the world—France, Holland, Ireland, Japan, Mexico, Spain, and the Philippines, among other countries—some by boat, some by car, one even by plane, I was told, taking up an entire row of business-class seats. It was a most incongruous scene, this pageant of Marys, each one perched on a single pedestal, dodging shadows cast by New York City's Financial District (figure 6.2). At a designated hour they were carefully loaded onto speedboats and leisure crafts. Lined up in flotilla formation on the Hudson River, they proceeded around the tip of Manhattan to the United Nations. There, the icon of global citizenship was consecrated to Our Lady of All Nations.[3]

The images of Mary brought, flown, and carried to Battery Park doubly signified. They were iconographic signs of the Holy Mother at the same time that they indexed their nationalized places of origin: Our Lady of Guadalupe from Mexico, Our Lady of La Salette from France, Our Lady of Akita from Japan, and so on. As such, the procession of Marian images along the tip of Manhattan appeared as much an envoy of national emblems as a parade of religious symbols, convening together in a cosmopolitan sphere. Furthermore, the great effort it took to bring these images together (often mentioned by the speakers at the event in terms of hardship), the distance the images and their caretakers had to travel, and an emphasis on the images' and participants' journey, suggested a pilgrimage of sorts, one that projected a particular world picture that privileged the United States as a singularly significant destination.[4]

But whose world picture was this? Despite the centrality of such symbolically significant sites as the United Nations to the stated aspirations of the celebration, it was not in New York, but Manila, that I first learned of the World Marian Peace Regatta. In the *Philippine Daily Inquirer* a brief article announced the celebration a few weeks before it was to take place.[5] The regatta was dreamed up by a woman named Maria Luisa Fatima Nebrida, also known as "Baby," a Filipina born, raised, and currently residing in Manila. It was her devotional organization, Mary's Army to Save Souls (MASS) Media Movement, that planned and executed the entire event. As I would later note at the celebration, the participants and attendees of the celebration were not all Filipino or Filipino American, but the salient presence of Filipinos was often remarked upon. Thus, for all its global pretenses, the World Marian Peace Regatta unwittingly called attention to the particular attributes of Filipino Catholicism. By presenting a picture of the world in which nations appeared representable by figures of the Virgin Mary and the United States existed as the "center" (in the words of the head organizer herself), the event stood not only as a religious celebration but also as the articulation of a certain Filipino imaginary.

This imaginary is deeply class based, rooted in a history of the migration of professional, middle-class Filipinos to the United States from the mid-1960s through the 1980s, and in the transnational networks of immediate and extended kin that ensued.[6] Nebrida's own life history reflects this, as she has spent the past forty years going back and forth from the East Coast of the United States to Manila for employment opportunities, family, and love. During an interview in Manila, two years after the World Marian Peace Regatta, Baby Nebrida recounted her adult life as a flurry of jobs and professional achievements, relationships that were made and broken, and a faith that would wax and wane. She also noted the dangerous environment of martial law under the Marcos regime, which led her to seek political asylum in the United States in the 1970s and, ultimately, to migrate.

The "turning point" in Nebrida's conversion took place while on a pilgrimage tour to the shrine of Our Lady of Montserrat in Spain. Kneeling, she said, at the same spot where St. Ignatius of Loyola had knelt nearly five hundred years before, she heard a man's voice telling her, "FIGHT FOR ME." "That's when the army thing came," Nebrida affirmed, "that we have to start an army, we are Mary's army, because the commander in chief, the one that's going to crush the head of the serpent is really Mary."[7] We are at war, she interpreted the mysterious locution to have declared: "When you wake up in the morning, there's a battle, a spiritual battle all the time."[8] Having spent most of her professional life working for the press, as a screenwriter, or in media production, Nebrida knew then that her role to play in this war would be that of propagandist.

Soon after, the MASS Media Movement was born, and then the World Marian Peace Regatta. Any incongruity or contradiction between the movement to wage battle and the event to promote peace was overlooked, and perhaps reasonably so, given that the former was framed as taking place in the realm of the spiritual and the latter in a worldly domain. At the event in Battery Park, however, it was not immediately clear how Nebrida's marshaling of the media for devotional work was to intersect with the more traditional format of the religious procession. I discovered this conjugation of religious mediation (in the replicated figure of Mary) and the mass media when, seeking momentary refuge from the crowd, I headed toward the periphery of the congregation. The mass of devotees did not thin out to a grassy respite but instead gave way to the conspicuous presence of equipment and a few small clusters of "techies." Stereotypically blasé, these technicians had spent the entire day perched on clunky scaffolding, supervising, and operating the cameras, lights, and speakers that had been taking in the scene. They were documenting the entire World Marian Peace Regatta as it took place in New York and beaming it live via satellite back to the Philippines.

Thus, on the one hand, we had the symbolism and world picture I outlined before: each image representing a nation, converging at the "center" of the world, with a big deal made of the distance they needed to travel, the importance of the physical location of New York City, and so forth. On the other hand, the deployment of the mass media simultaneously portrayed and undermined the temporal and spatial continuum that dictated these symbolic movements. But that was not all. For the capture of the images and the event on video secured their transmission to posterity. The images of the Battery Park event could and would play again—someday. And this in fact they did, in the wake of an event that would happen at the same place and on the exact same date as the World Marian Peace Regatta, only two years later, when the twin towers of the World Trade Center fell on September 11, 2001.

THE WOMEN OF MARY'S ARMY

Baby Nebrida's enlistment into Mary's Army reveals several compelling dimensions of contemporary Filipino Marian devotion, some of which have been examined elsewhere in this study, some of which require elaboration. For one, the location of Nebrida's mysterious encounter underscores the supranational dimension of Marian devotion in the Philippines as it has evolved over the past few decades. It was not in the Philippines that Nebrida received her inspiration but while on pilgrimage at the shrine of Our Lady of Montserrat in Spain, one of the most popular shrines in all of Europe, renowned for its place in the history of the powerful order of the Society of Jesus (the Jesuits). Indeed, when Nebrida heeded the call to wage spiritual battle she placed herself, quite self-consciously, in relation to the great founder of the order, Ignatius of Loyola, who was said to have laid his military vestments at Our Lady's feet, exchanging a life of worldly achievement for one of penance and asceticism.[9]

Yet even as the militant tone of "Mary's Army" might hearken back to the context of Counter-Reformation out of which the Society of Jesus emerged, Nebrida's experience of revival drew as much from modern Marian apparitions as it did from moments in the life of St. Ignatius. During our interview in Manila, right after she described the voice at Montserrat, Nebrida described the "dancing sun" that followed her and four of her fellow pilgrims to Portugal and back to Spain. She gave no explanation of what it might have meant, except to note that others in her group could not see it and might have thought her crazy. She assumed, in other words, that I knew to interpret the occurrence as a particularly Marian sign, an endorsement of the command that hounded Nebrida throughout her trip. Indeed, solar manifestations in which the sun appears to spin, dance, or emit brilliant colors, or can be observed directly without harming the eyes, are distinctly associated with two twentieth-century apparitions of Mary: at Fátima, Portugal, in 1917, and in Medjugorje, today in Bosnia and Herzegovina, from 1981 to the present.[10]

These and other modern apparition events from around the world have shaped the devotional journeys of Filipina Marians like Baby Nebrida and the organizations they formed in the 1990s. Sometimes the advocations of Mary that came from these apparitions served as inspiration. In 1997, for example, Nebrida organized the first daylong celebration of the Virgin Mary's birthday (Araw ng Papuri sa Kaarawan ni Inang Maria, or Day of Praise for Mary's Birthday) with a fluvial procession of Marian images along the Pasig River in Manila. (It, too, was simultaneously broadcast and served as the model for the World Marian Peace Regatta in New York two years later.) After the event, Nebrida brought the image of Our Lady of Fátima— her namesake—home, whereupon it started to weep. "That's when the name 'Mary's Army' came into the picture," she said: "Mary's Army to Save Souls—

MASS—Media Movement."[11] Sometimes, as we have seen already, phenomena associated with other apparitions played out before the devotees. At the next birthday celebration for Mary in 1998, also held along the Pasig, rain threatened to ruin the event. Miraculously, at dawn, the skies opened and the sun rose, dancing, then transforming into a host. "Look at the sun!" one of Nebrida's collaborators exclaimed. "It's like Medjugorje!"

Past apparitions of Mary, attendant phenomena, and their corresponding images make up a repertoire from which interpretations of other phenomena draw. Yet to assume a kind of facile derivativeness at work misses the imaginative effort it takes to make connections between past and present, between the Philippines and other Marian sites, and what might be circumvented in the process. For example, I asked Nebrida if "Mary's Army" was an old designation, thinking that perhaps, given Our Lady of Fátima's inspiration, Nebrida was adapting the name from the Blue Army of Our Lady of Fátima. This was a highly successful apostolate founded in the United States in 1946, dedicated to spreading the messages of Fátima as part of a broader movement of Catholic anticommunist action.[12] Nebrida immediately responded, "No, the idea came from her [Mary]," pointing out how "'Mary' and 'army,' if you look at the letters, are the same."[13] Likewise, it was Mary who chose Marikina (one of the cities that make up Metro Manila, named for the eighteenth-century governor-general Félix Berenguer de Marquina) as the stopping point for the fluvial procession, since "Marikina" combines the words "Mary" and the Tagalog word for "mother," or *ina*.

As we have seen elsewhere, the belief that Mary chooses the spot at which she wishes to appear or have something take place in her name is nothing new. The specifically modern twist is how devotees like Nebrida navigate the epistemological terrain that lies between Mary's agency and what in a non-Marian world we might simply call coincidence. One of the recurring motifs in the stories told by Filipina upper-middle-class women like Nebrida who were called to serve Mary in the late 1980s and 1990s is that there is something too compelling to ignore in the connections and coincidences between words, names, numbers, and dates, and that these connections and coincidences ultimately bring one to Mary.

This was certainly Lydia Sison's experience. Sison was the cocreator of the now-defunct Rosary Theater, "the world's first animated diorama of the life of Jesus,"[14] which once occupied retail space in a posh Manila mall. Like Nebrida, she became fully involved in Marian organizations through a geographically circuitous route, via the apparitions of the Virgin Mary at Medjugorje.[15] "Without realizing it at the time," she told me, "I formed the first group [of Filipinos] that went to Medjugorje."[16] I often heard devotees frame their narratives with this assertion of the unbeknownst; it produced the effect of imbuing what followed with the sense of the foreordained. The year was 1987, and Sison was standing in line at the American embassy with her three sons. She ran into a former classmate, who apropos of nothing said, "You know, Our Lady is appearing in Medjugorje." Sison replied, jokingly, "What? Medju what? You know, if Our Lady is going to appear why is she going to appear in a place that's so hard to remember?" Two days later, at a relative's birthday party, another friend she had not seen in a while directed her to sit beside Fr. Rodger Fleming, an American priest and champion of the Medjugorje apparitions, who happened to be in attendance. Soon after this encounter, Sison traveled to the United States with her sons. They visited a friend, who, it turned out, had just arrived from Medjugorje. The friend played a tape for them of the "dancing sun," and Sison burst into tears. "My God, it's true!" she recalled. "You could see the image of Our Lady in the sun!" Ten days later she met an American who showed her a picture of Cross Mountain in Medjugorje, insisting that Sison had to go there.[17] Finally convinced, Sison went, leading a group of Filipino laypeople accompanied by a priest. For her, the road from skepticism to belief was paved with repetition.

Although it seems clear that at this moment there was already a burgeoning interest in Medjugorje among Filipinos at home and abroad, Sison told the story in a manner that suggested a string of incredible, yet meaningful, coincidences that took on the force of an injunction: you must go to Medjugorje. She heeded the injunction, and as she tells it, when she arrived, she was allowed into one of the rooms where Mary allegedly appeared, on the condition that she write about her experience for Filipinos when she returned to Manila. Sison was apprehensive as she was not the type to "run after people" and had implored Mary to "send the people" to her. Yet she did her part to solicit interest by writing an article about the apparitions of Mary at Medjugorje that was published in at least two English-language papers. The article garnered so much interest that invitations for her to talk about her experience flooded in. According to her, in the years immediately following her 1987 pilgrimage, she gave talks to upward of two thousand people at a time, in venues from banks to schools to churches, and sometimes two or three talks in a day, crisscrossing the island of Luzon. The demand for such testimony shocked her—who would have imagined such enthusiasm? It was another instance of the unbeknownst.

Surprise at the sudden coalescence of signs or at the repetition of interest in Mary often catalyzed the devotional efforts of women like Nebrida and

Sison, who came (or came back) to Mary in the 1980s and 1990s. Interpreting this coalescence as a call to mission, they responded with the formation of Marian enterprises that made use of the "gifts" they already possessed. We might expect that such a call to mission would entail leaving one's home, and even, perhaps, one's nation.[18] But subtending these particular enterprises is a unique kind of internationalism not only instantiated by the various apparition sites that inspired the women but also generated by their own physical circulation and that of their peers. They moved as pilgrims, of course, but also as sojourning professionals, visa holders, and visitors to migrant friends abroad, long before their personal conversions. The logic of coincidence thus takes on an additional dimension here, as two ostensibly distinct worlds—that of pilgrimage and that of the movement of global Filipinos—converge.

Still, Sison's initially sarcastic reaction to the Medjugorje phenomenon is instructive. Upper- and upper-middle-class conservative Filipino Catholics have long held devotions to the Marys of established advocations such as Our Lady of Fátima and Our Lady of Lourdes. Taking a cue from her, why, indeed, would Filipinos of that status attend with such zeal the news that the Virgin Mary was appearing in a place that was barely on the edges of Europe, with a name that was so hard to remember?

THE DIALECTICS OF A MASS MOVEMENT

To begin to answer this question I turn to a 2012 article in the *Philippine Daily Inquirer* by June Keithley Castro, a well-known Filipina journalist who served as the emcee for the World Marian Peace Regatta in 2001. Written as a "gift" to Mama Mary on the occasion of Mary's birthday (celebrated on September 8), the article was Keithley's story of her conversion. It "started in Medjugorje," Keithley wrote, "and continues to this day." "A number of people who had come to visit me kept asking why I had become such a passionate Marian devotee. I have kept silent about this for almost 20 years, as I felt that there was so much more to say about the messages and history of Marian apparitions, and that what happened to me wasn't important."[19] In this opening, Keithley was referring to her prolific production of documentaries, articles, and books on apparitions of the Virgin Mary throughout the world, which included—recall from chapter 4—a full-length feature on the apparitions of Mary to a Carmelite novice in Lipa, Batangas. Indeed, before her death in 2013, Keithley was for decades the most visible and vocal champion in the Philippines of Marian devotion, dogma, and phenomena.

But Keithley was not only famous for her fervent Marian advocacy. In

1986, as Ferdinand Marcos's military loyalists tried to advance to the two military camps where his administration's major defectors, defense secretary Juan Ponce Enrile and the general Fidel Ramos were holed up with their own military men, Keithley took to a secret location and broadcast messages from Enrile and Ramos to the people to block the Marcos forces. For her role in the People Power revolt, Keithley was heroized, lauded with presidential honors and titles, and for a while most closely associated with Radyo Bandido (Radio Outlaw), the name given to the clandestine station.[20]

In her published conversion story, Keithley gestured to this political part of her past, curiously enough, with a scene that takes place on a train.[21] The year was 1987, and she was in Rome with her son, Diego, for the canonization of Lorenzo Ruiz, the first Filipino saint. There, her son was going to perform for the pope the role of Francisco in a play about the apparitions of Our Lady at Fátima (Francisco was one of the three child visionaries). But among the Filipinos in attendance, something else was afoot: "All the Pinoys [slang for "Filipinos"] were talking about going to this little village in Yugoslavia where Mama Mary was said to appear[,] . . . even urg[ing] me to change my plans and go with them. But I would have none of that! My first time in Europe would not be wasted in some poor village."[22] So Keithley and her son continued on with their scheduled itinerary, making their way to Geneva. On the train, she says, "Diego and I were in a compartment seated in front of an elderly couple, and the lady was reading a newspaper with 'Medjugorje' and a photo of a Marian image on the front page . . . The couple was from Costa Rica, and was thrilled to discover that we were Filipinos!" The Costa Rican couple exclaimed, "Oh, you have given hope to the world! Because of your People Power you have shown us that we do not have to go up in flames!" And Keithley concluded, "Of course, I got to borrow the paper."[23] By chance, right after Keithley shrugged off a group of Filipinos going to Medjugorje, a stranger in a train compartment happened to be reading about the apparitions allegedly taking place there. By chance, this stranger and her companion happened to be sitting across from one of the main figures in the peaceful revolt that forged a new paradigm for popular movements the world over. But for Keithley, at least in retrospect, this point of communion was but a vehicle to obtain more information about the intriguing apparitions of Mary in the Yugoslav village.

When I conducted a lengthy interview with June Keithley in 2007, she spoke more forthrightly about the role that the People Power revolt (also known as EDSA, or Epifanio de los Santos Avenue, the main highway where it took place) played in her conversion. She started by talking about her mother, whom she adored and described as "loving" and "wonderful":

That was what I wanted to be for my son. And so I did what I did in EDSA precisely because I knew that I had to do something. If not, where would my son grow up? Would he grow up in the States in a culture that I thought was not Filipino? That wasn't mine? As much as I may be American in the way I speak, the way I think and respond to stimulus, I'm really very Filipina. So I did what I did in EDSA precisely because I wanted a future for my son in this country. And so, that's what he [referring to God], used. And it was at EDSA, I guess you could say, that's where it [her conversion] began. Because I knew I could have died. I knew afterwards that they [Marcos's forces] were going to come and pick me up . . . So I was trying to bribe God, and I said to him at the last moment, "I know I cannot ask you for anything," at the moment just before I turned on the console to go on the air. It was the ultimate act of Marian surrender. I said to him, "I know I cannot ask you for anything; at this point all I can do is trust." And so I went on the air.[24]

What Keithley calls "Marian surrender" is meant to evoke the Annunciation, when the angel Gabriel delivered the message that Mary would bear the Son of God.[25] Before arriving at this submission to God's will, however, Keithley's spirited narrative instantiates themes common to the Marian conversions that took place either during or in the wake of the EDSA revolt, where motherhood and feelings of nationalism converged, and where one's own motherhood resonated with that of Mary's.

Take as another example of this the testimony of one woman who was at EDSA, described as a "wife and mother," and her recitation of the Hail Mary prayer:

Especially the part which goes "pray for us at the hour of our death." That seemed the same at that moment: "now . . . the hour of our death." I really knew then what that means to ask the Blessed Mother to be with me—will [sic] all of us—at the hour of our death.

She immediately followed with:

My deepest concern was for my daughter because she is so young, only 17. I looked at her with pain and said: She's only 17, and she is going to die. Then I also thought: But if she dies for the country, then it is a good way to die. I think a lot of people were there for the same reason.[26]

For this participant at EDSA, the words of the famous prayer rang uncannily precise to her experience in that moment. This was not performative speech, nor even a miracle, but another coincidence, one that gave rise to a collective "we," all of those ready to make the same sacrifice.[27]

Numerous publications and documentaries have revisited, sometimes critically, sometimes in celebration, the Marianism of the EDSA revolt.[28] Scholars have understood the Christianity of the event as continuous with its long legacy in the history of the Philippines and Philippine nationalism, and as having supplied a repertoire of narratives, symbols, and iconography that were deployed to liberatory, yet ultimately limiting, ends.[29] Catholic apologists, meanwhile, have proclaimed the event nothing short of a "Marian victory."[30] Supporting this perspective were a number of claims that the Virgin Mary appeared at EDSA to stop one of Marcos's tanks from reaching the defectors' camp. Perhaps in response to these claims, representatives of the church hierarchy issued more prudent statements that Mary's presence "did not come in the manner of Lourdes or Fatima or Guadalupe [because] [t]he millions of Filipinos at EDSA . . . believed she was already with them."[31] This belief in the presence of Mary during the revolt was so dominant that a colossal metal sculpture, *Our Lady of EDSA*, was constructed at the intersection where part of the revolt took place.[32] And much of the visual archive of the People Power revolt is complicit with this pious historiography, with numerous photographs taken of the event attesting to the ubiquitous presence of iconography of the Virgin Mary, protesters praying the rosary, and the like.[33]

The revival of devotion to the Virgin Mary in the past thirty years among some Filipino Catholics—especially Manileños of the middle and upper classes—owes a great deal, thus, to how people experienced the People Power revolt and participated in its construction as an event of divine inspiration, if not outright divine intervention. Yet this would hardly be the first time in the history of the Philippines that the struggle for regime change took place as a numinous experience.[34] What made the EDSA revolt distinct in this regard from past "popular uprisings" was the availability and adoption of a nonvernacular, generalizing rubric—that of the "Marian"—for summing up the nature of the event.

Thus, to understand the enthusiasm for the Medjugorje apparitions among Filipinos—an enthusiasm that, per my interlocutors' recollections, took off only in 1987—we must situate it in the local context of renewed devotion to Mary after the People Power revolt. At the same time, as I have just suggested, the sanctification of this revolt as "Marian" makes sense only in an internationalist arena of modern apparitions, their resultant devotions, and theological underpinnings. This dialectic is precisely what defines Filipino Marianism as a mass movement at the turn of the millennium.

Like all conversion stories, Keithley's was teleologically structured, so that incidences and events appeared driven in retrospect by destiny, giving the impression of the "unbeknownst." Approximately halfway through my interview with her, she returned to the subject of why she did what she did at EDSA. It was not over those days in February 1986, as she claimed previously, that her conversion truly began, but rather on December 8, 1985, at Luneta Park (one of the most important historical spaces in Manila and a common staging ground for mass rallies, such as those discussed in chapter 5), where more than two million Filipinos gathered to conclude what Cardinal Jaime Sin had declared as the Marian Year.[35] By this point in her life, Keithley had become a born-again Christian, but she insisted that her son Diego attend Catholic school and Mass. For his role as Francisco in the story of Fátima he stood front and center before the massive crowd with the cardinal and helped lead the rite known as the consecration to the Virgin Mary. This rite can take many forms, but it is a voluntary act of submission designed to renew one's faith, and it usually consists of a prayer in which those who recite it or those on whose behalf it is recited are wholly entrusted to Mary for protection and guidance.[36] Keithley said:

> I, as his mother, had one of the seats of honor behind the cardinal. I could not *not* read the consecration, because that was my son up there, *kawawa* [poor thing], my son . . . These are [just] words anyway [I told myself]. So I consecrated myself to Mary on December 8, 1985. Within weeks, a week or two, I began crying, crying everywhere, crying in the movie house, crying while I'm driving . . . Now I understand it's because I had consecrated myself to her. And so she took that consecration, used me, used my motherhood, because this was for my son and set that whole thing in motion, and in the end, it was good . . . Yes, God was able to do something for a nation. But my God, what was done for me![37]

Although the Marian Year was executed down the ranks of the hierarchy, from the cardinal through the dioceses and parishes, Keithley's personal experience demonstrated to a heightened extent how these Marian practices—how Mary—could work upon the laity. It is clear from the many stories of conversion I heard that this influence was felt most potently in relation to one's motherhood. And indeed, Keithley's competing claims regarding the true moment of her conversion encapsulates the politics of motherhood, and thus the politics of gender, in the Marian revival post-EDSA. In her first description, her "Marian surrender" is an extension of a prior, maternal will to sacrifice: "I did what I did in EDSA precisely because I wanted a future for my son in this country." In her modified narrative, she is a passive recipient of God's beneficence, a mere conduit for other transmissions. The women of Mary's Army have waged battle using the instruments they know best: the mass media. But they have done so in their capacity as instruments, their mediatic power circumscribed by male agents of the church.

PARABLES OF THE PROSTHETIC

Returning to the World Marian Peace Regatta, we witness in its setup and execution an interaction between Mary and the mass media that comes closest to that of instrumentality: the media is not yet the message. Yet it was not only in the simultaneous transfer of the religious images and messages of the event via satellite that the technological reproduction and transmission operative in the mass media was utilized. Here I turn to one segment of the celebration that illustrates the capacity of mass-mediated transmissions to actually intensify, if not provoke, religious experience. To fully appreciate these effects, I must first provide the backdrop against which this partial enabling of divine presence could take place.

So, to begin again, it is September 11, 1999, and the World Marian Peace Regatta is under way on the grounds of Battery Park, at the south end of Manhattan (figure 6.3). Fr. Jerry Orbos has just taken his place at the podium before the crowd. Highly charismatic, deep dimpled, with a voice like a DJ on the midnight shift, Fr. Jerry is extremely popular among Marian groups in Manila, and he is familiar to the middle-class readership of the *Philippine Daily Inquirer* for his weekly column, *Moments*. He is representative of Filipino priests who preach by appealing to sentimentality, professing a relationship to the Virgin Mary that is far more personal than theological. The exempla he employs in his homilies and talks about Mary are always emotional stories of mother love and sacrifice in which congregants can see themselves reflected as either mothers or children, or both. His mode of transmitting scriptural messages is thus one driven by the imperative to provoke identifications between his listeners and Mama Mary, mediated by the subjects of his tales.

On this particular day at Battery Park, Fr. Jerry cheerily began his talk by giving praise for being "still alive at this moment." He then asked everyone in the congregation to turn to their neighbor and tell him or her, "I'm happy you're here, I'm happy you're alive." Throughout this first part of his address he frequently paused, requesting that the listeners give rounds of applause to Mama Mary. At these moments he referred not to any particular image but merely to "her presence," which we, the congregation, found ourselves "in." After a few more brief acknowledgments, and having warmed up the crowd with his informal jocularity, he began to tell a story:

FIGURE 6.3 World Marian Peace Regatta, September 11, 1999. Photograph by Loren Ryter.

This is a story about a little girl who was born minus one—minus one ear. And this girl was growing up, she was very shy because she was very insecure because of that defect, and people were always laughing at her. She was always hurt, but there was also one person who was always hurt seeing that little girl. This, of course, was the mother. I mean, which mother would like to see their child hurt? And according to this story, on her eighteenth birthday, the mother said, "My dear child, everything is ready, we're going to the hospital." And according to this story, the girl had an ear transplant operation, according to this story. And it was very successful, according to this story. And from that moment on, she became a very happy person, she met the man of her dreams, and to cut this story short, she was getting married. The night before the wedding, she went to her mother and said, "Mama, tomorrow I'm getting married, and things are unfolding so beautifully in my life!" And according to this story, she embraced her mother so tight, but when she embraced her mother, she felt something very strange. For the first time she found out that her mother no longer had one ear!

[*Small gasps resounded throughout the crowd.*]

And she never knew. And she said, "Mama, you never told me it was you who gave your ear to me, and there were so many times in the past I hated you,

I shouted at you, I took you so for granted, I never knew how much you have sacrificed for me."

[At this point an elderly Filipina turned to me and, placing one hand on my fore-arm squeaked, "That's the love of a mother!"]

Dear friends, especially you mothers who are here, you know how it is like to love a child and how painful it is when the child grows up, hurting you, shouting at you, cursing at you. This is the story of each and every one of us, in many ways, towards our own mother Mary.[38]

Fr. Jerry opened with repeated reference to the "story" as a mode of en-framement. In doing so, he elevated the story to the level of the general rather than the particular; as a result, the truth of the story became immaterial. This is not to say that the details of this story were unimportant, but that bringing the story frame into constant relief converted the details into terms for which one could substitute one's own details. This is the strategy of all effective homilists, that of establishing structures that enable resemblances, so that, as Fr. Jerry declared, one can ultimately apprehend this story as "the story of each and every one of us." In this case, the "I" of the listener could substitute him- or herself into this story frame—as the parent or the child of the story, or both—as well as perceive his or her relationship to Mary as bearing the elements of another story, that person's own. With the goal to provoke identifications, Fr. Jerry's oral performance encircled its listeners in a narrative hall of mirrors. Yet this was not the only way in which substitution asserted itself. Let us not forget that this was, after all, a story about a transplanted ear. Read closely, the story reveals as much about the limits of substitution as its possibilities.

The daughter in the story bears a foundational defect. And although grafting her mother's ear performed a certain degree of restoration, the corporeal unity of the daughter would always be supplemented by the foreign flesh. The grafted ear may make the daughter appear, and perhaps even feel, whole, but it would always stand as a reminder that she once was not. Even if the mother gives with neither desire nor possibility for return, her sacrifice is incapable of bringing about a total reversal of her daughter's condition. Put another way, the mother can give up the ear for her daughter, but she can never give in a way that takes away her daughter's once having been without an ear. Hence the new ear, although an object of sacrifice, locates the limit of sacrifice in the uncanny overlay of imperfect substitution.[39] The congenial will never take the place of the congenital, no matter how much they look alike.

The prosthetic ear draws attention to another implicit truth. The daughter, although earless, was never "hearless." She never lacked the auditory sense of perception. Bearing this in mind, we can see the grafting procedure as (re)marking an already-denaturalized relationship between sense perception and the physical organ of that perception. Moreover, we can see how the transplant, in fact, exacerbated this alienation. The cost of the fleshly protuberance was precisely the failure, if not of hearing, then of receptivity, in this case to the mother, who henceforth suffered her daughter's hatred and neglect. The moment the daughter realized the identity of the donor—that is, the moment she properly receives the gift through recognition—is the moment receptivity itself is restored. By receiving the gift, the prosthetic nature of the ear is realized as an artificial instrument of reception instead of the natural organ of hearing.

As previously noted, the intent to provoke identifications between the listeners of Fr. Jerry's tale and its characters effectively doubled the effects of what lay solely within the story frame. Those of us who listened to the story that day were suddenly made aware of our own ears and the figurative deafness that might afflict us in relation to another's generosity.[40] With heightened awareness of this particular mode of perception—ears burning—passive hearing became active listening, which became more than just paying attention. With our ears like receivers tuning in, listening became a mode of anticipatory response to sounds and signals—most especially from the mother—yet to arrive. And arrive now she would.

Here is what happened next at Battery Park. Having thus declared that the story told was our own, Fr. Jerry concluded by asking the congregation once again to acknowledge Mama Mary by giving her a big round of applause:

> Thank you, Mama Mary, for being here!
>
> Dear friends, I would like to end with a simple prayer for all of us. There is a song from Mama Mary for all of us here. And she's asking all of us to pray. Right now, I'd like to ask you all to bow your head in prayer, and I invite you now dear brothers and sisters, to put your right hand over your heart, and close your eyes in humility. Let Mama Mary bless you now, in a very special way. Listen and pray, listen to your mother.

About midway through this final benediction, music faded in over PA systems that had been placed along the perimeter of the audience. It was a simple tune, a lone woman's voice accompanied by a single acoustic guitar, singing: "I am here. I am your mother. Do not fear, for I am here." The discursive mode shifted radically from that of narration to one of mimesis. Whereas Fr. Jerry's strategy was to surround the audience with a narrative hall of mirrors, the initial effect produced by being enveloped by Mary's voice was the foreclosure of reflexivity. Unlike the rest of the music performed that day, for this song there was no musician or singer on stage. There appeared, in other words, no body to which this sweet voice could properly belong. This absence lent the voice a distinct quality of being everywhere and nowhere, an enveloping field of sound. I watched as the crowd grew silent and contemplative, lulled by the disembodied voice of this female "I" that came, truly, from out of the blue. At first, during Mary's lullaby, the response of many people in the audience seemed to be one of introspection. Following Fr. Jerry's instructions, congregants sat with their eyes shut and their hands over their hearts, giving physical gesture to this containment.

Weeping is the utmost expression of emotional ambivalence. When a number of women and men started weeping silently, it was impossible to know at the time whether this response expressed blissful relief found in the voice of Mary or mournful acknowledgment of its simulation.[41] Like the transplanted ear of the girl in Fr. Jerry's story, the audiotape-recorded voice of Mary that enveloped the crowd marked the limit of fully realizable presence. Although the song enabled a certain appearance of Mama Mary, it also bore within itself traces of dissimulation and inauthenticity.

Still enveloped in Mary's "I am here!" those who were weeping began crying aloud. I watched one woman, whose red hair and pink sweater had earlier exuded a cheery disposition, lift her head as her mouth dropped open, wailing openly, her shoulders shaking. For her and others who began crying audibly, something of a crisis seemed to arise, a rupture in their own sealed, interiorized experience. The externalization of weeping into crying out loud gave expression to a more articulate, more explicitly mournful, form. But what exactly was being mourned—the fantasy of the maternal voice, or the momentarily lost subject—was impossible to determine for sure.[42]

It was difficult to make sense of this outpouring of emotion until I took note of what happened next, when Fr. Jerry stepped in, as if to rescue the affected members of the audience from their free fall in this gap of indeterminacy. Drawing from his authority, Fr. Jerry brought the affected and distressed congregation back into the realm of the individual and the orderly by introducing, as he had done with the inspirational talk, the reflective field by means of which congregants could safely reestablish positions of subjectivity. Before the song ended, as the expressions of many in the crowd became audible and their outbursts of grief unbearable, Fr. Jerry began echoing the voice of Mary, his own now responding with "I am here!" Over the song he asked those in the congregation to turn to one another and declare, "I am with you. I am your brother [or sister]!" The weeping and wailing died down. Each "I" of the individual devotees established a symbolic frame that both marked and mitigated their collective separation from Mary's voice.[43]

The outcome of this was wondrous. No longer enveloped by Mary's voice, the audience opened up to receive external signs from her. Led by Fr. Jerry in singing "Immaculate Mother" (a traditional Marian hymn), the entire congregation was on its feet, raising their handkerchiefs high in the air, waving at the sky. There was a small commotion in the crowd as a couple of women started jumping up and down, heralding with cries and shouts the visible and familiar sign sent by Mary: the "dancing sun" that spun and shook. Exorcised by Fr. Jerry, the interior voice generated by technological fidelity cast itself out from the intimate realm of sound far away into the distant dominion of sight.

The transplanted ear, the tape-recorded voice, the television image—all prosthetic forms, they are offered or present themselves as substitutes for the "real" thing, for "real" presence. As substitutes they stubbornly retain something of those losses or absences that necessitate them. Such prosthetic forms are thus as distressing as they are restorative; they cause anxiety as much as they do relief. This distress and anxiety can be contributed in part to losses that took place, that have been placed, in the past, and that presently haunt the space of disjuncture or lack that the prosthetic form can never fully cover over, or overcome. But this is not all. For at least with the latter two of these forms, produced by means of electronic reproduction and as archival storage, posterity is their intended purpose. The present (presence) that the tape-recorded voice and the television image convey have been captured as future losses. The distress and anxiety provoked by the appearance of these forms expresses itself as dread or anticipatory fear. These appearances cannot but become, someday, echoes and visions recuperating and recollecting what will have passed. There is something thus vaguely prophetic in all prosthetic media, a foretelling of that which is unforeseeable in its specificity, of death that haunts from the future.

PROPHECY AND THE ASSURANCE OF PROTECTION

D new york n d Washington bombings were planned long ago nd d FBI now knows d mastermind. Dey r now hunting down NOSTRADAMUS.[44]

—TEXT MESSAGE CIRCULATED IN MANILA AFTER SEPTEMBER 11, 2001

"The current New York project is Mary's Army's [the MASS Media Movement's] biggest. The World Marian Peace Regatta is a prayer rally for peace in a world suffering from 40 wars at present. It strives to achieve peace through the protection of the Virgin Mary."[45] The souvenir program of the World

Marian Peace Regatta articulates this mission in several different ways, as it was the primary motivation stated for the ceremonial procession of Marian images and consecration of the United Nations to Our Lady of All Nations. It was also one of the justifications for holding the event on September 11, three days after the traditional date celebrated as Mary's birthday and three days before the opening of the General Assembly at the United Nations that was to take place that year, 1999.

Exactly two years later, the realization that might have seemed evident to many—that the ritual procession intended to invoke and secure Mary's shield of protection had catastrophically failed—was itself preempted by an alternate vision proffered by one Manila-based community of Filipino Marian devotees. For this group, the events of September 11, 2001, stood as evidence not of failure but of prophecy, in this case revealed by several internationally known European visionaries.

The community was organized around a weekly rosary prayer meeting, or as it was called, a cenacle.[46] My introduction to the group was first facilitated by several of the participants' own involvement with the World Marian Peace Regatta (some of them were relatives of the organizers), but my enduring interest was that this group represented all that seemed to have fallen in the blind spot of scholarship on Filipino Catholicism. Young, urban, professional, educated, upper middle class and upper class, the members of this group were the antithesis of the "folk" figured by "folk Catholicism," the paradigm that has long dominated studies on Filipino Christian devotion and experience.[47] They were not converts to the Marianism that flourished as a result of the People Power revolt but its inheritors. They were as likely to have made a pilgrimage to Lourdes, say, as they were to have frequented shrines to Mary in the Philippines. They closely monitored missives on prayer and doctrine that were dispatched by the Holy See at the same time that their devotional practices and spiritual exercises were sometimes influenced by the variant of charismatic Catholicism that has become more prevalent in the Philippines. It would not have been unheard of, for instance, to witness at one of these meetings a participant being "slain in the Holy Spirit," followed later by an in-depth dialogue on how the latest encyclical letter from the pope might affect the worldwide campaign to declare the fifth Marian dogma (more on this later).

Our prayers were in English, although the lingua franca of the group was the hybrid known as Taglish (Tagalog-English), with varied inflections that betrayed the elite schools that many members of this group had attended. The format of the prayer meetings always began with the recitation of the rosary, preferably while kneeling for all fifteen decades.[48] On completing the long cycle of prayer, there were readings from the thick tome referred to as the "Blue Book," a compilation of messages given by Mary to an Italian priest named Fr. Gobbi via "interior locution," followed by the singing of popular church songs in both Tagalog and English. The devotional part of the evening would conclude by saying grace for the often elaborate meal that would follow. At this point the gathering would take a markedly convivial turn of joking, *tsika* (small talk), and *tsismis* (gossip).

At one of the meetings after September 11, 2001, however, the light conversation that usually concluded our gatherings was replaced by exegesis of the recent events. One of the most active members of the group, whom I'll call Joel, had brought along to the meeting a hefty book titled *True Life in God*, comprising daily entries written by a Greek Orthodox woman named Vassula Ryden.[49] These entries are based on messages Ryden claims to have received, also via interior locution. Opening up to a page that was a photocopy of her handwritten diary, dated September 11, 1991, Joel read: "The earth will shiver and shake—and every evil built into Towers will collapse into a heap of rubble and be buried in the dust of sin!"[50] He went on to talk about how the date for the World Marian Peace Regatta was chosen not only for its being a weekend falling conveniently between Mary's celebrated birth date and the opening of the UN General Assembly but also because the famous Irish visionary, Christina Gallagher, received a message from Mary in July of that year saying that the event had to be on September 11, 1999.[51] He then relayed the oft-repeated vision that appeared to Gallagher in 1992, during her first visit to the Philippines, in which she saw Mary perched on a globe, crushing the head of a black serpent. This vision was tied to the divine message that Gallagher had received at the end of her visit: that the triumph of Mary's Immaculate Heart would begin in the Philippines and then spread throughout the world.

Even snippets from popular culture could not escape prophetic suggestion. Backing down from his own intensity with a chuckle, Joel added: "Even the scene in *Godspell* the movie, where Jesus and John are singing 'All for the Best.' The camera pans out to show that they're on top of the World Trade Center."[52] He then broke into song: "Some men are born to live at ease, doing what they please, richer than the bees are in honey . . ." Joel mapped out this constellation of foreboding signs as we listened with rapt attention. In the wake of the cataclysm, he was providing an interpretive framework that would already account for its occurrence. The impact of this retrospective reading was most tellingly registered when one young woman sighed into the conversation: "It is *so* nice to feel prepared, *di ba* [isn't it]?"

Of course, such recourse to prophecy in making sense of the destruction in New York, Virginia, and Pennsylvania was not limited to this context. Although told in jest, the text message that circulated among Filipinos after September 11, 2001, was just a local version of what many entertained as a broader realization of prophecy. What interests me here is the particular path of associations tethered to prophecy that this group drew, and the power that the connections exerted to sidestep the question of the efficacy of the World Marian Peace Regatta. Where ritual mediation failed, other media—mediums, rather—appear in its place: a woman who claims to serve, quite literally, as Christ's instrument and a visionary to whom Mary's mantle of protection over the Philippines had long been revealed. Especially suggestive is how this latter vision inverted the symbolism of the World Marian Peace Regatta. Whereas the celebration at Battery Park presented a Filipino imaginary of the world and the representability of its nations, the Irishwoman's vision acted as an extranational agent, proclaiming to (certain) Filipinos the place of the Philippines in a global order, divinely authorized, of Marian redemption.

MARIAN INTERNATIONALISM, THE FIFTH MARIAN DOGMA, AND THE PHILIPPINES

Throughout my fieldwork I was bombarded with names that neither sounded remotely Filipino nor seemed, per my admittedly spotty recollection, to be part of the canon of Catholic saints: René Laurentin, Fr. Gobbi, Maria Valtorta, Mark Miravalle, Vassula Ryden, Christina Gallagher.[53] These names sometimes came up in interviews I conducted, marking a shift in the conversation whereupon my interlocutor would school me in the persons or reference works they believed indispensable to my research. The names were sometimes spoken in prayer groups like the one described earlier, as authors of texts that were read as an integral part of our practice. At the World Marian Peace Regatta, some of these names even appeared as participants in the program of activities for the day. They are the names of Catholic mystics and theologians, mostly contemporary, whose visions and words are closely attended to by Filipino devotees who self-identify as "Marian." Indeed, these producers of spiritual and doctrinal knowledge are partly responsible for strengthening the very category "Marian" in the Philippine context in recent years. In some respects, this strengthening has been quite superficial, remaining at a nominal level. Appearing in their book titles (e.g., *The Message of Medjugorje: The Marian Message to the Modern World*, by Mark I. Miravalle), or in the names of their associations (e.g., The Marian Movement of Priests, founded by Fr. Stefano Gobbi), the term "Marian" has filtered into quotidian usage among Filipino devotees who consume these texts and follow these groups, especially as they have formed and titled their own apostolates and produced their own media.[54] Yet, as we have anticipated in this study, there is more profound semiotic work being performed when Filipinos employ this term.

The best example of this work is the World Marian Peace Regatta itself, especially as the souvenir program encapsulates it. In its pages the following phrases appear: "Marian songs," "Marian authors and leaders," "the entire Marian assembly," "Marian dogma," "Marian visions and messages," "Marian prophecy," "Marian movement," "Marian workhorses," "Marian messenger," "Marian apostolates," "Marian team," "Marian history," "Marian hymns," "Marian apparitions," "Marian feastdays," "Marian doctrine," "Marian core group," and, of course, "Marian images." The abundant use of "Marian" as a modifier betokens a process of generalization, making a type or genre out of what has been in historical actuality a vast array of phenomena, beliefs, and practices. In several instances here the term is also clearly used as a distinct reification of identity. But what exactly does it signal in terms of what Filipino Marians hold to be the truth, and object, of their devotion?

We can approach this question by examining the last of these phrases, as it appears as the heading "Participating Marian Images," on one of the program pages. Beneath this heading is a long list divided into three sections. The first of these sections lists images of Mary from around the world except the Philippines (e.g., Our Lady of Guadalupe, Our Lady of Knock, Our Lady of Lourdes); the second section lists images of Mary that represent either names bestowed upon her (e.g., Mystical Rose, Queen of Peace) or one of the four dogmas of the Virgin Mary (Immaculate Conception); the last section lists images of Mary unique to the Philippines (e.g., Our Lady of Manaoag, Our Lady of Antipolo, Our Lady of Lipa). The page reads like a lineup of sponsors; under the rubric of "Marian images" these titles take on the formal appearance of a series.[55] It is the opposite of the litany of descriptions of Mary that we saw at the beginning of this book, in the eighteenth-century account by Bencuchillo about the Virgin of Caysasay, where the effusive recitation of Mary's qualities precisely marks the impossibility of a full rendition (in both senses of the term, if we recall the plot of the apparition tale). It is, in other words, the opposite of poetry.

In this context, to elaborate further, the opposite of poetry is doctrine. And it is an interest in doctrine—and even in Mariology, the theology of Mary—that makes organizations like the MASS Media Movement so radically distinct from other Filipino Christian denominations and groups. Among the stated "objectives" of the World Marian Peace Regatta was to "clarify the powerful role of Mary, who suffered with the Redeemer, who mediates grace, who prays for humanity."[56] This statement spells out in ordinary terms the three titles of Mary that have most concerned groups like Nebrida's and those in her international network. These titles are notably not those that have emerged from localized apparitions (e.g., Our Lady of ——) but rather the somewhat abstruse titles of Co-Redemptrix, Mediatrix, and Advocate. Together, these titles and the roles to which they refer constitute what Marian groups call the fifth Marian dogma. Currently there exist four Marian dogmas, that is, truths about Mary that Catholics are, by definition, obliged to believe. Clarifying the roles of Mary as Co-Redemptrix, Mediatrix, and Advocate is thus equivalent to campaigning for the dogma's solemn declaration by the magisterium of the Catholic Church.[57]

To understand what is at stake in this dogma for Filipinos, we need to briefly consider the other four and consider what makes this potential fifth dogma distinct and desired. The four Marian dogmas are as follows: her divine motherhood (*Theotokos*), her perpetual virginity, the Immaculate Conception, and her assumption into heaven. The first of these two date back to the early centuries of the church; the third and the fourth, to 1854 and 1950, respectively. All of them relate the exceptional status of Mary among humans. The fifth dogma departs from these definitions in the virtual suggestion that in Mary, insofar as she shares in Christ's role as redeemer of humankind, a fourth person could conceivably be added to the cornerstone of Christian theology, the Trinity.[58] In blunt terms, as Keithley explained it to me, the fifth dogma "defines [Mary] in her relationship to you and me. She is now the link to Jesus."[59] Or, as I heard it articulated on several occasions: *Siya ang nagpapasok ng mga tao sa langit* (Mary is the one who gets people into heaven), just as she saved the day at the wedding in Cana when she ordered Jesus to turn water into wine. In short, what makes the fifth dogma especially significant to these Filipino Catholics is that it provides theological heft to something that everyone already knows to be true.

Where it manifests, thus, Filipinos' interest in the doctrines of Mary should be taken not simply to indicate a greater aspiration to be more orthodox but rather to shape orthodoxy in a way that will ultimately affirm the emphasis on Mary as utterly instrumental to Christ's salvation of humankind, especially as performed through her motherhood. The prophetic words of visionaries from around the world underscore this by depicting Filipinos as divinely chosen to carry out this mandate. Mary's message to Irish visionary Christina Gallagher, that the Philippines would be the place from which the triumph of her Immaculate Heart would spread, was foretold in another message from Mary received via interior locution by the Italian mystic Fr. Stefano Gobbi:[60]

> Look at this immense archipelago and see how my work has also spread here, in an extraordinary way . . .
> Look at the hearts and the souls of all these children of mine: they are so faithful to Jesus, so devoted to me, and so united to the Church. Through them the light of my Heart is spreading through all the countries of this continent . . .
> I have a great design on this people.[61]

Couched in the patronizing idiom that depicts Filipino Catholics as deeply loyal to both divine and temporal authority, this message nonetheless conveys the idea of election, of the chosenness of Filipinos in advancing Marian mission.[62] But this recognition doesn't just come from without, for before Mary spoke of Filipinos through the words of foreign mystics, she revealed herself plainly to a young Filipina nun, in a Carmelite convent in the town of Lipa, Batangas, when she announced, "I am Mary, Mediatrix of All Grace."

Although deeply rooted in local history, the 1948 apparitions of Mary to Teresita Castillo in Lipa also have a role to play in the global efforts of organizations like the MASS Media Movement. Mary's proclamation at Lipa serves to ratify the theological concept of Mary as Mediatrix, a capacity whose title has been in circulation since at least the eighteenth-century writings of St. Louis Grignion de Montfort (whose name also carries significant currency in Filipino Marian circles).[63] At the same time, seen from a contemporary perspective, Mary's self-identification as Mediatrix takes on a prophetic significance all its own, pointing to a future when the Philippines would generate the final push to bring about the apogee, and even apotheosis, of Mary through the proclamation of her fifth dogma.

OVERCOMING COINCIDENCE

In this chapter, I have attempted to illustrate some of the ways in which various forms of religious mediation and the mass media reveal their affinities, at times enabling or intensifying one another's transmissions and capacities for signification, at others rescuing one from the consequences of a breakdown in mediation. At the Marian event that took place in New York City in 1999, the imagined efficacy of Mary's capacity to mediate peace and provide protection to the world was intensified and, to a certain extent, enabled by the power of the mass media to extend the reach of those images beyond their physical location.[64] In the vignette of Fr. Jerry's sermon and the disembodied singing voice of Mary, we witness how technologies of sound reproduction enhance, even produce, religious encounter and experience. And in the prayer meeting after September 11, 2001, we see how some Marian devotees associated with the World Marian Peace Regatta managed the possible implications of ritual failure via recourse to the prophecies of other divinity mediating figures, notably foreign to the Philippines.

Yet haunting these descriptions is a force that I found much more difficult to contain, one thematized throughout this chapter. The coincidence of dates and locale between the festive celebration and the mass destruction of the attacks on the United States produced a shock that at once fed back into the mechanics of production and modes of reception I outlined, and exceeded them.[65] In this milieu of unsettling repetition, Marian devotion of the sort I have been describing would always retain a power of preemption, of prior appropriation of the meaning of events. This preemptive power should not be reduced to a mere providentialist orientation, nor worse, to the culturalist assertion that Filipinos simply believe in a highly interventionist God. It is, rather, a deeply social and politically concocted claim for oneself and one's community of the privilege of preparedness—to draw from the comment of the young woman in the prayer group. Part of this privilege comes from participation in what I have been describing as Marian internationalism: access to engagement and the exchange of theological knowledge and media with Marian groups all over the world, resources to travel to congresses and shrines abroad, and time free from labor to dedicate to practicing and propagating devotion. But in the context of the global Philippines, whose emblem is the overseas Filipino worker, part of this privilege comes from enjoying a fundamental exemption from harm, the forms of which are all too familiar: abusive employers, discrimination and alienation, and, in the past decade especially, getting caught in the unpredictable violence of war.

The connection, thus, between the World Marian Peace Regatta and the kidnapping of Angelo de la Cruz is not just a field of interlinked dates and consequences—many links that we now know were forged by gross prevarications advanced by the George W. Bush administration—that bring them into relatedness. It is rather that the phenomenon of transnational labor emblematized by the latter serves as the enabling Other of the former. The harrowing vision of the abducted de la Cruz burst forth onto the Philippine mediascape as a reminder of the possibilities for peril that the state—with its massive bureaucracy dedicated to smoothly facilitating the movement of Filipino workers worldwide and remittances back home—continually suppresses. The Marian world conjured by the staging of the World Marian

Peace Regatta represented an alternative vision of international movement that, I would argue, was unimaginable without the history of the migration of Filipino citizens, including the astounding acceleration in the past thirty years of the deployment of sojourning workers around the globe. Yet the lure, and perhaps efficacy, of this alternative vision depended on its being an idealization, one that disavowed the movement of biological bodies across time and space by putting in their place images of Mary, a figure of perfect humanity, precisely invulnerable to violence and decay.

IMMACULATE TRANSMISSION, OR
THE PROMISE OF PRAYER

Although of a kind with the mediating capacities of Mary that I have examined in the World Marian Peace Regatta, the miraculous appearances of the bleeding statue and the dream-vision of Mary in the wake of the abduction of Angelo de la Cruz urged a different response to the crisis. Although we still saw the logic of substitution assert itself—where the mass media and, moreover, political mediation fails, religious mediation appears in its place—perfect substitution was not fulfilled. The bleeding statue was an openly indeterminate sign, whereas the dream-apparitions of Mary did not relay messages that specifically informed of the hostage situation. What both visions conveyed, or rather, were interpreted to convey, were injunctions to perform another kind of communication altogether, that of *prayer*.

And pray everyone did, so it seemed. There were local and nationwide vigils. There were special Masses. On at least one television network, there was a type of public service announcement interlude that ran between every regularly scheduled program. In it, a lone male voice beseeched the Lord while the words of the prayer—in Tagalog—scrolled up the screen:

> Lord, we pray, protect Angelo de la Cruz from being beheaded. Soften the hearts of his captors, that they may be overcome with pity [*awa*] for Angelo. Free his family's hearts from fear, so that they may withstand this ordeal. Merciful Father, guide each step of our government, of our president, in deciding how to achieve Angelo's freedom. Angelo represents [*kumakatawan*] the hardships endured by the Filipino worker abroad. Please don't let him meet the same fate as Flor Contemplacion, eight years ago. Please don't abandon all of our family members in Iraq and in other dangerous places in the Middle East, we implore you.[66]

This prayer does not mince words. Although the language retains some flourishes of more formal conventional prayers, it blatantly states the present danger: the beheading of Angelo de la Cruz. The prayer is not coy in declaring what is at stake in this potential act of violence: in using the word *kumakatawan*, one that draws upon the literal image of the body (*katawan*) to describe Angelo's relation to other OFWs, the prayer extends a single circumstance of danger into a general condition. The prayer refuses forgetting, finally: in invoking the name of Flor Contemplacion, the Filipino domestic worker who, accused of murdering a fellow domestic worker and her ward, was executed by hanging by the Singaporean state in 1995, it provides a grim reminder of the reality that has troubled the state-produced narrative of OFWs as the nation's "new heroes" (*bagong bayani*). Indeed, we might see the prayer as a script for the viewing—and notably Tagalog-speaking—public to directly voice a comprehensive commentary on the situation, at the same time that it served as a religious response to it. Furthermore, by addressing itself directly to God, the response suggests a desire for transcendent immediacy, or perfect transmission: transmission without the fear of mishearing or missed connection, such as that which had so bungled the hostage situation.

Three days of the media blackout passed before Arroyo finally broke her silence, ordering the immediate departure of all Filipino troops from Iraq. Within a couple of days, every Filipino of the "peacekeeping" mission had returned home. On Tuesday, July 20, more than two weeks after he had been abducted, Angelo de la Cruz was released. When at last Arroyo spoke to the press, one of the reasons she herself provided for her decision was divine assistance. It was to Mary, and in particular, to Our Lady of All Nations, whom Arroyo herself prayed the three days that her administration was silent. Her supplications to this particular patroness had precedent: in 2001, she had asked Our Lady of All Nations to help with the release of several vacationers kidnapped by the bandit group Abu Sayyaf, and "shortly after that," Arroyo noted to reporters, "the release [of the hostages came]. And so now, we're praying to her again."[67]

ALL ARROYO'S INSTRUMENTS

The national approval Arroyo received for the decision to withdraw the Filipino troops from Iraq was short lived. Already poised to undermine her legitimacy at the time of the hostage crisis were accusations of fraud in the May 2004 elections that returned her to power, and in the years between the hostage crisis and the end of her second term in 2010, criticism of her administration's abuses of power increased. Political repression worsened and extrajudicial killings multiplied, as several of the administrations' "counterinsurgency" and "antiterrorist" programs targeted students, journalists, activists, and workers.[68] Corruption scandals exposed the unscrupulous business practices of several of the administration's highest-ranking officials, including members of Arroyo's family. Rifts in the military, long in the making, deepened and gave rise to mutinies and recurring speculations over coups d'état. A state of emergency was declared in 2006. In this milieu of deteriorating conditions—sometimes compared to the martial law period of former president Ferdinand Marcos—the desire for immediacy seen in the televised prayer to God took another form: demands for transparency.

Emblematizing this demand was "truth," which became the watchword for opponents of the Arroyo administration. In the lead-up to several large rallies in February 2008 calling for Arroyo's resignation, unending references to "truth" issued from the lips of diverse participants, including ousted former president Joseph Estrada, members of the Catholic clergy, activist leaders, and leftist groups. In the face of this mobilization, some of Arroyo's provincial supporters decided to stage counterdemonstrations against what they claimed was just "political noise . . . isolated in the so-called imperial Manila."[69] Who should become part of these counterdemonstration efforts but Angelo de la Cruz himself, who traveled by bus to Manila from his hometown of Buenavista, Pampanga. "The President saved my life," one newspaper quoted de la Cruz as saying. "This is the time for me and fellow OFWs to show support for the President, who only has our welfare in mind."[70] Malacañang's Office of the Press Secretary elaborated in a statement reporting that "Dela Cruz [sic] said he went to Manila to send this message that it's not the 'time for us to be divided as a nation,' but . . . the right moment for the Filipinos to stand firm behind the President who brings growth, development, and economic miracles for the country."[71]

Having once represented the worst possible consequences of the Philippines' participation in the U.S. war in Iraq, Angelo de la Cruz gave a different spin to the idiom of sacrifice that so strongly resonates with the plight of OFWs. Whether out of a sincere sense of indebtedness or because he was outright enlisted, and whether these were in fact his words or those of the former administration's media machine, de la Cruz nevertheless lent his famous face to transmit the message that sacrificing dissent was necessary for the greater economic good. I conclude with this because it gathers together in one last series of substitutions the ideas I have sought to weave together throughout this chapter. Where there was recourse to foreign prophesiers to preempt questions of ritual efficacy, in this instance we see the resurrection of a national hero to buttress accusations of political ineffectiveness. Where it was Mary whose mantle of protection was sought in a time of "40 wars," it is here the female head of state to whom credit is given for saving lives. And in the place of divine intervention, we find the propagation of belief in miracles of a different sort: the "economic miracle," or the burgeoning value that may come from Filipino labor in a global economy. I do not present these as a sequence of occurrences that reveal some telos of secularization. On the contrary, the 2008 publicity stunt using Angelo de la Cruz brought together such familiar idioms of Catholic mediation that it confounded any easy distinction between the religious and the secular. But if these were repetitions, they were not ones that would give rise to marvelous coincidence. They were, rather, well-worn strategies for foreclosing the possibilities that might follow in crisis's wake.

Conclusion

In the introduction to this book I drew from William Christian Jr.'s marvelously evocative metaphor of a "sea bed" of apparition experience to help set up both the topical and the methodological parameters of this study. The preceding chapters have mapped a small archipelago in this vast ocean. But there are many islands to which I could not travel, for lack of time, resources (my own and what was available regarding a particular vision), or even, to conclude the metaphor, because of a missed connection at some point along my itinerary. This was the case with the visions of Emma de Guzman, about whom I learned during an interview with June Keithley in 2007.

Keithley had heard about de Guzman from a bishop in Canada, when she was traveling on one of her many tours to speak about apparitions of the Virgin Mary. Emma was born very poor in Cabanatuan City, in 1949. She married an older man who died when Emma was twenty-six, leaving her with three children. In 1984 she went to Singapore as a domestic helper. As Keithley tells it, Emma's yearlong contract as an overseas Filipino worker (OFW) was about to expire when a friend approached her, saying that she should try to get work in Canada, where there was a surge in demand for nannies and housekeepers. One day, soon after this encounter, while Emma sat on a park bench, a tiny piece of paper came fluttering down and landed in front of her. She picked it up and saw that written on it was, "Are you interested in working in Canada? Call this number!" Shortly thereafter, she obtained work as a live-in nanny in Kingston, Ontario.

In 1991, Emma traveled with friends to the Shrine of Our Lady of Fátima in New York. It was there that she had her first mystical experience. She had visions of Jesus, a monk, and Our Lady, who instructed that she confess to the monk. The monk, it turned out, was Padre Pio, the famous Italian mystic and stigmatic canonized by Pope John Paul II in 2002. As Keithley put it solemnly, "That was the beginning of it all." On Emma's days off she would sit in a park in Kingston. There, she met another Filipino and his daughter, a nurse named Sol Gaviola; they took Emma under their wing. Sol cultivated Emma's visionary powers by teaching her how to pray properly. She also cultivated Emma's following by spreading the word and forming prayer groups under the name La Pieta.[1]

In Keithley's retelling of Emma's story, she emphasized the visionary's simplicity in faith, which included not having any "real understanding" of Catholicism, knowing neither the Mass nor how to pray. This is a common motif in the biographies of modern visionaries. Such naïveté underscores the credibility of the seer, who, it is imagined, is incapable of inventing his or her experience. This is especially true in Emma's case with respect to some of her extraordinary manifestations, which included receiving and writing holy messages in Greek, Aramaic, and Latin. But this simplicity also serves as a counterpoint to the theological concerns upon which Keithley and her fellow Marian devotees expound in their public appearances. For Emma's gifts, or "charisms," are intensely corporeal: stigmata, bilocation, roses coming out of her chest, stones that pop out of her head, the ability to heal, and *escarchas* (glitter) that Emma leaves in her wake.

Listening to Keithley describe Emma and the worldwide ministry that her followers have created, I was simultaneously thrilled and daunted; thrilled at what appeared to be another extraordinary case of Filipino visionary experience to follow up on and daunted at the thought of doing new research at a time when I was tying up loose ends. I quickly imagined what pursuing this lead would entail: one more field site (or sites), one more round of chasing down contacts and negotiating access, one more set of interviews, one more string of events to attend. As if sensing my deliberations, Keithley suggested that I just look up "La Pieta prayer groups" on the Internet for more information.

In concluding fieldwork one has to draw the line somewhere, and it was with the Filipina visionary of Ontario that I drew mine. It seemed in any case that the phenomenon of the La Pieta group diverged in significant ways from the kinds of phenomena and organizations in which I had been interested. Indeed, I conclude with Emma for precisely this reason, for while her story and her ministry touch upon some of the major themes of this book, they also open up a range of questions that suggest future directions for research.

For one, both Keithley's narration and Emma's ministry return us to Filipino Catholics' investment in, and production of, religious orthodoxy. The emphasis on "real understanding" and "proper" prayer demonstrates recent efforts Filipinos have made in bringing their Catholic practices into greater conformity with the teachings of the church. In a brief introduction that appears on the La Pieta website, visitors are told that Emma is "absolutely obedient to the authority and teachings of the Roman Catholic Church and its Magisterium," and that "La Pieta International Prayer Groups espouse loyalty to the Holy Father, the Pope, and live out the traditional expression of prayer life, such as the utmost reverence when receiving Holy Communion on the tongue and the women wearing a white veil for Holy Mass."[2] Under the section of the website labeled "Testimonials," several scanned letters attest to Emma and La Pieta's standing in the estimation of church authorities. Among them is one letter from the archbishop of San Fernando, Pampanga (Philippines), officially certifying the prayer meetings conducted by Emma in several of that archdiocese's parishes, another from a pastor at a parish in Pennsylvania stating that "everything that was done [at one of Emma's prayer meetings] was in perfect harmony with the teaching and practice of Holy Mother the Church." Another letter is from the vicar-general of the archdiocese of Chicago, written in response to a request by one of La Pieta's members that the archdiocese confirm that La Pieta is a "legitimate Catholic organization . . . approved by the Archdiocese of Chicago," and another is from the Theology Department chair at Cardinal Newman High School in the diocese of Santa Rosa, inviting Emma to California to be present at a Eucharistic celebration and healing service.[3] It might seem odd that for a woman known to be a particularly gifted healer, the testimonial section of her promotional website is dominated by these endorsements, and not by actual cases of healing.[4] But it speaks to the convergent interests of the laity and clergy in the propagation of Marian devotion that this book has attempted to trace.

This book has focused primarily on lay actors in the growth of Filipino Marianism, although at times some discussion of church history and politics was needed to contextualize the shifts in devotional practice and attitudes documented herein. But there is much more that could be done in this regard; notwithstanding several sound analyses of church politics in the postcolonial Philippines, the fact of the matter is that a critical history or ethnography of the Philippine Catholic Church in the postindependence period has yet to be written.[5] I have often wondered why this is the case; if it is, for example, a matter of access, or that scholars have yet to develop the critical apparatus to effectively examine the complex institution in the same way that historians and anthropologists have been able to examine, say, the state, as a particular object of inquiry.

Attention to orthodoxy is one way this book has sought to provide an analysis alternative to the dominant paradigms of "folk Catholicism" and "popular religion." Another is through thinking about the relationship between religion and the mass media. Much of this book is devoted to understanding the "intermedium relationships" that have developed among technology, testimony, and figures of Catholic mediation in Philippine modernity.[6] But with the rapid ascendancy of digitally based technologies like the Internet, a new "discourse network" promises to link religious phenomena, discourse, archives, and bodies in unprecedented and powerful ways.

Emma's ministry provides a good point of departure for thinking about these transformations. There are two main websites where one can learn more about Emma and La Pieta International. The first is La Pieta International Prayer Group (http://www.lapietainternational.com), a rather rudimentary website that provides basic information about Emma and the founding of the organization, recent messages Emma has received, and an out-of-date calendar of events; the second is Mother of Joy House of Prayer (http://www.motherofjoy.com), a better-organized website with more comprehensive information that represents a chapter of La Pieta founded in upstate New York, after Pat and Bev Galtieri visited Emma in Canada and received five roses that had emerged from the center of her chest.[7] Both websites give us some indication of what has come of the supernatural in the digital age.

The promotional tenor of the websites is not so different from what we saw in chapter 5 with some of the material produced by the Family Rosary Crusade. These websites serve, above all, as a form of religious publicity, both for the La Pieta prayer groups and for the devotions they seek to propagate. But the websites betoken a different process of production and engagement with the public from what we saw in the FRC's use of the mass media and massive prayer rallies, and in the phenomenon of rose-petal showers in Lipa as engendered through the press. Virtual portals of information (and intercession, as any visitor can submit prayer requests by clicking on the mail icon), the websites are not quite virtual communities for public exchange. There is no forum on either of the websites where one can engage in a direct conversation with Emma or anyone in the Pieta prayer groups. There are links to other relevant websites, but no real reflexive discourse. The websites present a kind of hyper-topography, their content relaying La

Pieta events that have taken or will take place in physical locations in the United States, Canada, and the Philippines. Most curious in this regard is that in the early days of Emma's visionary experience, most of these events did not take place in public venues at all but occurred in individual homes. If, as anthropologist Paolo Apolito has suggested, this retreat of visionary phenomena into private spaces is a widespread trend, it is worth investigating the extent to which it may be an effect of a technological era in which the single screen, often at home, has become one of the primary sites from which people engage with the world at large.[8]

With the inclusion of pages for supporting documents, testimonies, messages of the apparitions, and galleries of photographs, the websites exist as their own self-constituted archives.[9] Following a prior logic whereby the archive is *the* locus of evidence, these pages attest to the truth of the miraculous visions and phenomena of Emma de Guzman. And yet I dare say that even the goriest images of Emma's stigmata appear trite; as Apolito has observed, "When [supernatural phenomena] are absorbed and processed by the technological *form*, they remain caught within a disconcerting immanence."[10] Unlike the haunting song of Mary that provoked an outpouring of emotion at the World Marian Peace Regatta, there is something decidedly *not* uncanny about the photographs of Emma de Guzman, as if the virtual medium has succeeded in flattening out the deeply corporeal phenomenon, without any spectral remainder.

This should hardly lead us to believe that we are finally at the threshold of disenchantment, however. This brings me to the final question the book has pursued: what happens when lay Filipinos take up the mantle of global mission? The latter half of this book is rife with stories of inspiration and conversion that relate the making of a new Filipino figure in Christian mission, that "righteous daughter (or son) of Mama Mary" who has assented to the church's fundamental claims of universality and made it his or her life's work to bring people around the world "to Jesus, through Mary."[11] In uncanny echoes of the early colonial period when native misrecognition of Spanish missionary intent resulted in an excess of zeal for some devotional practices over others, the emphasis on Mary as utterly instrumental to Christ's salvation of humankind reveals anew an assertion of difference in an otherwise orthodox sphere. In other words, even as there is an increased trend among Filipino Marian devotees to conceptualize and advocate for Mary more as a universal figure and less in her specific and local manifestations, this universalism is distinctly Filipino. The question is whether or not this Mary-centric Christianity, and especially the overtly sentimental emphasis on her maternal dimension (as opposed to, say, her perpetual virginity) simply represents an admissible instance of plurality still ultimately subsumed by Christian universalism or, by contrast, may actually serve to subvert the patriarchal and rationalized claims of the universal church. In the last chapter of this book, I took up this question by considering the vanguard role that some Filipino lay groups have taken in petitioning the Vatican to declare what is known as the fifth Marian dogma. Until this campaign succeeds or fails in its goals, this will remain an open question.

Notwithstanding this unresolved theological dispute, an important outcome of these efforts is that the Philippines has emerged as the place from which some believe Mary's triumph over evil will commence and spread throughout the world. The prophecies of mystics and visionaries worldwide have foretold it. But what exactly would be the status of the Philippines' "place" in this new global order? Would this divine election simply refer to the Philippines as the sending country for Marian mission groups, like those we have examined? Or might it entail something more?

At the end of 2001, while in a New Jersey home, Emma de Guzman relayed a message from the Blessed Mother. The message was, "There is a mountain waiting for you. I am going to take you to the mountain of peace, love, and joy. Many will come to the mountain."[12] This "mountain" was revealed to Emma soon after, during a medical mission that she and several La Pieta members made to the Philippines. Through a series of missed encounters and coincidences, Emma discovered the mountain in the province of Batangas that, with heart-pounding certainty, she knew to be the one to which the Blessed Mother had referred. One year later, on December 8, 2002, the feast of the Immaculate Conception, the Blessed Mother made her final appearance to Emma in North America, saying: "My son is leading you, my child, to your homeland, the Mountain of Salvation, a mountain of peace, love, and joy ... [I]f my children will open their hearts to listen to the message and follow my Son's call, He will reward His people and the country of the Philippines ... Your land will be an example of love and peace to the surrounding nations."[13]

Over the following two years the development of the Mountain of Salvation proceeded through fits and starts. Emma was certain that she had found the right mountain but unsure as to where upon this mountain the Blessed Mother would appear. One day in April 2003, she returned to the mountain; while descending on a steep trail, she suddenly heard the sound of running water. She followed its flow to the bottom of the mountain, where she discovered a small cave with fragrant water running through it. She knew then that this was the future apparition spot. But when would the Blessed Mother appear there?[14] Emma received her answer in 2004, back in Kingston, Ontario, when Sol, the woman who had nurtured Emma's gift and had since passed away, appeared to her accompanied by two angels and said, "The Blessed Mother will appear to you on your birthday [December 8]. This will be the start of your mission."[15]

It is tempting to read Emma's homecoming as a historical return to a time when sacredness was deeply rooted in physical space, localized, and tied to the earth. The "sacred mountain" figures prominently in Filipino folk literature and, indeed, in much historical and contemporary "folk Catholicism." But I would hesitate to assign this shift in Emma's practice to this designation so readily, since her life's trajectory, her mystical experience, and her ministry's commitments are densely imbricated in networks of transnational phenomena, affiliation, and authority that exceed and antecede this reenchantment of locality. I would suggest instead that in this case of spiritual return there is a literal enactment of the seismic shift of Christian mission from Europe and North America to the Global South in the twentieth and twenty-first centuries.

In the months between Sol's apparition and the scheduled apparition of Mary at the Mountain of Salvation, Emma and La Pieta International members readied themselves for the grand occasion. Emma went on what she called a "Marian Pilgrimage" through Luzon and orchestrated a reunion of the La Pieta International prayer groups. Workers constructed a foot trail down the mountain and an amphitheater at the apparition site for the pilgrims coming from Canada and the United States.[16] As promised, on December 8, 2004—the 150th anniversary of *Ineffabilis Deus*, the papal decree that declared the Immaculate Conception as dogma—Mary made her first appearance at the Mountain of Salvation, telling Emma:

> You are here my child, in this little humble mountain that my Son chose, like yourself, the little humble instrument of God, who will bring my children to come to the Mountain of Salvation of Peace, Love and Joy . . .
> You, my children, are here because God called you to be his instruments, to spread the message of love . . . I am calling my children to unite with me on this mission.[17]

To be an instrument is to submit to forces that one believes greater than oneself, to renounce a measure of agency, to be used. It is in these senses that most of the devotees—notably female—in this book have self-consciously, even triumphantly, employed the term. But if we listen closely to their stories, we will find that behind every act of submission there was doubt; behind every disavowal of agency there was a radical transformation of consciousness; behind every affirmation of being used there was the production of other transmissions. To put this in distinctly Marian terms: before Mary said, "Behold the handmaid of the Lord," she questioned, "How can this be?" In the vulnerable pause between question and answer lies a world of possibility from which a different meaning of instrument might emerge: this is the instrument that captures power as it is captivated by power, that allows itself to be possessed, and in so allowing says things that otherwise could not be said.

Notes

INTRODUCTION

1. This summary of the apparitions of Mary at Agoo draws from the following articles: "Devil's Advocate in Agoo," *Malaya* (Manila), February 16, 1993; "2M Pilgrims Expected in Agoo," *Manila Bulletin*, March 5, 1993; "The Virgin in Agoo," *Philippine Daily Inquirer*, March 5, 1993; "Agoo Pilgrims Assured Gov't Aid," *Manila Bulletin*, March 6, 1993; "Thousands Wait for Miracle Today," *Philippine Daily Inquirer*, March 6, 1993; "The Boy Who Sees the Virgin," *Philippine Daily Inquirer*, March 6, 1993; "'Apparition' Stirs Pilgrims in Agoo," *Manila Bulletin*, March 7, 1993; "A Million Trek to Agoo but Only Few See Vision," *Philippine Daily Inquirer*, March 7, 1993; "Blue Lights Streaked across the Sky," *Philippine Daily Inquirer*, March 8, 1993; "Shower of Flowers, Fragrance Reported," *Manila Bulletin*, March 8, 1993; "Church Notes More People Going to Mass," *Philippine Daily Inquirer*, March 9, 1993; "Omen from Heaven or Just Optical Illusion?" *Philippine Daily Inquirer*, March 10, 1993; "Two Church Bodies Probe Agoo 'Miracles,'" *Philippine Daily Inquirer*, March 10, 1993; "The New Marian Center of the Country," *Philippine Panorama*, March 14, 1993; "What If the Agoo Vision Were a Hoax?" *Manila Bulletin*, March 16, 1993; "The Agoo Apparitions," *Philippine Graphic*, March 22, 1993; "Himala sa Agoo: Gawa-gawa lamang o totoo?" *Pilipino Reporter Magasin*, May 2, 9, 16, 30 (*bilang* 378–382), 16, 30, 1993; "The Last Apparition," *Manila Bulletin*, August 29, 1993; "A Call for Caution," *Manila Bulletin*, August 30, 1993; "Agoo Miracle Marred by Devotees' Infighting," *Businessworld* (Manila), January 4, 1994.

2. "Agoo Miracle Marred by Devotees' Infighting."

3. "Probers Reject Agoo Apparitions," *Manila Bulletin*, September 7, 1995; "'Walang himala' sa Agoo," *People's Journal*, September 7, 1995.

4. In the writings of the early church fathers the idea of diabolical mimicry, or demonic plagiarism, was developed to account for the curious similarities they sometimes encountered between so-called pagan rituals and their own Christian rites. See, for example, Justin Martyr, First Apology, chap. 54, in *St. Justin Martyr, the First and Second Apologies*, trans. Leslie William Barnard (New York: Paulist Press, 1997), 61–62. I thank Donald S. Lopez Jr. for pointing this out in his discussion of the writings of seventeenth-century Jesuit missions as they described the adulation expressed to the Dalai Lama, so uncannily similar in form to Christian veneration of the pope. *Prisoners of Shangri-La: Tibetan Buddhism and the West* (Chicago: University of Chicago Press, 1998), 27–28.

5. "'Apparition' Star Judiel Nieva Is Now a Show Biz Star," *Philippine Daily Inquirer*, September 5, 2003.

6. William A. Christian Jr., "Afterword: Islands in the Sea: The Public and Private Distribution of Knowledge of Religious Visions," *Visual Resources* 25, nos. 1–2 (2009): 159.

7. *Oxford English Dictionary*, 3rd ed., June 2005, s.v. "Marian," http://www.oed.com/view/Entry /114079?rskey=NEb5Eq&result=3#eid.

8. Ibid., s.v. "Marianism," http://www.oed.com/view/Entry/114082?redirectedFrom=Marianism #eid.

9. For a genealogy and critique of the concept "world religions," see Tomoko Masuzawa's *The Invention of World Religions; or, How European Universalism Was Preserved in the Language of Pluralism* (Chicago: University of Chicago Press, 2005).

10. John Leddy Phelan, *The Hispanization of the Philippines: Spanish Aims and Filipino Responses, 1565–1700* (Madison: University of Wisconsin Press, 1967), 74; John N. Schumacher, "A Golden Age of the Filipino Church, 1700–1768," in *Growth and Decline: Essays on Philippine Church History* (Quezon City: Ateneo de Manila University Press, 2009), 34.

11. Masuzawa, *Invention of World Religions*.

12. There is, in the first place, the well-known thesis set down by Max Weber in *The Protestant Ethic and the Spirit of Capitalism*, trans. Talcott Parsons (1930; New York: Routledge, 2001). Critical to the further development of this literature has been Jean Comaroff and John Comaroff's *Of Revelation and Revolution*, vol. 1, *Christianity, Colonialism, and Consciousness in South Africa* (Chicago: University of Chicago Press, 1991), and Comaroff and Comaroff, *Of Revelation and Revolution*, vol. 2, *The Dialectics of Modernity on a South African Frontier* (Chicago: University of Chicago Press, 1997). More recent studies include Webb Keane's *Christian Moderns: Freedom and Fetish in the Mission Encounter* (Berkeley: University of California, 2007).

13. See Fenella Cannell, "The Christianity of Anthropology," *Journal of the Royal Anthropological Institute* 11, no. 2 (2005): 335–56; and Cannell, introduction to *The Anthropology of Christianity*, ed. Fenella Cannell (Durham, NC: Duke University Press, 2006), 1–50; and as these ideas inform a reading of Protestant mission in the early American colonial period, see Cannell, "Immaterial Culture: 'Idolatry' in the Lowland Philippines," in *Spirited Politics: Religion and Public Life in Contemporary Southeast Asia*, ed. Andrew C. Willford and Kenneth M. George (Ithaca, NY: Cornell Southeast Asia Program, 2005), 159–84.

14. This is not to suggest a lack of discussions of Catholicism and modernity, even as much scholarship on the topic takes as its starting point the recognition that Catholicism has been deeply marginalized in disciplines otherwise committed to explaining the impact of modernity on social, political, and religious life. Robert Orsi's meditations on doing religious studies scholarship in *Between Heaven and Earth: The Religious Worlds People Make and the Scholars Who Study Them* (Princeton, NJ: Princeton University Press, 2006), stand out in this regard, although the question of Catholic difference runs throughout his entire corpus. The same, too, can be said of the works of William A. Christian Jr., who pioneered the field of what is now referred to as the anthropology of Christianity with *Person and God in a Spanish Valley* (Princeton, NJ: Princeton University Press, 1972), the first ethnographic study of Catholicism in Europe. Most recently, historian Brian Porter-Szűcs has addressed this need for redress of bias, stating, "Catholicism's modernity may not look like liberalism's modernity, but it is no less modern for that." *Faith and Fatherland: Catholicism, Modernity, Poland* (New York: Oxford University Press, 2011), 83.

15. Victor Turner and Edith Turner, *Image and Pilgrimage in Christian Culture* (New York: Columbia University Press, 1978), 208.

16. The most notable among these include Thomas Kselman's *Miracles and Prophecies in Nineteenth-Century France* (New Brunswick, NJ: Rutgers University Press, 1983); David Blackbourn's *Marpingen: Apparitions of the Virgin Mary in a Nineteenth-Century German Village* (New York: Vintage Books, 1993); Turner and Turner's *Image and Pilgrimage*; Marina Warner's widely read classic *Alone of All Her Sex* (New York: Vintage Books, 1976); Ruth Harris's *Lourdes: Body and Spirit in a Secular Age* (New York: Penguin Books, 2000); and William A. Christian Jr.'s *Visionaries: The Spanish Republic and the Reign of Christ* (Berkeley: University of California Press, 1996). There are few book-length studies of modern apparitions of Mary outside of Europe, but one recent example is *Revolutions in Mexican Catholicism: Reform and Revelation in Oaxaca, 1887–1934*, by Edward

Wright-Rios (Durham, NC: Duke University Press, 2009). Recent articles have redoubled attention to apparitions of Mary as a particularly postmodern phenomenon. See, for example, Manuel A. Vásquez and Marie F. Marquardt, "Globalizing the Rainbow Madonna: Old Time Religion in the Present Age," *Theory, Culture, and Society* 17, no. 4 (2000): 119–43.

17. The most extreme example of the stance that Marian apparitions are simply displacements of human thought and action is the vitriolic volume by Nicolas Perry and Loreto Echeverría, *Under the Heel of Mary* (New York: Routledge, 1988).

18. Drawing from Élisabeth Claverie's study *Les guerres de la Vierge: Une anthropologie des apparitions* (Paris: Gallimard, 2003), on pilgrimage to the apparition site in Medjugorje, in the former Yugoslavia (today Bosnia and Herzegovina), Bruno Latour writes: "Even more difficult is when a pilgrim says, 'I came to this monastery because I was called by the Virgin Mary.' How long should we resist smiling smugly, replacing at once the agency of the Virgin by the 'obvious' delusion of an actor 'finding pretext' in a religious icon to 'hide' one's own decision? Critical sociologists will answer: 'Just as far as to be polite, it's bad manners to sneer in the presence of the informant.' A sociologist of associations meanwhile must learn to say: 'As long as possible in order to seize the chance offered by the pilgrim to fathom the diversity of agencies acting at once in the world.'" *Reassembling the Social: An Introduction to Actor-Network-Theory* (New York: Oxford University Press, 2005), 48.

19. This summary is taken from M. Aladel, C.M., *The Miraculous Medal, Its Origin, History, Circulation, Results*, trans. P.S., from the 8th French edition (Philadelphia: H. L. Kilner & Co., 1880). Aladel was Labouré's confessor, and his *Notice historique sur l'origine et les effets de la nouvelle médaille frappée en l'honneur de l'Immaculée Conception de la très sainte Vierge sous le nom de Médaille Miraculeuse* (first published in 1834) was instrumental in spreading the devotion. For more on the history of Labouré and Aladel, see René Laurentin, *Catherine Labouré: Visionary of the Miraculous Medal* (Boston: Pauline Books and Media, 2006).

20. Aladel, *Miraculous Medal*, 55.

21. Ibid., 57–58.

22. The basic story of the apparition of the Virgin Mary at Guadalupe in Mexico is as follows. In December 1531, an Indian was passing by a hill in Tepeyac (or Tepeyacac, now in the northern part of Mexico City) when he heard sweet music and saw a young woman who let him know that she was the Virgin Mary. She ordered him to tell the bishop that she wanted to have a chapel built in her honor at Tepeyac. Juan did as she commanded, but the bishop, Juan de Zumárraga, sent him away, telling him to return another day. On Juan's second return, the bishop told him that he must bring a sign of the apparitions. The Virgin assured Juan that a sign was forthcoming, and he went off to care for his uncle, Juan Bernardino, who was ill with the plague. The following Tuesday, the Virgin appeared to him again, demanding that he climb the hill at Tepeyac to collect roses and flowers, which he gathered in his cape. He took these to Bishop Zumárraga, and when he unfurled his cape the painted image of the Virgin miraculously appeared. This convinced the bishop, who ordered that the image be placed in the cathedral for public veneration. This synopsis draws from Miguel Sánchez's (1596?–1674) foundational text for the devotion to Our Lady of Guadalupe, *Imagen de la Virgen María, Madre de Dios de Guadalupe, milagrosamente aparecida en la Ciudad de México. Celebrada en su historia, con la profecía el capítulo doce del Apocalipsis* (Mexico: Imprenta de la Viuda de Bernardo Calderón, 1648).

23. See William A. Christian Jr., *Apparitions in Late Medieval and Renaissance Spain* (Princeton, NJ: Princeton University Press, 1981), which provides a survey of dozens of apparition cases, extracting from them general themes in local visions across the region.

24. Ibid., 76–80.

25. My thanks to Monique Scheer for her insight on the possible iconographical influences on the Miraculous Medal (e-mail communication, June 2, 2009).

26. Aladel, *Miraculous Medal*, 67; Laurentin, *Catherine Labouré*, 60. By the end of Labouré's life in 1876, more than a billion medals had been produced.

27. Aladel, *Miraculous Medal*, 71–72.

28. See, for example, Richard D. E. Burton's overview, quite dismissive in tone, of the Miraculous Medal in *Blood in the City: Violence and Revelation in Paris, 1789–1945* (Ithaca, NY: Cornell University Press, 2001), 118–29. Even in the more balanced study *Miracles and Prophecies in Nineteenth-Century France*, Thomas Kselman's discussion of Labouré and the Miraculous Medal focuses on the "millenarianism" of the Marian age, although he extends a more complex argument that this millenarianism dovetailed with French nationalism in the belief that France would play a role in the Second Coming (90–94).

29. See Carolyn Brewer's feminist reading of early conversion, *Holy Confrontation: Religion, Gender, and Sexuality in the Philippines, 1521–1685* (Manila: Institute of Women's Studies, St. Scholastica's College, 2001). See also Teresita Infante, *The Woman in Early Philippines and among the Cultural Minorities* (Manila: Unitas Publications, University of Santo Tomas, 1975); Evelyn Tan Cullamar, *Babaylanism in Negros, 1896–1907* (Quezon City: New Day Publishers, 1986); Alfred McCoy, "Baylan: Animist Religion and Philippine Peasant Ideology," in *Moral Order and the Question of Change: Essays on Southeast Asian Thought*, ed. David Wyatt and Alexander Woodside (New Haven, CT: Southeast Asia Studies, Yale University, 1982), 338–413; and Philippine historian F. Landa Jocano's "Ang mga Babaylan at Katalonan sa Kinagisnang Sikolohiya," in *Ulat ng Unang Pambansang Kumperensiya sa Sikolohiyang Pilipino*, ed. Lilia F. Antonio, Esther S. Reyes, Rogelia Pe, and Nilda R. Almonte (Quezon City: Pambansang Samahan ng Sikolohiyang Pilipino, 1976), 147–57. Neferti Tadiar, in her essay on the Filipina megastar Nora Aunor, has brought the historical figure of the *babaylan* to bear on a critique of mass culture. See "The Noranian Imaginary," in *Geopolitics of the Visible: Essays on Philippine Film Cultures*, ed. Rolando B. Tolentino (Quezon City: Ateneo de Manila University Press, 2000), 61–76.

30. No discussion of translation and conversion, in the Philippines or elsewhere, is possible without reference to Vicente Rafael's study *Contracting Colonialism: Translation and Christian Conversion in Tagalog Society under Early Spanish Rule* (Ithaca, NY: Cornell University Press, 1988).

31. Although there is widespread knowledge of pre-Hispanic society (including figures such as the *babaylan*), thanks to the nativist revival in some academic circles, rarely have I heard this casually stated as heavily informing contemporary Filipino devotion to Mary.

32. This passage comes from the *New American Bible* (online), http://www.usccb.org/bible/john/2.

33. See, for example, Martin Hengel, "The Interpretation of the Wine Miracle at Cana: John 2:1–11," in *The Glory of Christ in the New Testament: Studies in Christology*, ed. L. D. Hurst and N. T. Wright (Oxford, UK: Clarendon Press, 1987), 83–112.

34. Public talk delivered by Teresita Castillo, Marian Research Center, Lipa, September 1, 2001.

35. Daniel Wojcik, "'Polaroids from Heaven': Photography, Folk Religion, and the Miraculous Image Tradition at a Marian Apparition Site," *Journal of American Folklore* 109, no. 432 (Spring 1996): 129–48.

36. Paolo Apolito, *The Internet and the Madonna: Religious Visionary Experience on the Web* (Chicago: University of Chicago Press, 2005), 11.

37. The locus classicus for illuminating this logic remains Jacques Derrida's "Faith and Knowledge: The Two Sources of 'Religion' at the Limits of Reason Alone," trans. Samuel Weber, in *Religion*, ed. Jacques Derrida and Gianni Vattimo (Stanford, CA: Stanford University Press, 1998), 1–78. For an inquiry that brings this logic to bear on a specific phenomenon, see Hent de Vries, "Of Miracles and Special Effects," *International Journal for the Philosophy of Religion* 50, nos. 1–3 (December 2001): 41–56.

38. Wojcik, "'Polaroids from Heaven.'"

39. Louis-Marie Grignion de Montfort, *The Secret of the Rosary* (Bay Shore, NY: Montfort Fathers, 1965). St. Louis de Montfort was a French priest who lived from 1673 to 1716. Pope Leo XII canonized him in 1947.

40. In the Philippine literature, the term "folk Catholicism" has had a particularly a long career. The term appears as early as 1965, in an essay by Jaime C. Bulatao, Jesuit psychologist and profes-

sor at Ateneo de Manila University, titled "A Social-Psychological View of the Philippine Church," reprinted in his *Phenomena and Their Interpretation: Landmark Essays, 1957–1989* (Quezon City: Ateneo de Manila University Press, 1992), 12–22. See also his "Reflections on the Experience of God among Philippine Folk Catholics," in the same volume (72–78). Before that, the thesis that Filipino Catholicism was fundamentally syncretic had been elaborated in the conjunctive ideas of "Hispanizing the Philippines" and "Philippinizing Catholicism" put forth by historian John L. Phelan's indispensable work *The Hispanization of the Philippines.* American social scientists (mainly Jesuits) who served as permanent faculty at some of the Philippines' elite institutions also helped develop the paradigm. See, in particular, Frank Lynch, "Folk Catholicism in the Philippines," in *Philippine Society and the Individual: Selected Essays of Frank Lynch, 1949–1976,* ed. Aram A. Yengoyan and Perla Q. Makil, Michigan Papers on South and Southeast Asia 24 (Ann Arbor: Center for South and Southeast Asian Studies, University of Michigan, 1984), 197–207; and on syncretism, see John N. Schumacher, "Syncretism in Philippine Catholicism: Its Historical Causes," in his *Growth and Decline,* 107–25. Reynaldo Ileto's important and critical study of vernacular literature, *Pasyon and Revolution: Popular Movements in the Philippines, 1840–1910* (Quezon City: Ateneo de Manila University Press, 1979), brought "folk Catholicism" to a whole new level, as the primary idiom through which discontent and resistance to Spanish colonial rule could be articulated. "Lived religion" is a more recent analytical construct, coined by historian David D. Hall and richly developed in his *Lived Religion in America: Toward a History of Practice* (Princeton, NJ: Princeton University Press, 1997).

41. See Robert A. Orsi's extended critique of the category of "popular religion" in the introduction to the second edition of his classic *The Madonna of 115th Street: Faith and Community in Italian Harlem, 1880–1950* (New Haven, CT: Yale University Press, 2002).

42. John R. W. Smail, "On the Possibility of an Autonomous History of Modern Southeast Asia," *Journal of Southeast Asian History* 2, no. 2 (July 1961): 72–102. See also Harry J. Benda, "The Structure of Southeast Asian History: Some Preliminary Observations," *Journal of Southeast Asian History* 3, no. 1 (March 1962): 106–38. For an approach to Southeast Asian history that poses an altogether-different alternative to the externalist or autonomous approaches, see Victor Lieberman's *Strange Parallels: Southeast Asia in Global Context, c. 800–1830,* vol. 1, *Integration on the Mainland* (New York: Cambridge University Press, 2003); and Lieberman, *Strange Parallels: Southeast Asia in Global Context, c. 800–1830,* vol. 2, *Mainland Mirrors: Europe, Japan, China, South Asia, and the Islands* (New York: Cambridge University Press, 2009).

43. A revealing exception to this is the conclusion to the volume, written by coeditor Edilberto de Jesus. In it, he writes: "Quite apart from questions of training, resources and academic responsibilities, Filipinos will perhaps find a compelling psychological reason to force the leap from local to national history. It is more difficult for Filipinos to accept the reality that the nation-state is indeed a colonial creation . . . But if the reality of the nation is indeed rooted in the ideas shared by the people from whom it claims allegiance, Filipinos ought to continue the search for the beliefs that give substance to Philippine nationalism. The local national axis remains a most promising point of departure for this search." Conclusion to *Philippine Social History: Global Trade and Local Transformations,* ed. Alfred W. McCoy and Edilberto C. de Jesus (Honolulu: University of Hawai'i Press, 1982), 448. For a deeper reading of this historiographical turn, see Reynaldo C. Ileto, "On the Historiography of Southeast Asia and the Philippines: The 'Golden Age' of Southeast Asian Studies—Experiences and Reflections," proceeding of workshop "Can We Write History? Between Postmodernism and Coarse Nationalism" (Institute for International Studies, Meiji Gakuin University, March 9, 2002), http://www.meijigakuin.ac.jp/~iism/project/frontier/Proceedings/08%20Ileto%20Speech.pdf (accessed September 7, 2013).

44. See Fenella Cannell, *Power and Intimacy in the Christian Philippines* (New York: Cambridge University Press, 1999); Julius J. Bautista, *Figuring Catholicism: An Ethnohistory of the Santo Niño de Cebu* (Quezon City: Ateneo de Manila University Press, 2010); and Smita Lahiri, "Materializing the Spiritual: Christianity, Community, and History in a Philippine Landscape" (PhD diss., Cor-

nell University, 2002). In the past few decades there has been a veritable explosion of charismatic Catholic movements in the Philippines, little studied by scholars. An important foray into this field is Katherine Wiegele's *Investing in Miracles: El Shaddai and the Transformation of Popular Catholicism in the Philippines* (Honolulu: University of Hawai'i Press, 2005), the first book-length study on Filipino Charismatic Catholicism that focuses, among other things, on its urban and mass-mediated dimensions.

45. Oliver W. Wolters, *History, Culture, and Region in Southeast Asian Perspectives* (Ithaca, NY: Southeast Asian Program Publications, Cornell University, 1999), 57.

46. Francis Xavier, *The Letters and Instructions of Francis Xavier*, trans. M. Joseph Costelloe (St. Louis, MO: Institute of Jesuit Sources, 1992).

47. This persuasive hypothesis is not just anecdotal. In 2007, the Pew Research Center released the survey results of the massive study *U.S. Religious Landscape Survey*, as part of its Religion and Public Life Project. Among the many illuminating findings about belief in the supernatural, the study states that "nearly eight-in-ten American adults (79%) agree that miracles still occur today as in ancient times," and "seven-in-ten Americans (68%) believe that angels and demons are active in the world." See Pew Forum on Religion and Public Life, "Summary of Key Findings," *U.S. Religious Landscape Survey*, 2007, http://religions.pewforum.org/pdf/report2religious-landscape-study-key-findings.pdf (accessed September 15, 2013).

48. For an elaboration on the evocative theory of resonance, see Susan Lepselter's *The Resonance of Unseen Things* (Ann Arbor: University of Michigan Press, 2015).

49. Here it is worth recalling Weber's elaboration of "disenchantment" at length:

> Does it mean that we, today, for instance, everyone sitting in this hall, have a greater knowledge of the conditions of life under which we exist than has an American Indian or a Hottentot? Hardly. Unless he is a physicist, one who rides on the streetcar has no idea how the car happened to get into motion. And he does not need to know. He is satisfied that he may "count" on the behavior of the streetcar . . . but he knows nothing about what it takes to produce such a car so that it can move . . . The increasing intellectualization and rationalization do *not*, therefore, indicate an increased and general knowledge of the conditions under which one lives . . . It means something else, namely, the knowledge or *belief* that if one but wished one *could* learn it at any time. Hence, it means that principally there are no mysterious *incalculable* forces that come into play, but rather than one can, in principle, master all things by calculation. This means that the world is disenchanted. One need no longer have recourse to magical means in order to master or implore the spirits, as did the savage, for whom such mysterious powers existed. Technical means and calculation perform the service. This is above all is what intellectualization means.

"Science as Vocation," in *From Max Weber: Essays in Sociology*, ed. and trans. Hans H. Gerth and C. Wright Mills (New York: Oxford University Press, 1958), 139 (additional emphases mine).

50. Friedrich A. Kittler, *Discourse Networks 1800/1900*, trans. Michael Metteer (Stanford, CA: Stanford University Press, 1990).

CHAPTER 1

1. Here I have translated *imagen de bulto* as "fully bodied," in contrast to images sculpted *de bastidor*, meaning that only the head and hands are carved, and then attached to a frame that, in the case of religious images, is draped in fabric. See Regalado Trota Jose's *Simbahan: Church Art in Colonial Philippines, 1565-1898* (Manila: Ayala Foundation, 1991), 192-93. The original reads: "Es comparazión muy propria [*sic*] la de la escultura, que de piedra o de madera fabrica alguna imagen de bulto . . . y allí ver de aquel mármol duro o de aquel bronco tronco yr desbastando, el escultor con la escoda y pico en la piedra, y con la hacha y açuela en el madero, y, sobre la basta forma que le

dio con todo su trabajo, emprenderlo de nuevo en yrle perficionando [*sic*] parte por parte … hasta darle su forma de ojos, nariz, boca, y las demás facçiones, miembros y partes, y en el ropaje y vestido hasta los doblezes y pliegues, en llegando a este punto, ¿quién no quedara cansado de ver tanto cansançio y tanta menudenzia? ¡Y aún falta bruñir el mármol, y darle sus perfiles, si los a de llevar, y al palo blanquearle, encarnarle, y darle los colores y luçes! No es menos questo, sino mucho más, haçer Christianos de Infieles." Pedro Chirino, *Història de la província de Filipines de la Companyia de Jesús (1581-1606)* (Barcelona: Portic, 2000), 240. This *Història* is the more expansive version of the more readily available and commonly referenced *Relación de las Islas Filipinas*, a much-abridged version. *Història* is the only published edition of the entire Castilian manuscript.

2. In Spanish the idiom would read the same as in English: "en la imagen de Dios."

3. See John Leddy Phelan, *The Hispanization of the Philippines: Spanish Aims and Filipino Responses, 1565-1700* (Madison: University of Wisconsin Press, 1967), in particular chaps. 4 and 5, for a longer discussion of Spanish strategies of resettlement and their relation to conversion.

4. Ibid., 124. Although historians of the Philippines unanimously refer to the term *barangay* as designating the smallest unit of social structure in existence among various groups of the archipelago when the first European explorers arrived in the early sixteenth century, what this term might have encompassed when first heard by nonnative ears varies. Was it a kinship unit or a community settlement, or both? There is general agreement that what *barangay* did not denote was a fixed place of residence. Indeed, etymological evidence yields another meaning of the term, one that suggests the opposite of landed permanence, that is, seafaring mobility: *barangay* (*balangay* in some languages) also meant "boat." See William Henry Scott, *Barangay: Sixteenth-Century Philippine Culture and Society* (Quezon City: Ateneo de Manila University Press, 1994), 4-6; and Philippine archaeologist and social historian F. Landa Jocano's *The Philippines at Spanish Contact* (Manila: MCS Enterprises, 1975), 8-10.

5. William A. Christian Jr., *Local Religion in Sixteenth-Century Spain* (Princeton, NJ: Princeton University Press, 1982), 105.

6. For example, see Mary Ignazia S. Bunuan's *Gentle Woman: Mary to the Filipinos* (Pasay: Paulines Publishing House, 1997); Trota Jose's *Simbahan*; and from a more devotional perspective, Mary Anne Barcelona and Consuelo B. Estepa's *Inang Maria: A Celebration of the Blessed Virgin Mary in the Philippines* (Manila: Anvil Publishing, 2004).

7. For an introduction to the genres of the *awit* and *corrido*, see Damiana Eugenio, *Awit and Corrido: Philippine Metrical Romances* (Quezon City: University of the Philippines Press, 1987); Resil B. Mojares, *Origins and Rise of the Filipino Novel* (Quezon City: University of the Philippines Press, 1998), especially chap. 3; and Virgilio Almario, *Kung sino ang kumatha kina Bagongbanta, Ossorio, Herrera, Aquino de Belen, Balagtas, atbp.* (Manila: Anvil Publishing, 1992). The predominant figure in these discussions is that of Francisco Baltazar, more popularly known as "Balagtas," whose work *Pinagdaanang Buhay ni Florante at ni Laura sa Cahariang Albania* is regarded as the touchstone of true "Filipino" literature. See also Vicente Rafael, *The Promise of the Foreign: Nationalism and the Technics of Translation in the Spanish Philippines* (Durham, NC: Duke University Press, 2005), especially chap. 4; and John D. Blanco, *Frontier Constitutions: Christianity and Colonial Empire in the Nineteenth-Century Philippines* (Berkeley: University of California Press, 2009).

8. To date, there is no single source of comprehensive data on book publishing in the Philippines in the last half of the nineteenth century. But there are ample bibliographic sources from the turn of the twentieth century from which one can compile a fairly accurate picture of most genres and titles, especially when set against the historical context of censorship and the business of printing presses. Wenceslao E. Retana, Spanish historian, bibliophile, and one of the most interesting figures of late colonial modernity in the Philippines, published several titles, including *Aparato bibliográfico de la historia general de Filipinas* (Madrid: Imprenta de la Sucesora de M. Minuesa de los Ríos, 1906), vols. 1-3; *Archivo del bibliófilo filipino; recopilación de documentos históricos, científicos, literarios y políticos, y estudios bibliográficos* (Madrid: Imprenta de la Sucesora de M. Minuesa de los Ríos, 1895-1905), vols. 1-4; *La censura de imprenta en Filipinas* (Madrid: V. Suárez, 1908); *De la*

evolución de la literatura castellana en Filipinas: Los poetas, apuntes críticos (Madrid: Lib. General de Victoriano Suárez, 1909); *La imprenta en Filipinas: Adiciones y observaciones á la Imprenta en Manila de D. J. T. Medina* (Madrid: Imprenta de la Sucesora de M. Minuesa de los Ríos, 1899); *Noticias histórico-bibliográficas de el teatro en Filipinas desde sus orígenes hasta 1898* (Madrid: V. Suárez, 1910); and *Orígenes de la imprenta filipina; investigaciones históricas, bibliográficas y tipográficas* (Madrid: V. Suárez, 1911). Contemporary sources to which historians of the book in the Philippines may refer, especially with regard to the chapbook, include the catalog of the collection of Filipiniana in the library of the Colegio de Padres Agustinos in Valladolid, Spain: *Updated Checklist of Filipiniana at Valladolid*, 2 vols., compiled by Isacio R. Rodríguez (Manila: National Historical Institute, 1976); and the online catalog of the Biblioteca Nacional in Madrid (which has many *devocionarios* digitized and accessible via the web), at http://www.bne.es/es/LaBNE/. For recent publications on the history of the book in the Philippines, see Patricia May B. Jurilla, *Tagalog Bestsellers of the Twentieth Century: A History of the Book in the Philippines* (Quezon City: Ateneo de Manila University, 2008); and Vicente S. Hernández, *History of Books and Libraries in the Philippines, 1521-1900* (Manila: National Commission for Culture and the Arts, 1996).

9. Retana, *La censura de imprenta en Filipinas*, 3.

10. See, for example, excerpts from the meeting minutes for March 20, 1867, when the commission rejected Tissandier's *Teoría de la belleza* on the grounds that, although fundamentally Catholic in its ideas, it was too "ideological" in its Hegelian form of argumentation. Even the greatest work of Spanish literature was not exempt from possible bowdlerization: the commission agreed to take out the phrase "Feeble works of charity have no merit and are worth nothing" from chapter 36 of Cervantes's *Don Quijote*, qtd. in Retana, *La censura de imprenta en Filipinas*, 13.

11. "Miles los librillos de embrutecimiento religioso en lengua indígena, única que querían propagar los frailes, para que los naturales del país y los españoles no pudieran entenderse nunca." Ibid., 34.

12. Onofre D. Corpuz, *An Economic History of the Philippines* (Quezon City: University of the Philippines Press, 1997), 105-38. By the 1860s provincial ports had also opened to direct foreign trade. See Alfred W. McCoy and Ed. C. de Jesus, eds., *Philippine Social History: Global Trade and Local Transformations* (Honolulu: University Press of Hawai'i, 1982), 11.

13. Here a few words about literacy in the Philippines are warranted. Evidence of widespread literacy throughout the Spanish colonial period—and even prior to the arrival of the Spanish—is largely anecdotal but persuasive. Early missionary chronicles are rife with accounts attesting to the natives' fondness for reading and writing. For example, the Jesuit Pedro Chirino observed in the first decade of the 1600s that the *indios*' "passion for books is not limited to those printed in their language composed by the Religious but includes the sermons they hear, sacred histories, lives of the saints, prayers, and sacred poetry composed by them. Rarely is there a man or woman not in possession of one or more books handwritten in their language and script" (*su aficion á libros que no contentos con los impressos en su lengua, conpuestos [sic] por Varones Religiosos; de los sermones que oyen, de las historias sagradas, Vidas de Santos, Oraciones, y poessias [sic] a lo divino, compuestas por ellos: Apenas ay hombre y mucho menos muger que en su lengua y letra, y escritos de su mano, no tenga uno mas libros*). Francisco Colín, Pedro Chirino, and Pablo Pastells, *Labor evangélica, ministerios apostolicos de los obreros de la Compañia de Jesus, fundacion, y progressos de su provincia en las Islas Filipinas: Historiados por el padre Francisco Colín. Parte primera sacada de los manuscritos del padre Pedro Chirino, el primero de la Compañia que passó de los reynos de España a estas islas, por orden, y a costa de la catholica, y real magestad* (Barcelona: Imprenta y Litografía de Henrich y Compañía, 1900-1902), qtd. in D. R. M. Irving, *Colonial Counterpoint: Music in Early Modern Manila* (New York: Oxford University Press, 2010), 264. Although supplanting the Tagalog syllabary (the *baybayin*) with the Roman alphabet resulted in a period of widespread illiteracy in the seventeenth and eighteenth centuries, literacy was "restored" by the mid-eighteenth century, as more segments of the population aspired to gain access to European knowledge and as locals began to be admitted to seminaries. For this discussion, see Bienvenido Lumbera's *Tagalog Poetry, 1570-1898: Tradition and Influences*

in Its Development (Quezon City: Ateneo de Manila University Press, 2001), especially chap. 3. We can assume that the burgeoning of print through local presses and in local vernaculars from about the mid-nineteenth century onward correlated with and met a certain demand. Dean S. Fansler, an American folklorist who wrote on the *corrido* genre in the 1910s, noted that the small, cheap pamphlets "make up the body of most of the entertaining reading of the lower and middle classes." Fansler, "Metrical Romances in the Philippines," *Journal of American Folklore* 29, no. 112 (1916): 204. Later, Filipino anthropologist E. Arsenio Manuel confirmed: "The metrical romances became very widely popular and very soon every class had its share of this delightful literary fare. Even the farmer, home from his labor, found rest reading this cheap literary repast." Qtd. in Eugenio, Awit *and* Corrido, xvii. According to Eugenio, it was not uncommon for some titles to go through several editions or multiple printings. Furthermore, individual copies could have many lives, as seen in the prologue to one popular *corrido*, *Juan Bachiller*, whose author requests that the reader not throw away the copy of the tale but return it to its original owner for further loans (xviii).

14. Smita Lahiri, "Rhetorical Indios: Propagandists and Their Publics in the Spanish Philippines," *Comparative Studies in Society and History* 49, no. 2 (2007): 245.

15. Early missionaries identified a number of different types of oral versification in Tagalog, but as Bienvenido Lumbera has pointed out, over time they came to subsume many of these types under the rubric of *dalit*, transforming it into a capacious category akin to the English term "poetry." See *Tagalog Poetry*, 32. For a discussion of the *dalit* as it worked in "reciprocal and accelerated transculturation" with the written tradition of religious poetry coming from Spain, especially in the text and practice of the *pasyon* (the vernacular narrative of the Passion of Christ), see Blanco, *Frontier Constitutions*, 104-7.

16. Fenella Cannell has an example of this in her essay "Reading as Gift and Writing as Theft," in which she examines the dedicatory letter from the Bicolano translator of the *pasyon* to the archbishop who commissioned it. This letter appears as a preface to the main body of the *pasyon* text itself. See Cannell, ed., *The Anthropology of Christianity* (Durham, NC: Duke University Press, 2006), 134-62.

17. Resil B. Mojares, "Stalking the Virgin," in *Waiting for Mariang Makiling: Essays in Philippine Cultural History* (Quezon City: Ateneo de Manila University, 2002), 149.

18. *Epítome de la historia de la aparición de Nuestra Señora de Caysasay; que se venera en el pueblo de Taal, de la Provincia de Batangas, y su sagrada novena. Compuesta por el R. P. Fr. Francisco Bencuchillo, del Orden de S. Agustin. Sácala nuevamente á luz N.M.R.P. Ex-Provincial Fr. Ramon del Marco, del mismo órden; Vicario Provincial y Foráneo de la dicha provincia, y Cura Párroco actual del referido pueblo, quien la dedica á la misma Reina del Universo* (Manila: Imprenta de Ramirez y Giraudier, 1859).

19. To compare, see William A. Christian Jr.'s discussion of a seventeenth-century Dominican's survey of Catalan discovery legends in *Apparitions in Late Medieval and Renaissance Spain*, 15-25 (see also note 23 in the introduction to this book).

20. In his surrealist treatise on the profane miracle, André Breton writes of *la trouvaille*, or "the object found": "This *trouvaille*, whether it be artistic, scientific, philosophic, or as useless as anything, is enough to undo the beauty of everything beside it. It alone can enlarge the universe, causing it to relinquish some of its opacity, letting us discover its extraordinary capacities for reserve, proportionate to the innumerable needs of the spirit . . . Daily life abounds, moreover, in just this sort of small discovery." *Mad Love*, trans. Mary Ann Caws (Lincoln: University of Nebraska Press, 1987), 13-15 (originally published as *L'amour fou*, 1937).

21. For two takes on "virginal historiography," see Michael Taussig's "The Wild Woman of the Forest Becomes Our Lady of Remedies," in *Shamanism, Colonialism, and the Wild Man* (Chicago: University of Chicago Press, 1987); and Mojares's essay "Stalking the Virgin," 140-70. Both essays identify a miraculous image or appearance of Mary as a particular locus of dialogic encounter and historical production in the colonial context, as I try to do here. What further interests me, however, is why, of all the available figures in the Catholic pantheon, it is most overwhelmingly the Virgin Mary who occasions these mediations.

22. For a reading of the *Epítome de la historia de la aparición de Nuestra Señora de Caysasay* through the lens of Paul Ricouer's formulation of first and second "naïvetés," see Agustin Martin Rodriguez and Felice Noelle Rodriguez's "Apparition, Narration, and Reappropriation of Meaning," *Philippine Studies* 44, no. 4 (1996): 465–78.

23. Juan Catalina García López, *Biblioteca de escritores de la provincia de Guadalajara y bibliografía de la misma hasta el siglo XIX* (Madrid: Est. Tipográfico Sucesores de Rivadeneyra, 1899), 22; and Retana, *Epítome de la bibliografía general de Filipinas por W.E. Retana, parte primera, obras que posee el autor (Madrid 1898)* in *Archivo del bibliófilo filipino*, 4:31. Both sources corroborate that the first edition of the text was indeed published in 1754. The entry in García reads: *Epítome de la historia de la aparición de Nuestra Señora de Casaisai y su Novena en lengua tagala. Manila, con las licencias necesarias, en la imprenta de la Compañía de Jesus, por D. Nicolas de la Cruz. Bagai, 1754.* At a much later date I located one copy of an 1834 edition of Bencuchillo's text at the National Library of Australia, published by D. Cayetano Enriquez of Sampaloc, Philippines.

24. Policarpo F. Hernández, *The Augustinians in the Philippines* (Makati: Colegio de San Agustin, 1998), 90.

25. García López, *Biblioteca de escritores*, 21–22.

26. "Juzgaron algunos tan fácil de practicar la Poesía Tagala, quanto otros conocieron su dificultad, ó la aprendieron, en practicarla. Yo que no soy tan animoso como los primeros, pero ni tan cobarde como los segundos, escojeré caminar por el medio . . . [quoting Ovid] *Medio tustissimus* [*sic*] *ibis.*" Francisco Bencuchillo, *Arte poético tagalo* (Manila: Impresa de la Viuda de M. Minuesa de los Ríos, 1895), 3.

27. Lumbera, *Tagalog Poetry*, 56.

28. Ibid. See also the introduction to René Javellana's edited version of the famous *pasyon* (Passion of Christ), *Casaysayan nang Pasiong Mahal ni Jesucristong Panginoon Natin na Sucat Ipag-alab nang Puso nang Sinomang Babasa* (Quezon City: Ateneo de Manila University Press, 1988).

29. *Gagadolong lisa lamang* could more literally be translated as "only as small as a nit." See Sir John Bowring, "Popular Proverbs," in *A Visit to the Philippine Islands* (London: Smith, Elder & Co., 1859), 289.

30. I am relying here on Vicente Rafael's indispensable examination of how early Spanish missionaries attempted to "dominate the vernacular" by reducing it to Latin grammatical structures. *Contracting Colonialism: Translation and Christian Conversion in Tagalog Society under Early Spanish Rule* (Ithaca, NY: Cornell University Press, 1988), especially chap. 1.

31. This would be the Pansipit River, which runs from Taal Lake to the sea.

32. Here I have translated *lic-ha[ng]*, what would more conventionally be considered simply "creation" (often understood in relation to Ang Lumikha: the Creator, or God), more explicitly as "figurine," for "statue" (*estatua*) or "idol" (*ídolo*) is often found in Tagalog-Spanish vocabularies of the period. See Francisco de San Antonio, *Vocabulario Tagalo*, Pulong (1624; Quezon City: Sources for Philippine Studies, Ateneo de Manila University, 2000), 149. Even as late as the end of the nineteenth century, in Ferdinand Blumentritt's *Diccionario mitológico de Filipinas*, one finds *likha* defined as "word given to the small idols that the ancient [T]agalogs made in memory of their ancestors." *Diccionario mitológico de Filipinas*, in *La Solidaridad*, November 15, 1893, 1139.

33. This is referring to the iconography of the Immaculate Conception, the belief (later made dogma) that Mary was born without original sin.

34. Bencuchillo, *Epítome*, stanza 16.

35. Ibid., stanzas 19–20.

36. Ibid., stanza 22. In the last line of the stanza appears the word *cabecera*. This was the town of Taal.

37. Ibid., stanzas 31–36.

38. Here again we see the multiple temporalities of the poem, one purpose of which, recall, is to relate the founding of the town of Caysasay as the place where the Virgin appeared. Bencuchillo names the town in the time of the poem before it exists in the time of the legend.

39. Bencuchillo, *Epítome*, stanzas 39–42.

40. Ibid., stanzas 43–49.

41. Ibid., stanzas 51–57.

42. The nearby Taal Lake, an extraordinary geological formation that fills a large caldera known by the same name and holds within it an island that itself contains a lake that also contains a small island, was largely believed to have been a saline lake before a series of major volcanic eruptions beginning in the sixteenth century curtailed over time the mingling of fresh and salt water. It is now classified as a freshwater lake. Thomas R. Hargrove, *The Mysteries of Taal: A Philippine Volcano and Lake, Her Sea Life and Lost Towns* (Manila: Bookmark Publishing, 1991), 5.

43. Edgar Wickberg, *The Chinese in Philippine Life, 1850–1898* (1965; Quezon City: Ateneo de Manila University Press, 2000), 9.

44. Wickberg's study *Chinese in Philippine Life* still prevails as the standard text on this history. In it he argues that relations between the Chinese and the Spaniards were marked by "a pattern of distrust and latent hostility . . . basic [to which] was a prevailing condition of economic interdependence coupled with seemingly irreconcilable cultural differences." Thus, the word *Sangley*, he continues, "quickly came to apply to an invidious cultural stereotype . . . [becoming] not simply one of two ethnic groups of equal status under the Spanish [the other being the pejoratively named *indio*], but a despised cultural minority" (9). A sequel to Wickberg's classic is Richard T. Chu's *Chinese and Chinese Mestizos of Manila: Family, Identity, and Culture, 1860s–1930s* (Mandaluyong: Anvil Press, 2012).

45. The disproportionate system of taxing natives and Chinese, explains Wickberg, was one factor that often motivated the latter to convert: "Acceptance of baptism was a shrewd business move for a Chinese. Besides reduced taxes, land grants, and freedom to reside almost anywhere, one acquired a Spanish godparent, who could be counted upon as a bondsman, creditor, patron, and protector in legal matters." *Chinese in Philippine Life*, 16.

46. According to Wickberg, following a revolt in 1603 the entire population of Chinese in Manila—upward of twenty thousand people—were killed. Ibid., 10.

47. For further elaboration of this summary, see Wickberg, *Chinese in Philippine Life*, chap. 1.

48. Bencuchillo, *Epítome*, stanzas 69–70. This decree could refer to the massacre of Chinese that took place in either 1603 or 1639. Given the geographical reach of each massacre, the reference is most likely to the 1603 killings, since we know for certain that the Chinese fleeing Manila were pursued by Spanish forces well into the province of Batangas (where Taal and Caysasay are located). For a thorough examination of the primary accounts of this massacre, see José Eugenio Borao, "The Massacre of 1603: Chinese Perception of the Spaniards in the Philippines," *Itinerario* 23, no. 1 (1998): 22–39.

49. Bencuchillo, *Epítome*, stanzas 71–75.

50. Ibid., stanzas 77–79.

51. Ibid., stanza 84.

52. Ibid., stanza 86.

53. The Virgin Mary as a symbol of the church is indeed a long-standing tradition, reaching back to the early church fathers. See Thomas Livius, *The Blessed Virgin in the Fathers of the First Six Centuries* (London, 1893), chap. 6.

54. R. P. Fr. Casimiro Díaz, O.S.A., *Conquistas de las Islas Filipinas* (Valladolid, Spain: L. N. de Gaviria, 1890), book 1, chap. 12, 120–22. Díaz's volume was written from materials left by the better-known Augustinian chronicler, Gaspar de San Agustín.

55. One need look only at the current predicament of the "Chinese" in the Philippines to see the situation of the *Sangley* as a precursor. What were once physical expulsions are refusals of citizenship, and what before was a *Sangley* life cast in economic metaphors of borrowing and debt is now economic extortion of Chinese lives by extractive state policies and kidnap-for-ransom syndicates. Vulnerable to actual or symbolic jettison (from life, from land, from the nation-state) and repeatedly exposed to death, the Chinese in the Philippines are continually reproduced as that ele-

ment of internal exclusion that is crucial to the foundation of power. For a keen examination of this predicament, see Caroline S. Hau, "Kidnapping, Citizenship, and the Chinese," *Public Policy* 1 (October–December 1997): 62–89. Hau argues that the spate of kidnap-for-ransom cases seen in the post–People Power revolt period (from 1986—the end of the Marcos regime—onward) provides an exemplary site for understanding the historical conflation of Chinese capital and, ethnicity and class, and the continual estrangement of Chinese, even Philippine-born Chinese, from the nation-state. In addition to pointing out that the affinity between "alien" (in the sense of citizenship) and "alienating" (as in the movement necessary for the production of capital itself) in this case is by no means a linguistic coincidence, she demonstrates how even Chinese Filipinos' best-intended demands for political representation reveal at their core the state's own discourse of exclusion and interpellative power.

56. A survey of the iconography of Marian shrines in the Philippines reveals not only the provenance of many images to be from the Iberian Peninsula but also the formal qualities of those images (especially color, facial features, and dress) to be more "European." See, for example, the images of the country's most beloved patron saints in P. Yamsuan, L. Reyes, and V. Duavit, eds., *Pueblo Amante de Maria: The Filipinos' Love for Mary* (Manila: Reyes Publishing, 2012). This is not to say that over the course of hundreds of years there were not major transformations in the iconography of saints, especially as local (and especially, Chinese) artisans began the craft of sculpting them. But those images that remained the most publically venerated, that is, around which a shrine and devotional community could be built, largely retained "foreign" features.

57. The Litany of the Blessed Virgin is said to date from the twelfth century; it was approved by the Holy See in 1587. Today it consists of around fifty-one titles for Mary, each of which is followed in recitation by the phrase "pray for us." Some of the descriptions given the Virgin by Bencuchillo are lifted directly from the Tagalog version of the prayer.

58. Bencuchillo, *Epítome*, 17–22.

59. "Hasta hace muy poco tiempo, la vida de los naturales de Filipinas se asemejaba á las preciosas palmeras que hermosean las risueñas florestas de sus campos, mecidas por blanda brisa, al abrigo de un cielo bienhechor, y bajo la providencia de Dios, que envía lluvia y rocío para su crecimiento y lozanía. Así eran los pueblos filipinos ... Mas desde hace muy pocos años, las circunstancias van variando: el cielo, antes sereno, se cubre de nubarrones; la brisa se convierte en huracán; la lluvia tranquila, en aguacero torrencial; y todas las señales hacen creer que lo que ántes era un jardín, se convertirá muy pronto en campo asolado y triste ... Hasta hace muy pocos años, los naturales de Filipinas todos creían ciegamente las verdades de la fé, que habían aprendido de los Padres: si cometían pecados, eran pecados de debilidad, anejos a la condición de la naturaleza humana; pero su alma permanecía siempre dócil a las santas enseñanzas y á las verdades religiosas. Más hoy ¡oh dolor! ya se hoyen por los pueblos cierta clase de doctrinas, malévolamente sembradas por personas nacidas allende de los mares, quienes, en sus insensatez, creen medrar algunos codos ante la opinión de los indios, pretendiendo plaza de ilustrados, cuando no son sino malos deletreantes de algún periódico impudente ... Por fortuna, estas doctrinas hallan poco eco en los habitantes de Filipinas. Pero no faltan algunos desventurados filipinos, pocos por dicha, los cuales, sin entender ni saber lo que se dicen, repiten como papagayos estas doctrinas, creyendo que así hacen méritos para con los que se las enseñan, y serán por ellos exaltados á los destinos honoríficos de los pueblos, y sobresaldrán por este medio en la opinión de sus paisanos." Salvador Millán, *Breve noticia acerca de la aparición de Nuestra Señora de Manaoag, Patrona de Pangasinán, seguida de la Novena en honor de esta Señora, por el P. Fr. Salvador Millán, Dominico* (Manila: Establecimiento Tipográfico del Colegio de Santo Tomás, 1891), 11–13.

60. The historiography of the *ilustrados* has grown immensely in the past fifteen or so years, drawing out a number of fascinating dimensions of the class's formation and role in both the late Spanish colonial and early American imperial periods. See Benedict R. O'G Anderson, *Under Three Flags: Anarchism and the Anti-Colonial Imagination* (New York: Verso Books, 2005); John D. Blanco, *Frontier Constitutions: Christianity and Colonial Empire in the Nineteenth-Century Philippines* (Berke-

ley: University of California Press, 2009); Michael Cullinane, *Ilustrado Politics: Filipino Elite Responses to American Rule, 1898–1908* (Quezon City: Ateneo de Manila University Press, 2003); Paul Kramer, *The Blood of Government: Race, Empire, the United States, and the Philippines* (Chapel Hill: University of North Carolina Press, 2006); Resil B. Mojares, *Brains of the Nation: Pedro Paterno, T. H. Padro De Tavera, Isabelo de los Reyes and the Production of Modern Knowledge* (Quezon City: Ateneo de Manila University Press, 2008); Vicente L. Rafael, *The Promise of the Foreign: Nationalism and the Technics of Translation in the Spanish Philippines* (Durham, NC: Duke University Press, 2005); Raquel A. G. Reyes, *Love, Passion and Patriotism: Sexuality and the Philippine Propaganda Movement, 1882–1892* (Seattle: University of Washington Press, 2008); John N. Schumacher, S.J., *The Propaganda Movement, 1880–1895: The Creation of a Filipino Consciousness, the Making of the Revolution* (Quezon City: Ateneo de Manila University Press, 1997); and Megan C. Thomas, *Orientalists, Propagandists, and Ilustrados: Filipino Scholarship and the End of Spanish Colonialism* (Minneapolis: University of Minnesota Press, 2012).

61. Millán, *Breve noticia*, 13.

62. "Causa verdadero dolor, que apena el alma, el considerar que en cerca de trescientos años que lleva de existencia el Santuario de Manaoag, y no obstante la celebridad de que goza, que compite ventajosamente con los más famosos de Europa, no tenga todavía impresa su historia, la cual, á par que de edificación, sirva también para satisfacer la legítima curiosidad de los devotos." Ibid., 1.

63. "A treinta kilómetros del pueblo de Lingayén, capital de la provincia de Pangasinán, en dirección al Oriente, se encuentra un pintoresco valle, especie de anfiteatro, formado por pequeñas colinas que le cierran por todas partes, y le sirven de defensa contra los huracanes y contra las tormentas tropicales." Ibid., 23–24.

64. "Cierto día pasaba un indio devoto por el pié del montecito en que está erigido el Santuario, cuando oyó de pronto una voz de suavidad inefable, que le llamaba por su nombre. Miró hacia la cumbre del monte, de donde salió la voz, y quedó de repente sorprendido por la vista de una blanquísima y resplandeciente nube, que descansando en la copa de un árbol muy frondoso, se elevaba hacia el espacio, formando ondas vaporosas y trasparentes como de finísimo encaje. Dirigióse, no sin miedo, hacia el lugar que tanto llamaba su atención; y apenas hubo llegado, se presentó ante sus ojos una visión celestial, que llenando su alma de dulzura, atrajo á sí todas sus potencias y sentidos. En el centro de la nube apareció una señora vestida de blanco y radiante de belleza, y en sus brazos llevaba un niño de hermosura celestial. La señora tenía en su diestra un rosario, y tanto ella como el niño, fijaban dulcemente sus ojos en el indio afortunado. Dióle á entender la señora que era la Virgen del Rosario y su Santísimo Hijo, que deseaban se levantase un santuario en honor suyo en aquel mismo lugar, al cual pudieran acudir sus devotos en la sucesión de los tiempos, para implorar su maternal protección. Breves momentos duró la aparición celestial, al cabo de los cuales la nube fué elevándose poco á poco hácia el cielo, hasta desaparecer del todo de la vista del extático vidente. El cual, apenas repuesto de su profundo estupor, acercóse devotamente á besar el árbol santificado con el contacto de María; pero se detuvo al punto, porque entre sus ramas vió una imágen de talla de la Virgen del Rosario con el Niño, también de talla, en sus brazos. Avisó de todo al santo Misionero, el cual, acompañado de los cristianos de la Misión, fué al lugar por el indio señalado, y recogió cuidadosamente la imágen, llevándola a la iglesia de Santa Mónica, en donde estuvo expuesta á la veneración de los fieles, hasta que se levantó una iglesia de madera en el lugar de la aparición." Ibid., 27–29.

65. For an ethnographic elaboration of this formulation, see John Pemberton's *On the Subject of "Java"* (Ithaca, NY: Cornell University Press, 1994).

66. Speaking of voluptuous materiality, on the enormous Dominican compound that houses the shrine of Our Lady of Manaoag today is a museum where all the accoutrements donated to the Virgin over the years are displayed behind glass: jeweled crowns, gold rosaries, as well as a jaw-dropping collection of perfumes that sit on shelves lining an entire wall.

67. Sinibaldo de Mas, *Informe sobre el estado de las islas Filipinas en 1842* (Madrid: Imprenta de I. Sancha, 1843), 6.

68. Jose, *Simbahan*, 126.

69. This can surely be verified by any number of contemporary collectors of Philippine *santos*, who will entertain the exorbitant price that an image created, say, by an Asuncion or a Tampinco demands.

70. Esperanza Buñag Gatbonton, *A Heritage of Saints* (Manila: Editorial Associates, 1979), 168. For a more critical evaluation of the history of the Academia and the history of Philippine colonial art in general, see Patrick D. Flores, *Painting History: Revisions in Philippine Colonial Art* (Quezon City: Office of Research Coordination University of the Philippines; Manila: National Commission for Culture and the Arts), especially 277-87.

71. Jose, *Simbahan*, 126.

72. In an article titled "The Santo and the Rural Aristocracy," economist Victor Venida notes that "families would assign a portion of their landowning to the santo, the so called *lupa ng santo* [land belonging to the image]." Considering that anything resembling a rural aristocracy was inconceivable prior to the nineteenth century, we can safely assume that this is as far back as this "tradition" goes. "The Santo and the Rural Aristocracy," *Philippine Studies* 44, no. 4 (1996): 504.

73. For a hilarious send-up of the acquisitive elite's devotion to collecting *santos* in the late colonial period, see José Rizal's depiction of Capitan Tiago's home shrine in his famous satirical novel, *Noli me tangere*, trans. Soledad Lacson-Locsin (1886; Honolulu: University of Hawai'i Press, 1996), 33-34.

74. Jaime C. Laya, *Prusisyon: Religious Pageantry in the Philippines* (Manila: Cofradía de la Inmaculada Concepción, 1995), 85.

75. Gilles Deleuze, *Difference and Repetition* (New York: Columbia University Press, 1994), 1.

76. In the most comprehensive tome documenting the presence and activities of the Dominican Order in the sixteenth to mid-seventeenth centuries, Diego Aduarte's *Historia de la Provincia del Santo Rosario de la orden de predicadores en Filipinas, Japón, y China*, vol. 1 (1693; Madrid: Consejo Superior de Investigaciones Científicas, Departamento de Misionología Española, 1962), Manaoag is described as a settlement the Dominicans took over the from the Augustinians, with the Virgin of the Rosary as its patron (501-3).

77. Rosario Mendoza Cortes, *Pangasinan, 1572-1800* (Quezon City: New Day Publishers, 1974), 102. The Tagalog word for "call," *tawag*, shares the same root.

78. Owing to the vast diversity of languages, the perennial shortage of regular clergy, and the scattered nature of the native population, the Council of the Indies in 1594 instructed that the governor and the bishop divide the Philippines into missions defined by four religious orders: Augustinians, Franciscans, Jesuits, and Dominicans. See Phelan's *Hispanization of the Philippines*, 49-52 and 167-76.

79. See David Brading, *Mexican Phoenix: Our Lady of Guadalupe: Image and Tradition across Five Centuries*, especially chap. 15, 361-68.

80. *Historia at novena nang mahal na Virgin Ntra. Sra. de Guadalupe, pinag ayos at pinag husay sa uicang Castila nang isang religiosong Agustino* (Manila: Imp. de Ramirez y Giraudier, 1870).

81. Mateo de la Cruz, *Relación de la milagrosa aparición de la santa imagen de la Virgen de Guadalupe de México, sacada de la historia que compuso Br. Miguel Sánchez* (Mexico, 1660); Miguel Sánchez, *Imagen de la Virgen María Madre de Dios de Guadalupe* (Mexico, 1648). Both of these are reprinted in Ernesto de la Torre Villar y Ramiro Navarro de Anda, *Testimonios históricos guadalupanos* (Mexico City: Fondo de Cultura Económica, 1982), 267-81 and 153-267, respectively.

82. See Brading's *Mexican Phoenix* for the most exhaustive treatment of the historiography of Guadalupe; for more on Cruz's *Relación*, see Brading, *Mexican Phoenix*, 76-77.

83. *Historia at novena*, 6-19.

84. Ibid., 19-22.

85. Ibid., 23-42.

86. Mojares, "Stalking the Virgin," 155. In this essay, Mojares takes readers through an examination of the densely layered case of yet another icon of the Virgin of Guadalupe in the Philippines,

patrona of an area adjacent to Cebu City. Much like the story of Caysasay, the Virgin of Guadalupe of Cebu begins with the story of an image with a penchant for getting lost and found in the early colonial period. In its multiple versions, however, both oral and written, the story is rife with "indigenous" motifs of sacred topography and figures of power: caves, miraculous springs, tutelary spirits, chieftains, and earthly goddesses. The point well taken from Mojares's essay is that the Virgin of Guadalupe in Cebu has not one origin but is an "event tangled in obscure mediations[,] . . . an appearance densely contaminated rather than immaculate" (145).

87. For the most comprehensive list of Philippine *devocionarios* published in the nineteenth century, see Retana, *Archivo del bibliófilo filipino.*

88. *Historia at novena,* 7.

89. Ibid., 20.

90. See Thomas, *Orientalists, Propagandists, and Ilustrados;* and Mojares, *Brains of the Nation,* especially 43–68.

91. Benedict R. O'G Anderson, *The Spectre of Comparisons: Nationalism, Southeast Asia, and the World* (New York: Verso 1998), 39–40. See also Vicente Rafael's essay "White Love: Census and Melodrama in the U.S. Colonization of the Philippines," in *White Love and Other Events in Filipino History* (Quezon City: Ateneo de Manila University Press, 2000), 19–51.

92. For more on the category of "Tagalog" in the late nineteenth century and its relationship to the emergent category of "Filipino," see Kramer, *Blood of Government,* especially 35–86.

93. Anderson, *The Spectre of Comparisons,* 31.

94. Ibid., 36.

95. "Colección de noticias, publicadas ya ó todavía inéditas, acerca de las imágenes de la santísima Virgen más veneradas en el país, ilustrada con profusión de láminas. Comprende, además, en dos apéndices, la relación de todas las advocaciones marianas de las iglesias del archipiélago, y algunos datos históricos." Congregantes Marianos, *La Virgen Maria venerada en sus imágenes filipinas* (Manila: Imprenta de Santos y Bernal, 1904), title page.

96. Ibid., v.

CHAPTER 2

1. *Katipunan* is shorthand for Kataastaasan Kagalang-galang ng Katipunan ng mga Anak ng Bayan (The Highest and Most Venerable Society of the Children of the Land). Usually depicted as "proletarian," "plebian," and/or "of the masses," the Katipunan is the armed counterpoint to the *ilustrados,* the mestizo elite, largely educated in Europe, who pushed for secular reform of the colony in the latter half of the nineteenth century. The classic text on the Katipunan and its leader, Andres Bonifacio, is Teodoro Agoncillo's *The Revolt of the Masses: The Story of Bonifacio and the Katipunan* (Quezon City: University of the Philippines, 1956). A sharp critique of Agoncillo's text and much of the nationalist historiography of Bonifacio can be found in Glenn Anthony May's *Inventing a Hero: The Posthumous Re-creation of Andres Bonifacio* (Quezon City: New Day Publishers, 1997).

2. *Tandang* stems from *matanda,* or "elderly."

3. "Uno de ellos vió en sueños una hermosa Madre vestida al estilo de las campesinas de Balintawak que llevaba de la mano á un lindo niño, vestido de campesino con pantalon corto encarnado que esgrimía un reluciente bolo, gritando, LIBERTAD! LIBERTAD! La bella mujer se acercó al que soñaba y le dijo: 'OBRAD CON PRECAUCIÓN.' Al despertar el visionario, contó á sus compañeros lo que había soñado diciendo que la madre y el niño tenían cara de europeos aunque vestidos á lo filipino. Por esto no siguieron su propósito de regresar á Manila para sus oficios ordinarios y se propusieron esperar un poco en Balintawak. No tardó en llegar la noticia de que la Guardia Civil Veterana había requisado a imprenta del *Diario de Manila* y capturado á varios katipuneros." In Gregorio Aglipay, *Novenario de la Patria (La Patria se simboliza en la soñada madre de Balintawak) Escrito por el Emmo. Sr. Gregorio Aglipay y Labayan, Obispo Máximo de la Iglesia Filipina Independi-*

ente . . . aprobado por el Consejo Supremo de Obispos. Editor: Mons. Isabelo de los Reyes y Lopez, Obispo Rector de la Parroquia de María Clara en San Lázaro, Manila (Manila, 1926), back cover.

4. Gregorio Aglipay y Labayan was born in Batac, Ilocos Norte, in 1860. The son of farmers, he was raised by his maternal grandmother and her relatives when his mother died before Gregorio had reached the age of one and his father left town. One of few Ilocanos to receive a secondary education in Manila starting in 1876, Aglipay received a bachelor of arts from the illustrious Dominican University of Santo Tomas in 1881. He entered the seminary in Ilocos Sur in 1883 and was ordained a Catholic priest in 1889.

Aglipay's involvement in the Katipunan began when he founded the local chapter of the movement in Victoria, Tarlac Province, in 1897. When the revolution resumed in 1898, Aglipay was made military vicar-general of the Republican armed forces. He was excommunicated from the church by Manila archbishop Bernardino Nozaleda in October 1898 for "usurpation of authority" in several matters relating to his support of the Filipino clergy. See William Henry Scott, *Aglipay before Aglipayanism* (Quezon City: Aglipayan Resource Center, 1987), for a biography of the leader.

5. This newspaper succeeded *El Renacimiento*, one of the several nationalist periodicals that was published through 1910.

6. Aglipay, *Novenario de la Patria*, back cover.

7. See Rolando Tolentino's *"Inangbayan*, the Mother-Nation, in Lino Brocka's *Bayan Ko: Kapit sa Patalim* and *Orapronobis," Screen* 37, no. 4 (Winter 1996): 368–88. For a wonderful essay on imagining Filipino nationhood through the vernacularly rendered and gendered metaphor of motherland, especially in contradistinction to the photographed bodies of Filipino male patriots in the metropole, see Vicente Rafael, "Nationalism, Imagery, and the Filipino Intelligentsia in the Nineteenth Century," *Critical Inquiry* 16, no. 3 (Spring 1990): 591–611.

8. The origins of the concept of motherland or mother country are many, and tracing them historically could constitute a study unto itself. The *Oxford English Dictionary* includes sources from sixteenth-century translations of Ovid's *Metamorphoses*, as well as the definition "a country in relation to its colonies or dependencies; the country from which the founders of a colony came," whose oldest citation dates from 1732. The modern association of mother country or motherland with the nation-state is most likely a translation of *patria*, which, while stemming from *pater*, was feminized especially during the French Revolution with representations of the new republic. But the representation of motherland acquired particular potency in the era of nineteenth-century independence movements, with such iconography as Our Lady of Guadalupe in Mexico and the figure Bharat Mata, or Mother India. Although there is no dearth of scholarship on why nationalism demands that its love object be feminized, see Joan Landes's *Visualizing the Nation: Gender, Representation, and Revolution in Eighteenth-Century France* (Ithaca, NY: Cornell University Press, 2001), especially her chapter "Possessing *La Patrie*," for an analysis of this feminization and the iconography of the period. Given the geographical circulation and education of the *ilustrados*, we should not be surprised to find these concepts circulating in their own work. Important studies of gender and nationalism include Nira Yural Davis and Floya Anthias, *Woman, Nation, State* (Basingstoke, UK: Macmillan, 1989); and Mrinalini Sinha's *Colonial Masculinity: The "Manly Englishman" and the "Effeminate Bengali" in the Late Nineteenth Century* (Manchester, UK: Manchester University Press, 1995).

9. The best known among these studies is Reynaldo Ileto's *Pasyon and Revolution: Popular Movements in the Philippines, 1840–1910* (Quezon City: Ateneo de Manila University Press, 1979).

10. The Tagalog version of Flores's *Hibik ng Pilipinas sa Ynang España* can be found in a volume of prose and poetry titled *Philippine Literature Past and Present*, ed. S. Baltasar, T. Erestain, and Ma. F. Estanislao (Quezon City: Katha Publishing, 1981), 115–20. This is the version I use here. Original versions of del Pilar's *Sagot nang España sa Hibik nang Pilipinas* and *Katapusang Hibik ng Pilipinas* are reprinted in many compilations, including Bienvenido Lumbera's oft-cited *Tagalog Poetry, 1570–1898: Tradition and Influences in Its Development* (Quezon City: Ateneo de Manila University Press, 2001), 217–39, whose translations I draw from here.

11. For an abbreviated analyses of these three poems along these lines, see Reynaldo Ileto,

"Mother Spain, Uncle Sam, and the Construction of Filipino National Identity," in *Imperios y naciones en el Pacífico*, vol. 1, *La formación de una colonia: Filipinas* (Madrid: Consejo Superior de Investigaciones Científicas, 2001), 119–31; and Ileto, "Bernardo Carpio: *Awit* and Revolution," in *Filipinos and Their Revolution: Event, Discourse, and Historiography* (Quezon City: Ateneo de Manila University Press, 1998), 1–27.

12. "Frairocracy," translated from *frailocracía* in Spanish (*fraile* means "friar"), was a neologism popularized by del Pilar in the pamphlet "La Frailocracía," which he composed under the pen name Plaridel.

13. Lumbera writes, "The poem [del Pilar's *Sagot*] is for the most part pedestrian verse, not much better than its companion poem." *Tagalog Poetry*, 145.

14. Of the Philippine context, Lumbera writes, "The inspiration behind the design [of del Pilar's *Sagot*] seems to have come from the *loa*, the earliest form of Spanish drama performed in the colony. In certain *loas*, allegorical figures appeared and delivered speeches in flowery verse in praise of a guest of honor or of the occasion being celebrated." Ibid., 145.

15. Flores, *Hibik*, stanzas 9 and 13.

16. Ibid., stanza 5.

17. See Benedict R. O'G. Anderson, *Imagined Communities: Reflections on the Origin and Spread of Nationalism* (New York: Verso, 1991), especially chap. 2.

18. Del Pilar, *Sagot*, stanzas 5 and 8.

19. See Onofre D. Corpuz, *An Economic History of the Philippines* (Quezon City: University of the Philippines Press, 1997), especially chaps. 6–8; and John D. Blanco, *Frontier Constitutions: Christianity and Colonial Empire in the Nineteenth-Century Philippines* (Berkeley: University of California Press, 2009), especially chap. 1.

20. See Ileto, "Mother Spain" and "Bernardo Carpio."

21. See, for example, the entire section of Flores's *Hibik* (stanzas 30–43) that is dedicated to relaying the story of the assassination of Governor-General Bustamante in 1719, believed to be at the hand of friars.

22. Andres Bonifacio, *Katapusang Hibik*, reprinted in Lumbera, *Tagalog Poetry*, 234–39.

23. I have slightly modified Lumbera's translation here (originally "Filipinas has received nothing") to a more literal rendering of the verb *namana*, derived from the root word *mana*, or "inheritance." There is likely some etymological resonance with the more widely known definition of *mana* as a kind of power, but I have yet to see this traced out.

24. Ileto, *Pasyon and Revolution*, 105.

25. See, for example, René Javellana, *Casaysayan nang Pasiong Mahal ni Jesucristong Panginoon Natin na Sucat Ipag-alab nang Puso nang Sinomang Babasa* (Quezon City: Ateneo de Manila University Press, 1988), stanzas 1015–29 and 1762–1828.

26. Translation slightly modified in stanza 6, line 3 and stanza 11, line 4.

27. To compare, the canonical New Testament gospels include a total of a mere five mentions of Mary at the time of Christ's crucifixion (and none from the Gospel of Luke), situating her as only one figure at the scene. By contrast, in one of the more common versions of the *pasyon*, an entire scene consisting of fifteen stanzas is dedicated to portraying Jesus's separation from his mother on Holy Thursday. It includes a long dialogue between Jesus and Mary: he tells her of his need to save man from sin; she weeps inconsolably; he assures her she will not be alone but will be accompanied by John; they both cry together; and he departs, but not without one last glance behind him. This is not the only section, furthermore, in which the mournful Mary takes center stage; at the foot of the cross she even offers to take her son's place, so impossible to bear is the sight of his pain. See again Javellana, *Casaysayan nang Pasiong Mahal* and the devotional poem "Ang Pananangis ni Maria sa Paanan ng Krus" (Mary Weeps at the Foot of the Cross), in Aniceto de la Merced's *El libro de la vida*, in Lumbera's *Tagalog Poetry*, 209–15.

28. This is my main critique of Ileto's monumental work: it is still a rather Catholic reading of unorthodox Catholicism. Although his interpretation of vernacular texts brilliantly portrays the

political epistemology vastly different from that of "enlightened" nationalists, and while many of the motifs he elucidates in these texts (such as the recognized split between appearance and essence) reveal the real modernity of the "folk," Ileto still treats the *pasyon* as an unchanging form. In other words, even though "the pasyon was freed from its officially sanctioned moorings in Holy Week and allowed to give form and meaning to the people's struggles for liberation" (254), it is never allowed in Ileto's study to be free from itself. There are other religious sodalities of the period, relegated to footnotes by Ileto, which appropriated Catholic figures and narratives in ways that produced totally irrecuperable and incommensurable excesses of social and political signification, perceived as heretical by orthodox standards, yet outrageous even by the more routinized standard of the Catholic carnivalesque. The Guardia de Honor, to take an example pertinent to devotion to Mary, started with the local founding of a sodality (*cofradía*), originally sanctioned by the Dominican Order, that would devote itself to perpetual recitation of the rosary. Yet by the time of the Philippine-American War, the Guardia had settled the town of Cabaruan, Pangasinan, and had throngs of followers journeyed there after wreaking havoc across the countryside. The community of this New Jerusalem revolved around a God, a Jesus, a Virgin Mary, and twelve lieutenants known as "apostles." By most accounts, the Guardia had flummoxed every governing body that had ruled through the twenty or so years it was in existence for being impossible to pin down ideologically. Was it a provincial front for the Katipunan? Or a counterrevolutionary tool of the friars? A messianic cult that would wait out its last days as protocommunists? Or, as it would be soberly analyzed in the 1960s, a bona fide peasant rebellion? Simply put, the Guardia defied any thorough explanation of its allegiances and ideologies, and although it clearly had Catholic trappings, there was no syncretic or vernacular translation of Catholicism, and no compensatory assertion of "indigenousness," that would suffice to account for it. Hard to know, despite the years and theories later, was the exact call to which its leadership and members responded, except perhaps the call itself: the one sanctioned site they were known to hold sacred was none other than that of Our Lady of Manaoag. For a meditation on the Guardia de Honor, see Nick Joaquin's "Apocalypse and Revolution," in his *Culture and History: Occasional Notes on the Process of Philippine Becoming* (Manila: Solar Publishing, 1988), 162-93. And for a penetrating critique of Ileto's study along these lines, see Caroline Hau, "Literature and History," in *Necessary Fictions: Philippine Literature and the Nation, 1946-1980* (Quezon City: Ateneo de Manila University Press, 2000), especially 118-32.

29. For secondary writings on Aurelio Tolentino and his works, see the introduction to Edna Zapanta-Manlapaz, ed., *Aurelio Tolentino: Selected Writings* (Quezon City: University of the Philippines Library, 1975), 1-13; Esperidion Arsenio Manuel, *Dictionary of Philippine Biography* (Quezon City: Filipiniana Publications, 1970), 2:371-432; Felipe Fernando, "Aurelio Tolentino: Playwright, Poet, and Patriot," *Philippine Studies* 12 (January 1964): 83-92; and Resil B. Mojares, *Origins and Rise of the Filipino Novel* (Quezon City: University of the Philippines Press, 1998), 237-41.

30. Amelia Lapeña-Bonifacio, *The "Seditious" Tagalog Playwrights: Early American Occupation* (Manila: Zarzuela Foundation of the Philippines, 1972), 27.

31. Historians have rightly treated the seditious plays of the early twentieth century as some of the most compelling sites of resistance to the American occupation. See especially Vicente Rafael's essay "White Love: Census and Melodrama in the U.S. Colonization of the Philippines," in his *White Love and Other Events in Filipino History* (Quezon City: Ateneo de Manila University Press, 2000), 19-51, for a discussion of these dramas as they subverted the colonial project of represent and rule.

32. The consummate bibliophile W. E. Retana claims in his *Noticias histórico-bibliográficas de el teatro en Filipinas desde sus orígenes hasta 1898* that the first *comedia* written in the Philippines was staged in 1598 for the visit of one bishop Pedro de Agurto, cited in Nicanor Tiongson's comprehensive volume *Philippine Theater: History and Anthology*, vol. 2, *Komedya* (Quezon City: University of the Philippines Press, 1999), 2. Most of my comments on the *comedia* are drawn from Tiongson's text.

33. This runs very much against the general opinion held by scholars of Philippine performing

arts forms until very recently. In his authoritative volume *Komedya*, Nicanor Tiongson argues that the *comedia* functioned in the Spanish colonial period as an opiate for the masses, flourishing under church censors precisely because its plots advocated submission to hierarchy and the superiority of Europeans. One exception to this common dismissal can be found in Vicente Rafael's study of translation and nationalism, *The Promise of the Foreign: Nationalism and the Technics of Translation in the Spanish Philippines* (Durham, NC: Duke University Press, 2005), especially chap. 4, "The Colonial Uncanny: The Foreign Lodged in the Vernacular."

34. That Tolentino set his play in the same barrio that figures prominently in the legend of Mary's appearance to the Katipuneros is no coincidence; recall that it was Tolentino who related his fellow Katipunero's dream of the Madonna and Child.

35. *Luhang Tagalog* (Tagalog Tears), excerpted in its entirety as found in American naval officer and journalist Arthur Riggs's *The Filipino Drama* (1905; Manila: Ministry of Human Settlements, 1981), 91–92 (English) and 383–84 (Tagalog). Lamentably, the original Tagalog versions of many of the plays included in Riggs's study, including this one, no longer exist. The scripts he includes in the main body of the text are translations of Spanish versions into English, and although Tagalog versions are provided in the appendix, they themselves have been translated from the English only at the time of that volume's publication in the early 1980s. For these sections I have worked between the two translations. It is also worth noting that, since they were often written under censorship, even the scripts cannot do justice to what the performances themselves might have been; Riggs was furthermore hardly a neutral observer. For more on Riggs's study as instantiative of American colonial views that lowland Filipinos were singularly lacking in cultural signs of civilizational development, see Paul Kramer's *The Blood of Government: Race, Empire, the United States, and the Philippines* (Chapel Hill: University of North Carolina Press, 2006), 197–98.

36. *Luhang Tagalog*, in Riggs, *Filipino Drama*, 93 (English) and 385 (Tagalog).

37. The most common Tagalog words for "dream" are *panaginip* and *pangarap*. *Bangungot* derives from *bangon* (to rise) and *ungol* (to moan). Its association with death is evidenced by its colloquial usage as an explanatory term for someone who dies, unexpectedly, in his or her sleep. For more info on the history of the term's more popular usage, see social critic and medical anthropologist Michael Tan's *Revisiting Usog, Pasma, and Kulam* (Quezon City: University of the Philippines Press, 2008), especially chap. 3.

38. *Luhang Tagalog*, in Riggs, *Filipino Drama*, 91–93 (English) and 383–86 (Tagalog).

39. *Kahapon, Ngayon at Bukas*, 80–81 (original Tagalog). Although this play, too, appears in Riggs's edited volume, I draw from the Tagalog version based on the extant original script, which can be found in Zapanta-Manlapaz, *Aurelio Tolentino*, 15–142.

40. Ibid., 77–78.

41. This is referred to earlier in the play, in a conversation between Tagailog (literally "from the river," and often cited as the etymological root of "Tagalog") and his faithful defender Walangtutol (Obedient One), where they discuss "airships," "electric bullets," and "moveable fortresses" in preparation for revolt, should liberty not be granted them by Malaynatin. Ibid., 73.

42. Here I mean to invoke Benedict Anderson's reflection on the Tomb of the Unknown Soldier, which inspires his assertion that nationalism is always infused with death. *Imagined Communities*, 9–12.

43. In one scene Inangbayan appears to be grieving when the hero Tagailog approaches her. Insinuating that she should not weep, for her suitors (read: nations) are many, Inangbayan replies: "I am a wedded woman . . . [H]e is thy father, the richest and most beautiful in the entire world, with a love so true and most affectionate to all, he is the greatest, the son of all heavens and the true ruler of life . . . He is known as Kalayaan." Tolentino, in Zapanta-Manlapaz, *Aurelio Tolentino*, 82. The semantic breadth of Kalayaan has inspired several different readings of vernacular understandings of sovereignty in the late Spanish colonial period. In *Pasyon and Revolution*, Reynaldo Ileto traces the multivalence of *kalayaan* to the ambiguous root word *layaw*, which means "satisfaction from one's needs," "pampering treatment by parents," or "freedom from strict parental control" (87). The

familial logic asserts itself. For another reading of Kalayaan that acknowledges its debt to Ileto, yet significantly differs from it in profoundly associating Kalayaan with death, see the afterword to Rafael's *Promise of the Foreign*, 183–90.

44. For an abbreviated historical overview of the IFI, see Mary Clifford, "*Iglesia Filipina Independiente*: The Revolutionary Church," in *Studies in Philippine Church History*, ed. Gerard H. Anderson (Ithaca, NY: Cornell University Press, 1969), 223–55.

45. A prolific writer, de los Reyes is perhaps best known for folklorizing the Philippines in numerous articles and studies dedicated to documenting (presciently) what has been known only in anthropology as "local knowledge." De los Reyes's most interesting writings include *La religion antigua de los filipinos* (The Ancient Religion of the Filipinos), *La religion del Katipunan* (The Religion of the Katipunan), a vituperative tract titled *La sensacional memoria de Isabelo de los Reyes sobre la Revolución Filipina de 1896–1897, por lo cual fue deportado el autor al Castillo de Montjuich* (The Sensational Memoir of Isabelo de los Reyes and the Philippine Revolution, for Which the Author Was Banished to the Castle of Montjuich [Spain]), and the more scholarly *El Folklore Filipino* (translated and published in 1994 by the University of the Philippines Press). See Benedict Anderson's adoring treatment of de los Reyes in the prologue to *Under Three Flags: Anarchism and the Anti-Colonial Imagination* (New York: Verso Books, 2005), 8–25; Megan C. Thomas, *Orientalists, Propagandists, and Ilustrados* (Minneapolis: University of Minnesota Press, 2012), especially chap. 3; and Resil B. Mojares, *Brains of the Nation: Pedro Paterno, T. H. Padro de Tavera, Isabelo de los Reyes and the Production of Modern Knowledge* (Quezon City: Ateneo de Manila University Press, 2008), 253–380.

46. For more on Uchimura Kanzo and the Nonchurch Movement, see John F. Howes, *Japan's Modern Prophet: Uchimura Kanzo, 1861–1930* (Vancouver: University of British Columbia Press, 2005). A series of essays in part 3 of Robert E. Buswell Jr. and Timothy S. Lee, eds., *Christianity in Korea* (Honolulu: University of Hawai'i Press, 2006), serves as a good introduction to twentieth-century Protestant Christianity in Korea.

47. It should be noted that early on there were negotiations among de los Reyes, Aglipay, and several members of the American Bible Society. In the hopes of garnering some legitimacy in the eyes of the new colonial regime, perhaps, Aglipay had invited the American missionaries to discuss the possibility of their joining the Filipino secular clergy in leading the schism. Nothing came from these meetings, however, in part because the Protestants made particular demands, including giving the Bible theological priority, ending the celibacy of the clergy, and—important for our readings here—doing away with Marian devotion, or as they put it, "Mariolotry." Homer C. Stuntz, *The Philippines and the Far East* (Cincinnati, OH: Jennings and Pye, 1904), 489–90. For more on the IFI as one of several churches in a developing "transcontinental indigenous-Christian public sphere," see Adrian Hermann, "Transnational Networks of Philippine Intellectuals and the Emergence of an Indigenous-Christian Public Sphere around 1900," in *Polycentric Structures in the History of World Christianity*, ed. Klaus Koschorke and Adrian Hermann (Wiesbaden, Germany: Harrassowitz Verlag, 2014), 193–203.

48. For more on Isabelo de los Reyes's many activities during this period, see Mojares, *Brains of the Nation*, 270–87.

49. In early 1902 seventeen priests from the northern part of Luzon met with Aglipay and signed a document in which they resolved "to occupy exclusively" all bishoprics, parishes, and offices of the Catholic Church in the Philippines," adding, "In case the Delegate of the Pope should violate our rights . . . we will form a Filipino Church with the same dogmas as the Roman one." From Isabelo de los Reyes, "Historia documentada de la Iglesia Filipina," quoted in John N. Schumacher, S.J., *Revolutionary Clergy: The Filipino Clergy and the Nationalist Movement, 1850–1903* (Quezon City: Ateneo de Manila University Press, 1981), 231.

50. Pedro S. de Achútegui and Miguel A. Bernad, *Religious Revolution in the Philippines: The Life and Church of Gregorio Aglipay, 1860–1960*, vol. 1, *From Aglipay's Birth to His Death* (Manila: Ateneo de Manila, 1961), 434. Comprising four volumes that include valuable appendices of reprinted documents on the founding of the IFI, these tomes by two Jesuit scholars are among the most ex-

tensive histories written on Aglipay and his church, notwithstanding their bias. See also Isacio R. Rodriguez, *Gregorio Aglipay y los orígenes de la Iglesia Filipina Independiente (1898-1917)* (Madrid: Departamento de Misionología Española, Consejo Superior de Investigaciones Científicas, 1960).

51. Perplexingly, the Tagalog translation appears in print a year *before* the first published Spanish version does, but that could owe to any number of errors that are likely of little consequence. We can be certain that Spanish was the language in which the *Novenario* was originally penned by the bishop Gregorio Aglipay, because the Tagalog version reads on its title page, *Pagsisiyam sa Virgin sa Balintawak . . . sinulat sa wikang kastila ni Monseñor Gregorio Aglipay . . . at tinagalog ni G. Juan N. Evangelista* (Novena to the Virgin of Balintawak . . . written in Spanish by Monsignor Gregorio Aglipay . . . and translated into Tagalog by G. Juan N. Evangelista).

52. "¡Oh, Dios, nuestro verdadero Padre! Desde el fondo de nuestros corazones te elevamos los mas puros sentimientos de amor y gratitud por las incesantes pruebas de tu dulcísima paternidad. Cual padre afectuosísimo provees con admirable diligencia á todas nuestras necesidades por poco que trabajemos, y nos proteges de los peligros. Haznos, pues, buenos y merecedores de tanto cariño. Haz que cumplamos tus mandamientos de caridad y de trabajo, porque la caridad nos hará felices y nos librará de muchos disgustos, y el trabajo es el gran remedio que has puesto á nuestro alcance para satisfacer nuestras necesidades y nuestros justos deseos . . .

"¡O, Inteligencia suprema, faro esplendoroso del Universo! Con todo el fervor de nuestras almas te suplicamos nos prestes un rayo de tu luz increada, pará que por el camino de las ciencias conozcamos las maravillas de tu potencia suprema, entreveamos tu excelsa naturaleza y aprendamos las virtudes necesarias para nuestra dignificación y bienestar." Aglipay, *Novenario de la Patria*, 8.

53. (1) "Dios, según las antiguas religiones," (2) "Nuestra idea de Dios," and (3) "Lo que nos enseña la idea de Dios." Ibid., 8-12.

54. "Según esto el mundo empezó por una aurora que fué creada el primer día, lo cual es un enorme error, porque la aurora procede de la luz del sol que solo el cuarto día había surgir . . . No queremos siquiera hablar del cuento infantil que presenta á Dios como alfarero formando al hombre con el barro y sacando de sus costillas á la primera mujer." Ibid., 15.

55. "Dios es una Potencia inteligente, suprema y misteriosa que produce, da vida, dirige, mueve y conserva á todos los seres; es el gran alma del Universo; el principio de toda vida y del movimiento universal." Ibid., 10.

56. "Todas las energías al parecer perdidas por esos cuerpos extinguidos, en realidad habrán pasado en forma de electricidad, calórico, hidrógeno, etc.[,] . . . las leyes físicas y químicas prueban que nada desaparece: ni energía ni materia." This passage is strongly suggestive of nineteenth-century spiritist influences on the IFI. Ibid., 33.

57. "Si Jesús hubiese sido Dios, sus obras no tendrían tanto mérito." Ibid., 35.

58. [A Tagalog from a modest background, Apolinario Mabini is widely celebrated in nationalist historiography as the "brains of the revolution."]

59. "19a Lectura: Necesidad de una Iglesia Nacional y científica. Por las anteriores lecturas comprenderán los oyentes que por venerandas que sean las leyendas bíblicas y las enseñanzas de Jesús, no están exentas de muchos errores científicos y morales y que no pueden ser base de una Iglesia digna de los enormes progresos de la ciencia moderna, y además es muy necesaria una Iglesia Nacional que defienda el sacrosanto ideal de nuestra Independencia contra las maquinaciones de las corporaciones religiosas extranjeras que conspiran contra ella, y es preciso oponer las enseñanzas más modernas, científicas y patrióticas de Rizal, Mabini, y otros maestros filipinos á los cuentos judíos y paganizantes del neo-Cristianismo, que son completamente absurdos y contrarios á todas las ciencias. Hé aquí el motivo de la fundación de la Iglesia Filipina Independiente. No renegamos de Jesús ni de Moisés; y sólo corregimos los errores que se les atribuyen. En ese altar nuestro veis tres figuras monumentales, esto es, no les adoramos como ídolos, pues no somos salvajes que adoran en maderas, sino sólo las colocamos ahí como monumentos ó faros de nuestros ideales." Aglipay, *Novenario de la Patria*, 40-41.

60. "La Madre de Balintawak simboliza á nuestra Patria, y el Niño katipunero representa al

Pueblo Filipino, á la *rising generation* que ansía su independencia, y ambas figuras os recordarán constantemente los inmensos sacrificios de los redentores de nuestra patria." Ibid., 42 (emphasis and English in original).

61. This reading is excerpted from one of José Rizal's most famous writings, "Liham sa mga Kababaihan ng Malolos" (To the Young Women of Malolos). An English translation of this can be found in *Selected Essays and Letters of José Rizal*, ed. Encarnación Alzona (Manila: G. Rangel and Sons, 1964), 107-18.

62. For a fine discussion of this text, see Megan C. Thomas, "Orientalist Enlightenment: The Emergence of Nationalist Thought in the Philippines, 1880-1898" (PhD diss., Cornell University, 2002), 130-41.

63. Marcelo del Pilar, under the pen name Plaridel, wrote a series of poems parodying the most common Catholic prayers, including the Our Father and the Hail Mary. See "Dasalan at Tocsohan" (excerpts), in S. Baltasar, T. Erestain, and Ma. F. Estanislao, eds., *Philippine Literature Past and Present* (Quezon City: Katha Publishing, 1981), 114-15.

64. See Webb Keane, *Christian Moderns: Freedom and Fetish in the Mission Encounter* (Berkeley: University of California, 2007).

65. *Oxford English Dictionary*, 3rd ed., June 2005, s.v. "parergon," http://www.oed.com/view /Entry/137856?redirectedFrom=parergon#eid.

66. Jacques Derrida, *The Truth in Painting* (Chicago: University of Chicago Press, 1987), 56.

67. Immanuel Kant, *Religion within the Limits of Reason Alone* (New York: Harper & Row, 1960), 48.

68. Derrida, *Truth in Painting*, 9.

CHAPTER 3

1. "Official Statement on Reported Extraordinary Happenings at Carmel of Lipa," *Boletín eclesiástico de Filipinas: Organo oficial, interdiocesano, mensual, editado por la Universidad de Santo Tomas* 25 (1951): 287 (excerpts rearranged).

2. These are the volumes *English-Tagalog Dictionary* (Manila: Congregation of the Most Holy Redeemer, 1986) and *Tagalog-English Dictionary* (Manila: Congregation of the Most Holy Redeemer, 1977), both by Leo James English.

3. Interview with Teresita Castillo, Quezon City, September 27, 2001.

4. Ibid.

5. Walter Benjamin, "The Task of the Translator," in *Illuminations* (New York: Schocken Books, 1968), 69-82.

6. In English's *English-Tagalog Dictionary* the note of acknowledgment reads: "His [Fr. English's] principal assistant throughout the long period of preparation of the manuscript was Miss Teresita Castillo to whom a very special thanks are due. She not only typed the manuscript of nearly 4,000 pages [more pages than Teresita recalled in the interview] several times but also gave invaluable assistance in checking it, not merely for typographical errors, but also for any inaccuracies in translation and accentuation" (n.p.). The much-longer *Tagalog-English Dictionary* declares, "In the actual technical and lexicographical work my principal assistant during the entire eighteen years was Teresita Castillo. Her work was of such value that she deserves to be called the co-author of this dictionary" (n.p.).

7. The classic example of the force of narration comes from an analysis by Claude Lévi-Strauss in his famous essay "The Sorcerer and His Magic," in *Structural Anthropology* (New York: Basic Books, 1964), 167-85. Examining a case in which a boy accused of witchcraft is acquitted upon his compelling confession, Lévi-Strauss writes: "The warriors had become so absorbed by their interest in the narrative of the boy that they seemed entirely to have forgotten the cause of his appearance before them . . . Through the defendant, witchcraft and the ideas associated with it cease

to exist as a diffuse complex of poorly formulated sentiments and representations and become embodied in real experience. The defendant, who serves as a witness, gives the group the satisfaction of truth, which is infinitely greater and richer than the justice that would have been achieved by his execution" (173–74).

8. "Official Statement on Reported Extraordinary Happenings at Carmel of Lipa," 287 (emphasis mine).

9. The instructions in full read: "(1) No petals, nor water should be given out to any-one; (2) The statue of Our Lady (actually in the church) should be retired from public veneration; (3) All out-sisters must be admitted within the enclosure for the time being, excepting Sr. Elyzabeth, who shall remain outside to attend to the needs of the Community; and Finally (4) All visits are suspended temporarily, no letters will be allowed, until final decision on the matter will come from the Holy See." Rufino J. Santos, "Decree," April 12, 1951, private collection. The "petals" in the decree refer to the miraculous showers of petals that took place both inside and beyond the walls of the convent following the apparitions of Mary to Teresita. These are the subject of chapter 4. Although Santos concludes with a reference to the Holy See, the case likely never went beyond the Philippines.

10. Interview with Sr. Bernadette of the Mother of God, O.C.D. (Lydia Antonia Luz Bautista), Lipa, July 24, 2004.

11. There is ample documentation of the fruitless searches for the proceedings carried out by several parties, including some church officials who sought to reopen the case in the 1990s (the efforts of which are discussed in the next chapter). A letter faxed from the archbishop of Lipa to the archivist at the Vatican Secret Archives requesting materials related to the investigation was met with a perfunctory statement that access to sources is strictly limited to the period before the death of Pope Benedict XV. Archbishop of Lipa Gaudencio B. Rosales to Monsignor Charles Burns, January 28, 1995, private collection; Burns to Rosales, February 3, 1995, private collection. Furthermore, Rosales's predecessor, Mariano G. Gaviola, detailed his efforts to track down any proceedings from the investigation, including inquiries with the nunciature to the Philippines, the Archives of the Archdiocese of Manila, and the Generalate of the Carmelite Fathers in Rome, to no avail. See "Reflections on Mary Mediatrix of All Grace in Lipa Carmel Monastery from 1948 and Subsequent Years," April 16, 1995, private collection. Father Pablo Fernandez, O.P., former historian and archivist at the University of Santo Tomas, where much of the church's investigation of Teresita Castillo took place, described having found, in 1956, "some documents pertaining to the Lipa apparitions." They were in the papers of Fr. Juan Ylla, another Dominican who was likely involved in the investigation. Fernandez reported placing them "in the archives of the Dominican Fathers, thinking that they were safe there and that [the archives] were their fitting place." The documents disappeared, however, says Fernandez, likely during the years 1961–64, when he was in Spain. Fernandez to Gaviola, August 14, 1990, private collection.

12. Much of what does exist, furthermore, can be found only in private collections and scrapbooks belonging to individuals who either have quietly remained faithful to Mary Mediatrix over the years or grew interested in the case after it reentered the public sphere in the 1980s. Indeed, the case of Lipa provides an excellent example of an archive whose locus is not a building or an institution but a devotional community: laypersons, sympathetic clergy, and other religious who amassed documentation by circulating and duplicating what is out there while submitting to certain protocols of what could and could be spoken out loud.

13. Praxedes Villa, "*Kape* and How Batangas Coffee Made a Mark in the World Market," in *Batangas: Forged in Fire*, ed. Ramon N. Villegas (Makati: Ayala Foundation and Filipinas Heritage Library, 2002), 140–45. For a demystifying perspective on Lipa's "coffee boom," see Maria Rita Isabel Santos Castro, "Demythologising the History of Coffee in Lipa, Batangas in the XIXth Century" (M.A. thesis, University of Adelaide, 2003).

14. Teodoro M. Kalaw, *Aide-de-Camp to Freedom* (Manila: Teodoro M. Kalaw Society, 1965), 1–2.

15. For a treatment of these and other works carried out by Baras, see Manuel Sastrón, *Filipinas:*

Pequeños estudios; Batangas y su provincia (Malabon: Establ. Tipográfico del Asilo de Huérfanos de Ntra. Sra. de la Consolación, 1895), 165–69.

16. Praxedes L. Villa, "Lipa, the City with a Story" (unpublished article, n.d.).

17. Personal communication with Professor Ricardo Jose, Quezon City, August 2, 2004.

18. According to Professor Jose, this order was so horrifically outrageous that many of his own officers protested. Fujishige replied that he would take responsibility, but he refused to do so when the United States captured him. When he was later tried at the Yamashita war-crimes trial, many of his younger officers testified against him.

19. Ricardo T. Jose, "Panahon ng Hapon: Occupation and Liberation," in *Batangas: Forged in Fire*, ed. Ramon N. Villegas (Makati: Ayala Foundation and Filipinas Heritage Library, 2002), 236. The majority of these deaths, Jose notes, took place in February 1945.

20. This is not to be confused with the 1994 film by the same name about a family in Lipa who is murdered right before their father, an overseas Filipino worker, returns to the Philippines. I would not be surprised, however, if the filmmakers intended with the title to capitalize on the city's history of atrocity, or if, conversely, the popularization of the term for describing the atrocities of the 1940s derives in part from the film.

21. According to the a report filed by the Judge Advocate Section of the U.S. Army Forces in the Pacific (USAFPAC) in October 1945, approximately 2,298 civilians were killed in February of that year alone, although the report also notes: "Witnesses indicate that many more civilians also met death, but they have not been identified by name," and "the mayor of Lipa estimates that over ten thousand civilians of Lipa and vicinity were murdered by the Japanese," 1. USAFPAC, War Crimes Branch, Judge Advocate Section, "Report No. 84, Investigation of the Massacre of Approximately Twenty-Two Hundred and Ninety-Eight Filipino Civilians and the Looting and Destruction of Lipa, Batangas, P.I. in February 1945," bundle 7, vol. 84, Japanese War Crimes Closed Reports, National Archives of the Philippines. According to Japanese researcher Jintaro Ishida, this episode of killing resulted in an estimated 1,000 to 2,500 dead. Ishida's figure is based on oral histories he conducted with Lipa residents and former Japanese officers. *The Remains of War: Apology and Forgiveness* (Quezon City: Megabooks, 2001), 85.

22. USAFPAC, "Report No. 84," 36–54.

23. Ericson M. Josue, *Alfredo Verzosa, Obispo: The Life and Legacy of the Fourth Filipino Roman Catholic Bishop* (Lipa: Missionary Catechists of the Sacred Heart and Ericson M. Josue, 2007), 74–75. The seminary was erected in 1941, but owing to the war, the formation program was halted for a few months in 1942 and had been abandoned altogether by the time of the massacres in February 1945.

24. This is now referred to as the Pamintahan River, which runs through the center of Lipa. Descriptions of the killings come from the few men who survived the massacre at Pamintahan, mostly by pretending to be dead. See USAFPAC, "Report No. 84," 36–54.

25. The Discalced Carmelites (O.C.D.) is a mendicant order of contemplative nuns and friars established in 1593 in accordance with the reforms set forth by SS. Teresa of Ávila and John of the Cross for their chosen order, the Order of Carmelites.

26. Josue, *Alfredo Verzosa*, 70.

27. Mary Teresa Sideco, O.C.D., *The Roots of Teresa's Nuns in the Philippines* (Lipa: Association of Monasteries of Discalced Carmelite Nuns in the Philippines, 1999), 35.

28. Reference to Mary as Mediatrix, that is, as mediator or distributor of heavenly grace (usually interpreted as Jesus), dates back to at least the late Middle Ages, but on many levels—not least that of papal opinion—discourse on this particular dimension of her has increased significantly, worldwide, over the past two hundred years. The origin of her feast day dates back to 1921, when Pope Benedict XV granted the requests of Belgian bishops to hold a Mass and establish the Office of the Feast of the Blessed Virgin Mary, Mediatrix of All Graces, on May 31. See Mark I. Miravalle, *Mariology: A Guide for Priests, Deacons, Seminarians, and Consecrated Persons* (Goleta, CA: Seat of Wisdom Books, 2007), 448. Partly instigated by the apparitions of Mary at Lipa, wherein Mary announced

herself as Mediatrix of All Grace (singular), there is considerable theological debate, in which many Filipino Marians participate, as to whether the proper title should be "of Grace" or "of Graces."

29. Sideco, *Roots of Teresa's Nuns in the Philippines*, 38.

30. Sr. Mary Anne of Jesus, O.C.D. (Rosario Cuna), to addressee unknown, dated May 31, 1946, and printed in the program commemorating the Golden Jubilee of Carmel of Our Lady, Mary Mediatrix of All Grace, 1996, 13, author's personal collection.

31. Ibid.

32. Sr. Rosemary to Carmel Manila, dated June 6, 1946, in Golden Jubilee program, 13-14, author's personal collection.

33. Sideco, *Roots of Teresa's Nuns*, 43.

34. "Ang Benedicion ng Unang Bato ng Karmelo ng Lipa," in pamphlet "Carmel of Our Lady, Lipa, Batangas" (n.d.), Lipa Carmel Archives.

35. Sideco, *Roots of Teresa's Nuns*, 50.

36. "Address for the Laying of the Cornerstone of the Lipa Carmelite Monastery," in pamphlet "Carmel of Our Lady, Lipa, Batangas" (n.d.), Lipa Carmel Archives. The "Little Flower" refers to St. Thérèse of Lisieux, a Carmelite of the late nineteenth century who received her vocation when she was a small child, entering the contemplative order when she was only fifteen. She lived only twenty-four years.

37. Original: DAPAT MALAMAN NG LAHAT NA DITO NALIBING ANG MGA KALANSAY NG MGA TAO MAHIGIT NA ISANG LIBO (1000) BATA AT MATANDA PINATAY NG MGA JAPONES NOONG GUIERRA, MARZO 4, 1945[,] NA TAGARITO SA BO. LUMBANG, SOLOK AT PAGITAN. A photo of this monument can found in Ishida, *Remains of the War*, 86. While some of the most renowned treatments of World War II and the Japanese occupation were published within the first two decades of the postwar period—Teodoro Agoncillo's *The Fateful Years: Japan's Adventure in the Philippines* (Quezon City: R. P. Garcia Publishing, 1965) remains a classic text—the fiftieth anniversary of the war's end spurred a burgeoning of edited volumes and reconsideration of the period (as it had all over the world). Jintaro Ishida is just one of many Japanese scholars who collected testimonies from both Japanese army officers and Filipinos to piece together an on-the-ground view of the historical period.

38. This is the N. L. Villa Memorial Medical Center.

39. The root word of *pinagmumultuhan* is the Tagalog word for "ghost," or *multo*, derived from the Spanish *muerto*, or "dead."

40. In addition to having it confirmed to me by those closest to Teresita, I estimate the date of this first testimony from its opening lines, which read: "In loving obedience to the zealous lovers of Mama Mary whose love for her is beyond doubt . . . I will try my very best to write down the most I could remember after 42 years of complete silence." Teresita Castillo, original testimony (unpublished manuscript, n.d.), 1, private collection.

41. The basis on which some presume Mo. Cecilia's account to be from the time of the apparitions or soon after is that there exist two versions of it, one in English and one in Spanish. The assertion is that the Spanish version was produced for Alfredo Verzosa, bishop of Lipa at the time of the apparitions, who knew neither English nor Tagalog but only Spanish and Ilocano, his native language.

42. In the introductory chapter to *The Possession of Loudun* (Chicago: University of Chicago Press, 1996), Certeau writes, "History books begin with a present. They are constructed on the basis of two series of data: on the one hand, the 'ideas' we have about a past, ideas that are still conveyed by old material, but along pathways blazed by a new mentality; on the other hand, documents and 'archives,' remains saved by chance, frozen in collections that attach meaning to them that are also new . . . each of its halves says what is missing from the other, rather than its truth" (7-8).

43. Those seeking a straightforward timeline of the events may refer to Mo. Mary Cecilia of Jesus's account in appendix A of June Keithley's *Lipa* (Manila: Cacho Publishing House, distributed by Anvil Publishing, 1992), 179-204.

44. Much of this is summarized in Teresita's revised testimony, "My Life and Testimony" (unpublished manuscript, 1997), 1–3, private collection. Surprisingly, given the prominence of the Castillo family in provincial politics, little about them appears in secondary sources. Among the more salacious rumors that circulated at the time of the apparitions was that Teresita was engaged to Dr. Gil Angeles Laurel, the nephew of José P. Laurel, president of the Second Republic of the Philippines during the Japanese occupation. This would have caused some tension, since the Laurels and the Castillos were political rivals. In an interview with the author of one of the few extant books contemporaneous with the apparitions, Modesto Castillo, Teresita's father, denies this, noting, "I told Teresita . . . that if she wanted to marry Dr. Gil Angeles Laurel, as it was rumored, she should not hesitate to leave the monastery . . . But Teresita told me categorically that she did not want to marry, that she did not wish to go out of the monastery, and that she had decided to follow her vocation, to serve God, and to answer the call of God for the rest of her lifetime." Francisco Villanueva Jr., *The Wonders of Lipa* (Manila: Grand Avenue Bookstore, 1949), 30.

45. Castillo, original testimony, 1–2. Unless otherwise noted, the version of Teresita's testimony to which I henceforth refer is this first one she wrote circa 1990. Although the content is practically the same in both testimonies, Teresita's original version often employs a two-part structure to the dated entries, where the first part describes what happened to her, and the second part describes her reaction. The revised version in 1997 does away with this convention and thus reads more fluidly, with fewer grammatical errors than the first version. Where I find the structure and language of the first version more distracting than it is worth, I refer to the revised (1997) version. In 2008, Teresita's testimony underwent minor revisions again in a limited print run booklet titled *I Am Mary, Mediatrix of All Grace*, which was sold at the Lipa Carmel bookstore, author's personal collection.

46. Mo. Mary Cecilia, O.C.D., original testimony (English version) (unpublished manuscript, n.d.), 1, private collection.

47. Castillo, original testimony, 2.

48. Lévi-Strauss, "The Sorcerer and His Magic," 173–74.

49. We might understand this supernatural presence to be a kind of narrative voice, in the sense that Maurice Blanchot has written, as that whose neutrality, owing to its radical exteriority, is often confused with the "oblique voice of misfortune, or of madness," 387. "The Narrative Voice (the 'He,' the Neutral)," in *The Infinite Conversation* (Minneapolis: University of Minnesota Press, 1993), 379–87.

50. Castillo, original testimony, 2.

51. This again is why "madness" is often mistaken for the narrative voice: the detachment of voice from experience or identity.

52. Castillo, original testimony, 3.

53. Ibid., 2.

54. Ibid., 3.

55. Ibid. (emphasis mine). Devotional cards most frequently bear an image of a particular saint on one side and a prayer on the other. Although it is not clear to me exactly what kind of devotional cards would have these tarotlike inscriptions, there were "lesson cards" used more commonly in the past that illustrated scenes from the Bible with relevant scripture passages.

56. Ibid.

57. Certeau, *Possession at Loudun*, 31.

58. The association of the scent of flowers (in particular roses) with the Virgin is centuries old in Europe. Likewise, as Certeau details in the case of Loudun, there always exists the possibility of the scent of roses being cast like a spell by the devil in the first instance of possession. As for the folk belief that Teresita makes reference to, there are many variations on the theme that the scent of flowers is associated with death, acting either as a premonition of an impending death or as a sign of the presence of the dead.

59. Castillo, original testimony, 3.

60. Castillo, "My Life and Testimony," 9–10 (emphases mine). For reasons described earlier, I have referred to the revised version of Teresita's testimony for this excerpt.

61. Sideco, *Roots of Teresa's Nuns*, 40.

62. Castillo, original testimony, 6.

63. Ibid.

64. Castillo, "My Life and Testimony," 16.

65. Ibid., 18.

66. Ibid., 19.

67. A cilice is a penitential cloth or robe, traditionally made of haircloth but sometimes including thin wires.

68. Interior locution is a mode of private revelation in the Catholic tradition, wherein a person (often in a state of prayer) receives messages believed to be from a divine source but absent divine presence. St. Teresa of Ávila, founder of the Discalced Carmelites, was known to experience this, and the locutions are included in her famous guide to spiritual formation, *The Interior Castle*. See "Sixth Mansion," in *The Interior Castle*, trans. E. Allison Peers (New York: Doubleday, 1989), chap. 3. According to Mo. Cecilia's original testimony (n.d.), these locutions were as follows: "Have patience with your child. Three days she will be blind for the good of both," and "Love her much! Two more additional days of blindness for the salvation of her parents and for the beautiful destiny that is awaiting her in the next life. Do not leave your child from three to five p.m. It [*sic*] needs five days of sufferings and blindness for your good and hers. You will owe her much. Remain with her from eight until nine p.m. Give her good food. Love her much until the end! Patience!" (10).

69. Castillo, original testimony, 6.

70. Ibid., 21.

71. At the apparitions at Lourdes, Mary also asked Bernadette to visit her at the grotto for fifteen consecutive days, but she asked this on the third day, making eighteen the total number of apparitions. At Fátima, Mary told the three children—Lúcia, Francisco, and Jacinta—to return to the apparition site on the thirteenth of each month for five consecutive months, from June to October.

72. Castillo, original testimony, 12. In "My Life and Testimony," Teresita's 1997 version, she edits out the second parenthetical note, simply inserting "I picked up some grass and ate" (32).

73. Castillo, original testimony, 13.

74. Ibid., 20.

75. Ruth Harris, *Lourdes: Body and Spirit in a Secular Age* (New York: Penguin Books, 2000), 80–81.

76. For a survey of and exposition on the common motifs of apparitions in fifteenth- to seventeenth-century Spain, see William A. Christian Jr., *Apparitions in Late Medieval and Renaissance Spain* (Princeton, NJ: Princeton University Press, 1981).

77. Castillo, original testimony, 14–15.

78. Ibid., 17.

79. Ibid., 16.

80. Filipino linguist and scholar Andrew Gonzalez reports, "At the tail-end of the American period (1898–1935), after only thirty-seven years, the 1939 Census reported a total of 4,264,549 out of a total population of 16,000,303 or 26.6% who claimed the ability to speak English." The sense that this was, in his words, "surely an accomplishment," stems from the contrast to the number of Filipinos who commanded Spanish during the colonial period. *Language and Nationalism: The Philippine Experience Thus Far* (Quezon City: Ateneo de Manila University Press, 1980), 26.

81. Castillo, original testimony, 25.

82. "Hukbalahap" is an abbreviation for Hukbo ng Bayan Laban sa Hapon (People's Anti-Japanese Army); the term is commonly abbreviated further as simply "Huk." What began, as its name suggests, as a guerrilla movement against Japanese forces evolved into a peasant movement in the postwar period (during which they also changed their name to the Hukbong Mapagpalaya ng Bayan, or People's Liberation Army). Although its leadership was allied at times with Partido Komu-

nista ng Pilipinas (Communist Party of the Philippines), its demonization as a communist army, as opposed to very localized conflicts of peasant rebellion, was largely the result of the collaboration between the U.S. military and Central Intelligence Agency and the Philippine government operations to suppress the uprisings and use the rebellion as a kind of laboratory for the development of anticommunist strategy in the U.S.-led global Cold War. For a history of this collaboration, see Colleen Woods, "Bombs, Bureaucrats, and Rosary Beads: The United States, the Philippines, and the Making of Global Anti-Communism, 1945–1960" (PhD diss., University of Michigan, 2012). For other histories of the Huk rebellion, see Vina Lanzona, *Amazons of the Huk Rebellion: Gender, Sex, and Revolution in the Philippines* (Madison: University of Wisconsin Press, 2009); and Benedict Kerkvliet's locus classicus, *The Huk Rebellion: A Study of Peasant Revolt in the Philippines* (Berkeley: University of California Press, 1977).

83. Castillo, "My Life and Testimony," 34.

84. Castillo, original testimony, 25.

85. Castillo, "My Life and Testimony," 13. This statement does not appear in the original version.

86. Ibid., 17.

87. Ibid., 22–23.

88. Castillo, original testimony, 13.

89. It is a long-standing standard procedure to have investigations of supernatural phenomena carried out and decided at the diocesan level. Although a representative of the Holy See may well be involved (as was the case with the investigation of Lipa Carmel), cases rarely reach the Vatican.

90. Although the pope long held supreme authority in doctrinal matters, papal infallibility was officially promulgated as doctrine only at the Vatican Council of 1869–70.

91. See William A. Christian Jr., "Religious Apparitions and the Cold War in Southern Europe," in *Religion, Power, and Protest in Local Communities*, ed. Eric R. Wolf (Berlin: Mouton, 1984), 239–65.

92. Alfredo Ottaviani, "Cautela ante los falsos milagros," *Boletín eclesiástico de Filipinas* 25 (1951): 376–80. Not surprisingly, Ottaviani's article appears in the same issue as does "Official Statement on Reported Extraordinary Happenings at Carmel of Lipa."

93. The negotiations between the Japanese Military Administration and the Catholic Church in the Philippines were delicate, to say the least, given the presence of "enemy" clerics. The policy adopted by the Japanese commenced with the formation of a special "Religious Section," which comprised clergy, seminarians, and laity from the Catholic and Protestant communities in Japan; the primary policy architect was Taguchi Yoshigoro, bishop of Osaka. Bishop Taguchi devised a proposal for dealing with the church in the Philippines that addressed the pressing issues of religious instruction, respect for freedom of religion, the conduct of relations with the Vatican, and the Filipinization of the clergy. For an overview of this history, see Ikehata Setsuho and Ricardo T. Jose, eds., *The Philippines under Japan: Occupation Policy and Reaction* (Quezon City: Ateneo de Manila University Press, 1999), 215–46.

94. Santos would succeed Gabriel Reyes as archbishop of Manila upon Reyes's untimely death in 1953, and later would become the first cardinal of the Philippines, in 1960.

95. *Boletín eclesiástico de Filipinas* 23 (1949): 807.

96. The best biography of Archbishop O'Doherty is the querulous volume written by Columban priest Martin J. Noone, *The Life and Times of Michael O'Doherty, Archbishop of Manila*, part 5, vol. 3, *General History of the Philippines* (Manila: Historical Conservation Society, 1989).

97. These biographical notes are taken from Gary MacEoin and the Committee for the Responsible Election of the Pope, *The Inner Elite: Dossiers of Papal Candidates* (Kansas City, MO: Sheed Andrews & McMeel, 1978), 237–38.

98. "Message of the New Papal Nuncio," by Egidio Vagnozzi, *Boletín eclesiástico de Filipinas* 25 (1951): 285–86.

99. There is to my knowledge only one biography of Gabriel M. Reyes: Evelyn S. Reyes-Tirol's pious *Gentle Shepherd, Faithful Sentinel: A Biography of Gabriel M. Reyes* (Manila: Archbishop Gabriel M. Reyes Memorial Foundation, 1992).

100. Setsuho and Jose, *Philippines under Japan*, 241.

101. Arwin Paul Lingat, "1948–1975: From Diocese to Archdiocese of San Fernando," Roman Catholic Archdiocese of San Fernando, http://www.web.rcasf.com/about.php?history.

102. Biographies of Rufino Santos include Carmen Acosta, *The Life of Rufino Cardinal Santos* (Manila: Printed at Kayumanggi Press, Quezon City, 1973); and the most recent: Lord Francis Musni, Robert P. Tantingco, and Erlinda E. Cruz, eds., *Padre Pinong: First Filipino Cardinal, 1908–1973* (Angeles: Center for Kapampangan Studies, 2008).

103. "Archbishop Juan C. Sison," Catholic-Hierarchy.org, http://www.catholic-hierarchy.org /bishop/bsison.html.

104. "Bishop Vicente P. Reyes," Catholic-Hierarchy.org, http://www.catholic-hierarchy.org /bishop/breyesv.html.

105. Such is how Vagnozzi's surname brilliantly appeared in the interviews transcribed by my research assistant.

106. According to Teresita's testimony, the three points made in the statement were "(1) the apparitions were not true because they were just pure imaginations; (2) I invented the story so that I could win the affection of the whole community, and (3) I joined the Carmelite Order because of my family's feud with the Laurels." Castillo, original testimony, 29. As mentioned earlier in the chapter, the political rivalry between the Castillos and the Laurels, both political powerhouses, was the root of much speculation and opinion, positive and negative, about Teresita.

107. Ibid.

108. Ibid., 31.

109. Ibid., 29.

110. Ibid., 31.

111. This is to paraphrase—with a twist—the opening lines of Certeau's *Possession at Loudun*: "It always comes as a surprise when the nocturnal erupts into broad daylight. What it reveals is an underground existence, an inner resistance that has never been broken. This lurking force infiltrates the lines of tension within the society it threatens. Suddenly it magnifies them; using the means, the circuitry already in place, but reemploying them in the service of an anxiety that comes from afar, unanticipated . . . Is this the outbreak of something new, or the repetition of a past? The historian never knows which. For mythologies reappear, providing the eruption of strangeness with forms of expression prepared in advance, as it were, for sudden inundation" (1).

112. This is to echo Elias Canetti's famous dictum: "Secrecy lies at the very core of power." *Crowds and Power*, trans. Carol Stewart (New York: Noonday Press, 1996), 290.

113. Sr. Bernadette passed away in 2009.

114. Interview with Sr. Bernadette of the Mother of God, O.C.D. (Lydia Antonia Luz Bautista), Lipa, July 24, 2004.

115. The destruction of the image of Mary was not something that appeared in the written instructions given by Rufino Santos, apostolic administrator of the diocese of Lipa, upon delivering the negative decree.

116. Interview with Sr. Bernadette, Lipa, July 24, 2004.

117. Ibid.

118. As is the case with many a transnational monastic order, death circulars are very important documents for the religious, not only as memorials or information but also to convey the spiritual highlights of the deceased for the edification of the whole community.

119. Death circular for Sr. Bernadette of the Mother of God, O.C.D. (2009), author's personal collection.

120. The "Interior Castle" is how St. Teresa of Ávila conceptualized the soul, a multifaceted, crystalline structure of mansions and rooms, hallways, and chambers leading to a secret, most interior place where God lay in wait.

121. The nuns' citation of the poem "The Dark Night" (sometimes known as "The Dark Night of the Soul") by St. John of the Cross, the confessor of Teresa of Ávila, bespeaks an apprehension

of the dolorous circumstance in the terms of the centuries-old chronicle itself: as a passage through suffering and abandonment—both of self and by God—in the process of purification that readies the soul to be filled and illuminated with God's love. A good version of this with introduction and thorough, verse-by-verse commentary can be found in John of the Cross, *The Collected Works of St. John of the Cross*, trans. Kieran Kavanaugh and Otilio Rodriguez (Washington, DC: ICS Publications, 1991), 353–460.

122. Castillo, original testimony, 20–21.

123. Ibid., 21. Note that I will switch between using "St. Thérèse" and "Thérèse" depending on context.

124. Castillo, "My Life and Testimony," 54. The original version lacks this whimsical detail.

125. This is a theology that one hundred years after her death, and much to the surprise of many outside observers, church authorities deemed worthy enough to confer upon St. Thérèse the unique status of doctor of the church. Only two other women in history share this designation: Thérèse's progenitor, Teresa of Ávila, and Catherine of Siena. There are many, many biographies of St. Thérèse, but the most serious (and enjoyable) scholarly study of her life in context is Thomas R. Nevin's *Thérèse of Lisieux: God's Gentle Warrior* (New York: Oxford University Press, 2006), which includes a quite exhaustive annotated bibliography.

126. Castillo, original testimony, 24a.

127. Thérèse of Lisieux, *Story of a Soul: The Autobiography of St. Thérèse de Lisieux*, trans. John Clarke (Washington, DC: ICS Publications, 1996), 188. It appears that Thérèse actually reformulated this passage, since many versions of the Bible use the term "simple" rather than "little."

128. One of the oft-quoted passages from Thérèse's autobiography reads: "Great deeds are forbidden me . . . Love proves itself by deeds, so how am I to show my love? . . . The only way I can prove my love is by scattering flowers and these flowers are every little sacrifice, every glance and word, and the doing of the least of actions for love." *The Autobiography of Saint Thérèse de Lisieux, Story of a Soul*, trans. John Beevers (1957; New York: Doubleday Books, 2001), 163. As famous as this quote is, it is also highly problematic from a primary-source perspective, since it comes not from the translation of Thérèse's unpublished manuscripts (she wrote three in total, addressed to three different people), but from the single autobiographical volume edited from the three manuscripts into eleven chapters by her sister Pauline. (Thomas R. Nevin notes in his annotated bibliography that Pauline made at least seven thousand emendations to the manuscripts in compiling them; see Nevin, *Thérèse de Lisieux*, 387). It is this version that was published in 1898, a year after Thérèse's death, quickly becoming the phenomenon that would pave the road to her canonization. It is also this version that Carmelites of the early to mid-twentieth century would have had access to, including those sisters at Lipa Carmel.

129. Castillo, original testimony, 3.

130. Castillo, "My Life and Testimony," 28. The same basic description appears in the original testimony but is less fluidly written.

131. Ibid.

132. Thérèse of Lisieux, *Story of a Soul: The Autobiography of St. Thérèse de Lisieux*, 14. In contrast to the previously mentioned version of St. Thérèse's autobiography (translated by John Beevers), Clark's translation maintains as separate the three original manuscripts.

133. For a similar discussion, see Heather L. Claussen's depiction of contemporary Filipina Benedictine nuns studying and reenacting *The Life and Miracles of St. Benedict (Bennet) of Nursia* in *Unconventional Sisterhood: Feminist Catholic Nuns in the Philippines* (Ann Arbor: University of Michigan Press, 2001), 78–84.

134. Sideco, *Roots of Teresa's Nuns*.

135. Nevin, *Thérèse of Lisieux*, 66–67.

136. Quoted in Alison Weber, "Saint Teresa, Demonologist," in *Culture and Control in Counter-Reformation Spain*, ed. Anne J. Cruz and Mary Elizabeth Perry (Minneapolis: University of Minnesota Press, 1992), 184.

137. Indeed, at one point before the church's 1951 decree condemning the apparitions, the

chapter of Lipa Carmel, with the approval of its ecclesiastical superior, unanimously voted to place their monastery under the title and protection of Our Lady, Mediatrix of All Grace. Their statement to this effect was approved and signed by Bishop Verzosa. Statement of Sr. Mary-Cecilia of Jesus, O.C.D., October 11, 1949, private collection.

138. Monica Furlong, *Thérèse de Lisieux* (New York: Orbis Books, 1987), 121.

CHAPTER 4

1. In his study *The Apparitions of the Madonna at Oliveto Citra: Local Visions and Cosmic Drama* (University Park: Pennsylvania State University Press, 1998), Paolo Apolito writes, "The *world created* by the apparitions is not a totalizing, constricting, exclusive structure but rather a horizon—an ensemble of symbolic possibilities to which the actors have access" (74, emphasis in original).

2. One of the oldest newspapers in the Philippines, the *Manila Times* went through several owners and periods of hiatus before reappearing in 1945, when the Filipino literary giant Alejandro Roces put out a weekly edition of the paper. Demand swiftly increased, and within months the *Times* was converted into a daily, with the widest circulation of any Filipino newspaper. Buhain Dominador, *A History of Publishing in the Philippines* (Quezon City: Rex Bookstore, 1998), 48.

3. "Miracle of Rose Showers Drawing Crowds of Devotees," *Manila Times*, November 17, 1948.

4. "Notables in Throng Brave Rain to See Miracle of Roses," *Manila Times*, November 22, 1948.

5. "Army of Pilgrims Throngs Lipa to Witness Miracle of Roses," *Manila Times*, November 29, 1948; "Catholic Pilgrims See Petal Shower," *Manila Times*, January 10, 1949.

6. "Rose Petal Shower over Public Market," *Manila Times*, August 11, 1949; "More Miracles at Lipa Shrine," *Manila Times*, March 18, 1949; "Lipa-Inspired Phenomenon in Sampaloc Draws City Crowds," *Manila Times*, May 11, 1949.

7. "Heavy Shower Falls Anew in Lipa," *Manila Times*, February 4, 1949; "Cebu Pilgrims Expected in Lipa," *Manila Times*, February 20, 1949.

8. "Miracle Reported Anew in Lipa," *Manila Times*, February 17, 1949.

9. Michael Warner, "Publics and Counterpublics," in *Public Culture* 14, no. 1 (2002): 49–90.

10. "Shower of Roses in Lipa Convent Interests Scientists, Educators," *Manila Times*, November 20, 1948.

11. "The Miracles of Lipa," *Manila Times*, December 13, 1948.

12. "Book Written of Lipa Showers," *Manila Times*, May 12, 1949.

13. "Chief Justice and Noted Scientist Convinced Petal Shower a Miracle," *Manila Times*, January 24, 1949.

14. Ibid.

15. In May 1917, three children claimed that they saw the Virgin Mary at the Cova da Iria near the rural town of Fátima, Portugal. Although local authorities attempted to prevent the children from returning to the spot, they could not contend with the crowds that began to gather there, per Mary's instructions, every thirteenth of the month until October of that year. The apparitions resulted in the erection of a shrine approved by the church, yet received little attention beyond the region until the 1930s, when one of the visionaries, Lúcia Santos (who by that point had become a nun), wrote what she claimed to be the full version of Mary's messages to the children. The most important revelation in Sr. Lúcia's revised account was Mary's request that Russia be consecrated to her Immaculate Heart and that those devoted to her receive communion every first Saturday of five consecutive months for this purpose. By the late 1940s, the anticommunist message of Mary achieved wide recognition in the United States and resulted in increased devotion to Our Lady of Fátima. For overviews of Fátima and the history of American Catholic anticommunism, see Thomas Kselman and Steven Avella's "Marian Piety and the Cold War in the United States," *Catholic Historical Review* 72, no. 3 (July 1986): 403–24; and Una Cadegan's "The Queen of Peace in the Shadow of War: Fatima and U.S. Catholic Anticommunism," *U.S. Catholic Historian* 22, no. 4 (Fall 2004): 1–15. The best account of the apparitions, albeit from a pious perspective, remains

William Thomas Walsh's *Our Lady of Fatima* (New York: Doubleday, 1954). The link between the apparitions of Mary to Teresita Castillo and those at Fátima comes from the broad reference Mary makes to "pray for the conversion of sinners . . . for those who rejected me, and those who do not believe my messages in different parts of the world," concluding, "What I ask here is the same as in Fatima." Teresita Castillo, original testimony (unpublished manuscript, n.d.), 25, private collection.

16. Some of these speakers were noted anticommunists, like Stephen Breen Jr., who wrote frequently for the popular American Catholic magazine *The Scapular*. Others were like Julia Hughes, the daughter of an American colonel and a Filipina, and onetime golf champion of the Philippines, who drew in audiences with her firsthand accounts of the apparitions. See, for example, "Capacity Audience Hears Stephen Breen in Religious Address," *Biloxi (MS) Daily Herald*, March 2, 1950; "Speaker to Discuss Miracle of Lipa," *Racine (WI) Journal Times*, September 7, 1950; "Philippine Guest Speaks on Lady of Lipa Thursday," *Santa Fe New Mexican*, February 21, 1950.

17. "Lorraine Carr Lost Her Heart to the Philippines," *Los Angeles Times*, December 17, 1966.

18. Lorraine Carr, *To the Philippines with Love* (Los Angeles: Sherbourne Press, 1966), 169-70.

19. Ibid., 173.

20. Ibid.

21. Ibid., 176.

22. Ibid., 248.

23. For a critical reading of this genre of colonial memoir, see Vicente Rafael's "Colonial Domesticity: Engendering Race at the Edge of Empire, 1899-1912," in *White Love and Other Events in Filipino History* (Quezon City: Ateneo de Manila University Press, 2000), 52-75.

24. "Shower of Roses in Lipa Convent Interests Scientists, Educators," *Manila Times*, November 20, 1948; "Dr. Quisumbing, Botanist, Visits Lipa, Examines Retrieved Petals," *Manila Times*, November 30, 1948; "The Showers of Petals," *Manila Times*, December 5, 1948.

25. Unless you count the ideology of the scientific method itself, of course.

26. "The Showers of Petals," *Manila Times*, December 5, 1948.

27. Ibid.

28. Ibid.

29. For perspectives from other vernacular publications, see my "The Mass Miracle: Public Religion in the Postwar Philippines," *Philippine Studies* 62, nos. 3-4 (2014), 425-44.

30. Interview with Guillermo Milan (in Tagalog), Lipa, July 28, 2004.

31. Interview with Mely Kison, Lipa, July 23, 2004.

32. June Keithley, "The Petals of Lipa," in *Batangas: Forged in Fire*, ed. Ramon N. Villegas (Makati: Ayala Foundation and Filipinas Heritage Library, 2002), 128.

33. "Rose Petals from Lipa Are Reported Working Cures Abroad," *Manila Times*, June 26, 1949; "More Miracles at Lipa Shrine," *Manila Times*, March 18, 1949; "Mystic Rose Petals Fall in Philippines," *Cincinnati Telegraph Register*, April 8, 1949; "A Message for America," *The Scapular*, September-October 1949.

34. Veronica's Veil refers to the relic—the authenticity of which, like the Shroud of Turin, has yet to be either confirmed or denied by the church, despite the application of the most sophisticated of scientific tools—believed to have wiped the face of Christ on the road to Calvary, his sweat miraculously and permanently imprinting an image of his face. For a brief discussion of both Veronica's Veil (as rendered in Philippe de Champaigne's 1654 work *Veil of Veronica*) and *acheiropoietos*, put to the service of exploring "the modernist desire to paint the end of painting," see Keith Broadfoot, "Abstraction and Aura," *South Atlantic Quarterly* 101, no. 3 (Summer 2002): 459-78.

35. Walter Benjamin, "The Work of Art in the Age of Mechanical Reproduction," in *Illuminations* (New York: Schocken Books, 1968), 219.

36. A simple Google search for "Lipa petals" yields nearly two hundred hits, the majority of which lead to websites that have photos of the petals posted on them.

37. See, for example, "Petal Shower Stages Big Show," *Manila Times*, February 27, 1949; "Lipa Petal Cures American Patient," *Manila Times*, March 29, 1949.

38. Francisco Villanueva Jr., *The Wonders of Lipa* (Manila: Grand Avenue Bookstore, 1949), 48–49.

39. Ibid., 50–51.

40. Ibid., 53.

41. See, for example, "Syracusan Has Rose Petals from Lipa," *Syracuse (NY) Post Standard*, February 19, 1951.

42. "Rose Petals from Lipa Are Reported Working Cures Abroad," *Manila Times*, June 26, 1949.

43. "Lipa Petal Cures American Patient," *Manila Times*, March 29, 1949.

44. This story is the subject of "Lipa-Vadillo," a two-part article found in *Santo Rosario*, the bilingual (English-Spanish) monthly magazine published by the University of Santo Tomas (Manila): *Santo Rosario* 4, no. 5 (1949): 39–42; and *Santo Rosario* 4, no. 8 (1949): 42–43.

45. "Suceso prodigioso," *ABC*, March 30, 1949, morning edition, 15.

46. Ibid.

47. "Lipa-Vadillo," *Santo Rosario* 4, no. 5 (1949): 41.

48. Ibid.

49. "Lipa-Vadillo," *Santo Rosario* 4, no. 8 (1949): 42.

50. Following Benjamin, I understand "aura" to be the "unique phenomenon of a distance however close it may be," where distance is measured not necessarily in spatial terms but in terms of its "unapproachability." This "unapproachability," read in the context I am examining here, I take to be none other than a quality of the sacred. See Benjamin, "Work of Art," 243n5.

51. I thank Juan Obarrio for this suggestion.

52. "Lipa-Vadillo," *Santo Rosario* 4, no. 5 (1949): 42.

53. Ibid., 39.

54. Martin Heidegger, "The Age of the World Picture," in *The Question Concerning Technology and Other Essays* (New York: Harper & Row, 1977), 115–54. In this classic essay Heidegger argues that the quintessence of modernity is the ability to conceive of the world "as a picture," that is, to make an object of the world such that its representability—as a whole and in its parts—can be apprehended. In this case of Lipa we might advance a slippage between the *supernatural* and the *supranational*, a conceptualization of spiritual patronage that presupposes a nationalized site of origin, only to supersede it.

55. Letter from Fr. Alphonse Heckler, April 24, 1951, Marian Library, Apparitions—False, University of Dayton.

56. Francisco Dychangco, *My Diary on the Work for Our Lady, Mary Mediatrix of All Grace* (unpublished diary, 1982–93, prelude, p. B), private collection.

57. Mary Teresa Sideco, O.C.D., *The Roots of Teresa's Nuns in the Philippines* (Lipa: Association of Monasteries of Discalced Carmelite Nuns in the Philippines, 1999), 491.

58. Dychangco, *My Diary*, B.

59. Ibid.

60. Take the first three entries of Ka Paco's diary (ibid., 1), which are typical of the rest of the entries that follow:

July 3, 1982—I go to Lipa Carmel and meet Sis. ——, O.C.D. She says that she feels Our Lady is coming back to Carmel. With ——, I proceed to Manila.

July 4 (Sunday)—I attend Mass with —— at San Sebastian church. Then we proceed to the Holy Face Convent at R. Hidalgo St. Quiapo to see Mother ——. With ——, we discuss on how we can work for the re-investigation of the alleged apparitions of Our Lady at Lipa Carmel in 1948 so that they can be approved by the Church.

July 5—I receive the written testimony of Col. —— on his witnessing of the showers of petals at the Carmelite grounds in Lipa in 1948.

61. The role of the Catholic Church, and most spectacularly that of Cardinal Jaime Sin, in the People Power revolt of 1986 is well known. When defense secretary Juan Ponce Enrile and General

Fidel Ramos were on the verge of being crushed by the loyal contingent of Marcos's military, they called upon Cardinal Sin to galvanize his flock. The cardinal took to the airwaves (on Radio Veritas, the official radio station of the church) and urged Catholic followers to flood the major highway (Epifanio de los Santos Avenue, or EDSA, as it is most commonly known) and block Marcos's forces from entering the camp where Ramos and his contingent of military defectors had retreated. For four days millions of civilians stood face-to-face with Marcos's forces, in a protest against the regime that was widely covered by the international press and set a new paradigm for popular movements worldwide. As the visual archive indicates, the event known as People Power was saturated with Catholic iconography and heralded by more devout participants as a "Marian miracle."

62. Dychangco, *My Diary*, 45. This is likely a reference to Vatican II.

63. The questions Ka Paco included in this poll, which received the approval of one of the local bishops, were "(1) Are you aware of the strange happenings in the Carmelite monastery in the years 1948-49, concerning Mary Mediatrix of All Grace? (2) Do you personally believe that Our Lady really appeared there and gave messages—Ans. yes or no. (3) Please give your remarks or reasons for your answer." Ibid., 4.

64. Ibid., 72.

65. Ibid., 20.

66. Ibid., 20-21.

67. Ibid., 36.

68. Ibid., 56.

69. According to Archbishop Gaviola's written report on the case of Lipa, the decision to bring out the original statue was entirely spontaneous: "On the morning of May 21st [the day after Sr. Alphonse passed away], while taking my shower, I suddenly decided to have the image of Our Lady exposed in public during the funeral mass and throughout that day, until 6:00 p.m. In hindsight, I myself was surprised by this decision. Why did it come to me so spontaneously? How come I did not for a moment think of consulting anyone? But the Lord God knows I was truly grateful to the Holy Spirit, Mary's divine Spouse, for this singular inspiration." Mariano G. Gaviola, D.D., archbishop emeritus of Lipa to Most Rev. Salvador Q. Quizon, D.D., auxiliary bishop of Lipa, "Reflections on Mary Mediatrix of All Grace in Lipa Carmel Monastery from 1948 and Subsequent Years," 14, April 16, 1995, private collection.

70. "Oh Those Wild and Crazy Hoaxes!" *Weekend*, December 26, 1982, 16-20.

71. "Wanted: Testimonies for or against the Lipa Event," letter from Francisco Dychangco, *Weekend*, January 30, 1983, 1.

72. There are numerous books and accounts of the People Power revolt and its history. For a good, albeit pious, account of the event through the testimonies of several of its main participants, see Monina Allarey Mercado, ed., *People Power: An Eyewitness History* (Manila: James B. Reuter, S.J., Foundation, 1986). For a political and historical overview of the anti-Marcos movement that culminated in People Power, see Mark R. Thompson, *The Anti-Marcos Struggle: Personalistic Rule and Democratic Transition in the Philippines* (New Haven, CT: Yale University Press, 1995).

73. June Keithley, *The Keithley Report: The Woman Clothed with the Sun* (Manila: Center for Peace Asia, 1991). EDSA is short for Epifanio de los Santos highway, the location of the People Power revolt in 1986. "EDSA" in conjunction with "revolt" or "uprising" is often used to describe that event.

74. June Keithley, *Lipa: With the Original Account of the Events at Lipa Carmel in 1948 by Mother Mary Cecilia of Jesus, O.C.D.* (Manila: Cacho Publishing House, 1992), 7-10.

75. No exact date is given by Archbishop Gaviola of the commission's founding in his report to Auxiliary Bishop Quizon, except to note that it was "a year or so before Archbishop Rosales assumed his post." Gaviola, "Reflections," 3. According to Gaviola's notes, this special commission was constituted by secret ballot, with the identity of the resulting members of the committee also kept secret. The charge of the committee was to "focus their investigation only on reports about Lipa

Carmel that took place *after* the promulgation of the same Decree of 1952 [*sic*]," with its main purpose being to "verify cases of physical healings that were attributed to Our Lady Mary Mediatrix of All Grace after the Decree" (16–17).

76. Ramon C. Argüelles, D.D., archbishop of Lipa, "Declaration," Mary, Mediatrix of All Grace Parish, April 17, 2005, http://marymediatrixofallgrace.com/about/the-philippine-bishops-and-the-mediatrix/ (accessed September 27, 2014).

77. Ramon C. Argüelles, archbishop of Lipa, "Decree," Cenacle World Prayer Group, November 12, 2009, http://www.cenacleworldprayergroup.com/bull-our-lady-mediatrix-of-all-grace.html (accessed June 4, 2013).

78. Lourdes Policarpio, "The Apparitions of Our Lady of Lipa: Making Headway," and "Interview with Archbishop Arguelles," Totus Tuus, Maria, http://www.all-about-the-virgin-mary.com/our-lady-of-lipa.html (accessed July 31, 2012).

79. Argüelles, "Decree," November 12, 2009; Argüelles, "Declaration," April 17, 2005.

80. Lipa became an archdiocese in 1972.

81. Since the statue of Mary was brought out under the directive of former archbishop of Lipa Mariano Gaviola, September 12 has been an important date for devotees of Mary Mediatrix, as it commemorates the Virgin Mary's first appearance to Teresita in 1948.

82. Interview with Fr. Rodem Ramos, Lipa, June 1, 2007.

83. This phraseology has been used to describe the relationship of Eastern Orthodox and Roman Catholic Christianities, with specific reference made in the papal encyclical on ecumenism, *Ut unum sint*, issued by Pope John Paul II, on May 25, 1995. The text of this encyclical is at the website of the Holy See, http://www.vatican.va/holy_father/john_paul_ii/encyclicals/documents/hf_jp-ii_enc_25051995_ut-unum-sint_en.html (accessed September 27, 2014).

84. Interview with Fr. Rodem Ramos, Lipa, June 1, 2007.

85. This was made even more emphatic by having the image of Mary Mediatrix join the Blessed Sacrament in the dawn procession that officially began at the San Sebastian Cathedral, the seat of the archdiocese of Lipa. See "Lipa Gears for First National Marian Prayer Congress," *Archdiocese of Lipa: Chronicles of Events in the Archdiocese of Lipa, Managed by Fr. Nonie Dolor* (blog), https://fathernonie.wordpress.com/2010/09/06/lipa-gears-for-first-national-marian-prayer-congress/#more-323 (accessed December 1, 2014). On February 7, 2014, the parish Mary, Mediatrix of All Grace, was officially consecrated. Although the image of Mary Mediatrix remains at the chapel of Lipa Carmel, from the most recent program of events it appears that every annual national pilgrimage to Lipa (which takes place over several days and ends on September 12) includes this ceremonial procession of Mary Mediatrix from the cathedral to the new parish. See "11th National Pilgrimage to Lipa," Mary, Mediatrix of All Grace Parish," http://marymediatrixofallgrace.com/pilgrimage/event-update/ (accessed December 1, 2014).

86. The Mariological literature proves this not to be exactly correct. Yes, the feast day of the Visitation (when Mary visited her cousin Elizabeth, then pregnant with John the Baptist) is May 31, but nothing of Benedict XV's writings on Mary as Mediatrix that I have located directly links these two aspects of Mary. For further explication, see Mark I. Miravalle, *Mariology: A Guide for Priests, Deacons, Seminarians, and Consecrated Persons* (Goleta, CA: Seat of Wisdom Books, 2007), 447–48.

87. In a further display of dogmatic reach the congress not only was open to the general public but also was webcast via the new parish website, at http://www.marymediatrixofallgrace.com.

88. Excerpted from "Project Goals/Objectives, Mariological Society of the Philippines," Mary, Mediatrix of All Grace, Parish, http://marymediatrixofallgrace.com/pammsphil/project-goals-objectives/ (accessed March 5, 2015).

89. The history of authenticating relics has yet to be comprehensively told by scholars, owing in part to the very messy, and at times, ad hoc, manner in which protocols of authentication developed, especially in the Counter-Reformation period. (My thanks to Katrina Olds for her insight; for

an example of this, see her article "Ambiguities of the Holy: Authenticating Relics in Seventeenth-Century Spain," *Renaissance Quarterly* 65, no. 1 (Spring 2012): 135–84.

90. André Breton, *Mad Love*, trans. Mary Ann Caws (Lincoln: University of Nebraska Press, 1987), 13–15 (originally published as *L'amour fou*, 1937).

91. *Boletín eclesiástico de Filipinas* 25 (1951): 287.

CHAPTER 5

1. Readers can view this message at "Please Pray the Rosary," YouTube video, 0:17, posted by "dwayne anderson" on April 27, 2010, http://www.youtube.com/watch?v=oCB9HuVLnwA (accessed November 28, 2014).

2. For a broad overview of Peyton's life and activities, see Patrick Peyton, *All for Her: The Autobiography of Father Patrick Peyton, C.S.C.* (Garden City, NY: Doubleday, 1967); and Richard Gribble, *American Apostle of the Family Rosary: The Life of Patrick J. Peyton* (New York: Crossroad Publishing, 2005).

3. Gribble, *American Apostle*, 107.

4. An additional prayer that dates from the apparition of the Virgin Mary at Fátima is sometimes inserted here. Known as the Fátima Prayer, it follows: "Oh, my Jesus, forgive us our sins, save us from the fires of hell, and lead all souls to heaven, especially those in most need of your mercy."

5. In October 2002, Pope John Paul II, seeking to encourage renewed devotion through rosary prayer, declared the rest of that year and the coming year to be the Year of the Rosary. In the apostolic letter containing this pronouncement, *Rosarium Virginis Mariae*, the pope also announced that he would be altering the six-hundred-year-old tradition of the fifteen mysteries by introducing a fourth set, named "Luminous." These depict milestones in Christ's adult life and mission. I have chosen here not to include them in my discussion, for all historical and ethnographic research on rosary prayer in this book predated this change, and, the changes being so recent, many who pray the rosary both individually and in groups have yet to adopt these additional mysteries. The full text of this letter can be found on the Vatican's official website at http://www.vatican.va/holy_father /john_paul_ii/apost_letters/documents/hf_jp-ii_apl_20021016_rosarium-virginis-mariae_en.html.

6. One of the most common versions of the Apostles' Creed is this: "I believe in God the Father almighty, creator of heaven and earth. I believe in Jesus Christ, his only Son, our Lord. He was conceived by the power of the Holy Spirit and born of the Virgin Mary. Under Pontius Pilate, he was crucified, died, and was buried. He descended to the dead. On the third day he rose again. He ascended into heaven and is seated at the right hand of the Father. He will come again to judge the living and the dead. I believe in the Holy Spirit, the holy catholic Church, the communion of saints, the forgiveness of sins, the resurrection of the body, and life everlasting. Amen."

7. The most common doxology is as follows: "Glory be to the Father, and to the Son, and to the Holy Spirit. As it was in the beginning, is now, and ever shall be, world without end. Amen."

8. The "Luminous" mysteries introduced by Pope John Paul II would insert themselves here as the second set, making the "Sorrowful" mysteries the third set.

9. Marc Tremeau, *The Mystery of the Rosary* (New York: Catholic Book Publishing, 1982), 33 (emphasis mine).

10. Louis-Marie Grignion de Montfort, *The Secret of the Rosary* (Bay Shore, NY: Montfort Fathers, 1965), 89.

11. Pope Paul VI, *Marialis cultus*, in *17 Papal Documents on the Rosary* (Boston: Daughters of St. Paul, 1980), 62.

12. Some theorists have argued that there is in fact an inherent mechanicity to "religion," one that can be seen in the first instance in the term's etymology, with the affix "re-," denoting repetition. Jacques Derrida states: "the technical is the possibility of faith, indeed its very chance." "Faith and Knowledge: The Two Sources of 'Religion' at the Limits of Reason Alone," trans. Sam-

uel Weber, in *Religion*, ed. Jacques Derrida and Gianni Vattimo (Stanford, CA: Stanford University Press, 1998), 47. The relationship between religion and media is not, therefore, merely one of instrumentality (i.e., the use of mechanical reproduction for the dissemination of religious content) but of mutual enablement (ibid.).

13. These conditions were enacted as part of the Bell Trade Act, which U.S. Congress passed on July 2, 1946, two days before the Philippines was officially granted independence.

14. Here I am referring to the accusation against Lucille Ball, first made public on September 6, 1953, that she was an active member of the Communist Party. Even when the House Un-American Activities Committee (HUAC) lifted its original ban on televised coverage of the hearing sessions, those accused members of the entertainment industry who actually took the stand before the cameras were not major celebrities but lesser-known behind-the-scenes types. See Thomas Doherty's *Cold War, Cool Medium: Television, McCarthyism, and American Culture* (New York: Columbia University Press, 2003), especially chap. 6, for an analysis of the coevality of the communist scare and the "golden age" of television in the United States.

15. Here I am referring to *The Twilight Zone*, *The Addams Family*, *I Dream of Jeannie*, *Bewitched*, and *Hogan's Heroes*.

16. Raul Rodrigo, *Kapitan: Geny Lopez and the Making of ABS-CBN* (Quezon City: ABS-CBN Publishing, 2006), 12.

17. Elpidio Quirino hailed from the town of Vigan, in the province of Ilocos Sur. Vice president in the administration of Manuel Roxas, Quirino became president when Roxas died unexpectedly in 1948.

18. John A. Lent, ed., *Broadcasting in Asia and the Pacific: A Continental Survey of Radio and Television* (Philadelphia: Temple University Press, 1978), 178.

19. Charley Agatep, now a public relations mogul in the Philippines, studied journalism at the University of Santo Tomas in Manila before receiving a Fulbright scholarship to study broadcast journalism at Boston University. It was immediately upon his return to the Philippines that he helped set up DZAQ. For more on him, see Ferdie Bautista, "Charlie Agatep: President, Agatep Associates, Inc.: A Hands-On, Results-Driven PR Executive," *Philippine Star*, January 4, 1999, http://charlieagatep.wordpress.com/2012/09/20/charlie-agatep-president-agatep-associates-inc-a-hands-on-results-driven-pr-executive/ (accessed November 9, 2013).

20. Charley Agatep, "Lights, Camera, and How Philippine TV Began," *Philippine Star*, September 23, 2003.

21. *Kundiman* are ballads sung in the vernacular, usually of love and lament. Ibid.

22. Ibid.

23. The classic and most comprehensive study of the Hukbalahap remains Benedict Kerkvliet's *The Huk Rebellion: A Study of Peasant Revolt in the Philippines* (Berkeley: University of California Press, 1977).

24. Magsaysay's popularity stemmed from his own self-representation as a man of the common *tao* (people), his humble origins (compared to the oligarchic roots of leaders at that time), and his frequent forays into provincial barrios. Even the most scrupulous biographers praise the farm-boy president for ushering into the young nation a new and noble form of leadership (though with varying degrees of success in execution), one that aspired to bring government to the people, to rid its ranks (including the military) of nepotism and corruption, and to attract an alienated peasantry back into the fold of citizenry through plans of rural development and public works. Nevertheless, he held unwavering loyalty to his American friends. This "friendship" would reverberate as "neo-imperialism" long into the latter part of the twentieth century, especially with regard to the hot-button issue of U.S. control over military installations in the Philippines. Among the many biographies of the former president, the most detailed is Jose Abueva's *Ramon Magsaysay: A Political Biography* (Manila: Solidaridad Publishing House, 1971).

25. According to one history of Philippine television, this changed in the early 1960s, such that by "1962, the television was the most salable appliance in urban areas, with the electric fan far sec-

ond," and "by 1966, there were about 200,000 TV sets in the country, [w]ith one million people watching 18 stations during the prime time hours of 7–10 p.m." Cecille Matutina, *Pinoy Television: The Story of ABS-CBN* (Quezon City: ABS-CBN Broadcasting, 1999), 79.

26. Gribble, *American Apostle*, 107. Gribble's biography of Peyton is the most comprehensive and balanced portrayal to date.

27. For an outline of the crusades as proposed for the Philippines, see Fr. Patrick Peyton to archbishop of Manila Gabriel Reyes, January 13, 1952, Fr. Peyton's Visit to the Philippines, Archives of the Holy Cross Family Ministries (AHCFM). It would not be until 1959 that the first crusade in the Philippines was held. For an outline of the 1959 crusade, see "Family Rosary Crusade, Archdiocese of Manila," Reports, 1961–62, AHCFM.

28. Gribble, *American Apostle*, 107.

29. "Family Rosary Crusade Souvenir Program, Diocese of San Fernando, January 1, 1962, to February 11, 1961," Publicity and Outdoor Advertising, 1959–62, AHCFM.

30. "Crusader for Prayer Coming to S.F. [San Fernando, Pampanga]," "Archbishop Santos Writes on Crusade," November 1, 1959, "Information for Newsmen Regarding Family Rosary Rally," "Bus Companies," and "Contract for the Aerial Services," Publicity and Outdoor Advertising, 1959–62, AHCFM.

31. "Suggested Plan for the Celebration of the 1959 Family Week," Annex B, Reports, 1961–62, AHCFM.

32. Previously known as the Bagumbayan, the Luneta was the site of the execution of the three secular Filipino priests, Mariano Gomez, José Burgos, and Jacinto Zamora, wrongly accused of inciting the Cavite Mutiny in 1872, and the execution of José Rizal, in 1896. For an overview of the 1959 crusades from Peyton's perspective, see Fr. Patrick Peyton, "Diary of the Great Blessings of God and Our Lady on the Family Rosary Crusade in the Archdiocese of Manila," December 8, 1959, Reports, 1959, AHCFM.

33. The cities were Manila; Balanga (Bataan); San Fernando (Pampanga); Cabanatuan (Nueva Ecija); Daet (Camarines Norte); Naga (Camarines Sur); Masbate City, Sorsogon, Legaspi, and Virac (Bicol); Calbayog and Borongan (Samar); Maasin, Palo, and Tacloban (Leyte); San Jose (Antique); Jaro (Iloilo); Dumaguete (Negros Oriental); Tagbilaran (Bohol); Cebu City (Cebu); Bacolod (Negros Occidental); Kalibo (Aklan); Roxas (Capiz); Butuan (Agusan del Norte); Tagum (Davao del Norte); Digos (Davao del Sur); Dipolog (Zamboanga del Norte); Cagayan de Oro (Misamis); Marbel (South Cotabato); Jolo (Sulu); and Ozamis (Misamis Occidental). "Family Rosary Crusades in the Philippines" (1962) and "The 50th Anniversary of the Family Rosary Crusades in the Philippines, 1951–2001" (2001), FRC Philippines Archives.

34. "Family Rosary Crusades in the Philippines" (1962), FRC Philippines Archives.

35. Ian Hacking, *The Taming of Chance* (New York: Cambridge University Press, 1990).

36. "1 (M) Attend Rosary Rally," *Manila Times*, December 7, 1959.

37. This reading is informed by Jeffrey T. Schnapp's examination of panoramic photographs of crowds in fascist Italy. See "Mob Porn," in *Crowds*, ed. Jeffrey T. Schnapp and Matthew Tiews (Stanford, CA: Stanford University Press, 2006), 1–45.

38. For a discussion of political rallies, see Reynaldo Ileto, "Orators and the Crowd: Independence Politics, 1910–1914," in *Filipinos and Their Revolution: Event, Discourse, and Historiography* (Quezon City: Ateneo de Manila University Press, 1998), 135–63.

39. For an overview of the International Eucharistic Conference, see Agripino D. Bautista, *The Greatest International Event in the Orient* (Manila: Agripino D. Bautista, 1938). Eucharistic congresses grew out of the tradition of pilgrimage and spectacular gatherings of ecclesiastics and the laity "for the purpose of celebrating and glorifying the Eucharist" in a collective and organized response to increasing secularization. *The Catholic Encyclopedia*, s.v. "Eucharistic Congresses," http://www.newadvent.org/cathen/05592a.htm. The first congress was held in 1881, in Lille, France. For a brief and pious history of the congresses until 1930, see L. Gallagher, *The Eucharistic Congress: Its History and Organisation* (Dublin: Office of the "Irish Messenger," 1930).

40. One case in point comes from Spain's Canary Islands. In the 1950s, at a rosary rally held on the island of Fuerteventura, one man, alarmed by the fervor of the crowd, turned to his wife and urged, "Ámanos, Minga, que nos echan cuerpo a tierra!" (Let's go, Minga, before they throw us flat on the ground!). The inspiration for this warning was the arresting images, engrained in the popular imagination of those living in Franco's Spain, that came out of the 1955 International Eucharistic Congress of Barcelona, where 840 priests were ordained simultaneously. Lying face down had long been one gesture in the rite of consecrating a priest, but the striking formation of hundreds of bodies prostrate, framed by a stadium crowd, transformed the act into an image of aestheticized submission that the gentleman of Puerto del Rosario clearly feared was the direction in which the rosary rally was headed. Interview with Josefa Martínez Berriel, July 22, 2010, Palo Alto, CA. Notably, the reason Martínez Berriel knows this is because "Ámanos, Minga" became an expression in the local idiom.

41. To best convey the sense of spectacle of the Philippine crusades, I have opted in this section to present a composite picture. Sources I've drawn on include the following: "Family Rosary Rally," Lilia J. de Jesus's "A Knight and His Crusade—In Retrospect," "Iloilo Rally, Feb. 4, 1962," "Extract from Father Peyton's Letter of February 7, 1962," and "Family Rosary Crusade (Cavite, Bulacan, and Rizal Province)," Reports, 1961–62, AHCFM; "Family Rosary Crusade Souvenir Program, Diocese of San Fernando, January 1, 1962 to February 11, 1961," "One Million Attend Family Rosary Rally in Manila on December 6 [1959]," "1,500,000 Join Family Rosary Crusade Rally," and "Information for Newsmen Regarding Family Rosary Rally," Publicity and Outdoor Advertising, 1959–62, AHCFM; "Gran concentracion de la Cruzada del Rosario en Familia en Antique, Filipinas," and Fr. Patrick Peyton, "Diary of the Great Blessings of God and Our Lady on the Family Rosary Crusade in the Archdiocese of Manila," December 8, 1959, Reports, 1959, AHCFM; "Family Rosary Crusades in the Philippines" (1962), FRC Philippines Archives; "Big Bataan Crowd Hears Fr. Peyton Talk on Prayer," *Daily Mirror* (Manila), January 23, 1962; "Rosary Padre Arrives in Tagbilaran Tomorrow," *Manila Times*, January 23, 1962; "40,000 Hear Father Peyton in Bataan Rosary Rally," *Manila Times*, January 24, 1962; "200,000 Devotees Hear Peyton in Pampanga," *Manila Times*, January 30, 1962; "Peyton in Ecija Crusade," *Manila Times*, January 30, 1962; "Political Forum Caps Bohol Rosary Rally," *Manila Times*, October 24, 1963; and "Father Peyton Arrives for Imus Rally," n.d., "Peyton, Patrick" clippings file, Lopez Memorial Library.

42. "40,000 Hear Father Peyton in Bataan Rosary Rally," *Manila Times*, January 24, 1962.

43. Ibid.

44. Patrick Peyton, "Family Fortress," *Daily Mirror* (Manila), January 13, 1962.

45. Florencio Yllana, "Father Peyton's Grand Family Rosary Rallies," *Manila Times* (n.d.), reprinted in "Family Rosary Crusades in the Philippines" (1962), FRC Philippines Archives.

46. "40,000 Hear Father Peyton in Bataan Rosary Rally," *Manila Times*, January 24, 1962.

47. Florencio Yllana, "Father Peyton's Grand Family Rosary Rallies," *Manila Times* (n.d.), reprinted in "Family Rosary Crusades in the Philippines" (1962), FRC Philippines Archives.

48. Interview with Larry Ersuela, Manila, October 8, 2001. Ersuela was one of the FRC staff workers during a later series of crusades that took place between 1981 and 1983.

49. The classic analysis of this logic remains Vicente Rafael's *Contracting Colonialism: Translation and Christian Conversion in Tagalog Society under Early Spanish Rule* (Ithaca, NY: Cornell University Press, 1988).

50. Gribble, *American Apostle*, 107.

51. Ibid., 112.

52. "Our Family Rosary Pledge" (pledge card), Reports, 1961–62, AHCFM.

53. Ibid.

54. In describing the process of pledge gathering to teachers, Santos noted: "Each Pledge Card must carry at the top left-hand corner the name and address of the head of the family to be visited. This is a very painstaking job, in fact, it amounts to a Census-taking of the entire Parish." Most Rev. Rufino Santos to Teachers of Public and Private Schools, October 21, 1959, Reports 1959, AHCFM.

55. Most Rev. Rufino Santos, "Family Rosary Crusade—Pledge Gathering: Plan of Action for Vicar Forains [*sic*]," Reports 1959, AHCFM.

56. Ibid.

57. Most Rev. Rufino Santos to Teachers of Public and Private Schools, October 21, 1959, Reports 1959, AHCFM.

58. Ibid.

59. "The Family Rosary Crusade Souvenir Bulletin," Reports 1959, AHCFM.

60. "FRC Newsettes," in "The Family Rosary Crusade Souvenir Bulletin," p. B.

61. Ibid.

62. Family Rosary Crusade Archdiocese of Manila to Reverend Joseph M. Quinn, January 18, 1960, Correspondence, 1951–62, AHCFM.

63. Cited in Fr. Patrick Peyton to Rev. Joseph M. Quinn, March 3, 1962, Correspondence, Manhasset, 1959–62, AHCFM.

64. Sr. Mary of St. Rose Virginia to Fr. Patrick Peyton, February 5, 1961, Correspondence, 1960–65, AHCFM.

65. Mrs. Esperanza T. Buenconsejo to Fr. Patrick Peyton, October 20, 1959, Correspondence, 1951–62, AHCFM.

66. Family Rosary Crusade Souvenir Program, diocese of San Fernando, January 1, 1962–February 11, 1961, Publicity and Outdoor Advertising, 1959–62, AHCFM.

67. *Bakla* is a complex Tagalog term that gender theorist Martin Manalansan defines as "encompass[ing] homosexuality, hermaphroditism, cross-dressing, and effeminancy" (though not in that order and not necessarily all at once). Martin F. Manalansan IV, *Global Divas: Filipino Gay Men in the Diaspora* (Durham, NC: Duke University, 2003), ix.

68. First Anniversary Family Rosary Crusade Auxiliaries Souvenir Program, Correspondence, Ladies Auxiliaries, 1961–69, AHCFM.

69. Julie O. Campos to Fr. Patrick Peyton, March 8, 1960, Correspondence, 1951–62, AHCFM.

70. Ibid. In another report the Auxiliaries are described as raising funds for the importation of a "half million rosaries from Ireland." Family Rosary Crusade archdiocese of Manila to Rev. Joseph M. Quinn, January 18, 1960, Correspondence, 1951–62, AHCFM.

71. Nestora L. Benetua to Fr. Patrick Peyton, March 2, 1960, Correspondence, 1951–62, AHCFM.

72. Betty Velhagen to Fr. Patrick Peyton, February 28, 1960, Correspondence, 1951–62, AHCFM.

73. Melba Oliver to Fr. Patrick Peyton, February 25, 1960, Correspondence, 1951–62, AHCFM.

74. Lilia J. de Jesus, "A Knight and His Crusade—In Retrospect," Reports, 1961–62, AHCFM.

75. "The 50th Anniversary of the Family Rosary Crusades in the Philippines, 1951–2001" (2001), FRC Philippines Archives.

76. See the Family Rosary Crusade Philippines Functional Chart, appended to Mrs. Concepcion Martelino to Fr. Patrick Peyton, March 8, 1968, and Family Rosary Crusade First Report on Popular Mission–1968, Philippines Reports, AHCFM.

77. For more on the making of the films, see Gribble, *American Apostle*, chap. 6.

78. Interview with Larry Ersuela, Manila, October 8, 2001.

79. Interview with Ben de los Reyes, Manila, August 20, 2004.

80. Although they used Spanish actors, Peyton requested that the actors mouth the words in a kind of pidgin English. Gribble, *American Apostle*, 139.

81. Interview with Ben de los Reyes, Manila, August 20, 2004.

82. *Kamote*, from the Spanish *camote*, is a commonly eaten root vegetable.

83. Interview with Ben de los Reyes, Manila, August 20, 2004.

84. Ibid.

85. Ibid.

86. Ibid.

87. In the Philippines the manual for this was translated into Tagalog as *Mga tuntunin sa pag-papalabas ng mga pelikula ng Rosario ng mag-anak*, Philippines Report, AHCFM.

88. Ibid., 15.

89. Ibid., 38.

90. Interview with Ben de los Reyes, Manila, August 20, 2004.

91. Interview with Larry Ersuela, Manila, October 8, 2001.

92. Interview with Ben de los Reyes, Manila, August 20, 2004.

93. Ibid.

CHAPTER 6

1. "Statue of St. Therese in Baguio 'Weeps' Blood," *Sun Star Network Online*, July 14, 2004, http://www.sunstar.com.ph/static/net/2004/07/14/statue.of.st.therese.in.baguio.weeps.blood.html (accessed December 28, 2005).

2. Vincent Cabreza, "Little Flower 'Seen' Shedding Tears of Blood," *Philippine Daily Inquirer*, July 13, 2004.

3. Our Lady of All Nations is an advocation based on an apparition of Mary to thirty-nine-year-old Ida Peerdeman, in Amsterdam in 1945. Although the context of an occupied Netherlands is important to understanding the immediate import of Mary's early messages to the visionary (which included foretelling the date of Dutch liberation from the Nazis: May 5, 1945), the apparition's international pretentions were highly significant. To this day the cult of Our Lady of All Nations remains a controversial one, largely because of its theological implications, as the first apparition of Mary in modern times to demand that she be understood as "Co-Redemptrix," that is, that she be understood as being an active agent in Christ's plan of salvation. As Dutch scholar Peter Jan Margry has pointed out, this is most vividly rendered in the iconography of the Lady of All Nations, in which she is painted squarely against a crucifix, perched atop a globe, with light radiating from her outstretched hands and flocks of sheep at her feet. As is discussed later in this chapter, Our Lady of All Nations is important to contemporary Marian groups like the ones described here, for her messages herald the fulfillment of this role in the awaited declaration of the fifth Marian dogma. For a scholarly overview of the cult of Our Lady of All Nations, see Margry, "Paradoxes of Marian Apparitional Contestation: Networks, Ideology, Gender, and the Lady of All Nations," in *Moved by Mary: The Power of Pilgrimage in the Modern World*, ed. Anna-Karina Hermkens, Willy Jansen, and Catrien Notermans (Surrey, UK: Ashgate, 2009), 183–200.

4. To conceive of the world as picture, according to Martin Heidegger, is a defining act of modernity, one of objectification that enables the apprehension of the heterogeneity and systematicity of the world, thus making everything immanently representable. "The Age of the World Picture," in *The Question Concerning Technology and Other Essays* (New York: Harper & Row, 1977), 115–54.

5. "Devotees Mark Mary's 1st Global Birthday in NY," *Philippine Daily Inquirer*, August 7, 1999.

6. Known as the "brain drain," this mass migration of Filipinos owed itself to the following factors: the U.S. Immigration Act of 1965, the shortage of nurses in the United States, and the worsening social and political environment in the Philippines in the wake of Ferdinand Marcos's declaration of martial law in 1972. The hemorrhaging of Filipino labor at this time was not limited to the Filipino professional class, however. By creating new labor-export policies and the office of the Overseas Employment Development Board, the Marcos administration institutionalized the processing of overseas placement and made mandatory the remittance of a certain percentage of workers' salaries. These new policies were a swift response to the oil and building boom in the Middle East, which became one of the most common destinations of sojourning workers. Studies of globalization and its effects on Filipino migrants and contract workers have burgeoned in the past fifteen years, along with a broader scholarly interest in the Philippine diaspora. For a small sample of this scholarship, see Catherine Ceniza Choy, *Empire of Care: Nursing and Migration in Filipino American History* (Durham, NC: Duke University Press, 2003); Martin Manalansan, *Global Divas: Filipino Gay Men in the Diaspora* (Durham, NC: Duke University Press, 2003); Rhacel Sala-

zar Parreñas, *Servants of Globalization: Women, Migration, and Domestic Work* (Stanford, CA: Stanford University Press, 2001); Anna Guevarra, *Marketing Dreams, Manufacturing Heroes: The Transnational Labor Brokering of Filipino Workers* (New Brunswick, NJ: Rutgers University Press, 2009).

7. Interview with Maria Luisa Fatima Nebrida, Quezon City, January 25, 2001. The imagery Nebrida invokes comes from Genesis 3:15, which, according to the Catholic Douay Bible (notably the version translated during the Counter-Reformation), reads as follows: "I shall put enmity between you and the Woman, between your seed and her seed: she shall crush your head, while you will lie in wait for her heel." For devotees like Nebrida, the agent who destroys the serpent in the garden is unmistakably female, and unmistakably Mary. For a more elaborate discussion on the history and theology of Mary as a redemptory "second Eve," see Marina Warner's *Alone of All Her Sex* (New York: Vintage Books, 1976), 50-67.

8. Interview with Maria Luisa Fatima Nebrida, Quezon City, January 25, 2001.

9. The autobiography of St. Ignatius of Loyola reads: "He decided to watch over his arms all one night, without sitting down or going to bed, but standing a while and kneeling a while, before the altar of Our Lady of Montserrat where he had resolved to leave his clothing and dress himself in the armor of Christ." *The Autobiography of St. Ignatius Loyola, with Related Documents*, trans. Joseph F. O'Callaghan (New York: Fordham University Press, 1992), 31.

10. In what is the most frequently cited, albeit pious, account of the apparitions of Mary at Fátima, William Thomas Walsh describes the dancing sun phenomenon as follows: "The sun stood forth in the clear zenith like a great silver disk which, though bright as any sun they [the crowd] had ever seen, they could look straight at without blinking and with a unique and delightful satisfaction. This lasted but a moment. While they gazed, a huge ball began to 'dance' . . . Now it was whirling rapidly like a gigantic fire-wheel. After doing this for some time, it stopped. Then it rotated again, with dizzy, sickening speed. Finally there appeared on the rim a border of crimson, which flung across the sky, as from a hellish vortex, blood-red streamers of flame, reflecting to the earth, to the trees and shrubs, to the upturned faces and the clothes all sorts of brilliant colors in succession: green, red, orange, blue, violet, the whole spectrum in fact. Madly gyrating in this manner three times, the fiery orb seemed to tremble, to shudder, and then to plunge precipitately, in a mighty zigzag, toward the crowd." *Our Lady of Fatima* (New York: Doubleday, 1954), 145-46. At Medjugorje, witnesses often frame their experience of the dancing sun vis-à-vis the phenomenon at Fátima. For example, an article on one of Medjugorje's approved English-language web portals describes the first appearance of the "dancing of the sun" on August 2, 1981, as having been like that at Fátima in 1917, but with "considerably more facets." Ana Yeseta, "Signs and Wonders in Medjugorje," November 22, 2001, http://www.medjugorje.org/a_wonder.htm (accessed August 27, 2013). For several scientific takes on the "dancing sun" phenomenon at Fátima and elsewhere, see the eclectic set of essays in Fernando Fernandes, Joaquim Fernandes, and Raul Beneguel, eds., *Fatima Revisited: The Apparition Phenomenon in Ufology, Psychology, and Science* (San Antonio, TX: Anomalist Books, 2008), especially chap. 4.

11. Interview with Maria Luisa Fatima Nebrida, Quezon City, January 25, 2001.

12. A history of the Blue Army of Our Lady of Fátima can be found in the memoir of one of its American cofounders, John Haffert, *Dear Bishop: Memoirs of the Author Concerning the History of the Blue Army* (Washington, NJ: AMI International Press, 1982).

13. Interview with Maria Luisa Fatima Nebrida, Quezon City, January 25, 2001.

14. "Rosary Theater Finds New Home," *Manila Standard*, February 16, 1988.

15. The apparitions of the Virgin Mary at Medjugorje began on June 24, 1981, when six young people between the ages of ten and sixteen claimed to see a woman in white hovering above the ground on a hill. She continued to appear daily to the young adults, although over time the daily apparitions ceased for all but three of the visionaries (the other three still claim to receive visits from Mary on a yearly basis). The continued proliferation of commentary and studies on the case owe themselves in part to the ongoing—and notably serial—nature of the phenomenon. Social scientists have found in Medjugorje a fascinating window onto the shifting political tumult in the

region, commencing as it had in the immediate wake of the death of Tito and continuing through the period of the splintering of the region into ethnic conflict; see Mart Bax, *Medjugorje: Religion, Politics, and Violence in Rural Bosnia* (Amsterdam: VU University Press, 1995). French sociologist Élisabeth Claverie produced an extraordinary account of the phenomenon in its broader context, departing from the perspective of French pilgrims to Medjugorje in *Les guerres de la Vierge* (see note 18 in the introduction to this volume). A succinct overview of the apparitions and its relation to Croatian nationalism can be found in Zlatko Skrbiš's "The Apparitions of the Virgin Mary of Medjugorje: The Convergence of Croatian Nationalism and Her Apparitions," *Nations and Nationalism* 11, no. 3 (2005): 443–61. Among the most sober yet sympathetic theological accounts of the phenomenon are those volumes written by well-known Mariologist René Laurentin, *Is the Virgin Mary Appearing at Medjugorje? An Urgent Message for the World Given in a Marxist Country* (Washington, DC: Word among Us Press, 1984), and *Medjugorje—Thirteen Years Later* (Milford, OH: Riehle Foundation, 1994). On the Internet the most comprehensive clearinghouses for all information pertaining to the apparitions are Medjugorje Web (http://www.medjugorje.org) and Medjugorje: Place of Prayer and Reconciliation, the official website of the shrine (http://www.medjugorje.hr). In 1991, the Bishops' Conference of Yugoslavia declared that the supernatural events at Medjugorje could not be confirmed. But neither had they been proven false, and it is on this basis that the all the activity surrounding the apparitions is allowed to continue.

16. Interview with Lydia Sison, Pasig, February 5, 2001.

17. Cross Mountain is the name given to the hill above the town of Medjugorje, where a huge crucifix was erected in 1934. The official website for the Medjugorje shrine describes it as the "'Calvary' of the shrine where pilgrims remember the passion of Christ," and it is one of the places where visitors have regularly witnessed solar phenomena. Leonard Orec, O.F.M., "The Pilgrims' Gatherings in Medjugorje," 1996, Medjugorje: Place of Prayer and Reconciliation, http://www.medjugorje.hr/en/medjugorje-phenomenon/pilgrims-gatherings/ (accessed August 26, 2013).

18. To understand the origins of Christian mission, one can begin with the etymology of the term "mission" itself, which derives from the Latin *missio*, "to send." There is an abundance of references to "sending" in the New Testament, including that of Christ being, of course, he who has been sent, but also, in what some Christians term the "Great Commission," when Christ orders: "Go, therefore, and make disciples of all nations, baptizing them in the name of the Father, and of the Son, and of the holy Spirit, teaching them to observe all that I have commanded you" (Matthew 28:19–20, *New American Bible, Revised Edition*).

19. "Happy Birthday, Dearest Mother," *Philippine Daily Inquirer*, September 9, 2012, http://life style.inquirer.net/65442/happy-birthday-dearest-mother (accessed August 6, 2013).

20. During the snap presidential election of February 1986, Keithley was assigned to Radio Veritas, the Catholic station over which Cardinal Sin broadcast his call to the public to support the Marcos defectors. When their transmitters were destroyed, she resumed broadcasting over DZRJ, 810 AM, which to this day is known as Radyo Bandido.

21. The train epitomizes modernity's standardization of time, and thus repetition and all to which it may give rise, including coincidence. The classic treatment of repetition and train travel is found in Sigmund Freud's famous 1919 essay "The Uncanny," in *Writings on Art and Literature* (Stanford, CA: Stanford University Press, 1997), 193–232. See also the marvelous study by Wolfgang Schivelbusch, *The Railway Journey: The Industrialization of Time and Space in the 19th Century* (Berkeley: University of California Press, 1986).

22. "Happy Birthday, Dearest Mother," *Philippine Daily Inquirer*, September 9, 2012, http://lifestyle.inquirer.net/65442/happy-birthday-dearest-mother (accessed August 6, 2013).

23. Ibid.

24. Interview with June Keithley, Quezon City, June 12, 2007. Keithley's father was an American. See her brief biographical article, "My Life as a 'Kanang Pinay,'" *Philippine Daily Inquirer*, April 29, 2012. *Kanang Pinay* is slang for "American Filipina."

25. I often heard devotees like Keithley invoke the Annunciation as a model for their own

submission—and strength. For as Keithley noted during the interview, before Mary uttered those famous words "Behold, the handmaid of the Lord," she had enough wits about her to demand from the angel Gabriel how it was possible that she could be pregnant without having been with a man.

26. As quoted in Monina Allarey Mercado, ed., *People Power: An Eyewitness History* (Manila: James B. Reuter, S.J., Foundation, 1986), 124–25.

27. For more on the phenomenology of prayer during the People Power revolt of 1986, see my essay, "From the Power of Prayer to *Prayer Power*: On Religion and Revolt in the Modern Philippines," in *Southeast Asian Perspectives on Power*, ed. Liana Chua, Joanna Cook, Nicholas Long, and Lee Wilson (New York: Routledge, 2012), 165–80.

28. For examples of publications celebrating the Marian nature of the revolt, see Pedro S. de Achútegui and Loyola School of Theology, *The Miracle of the Philippine Revolution: Interdisciplinary Reflections: Symposium Organized by the Loyola School of Theology* (Quezon City: Loyola School of Theology, 1986); Socrates B. Villegas, ed., *EDSA Shrine: God's Gift, Our Mission* (Manila: Roman Catholic Archdiocese of Manila, 1999); and Mercado, *People Power*. For a trenchant critique of this perspective, see Neferti Tadiar's "'People Power': Miraculous Revolt," in *Fantasy-Production: Sexual Economies and Other Philippine Consequences for the New World Order* (Quezon City: Ateneo de Manila University Press, 2004), 185–224.

29. In "'People Power,'" Tadiar writes: "After the uprising, the revolutionary potential of the defiant Virgin was diffused. Instead of acting the part of subversive desire, that is, of the desiring subject, Cory [Aquino] was reduced by dominant interpreters to *being* the representation of the desired … The interpretation of 'people power' as God's power erased the people as historical subject, reducing them once again to that inert substance sometimes called the masses, whose shape and role is determined by greater and stronger forces transcending them." Ibid., 220–21.

30. As one woman described it: "The Filipinos' victory was a Marian victory … The Filipino was never more Christian than when he won fighting his most precious battle—the battle for freedom, democracy, and peace. Let no one write the history of this brave, noble revolution and forget that God was with his Filipino children and Mary led the battle." Quoted in Mercado, *People Power*, 250–51.

31. Bishop Socrates B. Villegas, "Our Lady of EDSA, Philippines 1986," http://www.balanga-diocese.com/Bishop'sMessages/ourladyofedsa.html (accessed on August 12, 2013). This was a talk given by one of the most important protégés of Cardinal Jaime Sin, then bishop of the diocese of Balanga, at the Asian Workshop Group of the Twenty-Second International Marian Congress in Lourdes, France (September 4–8, 2008), on the occasion of the 150th anniversary of the apparitions of Mary at Lourdes. The talk itself reads rather defensively, as if to combat specifically the rumors that Mary had "actually" appeared.

32. Officially called Shrine of Mary, Queen of Peace, the shrine at EDSA was completed in 1989, three years after the EDSA revolt. Once controversial for the "Asiatic" features of its thirty-five-foot bronze statue of Mary, and famous as the site of EDSA Dos, or People Power II, the large-scale protest that resulted in the ouster of then president Joseph Estrada in 2001, the shrine has suffered the fate of many monuments, becoming less and less conspicuous as more commercial developments have cropped up in the popular Ortigas area. A brief history of the EDSA shrine can be found at "The EDSA Shrine," http://edsashrine.com/edsa25/category/about-edsa-shrine/ (accessed on March 6, 2015).

33. For a discussion of this visual dimension, see JPaul S. Manzanilla, "Picturing Historical Subjects: The Photography of the EDSA People Power Uprising" (M.A. thesis, University of the Philippines, 2011).

34. The loci classici on "millenarian"-style popular uprisings in the Philippines are David R. Sturtevant's *Popular Uprisings in the Philippines 1840–1940* (Ithaca, NY: Cornell University Press, 1976); and Reynaldo Ileto's *Pasyon and Revolution: Popular Movements in the Philippines, 1840–1910* (Quezon City: Ateneo de Manila University Press, 1979).

35. A twentieth-century innovation, this is a period during which the ordinary liturgical year in-

corporates more Mary-related themes, devotions, and activities. The first Marian Year was declared by Pope Pius XII and celebrated in 1954. In his pastoral exhortation, Cardinal Sin minces no words in rationalizing the timing of the Philippine Marian Year of 1985:

> Perhaps not since the period of the Second World War have our people faced a year of such bleak prospects as they faced with the ending of 1984. For those socially and economically disadvantaged—that is, the majority of our people—1985 seems to promise perhaps even more privation, more widespread unemployment, increased inflation, greater hardships, with no end of the tunnel in sight. For so many who are suffering from difficulties and uncertainties, burdened by injustice and crushed by violations of human rights, the foreseeable future seems to bring little prospect of relief. In sum, the present year is hardly a year for facile optimism or bright hope.

Jaime Sin, "The Marian Year 1985: A Pilgrimage of Hope with Our Blessed Mother," CBCP Documents, http://www.cbcponline.net/documents/1980s/1985-pilgrimage_hope.html (accessed August 16, 2013). By the time the Marian Year concluded on December 8 (notably, the feast of the Immaculate Conception), Ferdinand Marcos had called for snap elections, which took place on February 7, 1986.

36. According to Sarah Jane Boss, voluntary consecration (in contrast to the consecration that takes place through the sacrament of baptism) in the modern period is almost exclusively to Mary and has been greatly influenced by the consecration recommended by St. Louis-Marie Grignion de Montfort (1673–1716). For a concise overview of Marian consecration, see Boss, "Marian Consecration in the Contemporary Church," in *Mary: The Complete Resource*, ed. Sarah Jane Boss (London: Continuum Books, 2007), 411–23.

37. Interview with June Keithley, Quezon City, June 12, 2007.

38. I have transcribed this verbatim (in its original English), using punctuation to convey the dramatic pauses in Fr. Jerry's speech. Talk delivered on September 11, 1999, New York City. In using the phrase "minus one," Fr. Jerry is playing on the popular Filipino name for karaoke.

39. Jacques Derrida writes: "Sacrifice supposes the putting to death of the unique in terms of its being unique, irreplaceable, and most precious. It also therefore refers to the impossibility of substitution, the unsubstitutable; and then also to the substitution of an animal for man; and finally, especially this, by means of this impossible substitution itself, it refers to what links the sacred to sacrifice and sacrifice to secrecy." *The Gift of Death* (Chicago: University of Chicago Press, 1995), 58.

40. The primary inspiration for my reading of the power of narrative in this sermon derives from James T. Siegel's remarkable readings of Lévi-Strauss in *Naming the Witch* (Stanford, CA: Stanford University Press, 2006).

41. My reading of this scene has benefited from Marilyn Ivy's analysis of the relationship among voice, memory, and grief in the practice of spirit mediumship on Mt. Osore, Japan. "Ghostly Epiphanies: Recalling the Dead on Mount Osore," in *Discourses of the Vanishing: Modernity, Phantasm, Japan* (Chicago: University of Chicago Press, 1995), 141–91.

42. As theorists Kaja Silverman and Julia Kristeva have noted, the maternal voice is marked by irreducible, irresolvable ambivalence. On the one hand, the maternal voice is a fantasy of absolute origination, of a time before the subject and identity, of the time, in other words, of pure gift. A "sonorous envelope," the maternal voice figures everything longed for and lost to the subject alienated by its own imago: plenitude, unity, protection, and satisfaction. On the other hand, for the alienated subject cajoled into such forgetting, the sound of the maternal voice may also induce unpleasant or downright distressing sensations of suffocation, entrapment, and wholly impotent interiority. For more on the maternal voice, see Silverman's *The Acoustic Mirror: The Female Voice in Psychoanalysis and Cinema* (Bloomington, IN: Indiana University Press, 1988); and Kristeva's "Place Names," in *Desire and Language: A Semiotic Approach to Literature and Art* (New York: Columbia University Press, 1980), 271–94. Kristeva's famous essay "Stabat Mater" brings this discussion to another level, literalizing in its textual layout this containment, embedding in an academic discussion of the para-

gon maternity of the Virgin Mary her own subjective and sensual impressions of being a mother. Kristeva, *Tales of Love* (New York: Columbia University Press, 1987), 234–63.

43. Jacques Lacan, "The Mirror Stage as Formative of the Function of the I as Revealed in Psychoanalytic Experience," in *Écrits* (New York: W. W. Norton, 1977), 1–7.

44. Or, "The New York and the Washington bombings were planned long ago and the FBI now knows the mastermind. They are hunting down NOSTRADAMUS."

45. Mary's Army to Save Souls (MASS) Media Movement, "World Marian Peace Regatta, New York[,] September 11, 1999," souvenir program, author's personal collection.

46. This is a specific type of prayer meeting, modeled after guidelines provided by Italian priest and mystic, founder of the worldwide Marian Movement of Priests, Fr. Stefano Gobbi, whose "Blue Book" of messages from Mary is a central feature of these meetings. In the book, Fr. Gobbi lays out the cenacle structure: (1) prayer with Mary (i.e., recitation of the holy rosary); (2) meditation aimed at "liv[ing] the consecration to the Immaculate Heart of Mary," during which time is usually "given over to the a communal meditation from the book of the Movement [of Priests]"; (3) "experience of a true fraternity," which, in the case of this group in Manila, very often consisted of lavish dinners which they referred to under the rubric of "agape meals." *To the Priests: Our Lady's Beloved Sons*, 17th special Philippine ed. (Manila: Marian Movement of Priests Philippines, n.d.), xxiv–xxv.

47. For further elaboration, see the discussion of the "folk Catholic" paradigm in Philippine historiography and ethnography in the introduction to this volume.

48. In 2002 Pope John Paul II added the "Luminous Mysteries" to the rosary, bringing the total number of decades to twenty. Most of the time I spent with this group was during 2001, however, before these mysteries were added.

49. Vassula Ryden is a contemporary mystic who claims that God revealed himself to her in 1985, while she was living in Bangladesh. She transcribes his messages in volumes of notebooks, most of which have been published under the title *True Life in God*. It is not clear how she came to the attention of Catholics, but in Marian circles she is widely read and has traveled to the Philippines on at least one occasion at the invitation of groups like MASS Media Movement. In 1995 the Congregation for the Doctrine of the Faith of the Catholic Church issued a notification regarding Ryden, pointing out a number of "doctrinal errors" contained in her messages. For the entirety of the statement, see "Notification," Holy See, http://www.vatican.va/roman_curia/congregations/cfaith/documents/rc_con_cfaith_doc_19951006_ryden_en.html (accessed August 30, 2013). For more on Ryden, see her website True Life in God, at http://www.tlig.org/en/ (accessed August 30, 2013).

50. For the entirety of this message, see "The Foundations of the Earth Will Rock," True Life in God, http://www.tlig.org/en/messages/654/ (accessed August 30, 2013).

51. Christina Gallagher is an Irish woman to whom the Virgin Mary allegedly appeared beginning in January 1988. Like Vassula Ryden, Gallagher claims that the messages she receives are prophetic in nature, and she travels extensively relaying messages that appear appropriately framed for each national context. More on her can be found at the Official Website of the Messages of Our Lady Queen of Peace through Christina Gallagher, at http://www.christinagallagher.org/en/ (accessed August 30, 2013).

52. For the film clip, see "'Yes, It's All for the Best' from Godspell," YouTube video, 0:53, posted by "Edward Oneill," September 11, 2012, http://www.youtube.com/watch?v=QL6d0ASmvfs (accessed August 30, 2013).

53. Fr. Stefano Gobbi, Vassula Ryden, and Christina Gallagher have already been discussed. René Laurentin is the most prolific, respected, and widely read theologian specializing in the doctrines of Mary and her modern apparitions. His early works focused on the more established apparitions of Mary such as those at Lourdes and Rue de Bac (the Miraculous Medal), and the biographical histories of their visionaries, but since the Medjugorje phenomenon he has focused more on advocating for that particular cult and comparative examinations of contemporary Marian apparitions worldwide. Exemplary of his corpus are *Bernadette Speaks: A Life of St. Bernadette Soubirous in*

Her Own Words (Boston: Pauline Books and Media, 1999) and *The Apparitions of the Blessed Virgin Mary Today* (Dublin: Veritas Publications, 1991). Maria Valtorta was an Italian mystic who over the course of several years in the 1940s wrote a narrative of Jesus's life titled *The Poem of the Man-God*, which some consider nothing less than a fifth gospel; Mel Gibson apparently drew from *Poem* in his making of the film *The Passion of the Christ* (2004). A brief biographical sketch of Valtorta appears at the beginning of *The Poem of the Man-God*, vol. 1, trans. Nicandro Picozzi (Isola de Liri, Italy: Centro Editoriale Valtortiano, 1986). Mark Miravalle is an American deacon and theologian who, like Laurentin, has published extensively in the areas of Mariology and Marian apparitions. Also a strong advocate of the Medjugorje apparitions, Miravalle has made the best use of the mass media in proclaiming his support of those visions and the fifth Marian dogma; in addition to many, many books on Medjugorje and Mariology, he can also be found across the Internet in brief instructional videos on all things Virgin Mary. His complete bibliography can be found on his official website (http://www.markmiravalle.com).

54. See, for example, the website Philippine Marian Site, at http://www.marianmessenger.ph (accessed August 30, 2013).

55. Directly facing this page, in fact, is "an additional listing" of "many helping hands" of individuals and offices that supported the event.

56. Mary's Army to Save Souls (MASS) Media Movement, "World Marian Peace Regatta, New York[,] September 11, 1999," souvenir program, author's personal collection.

57. The magisterium is the teaching authority of the church and includes the pope and the bishops. For further elaboration, see *The Catholic Encyclopedia*, s.v. "Tradition and Living Magisterium," http://www.newadvent.org/cathen/15006b.htm (accessed August 30, 2013).

58. See Margry, "Paradoxes of Marian Apparitional Contestation," 188.

59. Interview with June Keithley, Quezon City, June 12, 2007.

60. Although the "triumph of the Immaculate Heart of Mary" was popularized through the apparitions of Mary at Fátima, referring then to the consecration of Russia, the phrase has taken on a more general meaning of anything that will stave off the apocalypse.

61. Gobbi, *To the Priests*, 303-4.

62. For a specific discussion of apparitions and the idea of national election, see Skrbiš, "Apparitions of the Virgin Mary of Medjugorje."

63. St. Louis-Marie Grignion de Montfort (1673-1716) is the author of *A Treatise on the True Devotion to the Blessed Virgin (often abbreviated as The True Devotion to the Blessed Virgin)*, trans. Frederick William Faber (Sherbrooke, QC: St. Charles' Seminary, 1901), a small handbook that includes prescriptions for prayer (the rosary), elaboration on Mary's role in salvation, and recommended acts of consecration.

64. In her ethnography of El Shaddai, the charismatic renewal movement most popular among the urban poor in the Philippines, Katharine L. Wiegele similarly demonstrates the power of the mass media (namely radio and television) to transform the boundaries and scale of ritual space. *Investing in Miracles: El Shaddai and the Transformation of Popular Catholicism in the Philippines* (Honolulu: University of Hawai'i Press, 2005), 41-58.

65. See also John Pemberton, "The Specter of Coincidence," in *Southeast Asia over Three Generations: Essays Presented to Benedict R. O'G. Anderson*, ed. James T. Siegel and Audrey R. Kahin (Ithaca, NY: Cornell Southeast Asia Program Publications, 2003), 75-90.

66. "Bandila at panalangin para kay Angelo de la Cruz," ABS-CBN, 2004.

67. Gil C. Cabacungan Jr., Juliet Labog-Javellana, and Jerome Aning, "GMA: Buck Stops Here," *Philippine Daily Inquirer*, July 17, 2004.

68. Karapatan (Alliance for the Advancement of People's Rights), "Dangerous Regime, Defiant People: Year-End Report on the Human Rights Situation in the Philippines" (2007), Stop the Killings in the Philippines, http://stopthekillings.org/stknpv2/?q=resources/61/dangerous -regime%2C-defiant-people (accessed January 24, 2008).

69. Joel Guinto, "Arroyo Allies to Hold Prayer Rallies vs. 'Political Noise,'" *Philippine Daily In-*

quirer, February 21, 2008, http://newsinfo.inquirer.net/ breakingnews/nation/view/20080221 -120336/Arroyo-allies-to-hold-prayer-rallies-vs-political-noise (accessed March 27, 2008).

70. Ibid.

71. Office of the Press Secretary Online (Republic of the Philippines), "Famed OFW Angelo de la Cruz Stands Firm behind the President," February 21, 2008, http://www.news.ops.gov.ph /archives2008/feb21.htm (accessed March 28, 2008).

CONCLUSION

1. *La Pietà* is Michelangelo's sculpture of Mary cradling the body of the crucified Christ, and "La Pieta" was chosen as the name of the group in 1991, after Sol Gaviola found a replica at a garage sale. Jesus then appeared to Emma with the following message: "My Father gave the name 'La Pieta' to your group because you see My sufferings and My Beloved Mother's sufferings together. Through that icon, My people will open their eyes to see, and open their ears to listen. This mission will spread around the world." La Pieta International, "The La Pieta Group Story," http://www .lapietainternational.com/index.php/about-la-pieta (accessed October 17, 2013).

2. "About Emma," La Pieta International, http://www.lapietainternational.com/index.php /about-emma (accessed October 12, 2013).

3. "Testimonials," La Pieta International, http://www.lapietainternational.com/index.php/testimonials (accessed October 12, 2013).

4. On the La Pieta International Prayer Group website there are three cases of "documented healings," but they are brief and appear hastily written. "What They Say," La Pieta International, http://www.lapietainternational.com/index.php/testimonials (accessed October 12, 2013).

5. Examples of recent works on Philippine church history and politics include John N. Schumacher, *Growth and Decline: Essays on Philippine Church History* (Quezon City: Ateneo de Manila University Press, 2009); and Julius Bautista, "Church and State in the Philippines: Tackling Life Issues in a 'Culture of Death,'" *Sojourn: Journal of Social Issues in Southeast Asia* 25, no. 1 (2010): 29–53. One of the best analyses of the cultural sea change within the Philippine church post–Vatican II is found in Coeli Barry, "Transformations of Politics and Religious Culture inside the Philippine Catholic Church (1965–1990)" (PhD diss., Cornell University, 1996).

6. For more on "intermedium relationships," see William Mazzarella, "Culture, Globalization, Mediation," *Annual Review of Anthropology* 33 (2004): 345–67.

7. Mother of Joy House of Prayer, http://www.motherofjoy.com/about_us.htm (accessed October 12, 2013).

8. See Paolo Apolito, *The Internet and the Madonna: Religious Visionary Experience on the Web* (Chicago: University of Chicago Press, 2005), 85.

9. See especially the various web pages at the site Mother of Joy House of Prayer (http://www .motherofjoy.com).

10. Apolito, *Internet and the Madonna*, 5. For images of Emma de Guzman's stigmata, see "Miracles," Mother of Joy House of Prayer, http://www.motherofjoy.com/miracles.htm (accessed October 12, 2013).

11. These were phrases I often heard in prayer cenacles and public Marian events.

12. "Mountain of Salvation: The Story of the Mt. of Salvation in Batangas City," La Pieta International, http://web.archive.org/web/20130919040347/http://lapietainternational.com/index .php/mt-of-salvation (accessed March 16, 2015, 2013).

13. "Messages of Our Blessed Mother, Bloomsbury, New Jersey [2002]," La Pieta International, http://lapietainternational.com/index.php/messages/91-2002-messages (accessed October 14, 2013).

14. "Mountain of Salvation: The Story of the Mt. of Salvation in Batangas City," La Pieta International, http://web.archive.org/web/20130919040347/http://lapietainternational.com/index .php/mt-of-salvation (accessed March 16, 2015).

15. "March 7, 2004—Message to Emma from Soledad Gaviola," La Pieta International, http://www.lapietainternational.com/index.php/messages/90-2004-messages (accessed October 14, 2013).

16. "Mountain of Salvation: The Story of the Mt. of Salvation in Batangas City," La Pieta International, http://web.archive.org/web/20130919040347/http://lapietainternational.com/index.php/mt-of-salvation (accessed March 16, 2015).

17. "Message of Our Lady of Immaculate Conception to Visionary Emma C. de Guzman, Mountain of Salvation, Batangas, Philippines," La Pieta International, http://www.lapietainternational.com/index.php/messages/90-2004-messages (accessed October 14, 2013).

Bibliography

ARCHIVAL SOURCES

Philippines

Archdiocesan Office of Visions and Phenomena, Manila
Archives of the University of Santo Tomas, Manila
Asuntos Generales, General Administration, Archdiocesan Archives of Manila, Manila
Family Rosary Crusade Philippines Archives, Manila
Filipinas Heritage Library, Makati
Lipa Carmel Archives, Lipa
Lopez Memorial Museum and Library, Pasig
Miguel de Benavides Library, Filipiniana Section, University of Santo Tomas, Manila
Japanese War Crimes Closed Reports, National Archives of the Philippines, Manila
National Library of the Philippines, Manila
Rizal Library, Filipiniana Section, Ateneo de Manila University, Quezon City
Teodoro M. Kalaw Memorial Library, Lipa
University Library, University of the Philippines Diliman, Quezon City

Spain

Archivo de la Provincia Agustiniana de Filipinas, Valladolid
Arxiu Històric de la Companyia de Jesús a Catalunya, Barcelona
Biblioteca del Estudio Teológico Agustiniano, Valladolid
Biblioteca Nacional de España, Madrid
Real Academia de la Historia, Colección Cortes and Colección Traggia, Madrid

United States

Archives of the Holy Cross Family Ministries, North Easton, Massachusetts
Hatcher Graduate Library, Special Collections, University of Michigan, Ann Arbor
Kroch Library, Rare Books and Manuscripts, Cornell University, Ithaca, New York
Marian Library, University of Dayton, Dayton, Ohio

UNPUBLISHED WORKS

Castillo, Teresita. "'I am Mary, Mediatrix of All Grace.'" Revised testimony. Printed booklet, 2008.
————. "My Life and Testimony." Revised testimony. Unpublished manuscript, 1997.
————. Original testimony. Unpublished manuscript, n.d.
Dychangco, Francisco. "My Diary on the Work for Our Lady, Mary Mediatrix of All Grace." Unpublished diary, 1982–93.
Mary Cecilia of Jesus. Original testimony (English version). Unpublished manuscript, n.d.
Villa, Praxedes L. "Lipa, the City with a Story." Unpublished article, n.d.

PUBLISHED WORKS

Abueva, Jose. *Ramon Magsaysay: A Political Biography*. Manila: Solidaridad Publishing House, 1971.
Achútegui, Pedro S. de, and Miguel A. Bernad. *Religious Revolution in the Philippines: The Life and Church of Gregorio Aglipay, 1860–1960*. Vol. 1, *From Aglipay's Birth to His Death*. Manila: Ateneo de Manila, 1961.
Achútegui, Pedro S. de, and Loyola School of Theology. *The Miracle of the Philippine Revolution: Interdisciplinary Reflections: Symposium Organized by the Loyola School of Theology*. Quezon City: Loyola School of Theology, 1986.
Acosta, Carmen. *The Life of Rufino Cardinal Santos*. Manila: Kayumanggi Press, 1973.
Aduarte, Diego. *Historia de la Provincia del Santo Rosario de la orden de predicadores en Filipinas, Japón y China*. 1693. Madrid: Departamento de Misionología Española, Consejo Superior de Investigaciones Científicas, 1962.
Aglipay, Gregorio. *Novenario de la Patria (La Patria se simboliza en la soñada madre de Balintawak) Escrito por el Emmo. Sr. Gregorio Aglipay y Labayan, Obispo Máximo de la Iglesia Filipina Independiente . . . aprobado por el Consejo Supremo de Obispos. Editor: Mons. Isabelo de los Reyes y Lopez, Obispo Rector de la Parroquia de María Clara en San Lázaro, Manila*. Manila, 1926.
————. *Pagsisiyam sa Virgen sa Balintawak (Ang Virgen sa Balintawak ay ang Inang Bayan). Sinulat sa wikang Kastila at tinagalog ni Juan Evangelista*. Manila: I. de los Reyes y Lopez, 1925.
Agoncillo, Teodoro. *The Fateful Years: Japan's Adventure in the Philippines*. Quezon City: R. P. Garcia Publishing, 1965.
————. *The Revolt of the Masses: The Story of Bonifacio and the Katipunan*. Quezon City: University of the Philippines, 1956.
Aladel, M., C.M. *The Miraculous Medal, Its Origin, History, Circulation, Results*. Translated by P.S., from the 8th French ed. Philadelphia: H. L. Kilner & Co., 1880.
Almario, Virgilio. *Kung sino ang kumatha kina Bagongbanta, Ossorio, Herrera, Aquino de Belen, Balagtas, atbp*. Manila: Anvil Publishing, 1992.
Anderson, Benedict R. O'G. *Imagined Communities: Reflections on the Origin and Spread of Nationalism*. New York: Verso, 1991.
————. *The Spectre of Comparisons: Nationalism, Southeast Asia, and the World*. New York: Verso, 1998.
————. *Under Three Flags: Anarchism and the Anti-Colonial Imagination*. New York: Verso Books, 2005.
Apolito, Paolo. *The Apparitions of the Madonna at Oliveto Citra: Local Visions and Cosmic Drama*. University Park: Pennsylvania State University Press, 1998.
————. *The Internet and the Madonna: Religious Visionary Experience on the Web*. Chicago: University of Chicago Press, 2005.
Archdiocese of Manila. "Manila Archdiocesan Commission on Visions and Phenomena." *Vadecum: The Official Bulletin of the RCAM Offices and Ministries* 23, no. 5 (2000), 15–31.

Barcelona, Mary Anne, and Consuelo B. Estepa. *Inang Maria: A Celebration of the Blessed Virgin Mary in the Philippines*. Manila: Anvil Publishing, 2004.

Barry, Coeli. "Transformations of Politics and Religious Culture inside the Philippine Catholic Church (1965-1990)." PhD diss., Cornell University, 1996.

Barthes, Roland. *Camera Lucida*. New York: Hill and Wang, 1981.

Bautista, Agripino D. *The Greatest International Event in the Orient*. Manila: Agripino D. Bautista, 1938.

Bautista, Julius. "Church and State in the Philippines: Tackling Life Issues in a 'Culture of Death.'" *Sojourn: Journal of Social Issues in Southeast Asia* 25, no. 1 (2010): 29-53.

———. *Figuring Catholicism: An Ethnohistory of the Santo Niño de Cebu*. Quezon City: Ateneo de Manila University Press, 2010.

Bax, Mart. *Medjugorje: Religion, Politics, and Violence in Rural Bosnia*. Amsterdam: VU University Press, 1995.

Bencuchillo, Francisco. *Arte poético tagalo*. Manila: Impresa de la Viuda de M. Minuesa de los Rios, 1895.

———. *Epítome de la historia de la aparición de Nuestra Señora de Caysasay; que se venera en el pueblo de Taal, de la Provincia de Batangas, y su sagrada novena*. Manila: Imprenta de Ramirez y Giraudier, 1859.

Benda, Harry J. "The Structure of Southeast Asian History: Some Preliminary Observations," *Journal of Southeast Asian History* 3, no. 1 (March 1962): 106-38.

Benjamin, Walter. *Illuminations*. New York: Schocken Books, 1968.

Blackbourn, David. *Marpingen: Apparitions of the Virgin Mary in a Nineteenth-Century German Village*. New York: Vintage Books, 1993.

Blanchot, Maurice. *The Infinite Conversation*. Minneapolis: University of Minnesota Press, 1993.

Blanco, John D. *Frontier Constitutions: Christianity and Colonial Empire in the Nineteenth Century Philippines*. Berkeley: University of California Press, 2009.

Bonifacio, Andres. *Katapusang Hibik ng Pilipinas*. Reprinted and translated by Bienvenido Lumbera in *Tagalog Poetry, 1570-1898: Tradition and Influences in Its Development*, 234-39. Ca. 1896. Quezon City: Ateneo de Manila University Press, 2001.

Borao, José Eugenio. "The Massacre of 1603: Chinese Perception of the Spaniards in the Philippines." *Itinerario* 23, no. 1 (1998): 22-39.

Boss, Sarah Jane. "Marian Consecration in the Contemporary Church." In *Mary: The Complete Resource*, edited by Sarah Jane Boss, 411-23. London: Continuum Books, 2007.

Bowring, Sir John. *A Visit to the Philippine Islands*. London: Smith, Elder & Co., 1859.

Brading, D. A. *Mexican Phoenix: Our Lady of Guadalupe: Image and Tradition across Five Centuries*. Cambridge: Cambridge University Press, 2001.

Breton, André. *Mad Love*. Translated by Mary Ann Caws. Lincoln: University of Nebraska Press, 1987. Originally published as *L'amour fou*, 1937.

Brewer, Carolyn. *Holy Confrontation: Religion, Gender, and Sexuality in the Philippines, 1521-1685*. Manila: Institute of Women's Studies, St. Scholastica's College, 2001.

Broadfoot, Keith. "Abstraction and Aura." *South Atlantic Quarterly* 101, no. 3 (Summer 2002): 459-78.

Bulatao, Jaime C. *Phenomena and Their Interpretation: Landmark Essays, 1957-1989*. Quezon City: Ateneo de Manila University Press, 1992.

Bunuan, Mary Ignazia S. *Gentle Woman: Mary to the Filipinos*. Pasay: Paulines Publishing House, 1997.

Burton, Richard D. E. *Blood in the City: Violence and Revelation in Paris, 1789-1945*. Ithaca, NY: Cornell University Press, 2001.

Buswell, Robert E., Jr., and Timothy S. Lee, eds. *Christianity in Korea*. Honolulu: University of Hawai'i Press, 2006.

Cadegan, Una. "The Queen of Peace in the Shadow of War: Fatima and U.S. Catholic Anticommunism." *U.S. Catholic Historian* 22, no. 4 (Fall 2004): 1-15.

Canetti, Elias. *Crowds and Power*. Translated by Carol Stewart. New York: Noonday Press, 1996.

Cannell, Fenella, ed. *The Anthropology of Christianity*. Durham, NC: Duke University Press, 2006.

———. "The Christianity of Anthropology." *Journal of the Royal Anthropological Institute* 11, no. 2 (2005): 335–56.

———. "Immaterial Culture: 'Idolatry' in the Lowland Philippines." In *Spirited Politics: Religion and Public Life in Contemporary Southeast Asia*, edited by Andrew C. Willford and Kenneth M. George, 159–84. Ithaca, NY: Cornell Southeast Asia Program, 2005.

———. Introduction to *The Anthropology of Christianity*, edited by Fenella Cannell, 1–50. Durham, NC: Duke University Press, 2006.

———. *Power and Intimacy in the Christian Philippines*. Cambridge: Cambridge University Press, 1999.

———. "Reading as Gift and Writing as Theft." In *The Anthropology of Christianity*, edited by Fenella Cannell, 134–62. Durham, NC: Duke University Press, 2006.

Carr, Lorraine. *To the Philippines with Love*. Los Angeles: Sherbourne Press, 1966.

Castro, Maria Rita Isabel Santos. "Demythologising the History of Coffee in Lipa, Batangas in the XIXth Century." MA thesis, University of Adelaide, 2003.

Certeau, Michel de. *The Possession at Loudun*. Chicago: University of Chicago Press, 1996.

Chirino, Pedro. *Història de la Provincia de Filipines de la Companyia de Jesús (1581–1606)*. Barcelona: Portic, 2000.

Choy, Catherine Ceniza. *Empire of Care: Nursing and Migration in Filipino American History*. Durham, NC: Duke University Press, 2003.

Christian, William A., Jr. "Afterword: Islands in the Sea: The Public and Private Distribution of Knowledge of Religious Visions." *Visual Resources* 25, nos. 1–2 (2009): 153–65.

———. *Apparitions in Late Medieval and Renaissance Spain*. Princeton, NJ: Princeton University Press, 1981.

———. *Local Religion in Sixteenth-Century Spain*. Princeton, NJ: Princeton University Press, 1982.

———. *Person and God in a Spanish Valley*. Princeton, NJ: Princeton University Press, 1972.

———. "Religious Apparitions and the Cold War in Southern Europe." In *Religion, Power, and Protest in Local Communities*, edited by Eric R. Wolf, 239–65. Berlin: Mouton, 1984.

———. *Visionaries: The Spanish Republic and the Reign of Christ*. Berkeley: University of California Press, 1996.

Chu, Richard T. *Chinese and Chinese Mestizos of Manila: Family, Identity, and Culture, 1860s–1930s*. Mandaluyong, Philippines: Anvil Press, 2012.

Claussen, Heather L. *Unconventional Sisterhood: Feminist Catholic Nuns in the Philippines*. Ann Arbor: University of Michigan Press, 2001.

Claverie, Élisabeth. *Les guerres de la Vierge: Une anthropologie des apparitions*. Paris: Gallimard, 2003.

Clifford, Mary, B.V.M. "*Iglesia Filipina Independiente*: The Revolutionary Church." In *Studies in Philippine Church History*, edited by Gerard H. Anderson, 223–55. Ithaca, NY: Cornell University Press, 1969.

Comaroff, John L., and Jean Comaroff. *Of Revelation and Revolution*. Vol. 1, *Christianity, Colonialism, and Consciousness in South Africa*. Chicago: University of Chicago Press, 1991.

———. *Of Revelation and Revolution*. Vol. 2, *The Dialectics of Modernity on a South African Frontier*. Chicago: University of Chicago Press, 1997.

Compendio de la "Reseña Biográfica de los Religiosos de la Provincia del Santísimo Rosario de Filipinas," desde su fundación hasta nuestros días (1587–1895). Manila: Establ. Tip. del Real Colegio de Sto. Tomas, 1895.

Congregantes Marianos del Colegio de la Compañía de Jesús en Manila. *La Virgen María venerada en sus imágenes filipinas*. Manila: Imprenta de Santos y Bernal, 1904.

Corpuz, Onofre D. *An Economic History of the Philippines*. Quezon City: University of the Philippines Press, 1997.

Cortes, Rosario Mendoza. *Pangasinan, 1572–1800*. Quezon City: New Day Publishers, 1974.

Cruz, Deirdre de la. "Coincidence and Consequence: Marianism and the Mass Media in the Global Philippines," *Cultural Anthropology* 24, no. 3 (2009): 455-88.

———. "From the Power of Prayer to *Prayer Power*: On Religion and Revolt in the Modern Philippines." In *Southeast Asian Perspectives on Power*, edited by Liana Chua, Joanna Cook, Nicholas Long, and Lee Wilson, 165-80. New York: Routledge, 2012.

———. "The Mass Miracle: Public Religion in the Postwar Philippines." *Philippine Studies* 62, nos. 3-4 (2014): 425-44.

Cruz, Mateo de la. *Relación de la milagrosa aparición de la santa imagen de la Virgen de Guadalupe de México, sacada de la historia que compuso Br. Miguel Sánchez*. Mexico, 1660. Reprinted in Ernesto de la Torre Villar y Ramiro Navarro de Anda, *Testimonios históricos guadalupanos*, 267-81. Mexico City: Fondo de Cultura Económica, 1982.

Cullamar, Evelyn Tan. *Babaylanism in Negros, 1896-1907*. Quezon City: New Day Publishers, 1986.

Cullinane, Michael. *Ilustrado Politics: Filipino Elite Responses to American Rule, 1898-1908*. Quezon City: Ateneo de Manila University Press, 2003.

Deleuze, Gilles. *Difference and Repetition*. New York: Columbia University Press, 1994.

Derrida, Jacques. "Faith and Knowledge: The Two Sources of 'Religion' at the Limits of Reason Alone." In *Religion*, edited by Jacques Derrida and Gianni Vattimo, 1-78. Stanford, CA: Stanford University Press, 1998.

———. *The Gift of Death*. Chicago: University of Chicago Press, 1995.

———. *The Truth in Painting*. Chicago: University of Chicago Press, 1987.

Díaz, Casimiro. *Conquistas de las Islas Filipinas*. Valladolid, Spain: L. N. de Gaviria, 1890.

Doherty, Thomas. *Cold War, Cool Medium: Television, McCarthyism, and American Culture*. New York: Columbia University Press, 2003.

Dominador, Buhain. *A History of Publishing in the Philippines*. Quezon City: Rex Bookstore, 1998.

English, Leo James. *English-Tagalog Dictionary*. Manila: Congregation of the Most Holy Redeemer, 1977.

———. *Tagalog-English Dictionary*. Manila: Congregation of the Most Holy Redeemer, 1986.

Eugenio, Damiana. *Awit and Corrido: Philippine Metrical Romances*. Quezon City: University of the Philippines Press, 1987.

Fansler, Dean S. "Metrical Romances in the Philippines." *Journal of American Folklore* 29, no. 112 (1916): 203-34.

Fernandes, Fernando, Joaquim Fernandes, and Raul Beneguel, eds. *Fatima Revisited: The Apparition Phenomenon in Ufology, Psychology, and Science*. San Antonio, TX: Anomalist Books, 2008.

Fernando, Felipe. "Aurelio Tolentino: Playwright, Poet, and Patriot." *Philippine Studies* 12 (January 1964): 83-92.

Ferrando, Juan, and Joaquin Fonseca. *Historia de los Pp. Dominicos en las Islas Filipinas y en sus misiones del Japón, China, Tung-Kin y Formosa: Que comprende los sucesos principales de la historia general de este archipiélago, desde el descubrimiento y conquista de estas islas por las flotas españolas, hasta el año de 1840*. Madrid: Impr. y Estereotipia de M. Rivadeneyra, 1870.

Flores, Hermenegildo. "Hibik ng Pilipinas sa Ynang España." In *Philippine Literature Past and Present*, edited by S. Baltasar, T. Erestain, and Ma. F. Estanislao, 115-20. Quezon City: Katha Publishing, 1981.

Flores, Patrick D. *Painting History: Revisions in Philippine Colonial Art*. Quezon City: Office of Research Coordination University of the Philippines; Manila: National Commission for Culture and the Arts, 1998.

Florida, Nancy. *Writing the Past, Inscribing the Future: History and Prophesy in Colonial Java*. Durham, NC: Duke University Press, 1995.

Freud, Sigmund. "The Uncanny." 1919. In *Writings on Art and Literature*, 193-232. Stanford, CA: Stanford University Press, 1997.

Furlong, Monica. *Thérèse de Lisieux*. New York: Orbis Books, 1987.

Gallagher, L. *The Eucharistic Congress: Its History and Organisation*. Dublin: Office of the "Irish Messenger," 1930.

García López, Juan Catalina. *Biblioteca de escritores de la provincia de Guadalajara y bibliografía de la misma hasta el siglo XIX*. Madrid: Est. Tipográfico Sucesores de Rivadeneyra, 1899.

Gatbonton, Esperanza Buñag. *A Heritage of Saints*. Manila: Editorial Associates, 1979.

Gobbi, Stefano. *To the Priests: Our Lady's Beloved Sons*. 17th special Philippine ed. Manila: Marian Movement of Priests Philippines, n.d.

Gonzalez, Andrew. *Language and Nationalism: The Philippine Experience Thus Far*. Quezon City: Ateneo de Manila University Press, 1980.

Gribble, Richard. *American Apostle of the Family Rosary: The Life of Patrick J. Peyton*. New York: Crossroad Publishing, 2005.

Grignion de Montfort, Louis-Marie. *The Secret of the Rosary*. Bay Shore, NY: Montfort Fathers, 1965.

————. *A Treatise on the True Devotion to the Blessed Virgin*, trans. Frederick William Faber (Sherbrooke, QC: St. Charles' Seminary, 1901).

Guevarra, Anna. *Marketing Dreams, Manufacturing Heroes: The Transnational Labor Brokering of Filipino Workers*. New Brunswick, NJ: Rutgers University Press, 2009.

Hacking, Ian. *The Taming of Chance*. New York: Cambridge University Press, 1990.

Haffert, John. *Dear Bishop: Memoirs of the Author Concerning the History of the Blue Army*. Washington, NJ: AMI International Press, 1982.

Hall, David D. *Lived Religion in America: Toward a History of Practice*. Princeton, NJ: Princeton University Press, 1997.

Hargrove, Thomas R. *The Mysteries of Taal: A Philippine Volcano and Lake, Her Sea Life and Lost Towns*. Manila: Bookmark Publishing, 1991.

Harris, Ruth. *Lourdes: Body and Spirit in a Secular Age*. New York: Penguin Books, 2000.

Hau, Caroline S. "Kidnapping, Citizenship, and the Chinese." *Public Policy* 1 (October–December 1997): 62–89.

————. *Necessary Fictions: Philippine Literature and the Nation, 1946–1980*. Quezon City: Ateneo de Manila University Press, 2000.

Heidegger, Martin. "The Age of the World Picture." In *The Question Concerning Technology and Other Essays*, 115–54. New York: Harper & Row, 1977.

Hengel, Martin. "The Interpretation of the Wine Miracle at Cana: John 2:1–11." In *The Glory of Christ in the New Testament: Studies in Christology*, edited by L. D. Hurst and N. T. Wright, 83–112. Oxford, UK: Clarendon Press, 1987.

Hermann, Adrian. "Transnational Networks of Philippine Intellectuals and the Emergence of an Indigenous-Christian Public Sphere around 1900." In *Polycentric Structures in the History of World Christianity*, edited by Klaus Koschorke and Adrian Hermann, 193–203. Wiesbaden, Germany: Harrassowitz Verlag, 2014.

Hernández, Policarpo F. *The Augustinians in the Philippines*. Makati: Colegio de San Agustin, 1998.

Hernández, Vicente S. *History of Books and Libraries in the Philippines, 1521–1900*. Manila: National Commission for Culture and the Arts, 1996.

Historia at novena nang mahal na Virgin Ntra. Sra. de Guadalupe, pinag ayos at pinag husay sa uicang Castila nang isang religiosong Agustino. Manila: Imp. de Ramirez y Giraudier, 1870.

Howes, John F. *Japan's Modern Prophet: Uchimura Kanzo, 1861–1930*. Vancouver: University of British Columbia Press, 2005.

Hubert, Henri, and Marcel Mauss. *Sacrifice: Its Nature and Function*. Chicago: University of Chicago Press, 1964.

Ignatius of Loyola. *The Autobiography of St. Ignatius Loyola, with Related Documents*. Translated by Joseph F. O'Callaghan. New York: Fordham University Press, 1992.

Ileto, Reynaldo C. "Bernardo Carpio: *Awit* and Revolution." In *Filipinos and Their Revolution: Event, Discourse, and Historiography*, 1–27. Quezon City: Ateneo de Manila University Press, 1998.

————. "Mother Spain, Uncle Sam, and the Construction of Filipino National Identity." In *Imperios y naciones en el Pacífico*. Vol. 1, *La formación de una colonia: Filipinas*, edited by M. D. Elizalde, J. M. Fradera, and L. Alonso, 119–32. Madrid: Consejo Superior de Investigaciones Científicas, 2001.

———. "On the Historiography of Southeast Asia and the Philippines: The 'Golden Age' of Southeast Asian Studies—Experiences and Reflections." Proceedings of "Can We Write History? Between Postmodernism and Coarse Nationalism" at the Institute for International Studies, Meiji Gakuin University, March 9, 2002. http://www.meijigakuin.ac.jp/~iism/project/frontier/Proceedings/08%20Ileto%20Speech.pdf (accessed September 7, 2013).

———. "Orators and the Crowd: Independence Politics, 1910–1914." In *Filipinos and Their Revolution: Event, Discourse, and Historiography*, 135–63. Quezon City: Ateneo de Manila University Press, 1998.

———. *Pasyon and Revolution: Popular Movements in the Philippines, 1940–1910*. Quezon City: Ateneo de Manila University Press, 1979.

Infante, Teresita R. *The Woman in Early Philippines and Among the Cultural Minorities*. Manila: Unitas Publications, University of Santo Tomas, 1975.

Irving, D. R. M. *Colonial Counterpoint: Music in Early Modern Manila*. New York: Oxford University Press, 2010.

Ishida, Jintaro. *The Remains of War: Apology and Forgiveness*. Quezon City: Megabooks, 2001.

Ivy, Marilyn. *Discourses of the Vanishing: Modernity, Phantasm, Japan*. Chicago: University of Chicago Press, 1995.

Javellana, René B., ed. *Casaysayan nang Pasiong Mahal ni Jesucristong Panginoon Natin na Sucat Ipagalab nang Puso nang Sinomang Babasa*. Quezon City: Ateneo de Manila University Press, 1998.

———. Introduction to *Casaysayan nang Pasiong Mahal ni Jesucristong Panginoon Natin na Sucat Ipag-alab nang Puso nang Sinomang Babasa*, edited by René B. Javellana, 3–42. Quezon City: Ateneo de Manila University Press, 1988.

Jesus, Edilberto de. Conclusion to *Philippine Social History: Global Trade and Local Transformations*, edited by Alfred W. McCoy and Ed. C. de Jesus, 447–54. Honolulu: University of Hawai'i Press, 1982.

Joaquin, Nick. *Culture and History: Occasional Notes on the Process of Philippine Becoming*. Manila: Solar Publishing, 1988.

Jocano, F. Landa. "Ang mga Babaylan at Katalonan sa Kinagisnang Sikolohiya." In *Ulat ng Unang Pambansang Kumperensiya sa Sikolohiyang Pilipino*, edited by Lilia F. Antonio, Esther S. Reyes, Rogelia Pe, and Nilda R. Almonte, 147–57. Quezon City: Pambansang Samahan ng Sikolohiyang Pilipino, 1976.

———, ed. *The Philippines at Spanish Contact*. Manila: MCS Enterprises, 1975.

John of the Cross. *The Collected Works of St. John of the Cross*. Translated by Kieran Kavanaugh and Otilio Rodriguez. Washington, DC: ICS Publications, 1991.

Jose, Regalado Trota. *Simbahan: Church Art in Colonial Philippines, 1565–1898*. Manila: Ayala Foundation, 1991.

Jose, Ricardo T. "Panahon ng Hapon: Occupation and Liberation." In *Batangas: Forged in Fire*, edited by Ramon N. Villegas, 229–37. Makati: Ayala Foundation and Filipinas Heritage Library, 2002.

Josue, Ericson M. *Alfredo Verzosa, Obispo: The Life and Legacy of the Fourth Filipino Roman Catholic Bishop*. Lipa: Missionary Catechists of the Sacred Heart and Ericson M. Josue, 2007.

Jurilla, Patricia May B. *Tagalog Bestsellers of the Twentieth Century: A History of the Book in the Philippines*. Quezon City: Ateneo de Manila University, 2008.

Justin Martyr. *St. Justin Martyr, the First and Second Apologies*. Translated by Leslie William Barnard. New York: Paulist Press, 1997.

Kalaw, Teodoro M. *Aide-de-Camp to Freedom*. Manila: Teodoro M. Kalaw Society, 1965.

Kant, Immanuel. *Religion within the Limits of Reason Alone*. New York: Harper & Row, 1960.

Keane, Webb. *Christian Moderns: Freedom and Fetish in the Mission Encounter*. Berkeley: University of California, 2007.

Keithley, June. *The Keithley Report: The Woman Clothed with the Sun*. Manila: Center for Peace Asia, 1991.

———. *Lipa: With the Original Account of the Events at Lipa Carmel in 1948 by Mother Mary Cecilia of Jesus, O.C.D.* Manila: Cacho Publishing House, 1992.

———. "The Petals of Lipa." In *Batangas: Forged in Fire*, edited by Ramon N. Villegas, 122–28. Makati: Ayala Foundation and Filipinas Heritage Library, 2002.

Kerkvliet, Benedict. *The Huk Rebellion: A Study of Peasant Revolt in the Philippines*. Berkeley: University of California Press, 1977.

Kittler, Friedrich A. *Discourse Networks 1800/1900*. Translated by Michael Metteer. Stanford, CA: Stanford University Press, 1990.

———. *Gramophone, Film, Typewriter*. Stanford, CA: Stanford University Press, 1999.

Kramer, Paul. *The Blood of Government: Race, Empire, the United States, and the Philippines*. Chapel Hill: University of North Carolina Press, 2006.

Kristeva, Julia. *Desire and Language: A Semiotic Approach to Literature and Art*. New York: Columbia University Press, 1980.

———. *Tales of Love*. New York: Columbia University Press, 1987.

Kselman, Thomas. *Miracles and Prophecies in Nineteenth-Century France*. New Brunswick, NJ: Rutgers University Press, 1983.

Kselman, Thomas, and Steven Avella. "Marian Piety and the Cold War in the United States." *Catholic Historical Review* 72, no. 3 (July 1986): 403–24.

Lacan, Jacques. "The Mirror Stage as Formative of the Function of the I as Revealed in Psychoanalytic Experience." In *Écrits, 1–7*. New York: W. W. Norton, 1977.

Lahiri, Smita. "Materializing the Spiritual: Christianity, Community, and History in a Philippine Landscape." PhD diss., Cornell University, 2002.

———. "Rhetorical Indios: Propagandists and Their Publics in the Spanish Philippines." *Comparative Studies in Society and History* 49, no. 2 (2007): 243–75.

Landes, Joan. *Visualizing the Nation: Gender, Representation, and Revolution in Eighteenth-Century France*. Ithaca, NY: Cornell University Press, 2001.

Lanzona, Vina. *Amazons of the Huk Rebellion: Gender, Sex, and Revolution in the Philippines*. Madison: University of Wisconsin Press, 2009.

Lapeña-Bonifacio, Amelia. *The "Seditious" Tagalog Playwrights: Early American Occupation*. Manila: Zarzuela Foundation of the Philippines, 1972.

Latour, Bruno. *Reassembling the Social: An Introduction to Actor-Network-Theory*. New York: Oxford University Press, 2005.

Laurentin, René. *The Apparitions of the Blessed Virgin Mary Today*. Dublin: Veritas Publications, 1991.

———. *Bernadette Speaks: A Life of St. Bernadette Soubirous in Her Own Words*. Boston: Pauline Books and Media, 1999.

———. *Catherine Labouré: Visionary of the Miraculous Medal*. Boston: Pauline Books and Media, 2006.

———. *Is the Virgin Mary Appearing at Medjugorje? An Urgent Message for the World Given in a Marxist Country*. Washington, DC: Word among Us Press, 1984.

———. *Medjugorje—Thirteen Years Later*. Milford, OH: Riehle Foundation, 1994.

Laya, Jaime C. *Prusisyon: Religious Pageantry in the Philippines*. Manila: Cofradía de la Inmaculada Concepción, 1995.

Lent, John A., ed. *Broadcasting in Asia and the Pacific: A Continental Survey of Radio and Television*. Philadelphia: Temple University Press, 1978.

Lepselter, Susan. *The Resonance of Unseen Things*. Ann Arbor: University of Michigan Press, 2015.

Lévi-Strauss, Claude. *Structural Anthropology*. New York: Basic Books, 1964.

Lieberman, Victor. *Strange Parallels: Southeast Asia in Global Context, c. 800–1830*. Vol. 1, *Integration on the Mainland*. New York: Cambridge University Press, 2003.

———. *Strange Parallels: Southeast Asia in Global Context, c. 800–1830*. Vol. 2, *Mainland Mirrors: Europe, Japan, China, South Asia, and the Islands*. New York: Cambridge University Press, 2009.

Livius, Thomas. *The Blessed Virgin in the Fathers of the First Six Centuries*. London, 1893.

Lopez, Donald S., Jr. *Prisoners of Shangri-La: Tibetan Buddhism and the West*. Chicago: University of Chicago Press, 1998.

Lumbera, Bienvenido L. *Tagalog Poetry, 1570–1898: Tradition and Influences in Its Development.* Quezon City: Ateneo de Manila University Press, 2001.

Lynch, Frank. "Folk Catholicism in the Philippines." In *Philippine Society and the Individual: Selected Essays of Frank Lynch, 1949–1976,* edited by Aram A. Yengoyan and Perla Q. Makil, 197–207. Michigan Papers on South and Southeast Asia no. 24. Ann Arbor: Center for South and Southeast Asian Studies, University of Michigan, 1984.

MacEoin, Gary, and Committee for the Responsible Election of the Pope. *The Inner Elite: Dossiers of Papal Candidates.* Kansas City, MO: Sheed Andrews & McMeel, 1978.

Manalansan, Martin. *Global Divas: Filipino Gay Men in the Diaspora.* Durham, NC: Duke University Press, 2003.

Manuel, Esperidion Arsenio. *Dictionary of Philippine Biography.* Vol. 2. Quezon City: Filipiniana Publications, 1970.

Manzanilla, JPaul S. "Picturing Historical Subjects: The Photography of the EDSA People Power Uprising." MA thesis, University of the Philippines, 2011.

Margry, Peter Jan. "Paradoxes of Marian Apparitional Contestation: Networks, Ideology, Gender, and the Lady of All Nations." In *Moved by Mary: The Power of Pilgrimage in the Modern World,* edited by Anna-Karina Hermkens, Willy Jansen, and Catrien Notermans, 183–200. Surrey, UK: Ashgate, 2009.

Mas, Sinibaldo de. *Informe sobre el estado de las Islas Filipinas en 1842.* Madrid: Imprenta de I. Sancha, 1843.

Masuzawa, Tomoko. *The Invention of World Religions; or, How European Universalism Was Preserved in the Language of Pluralism.* Chicago: University of Chicago Press, 2005.

Matutina, Cecille. *Pinoy Television: The Story of ABS-CBN.* Manila: ABS-CBN Broadcasting, 1999.

May, Glenn Anthony. *Inventing a Hero: The Posthumous Re-Creation of Andres Bonifacio.* Quezon City: New Day Publishers, 1997.

Mazzarella, William. "Culture, Globalization, Mediation." *Annual Review of Anthropology* 33 (2004): 345–67.

McClintock, Anne. *Imperial Leather: Race, Gender, and Sexuality in the Colonial Context.* New York: Routledge, 1995.

McCoy, Alfred. "Baylan: Animist Religion and Philippine Peasant Ideology." In *Moral Order and the Question of Change: Essays on Southeast Asian Thought,* edited by David Wyatt and Alexander Woodside, 338–413. New Haven, CT: Yale University Southeast Asia Studies, 1982.

McCoy, Alfred W., and Ed. C. de Jesus, eds. *Philippine Social History: Global Trade and Local Transformations.* Honolulu: University Press of Hawai'i, 1982.

Mercado, Monina Allarey, ed. *People Power: An Eyewitness History.* Manila: J. B. Reuter, S.J., Foundation, 1986.

Merced, Aniceto de la. *El libro de la vida.* Reprinted in Bienvenido Lumbera, *Tagalog Poetry, 1570–1898: Tradition and Influences in Its Development,* 209–15. Quezon City: Ateneo de Manila University Press, 2001.

Millán, Salvador. *Breve noticia acerca de la aparición de Nuestra Señora de Manaoag, Patrona de Pangasinán, seguida de la Novena en honor de esta Señora, por el P. Fr. Salvador Millán, Dominico.* Manila: Establecimiento Tipográfico del Colegio de Santo Tomás, 1891.

Miravalle, Mark I., ed. *Mariology: A Guide for Priests, Deacons, Seminarians, and Consecrated Persons.* Goleta, CA: Seat of Wisdom Books, 2007.

Mojares, Resil B. *Brains of the Nation: Pedro Paterno, T. H. Padro De Tavera, Isabelo de los Reyes and the Production of Modern Knowledge.* Quezon City: Ateneo de Manila University Press, 2008.

———. *Origins and Rise of the Filipino Novel.* Quezon City: University of Philippines Press, 1998.

———. "Stalking the Virgin." In *Waiting for Mariang Makiling: Essays in Philippine Cultural History,* 140–70. Quezon City: Ateneo de Manila University Press, 2002.

Morris, Rosalind. *In the Place of Origins: Modernity and Its Mediums in Northern Thailand.* Durham, NC: Duke University Press, 2000.

Mrázek, Rudolf. *Engineers of Happyland: Technology and Nationalism in a Colony*. Princeton, NJ: Princeton University Press, 2002.

Musni, Lord Francis, Robert P. Tantingco, and Erlinda E. Cruz, eds. *Padre Pinong: First Filipino Cardinal, 1908–1973*. Angeles City, Philippines: Center for Kapampangan Studies, 2008.

Nevin, Thomas R. *Thérèse of Lisieux: God's Gentle Warrior*. New York: Oxford University Press, 2006.

Noone, Martin J. *General History of the Philippines*. Vol. 3, *The Life and Times of Michael O'Doherty, Archbishop of Manila*. Manila: Historical Conservation Society, 1989.

Olds, Katrina. "Ambiguities of the Holy: Authenticating Relics in Seventeenth-Century Spain." *Renaissance Quarterly* 65, no. 1 (Spring 2012): 135–84.

Orsi, Robert A. *Between Heaven and Earth: The Religious Worlds People Make and the Scholars Who Study Them*. Princeton, NJ: Princeton University Press, 2006.

———. *The Madonna of 115th Street: Faith and Community in Italian Harlem, 1880–1950*. 2nd ed. New Haven, CT: Yale University Press, 2002.

Ottaviani, Alfredo. "Cautela ante los falsos milagros." *Boletín eclesiástico de Filipinas: Organo oficial, interdiocesano, mensual, editado por la Universidad de Santo Tomas* 25 (1951): 376–80.

Parreñas, Rhacel Salazar. *Servants of Globalization: Women, Migration, and Domestic Work*. Stanford, CA: Stanford University Press, 2001.

Paul VI. "Marialis Cultus." In *17 Papal Documents on the Rosary, 23–74*. Boston: Daughters of St. Paul, 1980.

Pemberton, John. *On the Subject of "Java."* Ithaca, NY: Cornell University Press, 1994.

———. "The Specter of Coincidence." In *Southeast Asia over Three Generations: Essays Presented to Benedict R. O'G. Anderson*, edited by James T. Siegel and Audrey R. Kahin, 75–90. Ithaca, NY: Cornell Southeast Asia Program Publications, 2003.

Perry, Nicolas, and Loreto Echeverría. *Under the Heel of Mary*. New York: Routledge, 1988.

Pew Forum on Religion and Public Life. "Summary of Key Findings." *U.S. Religious Landscape Survey*. 2007. http://religions.pewforum.org/pdf/report2religious-landscape-study-key-findings.pdf (accessed September 15, 2013).

Peyton, Patrick. *All for Her: The Autobiography of Father Patrick Peyton, C.S.C.* Garden City, NY: Doubleday, 1967.

Phelan, John Leddy. *The Hispanization of the Philippines: Spanish Aims and Filipino Responses, 1565–1700*. Madison: University of Wisconsin Press, 1959.

Pilar, Marcelo del. "Sagot nang España sa Hibik nang Pilipinas." Reprinted in Bienvenido Lumbera, *Tagalog Poetry, 1570–1898: Tradition and Influences in its Development*, 217–39. Quezon City: Ateneo de Manila University Press, 2001.

Plaridel [Marcelo del Pilar]. "Our Father" and "Hail Mary." Reprinted in *Philippine Literature Past and Present*, edited by S. Baltasar, T. Erestain, and Ma. F. Estanislao, 114–15. Quezon City: Katha Publishing, 1981.

Porter-Szűcs, Brian. *Faith and Fatherland: Catholicism, Modernity, Poland*. New York: Oxford University Press, 2011.

———. "Hetmanka and Mother: Representing the Virgin Mary in Modern Poland." *Contemporary European History* 14, no. 2 (May 2005): 151–70.

Rafael, Vicente. "The Cell Phone and the Crowd: Messianic Politics in the Contemporary Philippines." *Public Culture* 15, no. 3 (2003): 399–425.

———. *Contracting Colonialism: Translation and Christian Conversion in Tagalog Society under Early Spanish Rule*. Ithaca, NY: Cornell University Press, 1988.

———. "Nationalism, Imagery, and the Filipino Intelligentsia in the Nineteenth Century." *Critical Inquiry* 16, no. 3 (Spring 1990): 591–611.

———. *The Promise of the Foreign: Nationalism and the Technics of Translation in the Spanish Philippines*. Durham, NC: Duke University Press, 2005.

———. *White Love and Other Events in Filipino History*. Quezon City: Ateneo de Manila University Press, 2000.

Retana, Wenceslao E. *Aparato bibliográfico de la historia general de Filipinas*. Vols. 1-3. Madrid: Imprenta de la Sucesora de M. Minuesa de los Ríos, 1906.

———. *Archivo del bibliófilo filipino; recopilación de documentos históricos, científicos, literarios y políticos, y estudios bibliográficos*. Vols. 1-4. Madrid: Imprenta de la Sucesora de M. Minuesa de los Ríos, 1895-1905.

———. *La censura de imprenta en Filipinas*. Madrid: V. Suárez, 1908.

———. *De la evolución de la literatura castellana en Filipinas: Los poetas, apuntes críticos*. Madrid : Lib. General de Victoriano Suárez, 1909.

———. *La imprenta en Filipinas: Adiciones y observaciones á la Imprenta en Manila de D. J. T. Medina*. Madrid: Imprenta de la Sucesora de M. Minuesa de los Ríos, 1899.

———. *Noticias histórico-bibliográficas de el teatro en Filipinas desde sus orígenes hasta 1898* (Madrid: V. Suárez, 1910).

———. *Orígenes de la imprenta filipina; investigaciones históricas, bibliográficas y tipográficas*. Madrid: V. Suárez, 1911.

Reyes, Isabelo de los. *El Folklore Filipino*. Translated by Salud C. Dizon and Maria Elinora P. Imson. Manila: University of the Philippines Press, 1994.

Reyes, Raquel A. G., *Love, Passion and Patriotism: Sexuality and the Philippine Propaganda Movement, 1882-1892*. Seattle: University of Washington Press, 2008.

Reyes-Tirol, Evelyn S. *Gentle Shepherd, Faithful Sentinel: A Biography of Gabriel M. Reyes*. Manila: Archbishop Gabriel M. Reyes Memorial Foundation, 1992.

Riggs, Arthur. *The Filipino Drama*. 1905. Manila: Ministry of Human Settlements, 1981.

Rizal, José. *Noli me tangere*. 1886. Translated by Soledad Lacson-Locsin. Honolulu: University of Hawai'i Press, 1996.

———. *Selected Essays and Letters of José Rizal*. Edited by Encarnación Alzona. Manila: G. Rangel and Sons.

Rodrigo, Raul. *Kapitan: Geny Lopez and the Making of ABS-CBN*. Quezon City: ABS-CBN Publishing, 2006.

Rodriguez, Agustin Martin, and Felice Noelle Rodriguez. "Apparition, Narration, and Reappropriation of Meaning." *Philippine Studies* 44, no. 4 (1996): 465-78.

Rodríguez, Isacio R. *Gregorio Aglipay y los orígenes de la Iglesia Filipina Independiente (1898-1917)*. Madrid: Departamento de Misionología Española, Consejo Superior de Investigaciones Científicas, 1960.

———. *Updated Checklist of Filipiniana at Valladolid*. 2 vols. Manila: National Historical Institute, 1976.

San Antonio, Francisco de. *Vocabulario Tagalo*. 1624. Quezon City: Ateneo de Manila University, 2000.

Sánchez, Miguel. *Imagen de la Virgen María Madre de Dios de Guadalupe, milagrosamente aparecida en la ciudad de México. Celebrada en su historia, con la profecía el capítulo doce del Apocalipsis*. Mexico City: Imprenta de la Viuda de Bernardo Calderón, 1648. Reprinted in Ernesto de la Torre Villar y Ramiro Navarro de Anda, *Testimonios históricos guadalupanos*, 153-267. Mexico: Fondo de Cultura Económica, 1982.

Sastrón, Manuel. *Filipinas: Pequeños estudios; Batangas y su provincia*. Malabon: Establ. Tipográfico del Asilo de Huérfanos de Ntra. Sra. de la Consolación, 1895.

Schivelbusch, Wolfgang. *The Railway Journey: The Industrialization of Time and Space in the 19th Century*. Berkeley: University of California Press, 1986.

Schnapp, Jeffrey T. "Mob Porn." In *Crowds*, edited by Jeffrey T. Schnapp and Matthew Tiews, 1-45. Stanford, CA: Stanford University Press, 2006.

Schumacher, John N. *Growth and Decline: Essays on Philippine Church History*. Quezon City: Ateneo de Manila University Press, 2009.

———. *The Propaganda Movement, 1880-1895: The Creation of a Filipino Consciousness, the Making of the Revolution*. Quezon City: Ateneo de Manila University Press, 1997.

———. *Revolutionary Clergy: The Filipino Clergy and the Nationalist Movement, 1850–1903.* Quezon City: Ateneo de Manila University Press, 1981.

Scott, William Henry. *Aglipay before Aglipayanism.* Quezon City: Aglipayan Resource Center, 1987.

———. *Barangay: Sixteenth-Century Philippine Culture and Society.* Quezon City: Ateneo de Manila University Press, 1994.

Setsuho, Ikehata, and Ricardo T. Jose, eds. *The Philippines under Japan: Occupation Policy and Reaction.* Quezon City: Ateneo de Manila University Press, 2000.

Sideco, Mary Teresa. *The Roots of Teresa's Nuns in the Philippines.* Vol. 2. Lipa: Association of Monasteries of Discalced Carmelite Nuns in the Philippines, 1999.

Siegel, James T. *Naming the Witch.* Stanford, CA: Stanford University Press, 2006.

Silverman, Kaja. *The Acoustic Mirror: The Female Voice in Psychoanalysis and Cinema.* Bloomington: Indiana University Press, 1988.

Sinha, Mrinalini. *Colonial Masculinity: The "Manly Englishman" and the "Effeminate Bengali" in the Late Nineteenth Century* (Manchester, UK: Manchester University Press, 1995).

Skrbiš, Zlatko. "The Apparitions of the Virgin Mary of Medjugorje: The Convergence of Croatian Nationalism and Her Apparitions." *Nations and Nationalism* 11, no. 3 (2005): 443–61.

Smail, John R. W. "On the Possibility of an Autonomous History of Modern Southeast Asia." *Journal of Southeast Asian History* 2, no. 2 (July 1961): 72–102.

Stuntz, Homer C. *The Philippines and the Far East.* Cincinnati, OH: Jennings and Pye, 1904.

Sturtevant, David R. *Popular Uprisings in the Philippines 1840–1940.* Ithaca, NY: Cornell University Press, 1976.

Tadiar, Neferti. *Fantasy-Production: Sexual Economies and Other Philippine Consequences for the New World Order.* Quezon City: Ateneo de Manila University Press, 2004.

———. "The Noranian Imaginary." In *Geopolitics of the Visible: Essays on Philippine Film Cultures,* edited by Rolando B. Tolentino, 61–76. Quezon City: Ateneo de Manila University Press, 2000.

Tan, Michael. *Revisiting Usog, Pasma, and Kulam.* Quezon City: University of the Philippines Press, 2008.

Taussig, Michael. *Shamanism, Colonialism, and the Wild Man.* Chicago: University of Chicago Press, 1987.

Teresa of Ávila. *The Interior Castle.* Translated by E. Allison Peers. New York: Doubleday, 1989.

Thérèse of Lisieux. *The Autobiography of Saint Thérèse de Lisieux, Story of a Soul.* Translated by John Beevers. 1957. New York: Doubleday Books, 2001.

———. *Story of a Soul: The Autobiography of St. Thérèse de Lisieux.* Translated by John Clarke, O.C.D. Washington, DC: ICS Publications, 1996.

Thomas, Megan C. "Orientalist Enlightenment: The Emergence of Nationalist Thought in the Philippines, 1880–1898." PhD diss., Cornell University, 2002.

———. *Orientalists, Propagandists, and Ilustrados: Filipino Scholarship and the End of Spanish Colonialism.* Minneapolis: University of Minnesota Press, 2012.

Thompson, Mark R. *The Anti-Marcos Struggle: Personalistic Rule and Democratic Transition in the Philippines.* New Haven, CT: Yale University Press, 1995.

Tiongson, Nicanor. *Philippine Theater: History and Anthology.* Vol. 2, *Komedya.* Quezon City: University of the Philippines Press, 1999.

Tolentino, Aurelio. "Kahapon, Ngayon, at Bukas." In *Selected Writings,* edited and with an introduction by Edna Zapanta-Manlapaz, 15–142. Quezon City: University of the Philippines Library, 1975.

———. "Luhang Tagalog." In *The Filipino Drama,* by Arthur Riggs. 1905. Manila: Ministry of Human Settlements, 1981.

Tolentino, Rolando. "*Inangbayan,* the Mother-Nation, in Lino Brocka's *Bayan Ko: Kapit sa Patalim* and *Orapronobis.*" *Screen* 37, no. 4 (Winter 1996): 368–88.

Torre Villar, Ernesto de la, and Ramiro Navarro de Anda. *Testimonios históricos guadalupanos.* Mexico City: Fondo de Cultura Económica, 1982.

Tremeau, Marc. *The Mystery of the Rosary.* New York: Catholic Book Publishing, 1982.

Turner, Victor, and Edith Turner. *Image and Pilgrimage in Christian Culture*. New York: Columbia University Press, 1978.

Valtorta, Maria. *The Poem of the Man-God*. Vol. 1. Translated by Nicandro Picozzi. Isola de Liri, Italy: Centro Editoriale Valtortiano, 1986.

Vásquez, Manuel A., and Marie F. Marquardt. "Globalizing the Rainbow Madonna: Old Time Religion in the Present Age." *Theory, Culture, and Society* 17, no. 4 (2000): 119–43.

Venida, Victor. "The Santo and the Rural Aristocracy." *Philippine Studies* 44, no. 4 (1996): 500–513.

Villa, Praxedes. "*Kape* and How Batangas Coffee Made a Mark in the World Market." In *Batangas: Forged in Fire*, edited by Ramon N. Villegas, 140–45. Makati: Ayala Foundation and Filipinas Heritage Library, 2002.

Villanueva, Francisco, Jr. *The Wonders of Lipa*. Manila: Grand Avenue Bookstore, 1949.

Villegas, Socrates B., ed. *EDSA Shrine: God's Gift, Our Mission*. Manila: Roman Catholic Archdiocese of Manila, 1999.

Vries, Hent de. "In Media Res; Global Religion, Public Spheres, and the Task of Contemporary Comparative Religious Studies." In *Religion and Media*, edited by Hent de Vries and Samuel Weber, 3–42. Stanford, CA: Stanford University Press, 2001.

———. "Of Miracles and Special Effects." *International Journal for the Philosophy of Religion* 50, nos. 1–3 (December 2001): 41–56.

Walsh, William Thomas. *Our Lady of Fatima*. New York: Doubleday, 1954.

Warner, Marina. *Alone of All Her Sex: The Myth and Cult of the Virgin Mary*. New York: Vintage, 1976.

Warner, Michael. "Publics and Counterpublics." *Public Culture* 14, no. 1 (2002): 49–90.

Weber, Alison. "Saint Teresa, Demonologist." In *Culture and Control in Counter-Reformation Spain*, edited by Anne J. Cruz and Mary Elizabeth Perry, 171–95. Minneapolis: University of Minnesota Press, 1992.

Weber, Max. *The Protestant Ethic and the Spirit of Capitalism*. Translated by Talcott Parsons. 1930. New York: Routledge, 2001.

———. "Science as Vocation." In *From Max Weber: Essays in Sociology*, edited and translated by Hans H. Gerth and C. Wright Mills, 129–56. New York: Oxford University Press, 1958.

Wickberg, Edgar. *The Chinese in Philippine Life, 1850–1898*. 1965. Quezon City: Ateneo de Manila University Press, 2000.

Wiegele, Katharine L. *Investing in Miracles: El Shaddai and the Transformation of Popular Catholicism in the Philippines*. Honolulu: University of Hawai'i Press, 2005.

Wojcik, Daniel. "'Polaroids from Heaven': Photography, Folk Religion, and the Miraculous Image Tradition at a Marian Apparition Site." *Journal of American Folklore* 109, no. 432 (Spring 1996): 129–48.

Wolters, Oliver W. *History, Culture, and Region in Southeast Asian Perspectives*. Ithaca, NY: Cornell University Southeast Asian Program Publications, 1999.

Woods, Colleen. "Bombs, Bureaucrats, and Rosary Beads: The United States, the Philippines, and the Making of Global Anti-Communism, 1945–1960." PhD diss., University of Michigan, 2012.

Wright-Rios, Edward. *Revolutions in Mexican Catholicism: Reform and Revelation in Oaxaca, 1887–1934*. Durham, NC: Duke University Press, 2009.

Xavier, Francis. *The Letters and Instructions of Francis Xavier*. Translated and introduced by M. Joseph Costelloe. St. Louis, MO: Institute of Jesuit Sources, 1992.

Yamsuan, Peachy, Louie Reyes, and Vilma Roy Duavit, eds. *Pueblo Amante de Maria: The Filipinos' Love for Mary*. Manila: Reyes Publishing, 2012.

Yuval-Davis, Nira, and Floya Anthias, eds. *Woman, Nation, State*. Basingstoke, UK: Macmillan, 1989.

Zapanta-Manlapaz, Edna. Introduction to *Aurelio Tolentino: Selected Writings*, edited by E. Zapanta-Manlapaz, 1–13. Quezon City: University of the Philippines Library, 1975.

Index